24/7 POLITICS

Politics and Society in Modern America

Gary Gerstle, Elizabeth Hinton, Margaret O'Mara, and Julian E. Zelizer, Series Editors

For a full list of books in this series see: https://press.princeton .edu/series/politics-and-society-in-modern-america

24/7 Politics

Cable Television and the Fragmenting of America from Watergate to Fox News

Kathryn Cramer Brownell

PRINCETON UNIVERSITY PRESS

PRINCETON AND OXFORD

Published by Princeton University Press
41 William Street, Princeton, New Jersey 08540
99 Banbury Road, Oxford OX2 6JX

press.princeton.edu

Library of Congress Control Number: 2023930207

All Rights Reserved

ISBN 9780691246666
ISBN (e-book) 9780691246680

British Library Cataloging-in-Publication Data is available

Editorial: Bridget Flannery-McCoy, Alena Chekanov
Jacket: Jessica Massabrook
Production: Erin Suydam
Publicity: James Schneider, Kathryn Stevens

Jacket Credit: Jacket images (from left to right): President Richard Nixon /
Danita Delimont; President Jimmy Carter (left) and First Lady Rosalynn Carter /
ZUMA Press, Inc.; Jane Fonda and Ted Turner / MARKA; President Gerald Ford and
Jimmy Carter / American Photo Archive; Television Image of President Gerald Ford's Casket /
joeysworld.com; Bill Clinton / Everett Collection Inc. All images courtesy of Alamy.

This book has been composed in Adobe Text Pro with Gotham

Printed on acid-free paper. ∞

Printed in the United States of America

10 9 8 7 6 5 4 3 2 1

To my mom, Terri Rohde Dunham

TABLE OF CONTENTS

ACKNOWLEDGMENTS

This book began with an idea and an interview. While finishing my first book and interviewing for my current position at Purdue University, I was curious about the connection between cable television and American politics and I had the good fortune to meet Robert Browning, the director of the C-SPAN Video Library. Our first half-hour conversation that January set me on a journey that has taken eight years and has been made possible by support from so many people who have shared their time, expertise, and experiences with me.

First, thank you to Robert Browning for sparking my research into Richard Nixon and the cable industry that has been foundational to this book. He has also built an archive central to my scholarship: the C-SPAN Video Library. When I first arrived at Purdue, Carolyn Curiel, a talented speechwriter for Bill Clinton who then established the Purdue Institute for Civic Communication, shared her insights into the media landscape and introduced me to Purdue's distinguished alumnus, Brian Lamb. During a phone conversation with Brian, he told me to look at the Clay Whitehead papers and see what I found. It was the first of many research tips he gave me, and I am so grateful for his time and generosity in opening conversations with cable industry figures and pointing me to archives to explore. Over the past eight years, it has been a privilege and pleasure working with the Brian Lamb School of Communication at Purdue University and the Center for C-SPAN Scholarship & Engagement (CCSE) that Robert Browning, Marifran Mattison, Connie Doeble, and Andrea Langrish have built. Collaborating on projects with Lamb School faculty like Stacey Connaughton and Jennifer Hoewe to connect scholarship in communication and history has been intellectually rewarding, and a reminder that working with supportive women matters professionally and personally.

Purdue University has provided substantial institutional support for this project from the beginning. The University Scholars program, the Center for Humanistic Studies, the Enhancing Research in the Humanities and Arts, and the ENGAGE and ASPIRE programs have all provided tremendous financial resources to help me build digital databases, travel to archives, hire research assistants, carve out time to write, and host a manuscript review. I also have had the privilege of writing this book as a member of the Purdue history department under the leadership of R. Douglas Hurt and Frederick Rowe Davis. My colleagues are some of the best historians in the country and I am so fortunate to have their critical eyes and sharp feedback to strengthen my work. Their humor, generosity, and kindness have also made me enjoy life inside and outside University Hall. Thank you especially to Cole Jones, Jennifer Foray, Randy Roberts, Stacy Holden, Margaret Tillman, and Wendy Kline. For the past seventeen years, David Atkinson has been such an amazing friend and colleague, and I can't imagine navigating the challenge of graduate school, the tenure track, and the second book project without tea breaks, burritos, venting sessions, and lots of laughs. He has endured countless hours of conversation about cable television and politics, and so much more. In the final days of writing the book, he also always took the time to help me find the right words to tell the story.

Thank you to all the archivists, librarians, and research assistants who have helped me pursue my research questions, especially during the challenging time of COVID-19. I am especially grateful for the George Mason University Special Collections library staff who took the extra effort to help me navigate the newly opened C-SPAN records as a nursing mom. Purdue librarians, and especially Albert Chapman and Kristin Leaman, have been so helpful in tracking down sources in all the research and writing stages. Caitlin Fendley, Bo Blew, and Vincent Szilagyi have also provided invaluable research assistance over the years, and I am grateful for their diligence and dedication to the project.

Words cannot express my gratitude for Brian Kenny, the director of the Barco Library at the Cable Center. He is firmly committed to making information available to scholars like me, and time and time again, he went above and beyond in answering my *many* research questions. I will always be grateful for his professionalism, expertise, and friendship. The Cable Center staff, especially the dynamic Diane Christman, and its many industry partners have been exceedingly open with their archival material. Before the pandemic interfered, I had the incredible experience of working as a scholar-in-residence at the Cable Center and learned so much from those in the industry who kindly shared their stories with me.

I have also benefited tremendously from an incredible scholarly community of historians willing to share sources and expertise. I am so grateful for generosity shown by Lily Geismer, Anne Blaschke, Allison Perlman, Brent Cebul, Brian Balogh, Reed W. Smith, Sage Goodwin, Clay Howard, Elizabeth Tandy Shermer, Kate Jewell, and Richard John. I have learned so much from Oscar Winberg's fantastic work on television and politics and am so grateful for his sharp editorial eye in the final stages of the book's production. James Baughman's collaborative spirit, support for junior scholars, and superb scholarship have influenced me in so many ways, and I am so fortunate to have gotten to know him before he sadly passed away in 2016. I have also been fortunate to share drafts of this material at a variety of works-in-progress seminars, conference panels, and roundtables, and the feedback from these conversations has continued to push me as a scholar. Brooke Blower, Sarah Phillips, and the entire *Modern American History* team, including five anonymous reviewers, helped me think through key arguments and historical questions and showed how academic publishing can be rigorous, supportive, and timely.

Nicole Hemmer, David Greenberg, Heather Hendershot, and Patrick Parsons—scholars whose work has paved the way for my own—all graciously read a very rough draft of the book during a manuscript review and offered constructive and supportive feedback on it, encouraging me to have the confidence to make the bold argument about American democracy the material warrants. Their feedback, along with thorough and penetrating comments from the anonymous reviewers at Princeton University Press, helped me transform anecdotes into a deeper analysis of political, media, and economic changes in modern America. Thank you to all these manuscript reviewers who truly embody the generous and collaborative environment of intellectual exchange that makes being a professional historian so exciting and rewarding.

Researching and writing this book coincided with the development of different initiatives in American political history, notably the launch of "Made By History" a history column at the *Washington Post* and the establishment of the American Political History Conference. Working with my brilliant collaborators in these venues—Nicole Hemmer, Brian Rosenwald, Carly Goodman, and Leah Wright Rigueur—has taught me how to be a better writer and historian, and I continue to be inspired by their work ethic and generosity. Brian Rosenwald has also taken many hours to talk about the book and to provide his fantastic editorial feedback in the project's many stages, and I am so grateful for his editorial skills, historical expertise, and friendship.

Princeton University Press has simply been incredible, offering me the rigor of an academic review process and the publishing reach of a trade press. I could not ask for a better production team with their diligence, support, and hard work. Margaret O'Mara has long inspired me as a historian with her research, her writing ability, and support of women in the field. Getting to work with her as a series editor has been an extraordinary experience. So too has working with the brilliant Bridget Flannery-McCoy, whose editing skills and instincts are truly remarkable and have sharpened the final project tremendously. From the beginning, Bridget and Margaret understood what I wanted to do with this book, even at times when I struggled to see the forest through the trees, and their dedication to the project has helped to make it into the book that it is today.

I would also like to thank the three people who have mentored me at different stages of my career, and who continue to be trusted advisors and treasured friends. Matthew Lassiter sparked my interest in history years ago at the University of Michigan, and he has since continued to inspire my work in public engagement and help me think through critical developments in American political history. Bruce Schulman's willingness to always pick up a phone call, extend a speaking invitation, travel to West Lafayette, or even do a last-minute read of a manuscript, reveals the depth and continuity of his mentorship that began in graduate school. Caroline Janney taught me how to climb the professional ranks of academia with kindness and empathy, and to do so while balancing life as a new mom. I will always strive to uphold their high standards of rigor and compassion as I work with undergraduate students, graduate students, and my colleagues.

Finally, thank you to my friends and family who endured way too many conversations about history, media, and politics over the years and have also made me enjoy life outside of work. I started writing this book while living on Nantucket and am so grateful for the enduring friendship of Rocky Fox, Justine Bistany, and my incredible mother-in-law Judy Brownell, all of whom continue to make summer visits to the island so enjoyable and worthwhile. I am also so fortunate to have met Maureen Orth, who has shared her personal archive and her experiences with me over many lunches and cocktail hours and continues to be a constant source of inspiration and support. Moving to the Midwest was no small feat, but friends like Jessi Zumdahl, Lindsay Perrault, Libby Richards, Mandy Rispolli, and Karen Regan have made Lafayette such a wonderful place to live and raise children. I even had the pleasure of finishing up the book project alongside my neighbor and fellow author, Vanessa Regan. My sisters, Sarah Cuppelli and Jamie Klusacek, and their families have provided housing, dinners, and lots of laughs during my stays in Denver, as have my favorite couple, Brandi Phillips and Meagan Bauer. My brother and sister-in-law, Chris and Katie Cramer, always made visits to Ann Arbor, and then later Grand Rapids, productive and entertaining.

My parents, Doug Cramer and Fred and Terri Dunham, have been a source of encouragement and support my entire life. My mom has endured so many conversations about the specifics of my research findings and she has always pushed me to make my work accessible to a broader audience. This book reflects my efforts to do so, and it has benefited from so many conversations with her about storytelling, and even her close reading of the material and editorial suggestions. Far more significantly, she has taught me how to be a strong and kind person and caring and compassionate mother. I will always strive to live up to the high standard she continues to set for me in her words and deeds every day. In gratitude for all she has done and continues to do for me and my family, this book is dedicated to her.

Lastly, I reserve my greatest gratitude for my husband, Jason, and daughters, Lillian and Jacqueline, both of whom were born while pursuing this project. They are the loves of my life and remind me that the best things happen when I turn off my computer and embrace the joy that only they can provide. Jason's support for my career has been surpassed only by his patience and hard work to keep our family functioning and flourishing every day. He is my rock, and he helps to make all I do possible. Thank you from the bottom of my heart.

24/7 POLITICS

Introduction

THE GREAT HIDDEN POLITICAL ASSET

Curiosity and excitement filled the air as Washington politicos gathered on March 1, 1984, to hear about a "great hidden political asset": cable television.[1] It was the first ever "Cable Television Political Workshop" and cable executives, operators, and lobbyists had a big message to sell to the officials, consultants, and congressional staffers they had invited that day: how broadcasting had failed democracy and how cable could save it.

Frustrated by the high cost of campaign advertisements on network television? Cable offered cheap, even free, options to have lengthy conversations with citizens. Unsatisfied with the boundaries of thirty seconds to make these television pitches? On cable, as Tom Wheeler, the president of the National Cable Television Association (NCTA), put it to the wide-eyed participants, "what you can do is only limited by your imagination." He stressed that successful candidates needed to "throw out all the old ideas about how you use television in political campaigns." Why? Because cable isn't just "more TV," he emphasized. "It is different television. It's a different medium and the key to using it is to open up your imagination and figure out new approaches."

The NCTA celebrated the political power of narrowcasting and targeting. Cable Americans, as market researchers called cable subscribers, consumed more goods than noncable households. They drank more wine, bought more items via mail orders, owned more video games, and used their American Express credit cards in higher volumes.[2] They were also more politically active. Compared to noncable subscribers, they were 28 percent more likely to vote, 50 percent more likely to work on a campaign, and 69 percent more likely to donate money to a candidate or a political cause. "The population of Cable America is politically active. They are literally hard wired into their communities," explained Richard Zackon, the vice president of the Cabletelevision Advertising Bureau (CAB). "The relationship between viewing and voting then is the answer to the question why is it politically important . . . to reach those people in Cable America." He encouraged candidates to customize their campaigns in the mold of successful cable networks, which had smaller, but more loyal and more vocal, audiences than the national broadcasting networks that still dominated television in the early 1980s.

For three and a half hours, cable businessmen—notably not one woman or person of color spoke—expressed the logic that other entrepreneurs had learned over the course of the twentieth century: consumer capitalism thrives on the perpetual pursuit of personal pleasure.[3] For decades, corporations had studied how to make psychological appeals to American consumers to encourage them to buy goods as a form of democratic empowerment.[4] Now, cable leaders were pushing politicians and their staffers to bring these principles to winning elections and governing. The economic stakes for the industry went beyond just tapping into hefty campaign advertising budgets. The workshop was also a way to generate goodwill, and then votes, for legislation to deregulate the cable industry.

It worked. The workshop was one of many events organized by the cable industry to teach Washington insiders how to use a technology that had long been an outsider in politics and television. It exposed the industry's most consequential lobbying strategy: highlighting the limits of broadcast television and lauding the civic possibilities of cable television. Wheeler ended the workshop with a speech titled "How the Electorate Wins in the End."[5] The premise was simple: more choice, information, and access to direct conversations between candidates and the public would engage and inform voters like never before. The workshop was never about enhancing democracy, however. It was about making money and forging strategic partnerships between an industry and the elected politicians who wrote the rules in which that industry operated.

This book explores how cable television evolved into a multibillion-dollar industry by tapping into political frustrations with broadcast television and promising that choice on the television dial would fulfill the promise of American democracy. Cable television began in the late 1940s simply to bring existing broadcast signals to Americans in small rural towns and western mountain regions who were otherwise unable to get programming from the three broadcast networks that dominated the television landscape— National Broadcasting Company (NBC), Columbia Broadcasting System (CBS), and American Broadcasting Company (ABC). Over the next four decades, a combination of political and business decisions enabled the cable industry to challenge the broadcasting oligopoly rather than just expand its reach. By the 1970s, cable operators and industry lobbyists promised the public and politicians that their medium would deliver a different form of news and entertainment— one that was more authentic, accessible, and adaptable to the needs of elected officials. Distinguishing cable from broadcast television became both a business and political strategy, with the public interest frequently invoked but seldom taken seriously.

Challenging the broadcasting industry was no small feat, and the consequences of cable television's triumph reverberate in the twenty-first century. Broadcasting—on radio and then television—had created a shared entertainment culture that erased many regional and economic divides and helped citizens to see themselves as consumers.[6] Such a national identity privileged the perspective of straight, white men and became a tool to further buttress a political establishment growing more media savvy.[7] Network broadcasting executives searched for programs that appealed to the masses—which they understood to be white, middle class, and heterosexual—and built newsrooms that relied on elite men to shape conversations about public affairs. This shared culture created by broadcasting was powerful but also ideologically exclusionary and built on racial, ethnic, and gendered stereotypes, which it then perpetuated.[8]

Cable television thrived by promising to bring diversity and new perspectives into American politics and culture and to tear down the gatekeepers of network broadcasting with market forces. Even as cable companies became more consolidated, programming on the medium remained decentralized compared to the film and broadcast industries, ultimately emerging as a vehicle for anti-establishment political forces. Cable news programs called out the elitism of network news and eagerly challenged and disrupted mainstream institutions and journalistic practices. Eschewing the half-hour evening news program narrated by the likes of Walter Cronkite, cable networks like C-SPAN offered an unfiltered view of the House of Representatives, whose empty chamber was used by figures like Newt Gingrich (R-GA) and Robert Walker (R-PA) to build a small but outspoken conservative audience. Lengthy cable talk shows allowed presidential candidates to evade the Washington press corps and talk directly to narrow segments of the population about the very issues polls showed audiences cared about, whether specific policies or music interests.

Such programs took on a feeling of authenticity because they differed so dramatically from the curated network news programs. And yet, they simply introduced a different political filter, one that often entertained rather than informed viewers and overwhelmingly did so by stressing divisions rather than finding common ground.[9]

Cable promised to empower people, politicians, and perspectives not included in network broadcasting. And it did. It seduced political leaders, who saw television as central to winning elections and governing and wanted more media access than network television would provide. It mobilized a public willing to pay for newer and better television. It encouraged a different approach to television that made citizens and politicians rely on the marketplace to interact with one another, ultimately making political success dependent on generating good ratings, not necessarily crafting effective policy.

The history of cable television *does* reveal how a more accessible and expansive medium can bring new voices to political conversations and stimulate civic engagement. That's certainly what happened in 1972 as ordinary citizens creatively produced their own election night coverage of local city council races on public access channels using "roving reporters" donning portapaks to interview candidates and analyze voting patterns.[10] Two decades later, MTV lauded how its "Choose or Lose" initiative registered thousands of young voters. But such efforts were always about advancing the bottom line of a highly regulated industry looking to demonstrate to elected officials why they should encourage, rather than limit, the growth of cable television.[11]

The development of cable television—from its political awakening in the 1960s to its dominance in the 1990s—exposes the ways in which American political institutions and values are deeply intertwined with media industries. This has always been the case.[12] During the early republic, concerns about the circulation of misinformation through pamphlets and the printing press proliferated, even motivating legislators to pass the Sedition Act of 1798, which prohibited "false, scandalous and malicious writing or writings against the government of the United States."[13] The law exposed the deep concern about public opinion, which the founding generation saw as playing an important, but perpetually flawed, role in American government.[14] Elected officials needed to communicate with their constituents and represent their interests, but what tools should they use to do those jobs?

Twentieth-century technological developments—notably motion pictures, radio, and then television—brought new opportunities for political leaders to sell ideas to voters and build national constituencies.[15] Yet, access to this audience involved establishing and sustaining a particular corporate structure upheld by federal government regulations to serve the public interest. Over the course of four decades, cable television fundamentally challenged and changed this arrangement. As cable knocked down the hierarchies and rules embedded in the broadcasting era, it helped to create a privatized public sphere where notions of "efficiency" and "consumer choice" reigned supreme, and earlier expectations that corporations had a civic responsibility increasingly faded. Regulators, elected officials, and millions of Americans became convinced that a deregulated media marketplace could advance democracy, and as the CAB understood with the slogan that it promoted during the 1984 workshop "E = MC2," effectiveness equaled more cable.[16]

As a result, the politicians who once looked down on the industry during the 1960s had their media consultants studying it during the 1980s, and over the next decade, they eagerly accepted invitations to appear on new cable channels like CNN, C-SPAN, Comedy Central, and even Nickelodeon. Ignoring criticism that MTV News contributed to the "junkification" of American life, Bill Clinton used the cable channel's new foray into presidential politics to talk about student loan policies on the campaign trail in 1992, and yes, even his underwear choice during a presidential town hall two years later.[17] Others bought advertisements on ESPN, invited C-SPAN cameras to their congressional offices for interviews, and held electronic town halls.

Not only did cable television furnish the tools to build new types of electronic coalitions, its expansion also built faith in and loyalty to the idea of the free market itself.[18] Cable operators promised to deliver programming that would educate and empower individuals by expanding media choice. They did, but such programs prioritized keeping viewers' attention rather than informing citizens. In the end, more Americans became engrossed in watching sports and movies and ignored politics altogether, ultimately affording an outsized role for more extreme voices to shape the political process.[19]

Donald Trump's divisive presidency was a culmination of the shifting media culture propelled by cable television and a consequence of this bipartisan embrace of the marketplace as the arbitrator of democracy.[20] Trump launched his political career by appearing on Fox News and using his celebrity status created on a reality television program, a programming style that the cable dial first revealed could be profitable.[21] His obsession with ratings and his disregard for democratic institutions has exposed a fundamental conflict at the heart of modern American politics.[22] The information age has ushered in a decentralized and open public sphere, but one driven by performative politics and the constant search to exploit new media to gain personal power. How the latter impulses were baked into the former is the story of this book.

In the twenty-first century, it is easy to lament how this multi-channel medium has contributed to corporate consolidation, partisan polarization, voter apathy, and media excess.[23] But this was not preordained. As John M. Culkin, a colleague of famed media scholar Marshall McLuhan, once observed about new media technology, "We shape our tools and, thereafter, they shape us."[24] For decades, federal regulators, elected officials, and entrepreneurs engaged in a debate over how to structure television as a political institution. Our current political and media landscapes reflect their experimentations, compromises, and ultimate adherence to a belief that consumer choice could fuel democracy, ignoring the ways in which it could also sow the seeds for its upheaval.[25]

The rise of Cable America is also a legislative story full of strange bedfellows and unanticipated consequences. When a young Democratic representative from Colorado, Timothy Wirth, came to Congress in 1974 on the heels of Watergate, he certainly didn't envision working with the conservative senator from Arizona, Barry Goldwater, to deliver cable legislation that would put him at odds with his fellow "New Democrat" from Tennessee, Albert Gore Jr. Wirth even sided with President George H. W. Bush on the issue in the fall of 1992—as he helped to run the Clinton-Gore campaign. When Democratic Chief Deputy Whip William Alexander launched a congressional experiment to connect to local news outlets through C-SPAN, he did not anticipate that members on the conservative fringe of the Republican Party would use these same tactics to undermine the credibility of Democratic Speaker of the House Thomas "Tip" O'Neill. Such instances show the limits of seeing ideological battles between liberalism and conservatism as driving changes in recent American political history.[26] For elected officials, constituent pressures and self-interest frequently determined their legislative decisions, particularly when it came down to how to structure media institutions that they increasingly saw as central to political power.

That's why Richard Nixon—a man obsessed with media politics—played such a central role in shaping the trajectory of cable television. The 37th president viewed the medium as a political weapon to undermine the political, economic, and social authority of television networks he felt were biased and out to get him. Cable could also provide embattled political leaders like himself more control over media messaging. Even as he retreated to Southern California in disgrace, such ideas resonated with politicians across the political aisle, something savvy cable operators recognized as they worked to ingratiate the industry into operations of government and campaigns. For the next two decades, the industry celebrated narrowcasting, targeting, and the ability of the market to deliver civic goods and services, and politicians and the public alike bought into that promise. Cable television's political triumph by the end of the twentieth century deepened the connection between democracy and the marketplace, ultimately creating the segmented, sensationalized, and privatized public sphere that exists today.

In 1958, prominent newscaster Edward R. Murrow famously feared a future in which public affairs became shaped by "an incompatible combination of show business, advertising and news."[27] Less than four decades later, cable television made that world a reality. Cable pioneers didn't set out to transform American democracy. But they did, unleashing a media-driven battle for ratings that has now overtaken the political process. This is the story of how citizens learned to vote with their remote, with stark consequences for American politics.

A Political Awakening

It all started in the late 1940s when some engineers and appliance store salespeople in Oregon, Arkansas, and Pennsylvania experimented with a way to tap into the burgeoning television market by bringing broadcast signals to rural and distant communities.[1]

The premise was simple: put an antenna on top of a building or a mountain to get the television broadcast signals coming in from a nearby city and then run a cable—hence the name the technology would later take on—into hotels, bars, and even individual homes for a monthly fee. It was hard work to trek up a hilltop with an antenna, generator, and television set to even find a signal. Bringing that signal into town required creative technology, notably amplifiers to boost it along the way. It was risky and expensive. Some of the first operators mortgaged everything they had to purchase miles and miles of coaxial cable.

The gamble paid off.

Residents of small towns were thrilled and eagerly signed up so they could purchase newly available television sets. Known first as "community television," these systems soon took on the name CATV—derived by combining the terms community antenna and television. Initially it was a win-win for local broadcasters and CATV

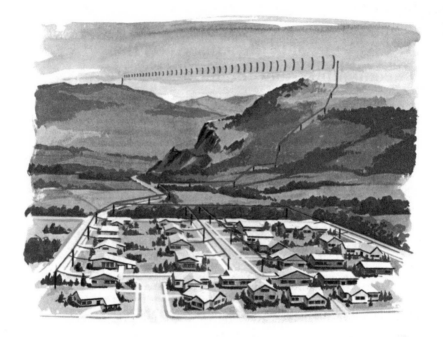

A rural mountain diagram composed by the National Community Television
Association in 1966 to demonstrate how cable systems functioned.
Photo Credit: Barco Library, The Cable Center.

operators, what Federal Communications Commission (FCC) Chairman Newton Minow called a "love affair."[2] Broadcasters depended
on advertising to pay the bills for programs they then disseminated
for free to viewers. Larger audiences, then, could only help them
justify charging higher prices. Operators of CATV systems didn't
need to create any programming; they just had to deliver it. These
entrepreneurs faced high startup costs and had to negotiate with
local government and telephone companies to hang their wires on
utility poles. However, once a household hooked up to the system,
operators knew they had a dependable monthly income. Americans
in small towns and cities alike loved their television sets and, if tough
times hit, they would forgo paying other bills before canceling a
subscription.[3]

   To Bill Daniels—the man his colleagues would affectionately call
"the father of cable television"—simple economics fueled the growth

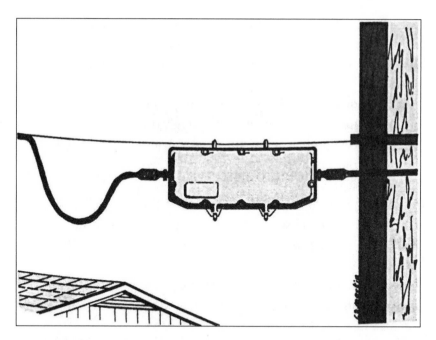

A drawing of the amplifiers used to boost the signals about every two thousand feet.
Photo Credit: Barco Library, The Cable Center.

of CATV into the modern cable television industry, which decades later would directly compete with broadcasting networks for viewers, advertising dollars, and political prestige.[4] As he built a powerful and profitable investment firm that forged deals to grow the cable industry, Daniels repeatedly emphasized that cable television had two friends: Main Street and Wall Street.[5] The public wanted television and investors saw the profits that could be made by tapping into such an obsession.

And yet, Daniels—who would later climb the ranks of the Republican Party and launch an unsuccessful bid for the Colorado governorship—also understood that cable's success depended on another factor: politics. Across the country cable operators quickly learned that the state mattered as they encountered tax bills from the IRS, antitrust investigations from the Department of Justice into business partnerships between cable operators and equipment suppliers, and rules from the FCC limiting what programs they could show and where they could even build systems. And so, like other industries, they formed a trade association to grapple with these shared political concerns.[6]

Through the National Community Television Association (NCTA), these men—and overwhelmingly they were men—battled over what community television even was and what it could be. At first, to avoid taxes, NCTA members agreed on a narrow definition of cable television. They sold CATV as a "passive antenna" that merely extended broadcasting signals rather than working as a "wire and equipment service" that would have incurred an 8 percent federal excise tax. It worked, resulting in lower taxes when the courts agreed in 1957.[7]

Eventually members like Bill Daniels saw this vision for cable as too constricting and pushed another view of the technology to tap into new markets: cable as an alternative to broadcasting and its handful of channels.[8] Such an approach to cable put it in direct opposition to entrenched interests that shaped the postwar media and political landscapes, ultimately forging a rivalry that would transform both over the next few decades.

By 1990, Bill Daniels could reflect on how far cable had come by rattling off everyone who'd tried to stop them: "ABC, NBC, CBS, the telephone company owners, the movie producers, the local TV stations."[9] The list went on to include city councils, state governments, power companies, lawyers, and lobbyists. Daniels recalled a particular challenge came from congressional representatives who "didn't like us because their broadcast buddies at home who they were dependent on to get re-elected didn't like us." To Daniels, though, all that bad blood spelled opportunity. "We figured that if all of these people were trying to stop us, we must have something."

As Daniels made clear, the cozy relationship between broadcasters and CATV operators quickly dissolved amid debates over the legality of pay television, the types of signals operators could import, and FCC ownership rules. Unexpectedly, it was the most

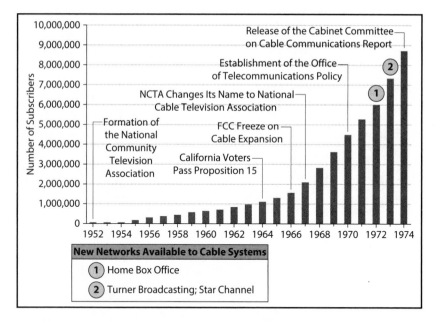

A snapshot of the cable television industry's growth from 1952 to 1974.
Sources: Television & Cable Factbook; SNL Kagan; Larry Satkowiak, *The Cable Industry: A Short History through Three Generations*, Barco Library, The Cable Center.

powerful man in the country who delivered the final blow to this relationship: President Richard Nixon, who used cable television as a weapon to wage war on network television with sweeping consequences.

1

The Power of Broadcasting

In the early days of 1961, the news broke that Newton Minow would be joining John F. Kennedy's upcoming administration as the new Federal Communications Commission (FCC) chairman.[1] As a young lawyer from Chicago, he was excited about the opportunity even though he knew little about the broadcast industry he would soon oversee. Before the January inauguration, he received a phone call from a familiar voice, J. Leonard Reinsch. The Cox Broadcasting executive who had also climbed the ranks of the Democratic Party wanted to set up a meeting to share his insights on the industry that Minow would soon be regulating.[2]

Although almost twenty years apart in age, the two men had both hailed from the Midwest and had attended Northwestern University. They also shared a conviction that mass media—notably radio and then television—could enhance the democratic process. Reinsch had made a name for himself during the 1944 election when he urged Franklin Roosevelt to make short and entertaining radio spots—many of them featuring celebrities like Humphrey Bogart and Frank Sinatra—to bring his campaign message to new voters.[3] It worked, and he quickly became a highly sought-after media adviser in the Democratic Party. Working on Adlai Stevenson's failed bids for the presidency in 1952 and 1956, Minow and

Reinsch got to know one another.[4] In 1960, they were finally successful in helping the party recapture the White House, and now the broadcaster wanted to offer the ambitious Minow some advice for his new job.

Reinsch brought Frank Stanton, the president of CBS, to the meeting. Over breakfast, the three men discussed the future of television. One thing surprised Minow during the conversation. Both broadcasters predicted, privately, that one day American television would be predominantly delivered via a wire rather than over the air. It was a bold forecast, given that the entire television system hinged on protecting and preserving the airwaves for broadcasters. It revealed the close attention that broadcasting executives paid to cable television—which was only a blip on the TV radar at the time—and many of them, Reinsch and Stanton included, invested in CATV systems over the next few years.[5] Indeed, the meeting made one thing clear: the existing over-the-air television system and the monopoly structure it engendered were fundamentally vulnerable.

Minow attempted to address this issue at the FCC. He saw the importance of bringing more choice to the television dial and believed that would help the medium fulfill its democratic potential. He was especially passionate about educational television and would continue to be a leader in fostering public and private support for it throughout his career (even becoming chair of PBS in 1978). He also encouraged the growth of new technology—including expanding the broadcasting spectrum and launching a communications satellite—and pushed the FCC to reconsider regulatory policies that limited the growth of experimental approaches to television, like proposals to have viewers pay directly to receive additional programming over the air or through a wired connection.[6]

Perhaps just as significantly, he pressed the network broadcasting industry to live up to its civic responsibilities. His first address to the National Association of Broadcasters (NAB) that May tackled this very issue. "Ours has been called the jet age, the atomic age, the space age. It is also, I submit, the television age," he began in a speech that has since become enshrined in television history. The question remained, he observed, as to whether "today's broadcasters employed their powerful voice to enrich the people or to debase them." Minow believed that television was failing the American people with its embrace of brash commercialism and formulaic programs—quiz shows, westerns, and situation comedies—that generated profits but not knowledge of public affairs. "Keep your eyes glued to that set until the station signs off. I can assure you that what you will observe is a vast wasteland."[7]

The "vast wasteland" phrase instantly became famous, but Minow had actually wanted to hammer home a different message that day: the public interest responsibilities broadcasters had in exchange for what he called the "extraordinary privilege" they had in using public airwaves, for free, to make money.[8] He admonished broadcasters for eschewing their responsibility "to teach, to inform, to uplift."[9] As a "slave" to ratings, broadcasters catered to what the public wanted, not what it needed. After all, he added, "if parents, teachers, and ministers conducted their responsibilities by following the ratings, children would have a steady diet of ice cream, school holidays, and no Sunday school." Broadcasting must do better, he implored on that spring day. Minow also proposed a specific solution to the public interest problem by expanding public affairs programming. Such civic expectations were enshrined in FCC regulations, but they were scarcely enforced. Minow let broadcasters know he would be paying close attention to the issue, however.

Over the next few years, the networks responded with a massive investment into their newsrooms—notably dedicating more time for documentaries and evening news programs—to show their commitment to Kennedy's New Frontier agenda.[10] This did more than help broadcasters evade FCC scrutiny; it actually strengthened their political and economic power by ingratiating broadcasting into the very operations of government and the global Cold War battle against communism.[11] Such mutually beneficial relationships between elected officials and broadcasters also limited business opportunities for early cable television systems, revealing the deep interconnectedness between American political and media institutions.

———

The commercialism that Minow so lamented was the product of a regulatory system decades in the making. During the 1920s, policymakers implemented an "American System," which allowed corporations to dominate radio (and then later television) broadcasting—a marked departure from the government-funded regulatory structure of communications that took hold in other countries like Great Britain.[12] This system depended on certain technical assumptions, notably the principle of scarcity. Understanding the broadcast spectrum to be a limited and valuable resource, government officials decided to divide it into different frequencies and then assign licenses to those who wanted to use specified frequencies.

In 1927 Congress created the Federal Radio Commission (FRC) to make determinations over spectrum placement and hours of operation for local license applicants. In practice, the five-member independent regulatory commission gave prime spectrum placement (access to signals that reached larger audiences) to corporate and commercial interests with stronger signals rather than nonprofit and educational ones.[13] Applicants for an FCC broadcast license then had a better shot at receiving it if they were affiliated with a national network that disseminated commercially sponsored programming or could demonstrate substantial financial resources to underwrite broadcasting operations.[14]

Affiliation required local broadcasters to cede significant authority to the networks to craft the programming schedule each day. Such an arrangement with local affiliates also required negotiations with another corporation, the American Telephone and Telegraph Company (AT&T), which operated what was known as the Bell System until its breakup in the 1980s. Frequently referred to as Ma Bell, the company coordinated regional telephone systems—all of which purchased equipment from Western Electric, a subsidiary of

AT&T—and then delivered network programming to local affiliates.[15] At every step of the way, from acquiring a license to operating a station, corporate interests dominated.

While commercialism prospered in this regulatory framework, government played a key role in overseeing it and manipulating it for personal and political gain.[16] First, the Radio Act of 1927, which established the FRC, clearly stated that the public owned the airwaves, and thus, that access to them was a privilege that technically required broadcasters to serve the public interest (although it didn't specify how). Second, the law also mandated that political candidates would have access to radio by requiring that stations afford equal time to all candidates seeking office.[17]

When President Franklin Roosevelt worked with Congress to create the Federal Communications Commission in 1934, these policies remained in place. Despite the emergence of a broadcast reform movement advocating for a more noncommercial approach, Roosevelt had little interest in changing a communications system that prioritized national interests over local ones. After all, such a regulatory structure provided a coast-to-coast audience for his groundbreaking "Fireside Chats."[18]

Over the next decade, it became clear that broadcasters prioritized popular entertainment programs, frequently ignoring the public service requirement that came along with their licenses. Many critics lamented the advertising-based system that kept network executives focused on sponsor contracts rather than the needs of their listeners—a criticism made famous by Frederic Wakeman's 1946 best-selling novel about greed driving radio operations, *The Hucksters*. Others noted that despite growing labor unrest, any radio news coverage that did appear had a more conservative and corporate bent. Organizations like the National Negro Congress and the National Urban League also called out both discriminatory practices in hiring and the negative stereotypes that proliferated on popular programs like *Amos 'n Andy*.[19]

In the end, media reform efforts during the 1930s and 1940s failed to displace the corporate interests driving broadcasting. But such activism did result in several important developments that established specific rules to make the commercialized public sphere of broadcasting responsive to civic issues.

The first was the establishment of ownership rules designed to bring greater diversity of perspectives to the air by breaking up the monopolistic control of the medium by a dominant electronics company, Radio Corporation of America (RCA), which owned two different National Broadcasting Company (NBC) networks that disseminated programming, the Red and the Blue. The FCC ruled that one organization could not own more than one network, and it mandated the breakup of NBC. When the Supreme Court upheld this order, NBC had to sell off its Blue network, giving birth to a new competitor, the American Broadcasting Company (ABC).[20] Such a ruling went beyond questions of ownership and also upheld the right of the FCC to weigh in on programming itself.[21] When the FCC then looked into the specifics of educational and public affairs programming, it found that many stations promised such programming but failed to deliver it. The FCC's 1946 report, *Public Service Responsibilities of Broadcast Licensees* known colloquially by the color of its cover as the "Blue Book," created more specific program standards, including the importance of delivering news and noncommercial programming, even if such shows generated less profit than entertainment ones did.

Another change focused even more specifically on political content. The FCC had continued the FRC's rule about equal time to require radio stations to provide all legally qualified candidates equal access to airtime at the same price (whether paid or provided freely). However, concerns about political editorializing by broadcasters proliferated during the 1930s as controversial figures like Father Charles Coughlin—whose program was wildly popular—used the airwaves to attack Jews, the New Deal, and the idea of intervention in the battle against fascism.[22] In 1941, the FCC made its Mayflower decision, which aimed to stop such political rants by stating: "In brief, the broadcaster cannot be an advocate."[23] The decision paved the path for the Fairness Doctrine of 1949—a policy that many progressives celebrated and some conservatives hated in the decades to come.[24] With this rule, the FCC removed the ban on editorializing. Instead, it required broadcasters to cover "controversial issues of public importance" but emphasized the obligation to present contrasting views on these issues.

Such changes heightened expectations that radio broadcasters had a responsibility to serve the public interest, even as these rules prioritized the rights of media owners and producers (rather than consumers). While corporate networks promised to self-regulate and fulfill their social responsibility, they frequently ignored the Blue Book programming standards.[25] The FCC rarely enforced them when stations submitted license renewal requests.[26] Nevertheless, consequences of the Fairness Doctrine reverberated in the postwar period, notably censoring topics and viewpoints on the left and right fringes of the political spectrum while also bolstering the authority of and messaging from the political establishment.[27]

———

Amidst these rule changes, television emerged.[28] After decades of experimentation, the new medium exploded in popularity in the postwar period, and it did so following radio's regulatory and business structure. Local broadcasters secured FCC licenses and affiliated with a national network (overwhelmingly the radio networks now experimenting with "telecasts"), which then provided programming underwritten by corporate sponsors.[29]

As with radio, commercial and corporate interests reigned once again. As the journalist Les Brown noted in his 1971 book *Televi$ion: The Business Behind the Box*, "Television is not so much interested in the business of communication as in the business of delivering people to advertisers."[30] Early television programming was initially created by advertisers with soup or cigarette references baked into elements of the program. (Think: Camel News Caravan, Lucky Strike Hit Parade, and The Campbell Playhouse.) Later, advertisements would run during commercial breaks, but the main goal was always to use programming as "bait" to gather audiences. "The consumer, whom the custodians of the medium are pledged to serve, is in fact served up," wrote Brown. The bigger the audience, the more network executives and their local affiliates could command for advertising time.

The FCC quickly became overwhelmed with applications for new broadcast television licenses.[31] It needed to figure out how to organize and allocate time on the spectrum, which consisted of the limited Very High Frequency (VHF) band with signals that allowed for more accessible and longer wavelengths, and the Ultra High Frequency (UHF) band, which had signals with lower-quality reception. Since the FCC initially only authorized VHF channels to operate, television companies had built sets to receive the VHF signals, which meant that accessing the UHF band required a special converter on televisions that cost $25–$50 (roughly $300–$600 in 2022 dollars).[32]

Initially, the agency anticipated it could resolve the spectrum issues in just six months, by the end of 1948. It took four years. During this time, the FCC decided that the UHF spectrum would deliver opportunities for different types of programming, including educational ones. But the agency never invested fully into developing the UHF spectrum, allowing the promise of diversity on the dial to go unfulfilled. Instead, advertisers, which funded programming, flocked to CBS and NBC, which reached larger audiences because their affiliates used the stronger signals on the VHF spectrum.

Between 1948 and 1952, many people lived "on the fringe" of television reception. They had heard of this new home entertainment device, and perhaps had witnessed it at a demonstration or local appliance store. But they could not access the signals in their homes.[33] Grace Parsons was one such person. She saw the new medium in action when she accompanied her husband Ed, a radio station operator in Astoria, Oregon, to Chicago for a convention. When they returned to the West Coast, she wanted to buy a television set. It was useless—Astoria, a fishing town of about ten thousand people, was well out of range of any television signals. When they heard about a new television station being launched in Seattle, Grace pushed her husband, with all of his radio and engineering experience, to find a way to access a channel. And so, Parsons built an antenna on top of a local hotel room and was able to amplify the signal from Seattle and then convert it via wire for reception on his wife's newly purchased television set.[34]

Soon, the Parsonses' household was overrun with neighbors hoping to catch a glimpse of television. Overwhelmed, Ed Parsons worked with the hotel manager to bring the rooftop signal into the hotel lobby with a wire in the elevator shaft. When curious television observers overcrowded the hotel, Parsons went to the music store next door and the owner, Cliff Poole, became his first customer. Soon bar owners wanted their own television sets to bring in new patrons. Community television, or CATV, had taken root.

The demand intensified, and soon people wanted a wired connection to their individual houses. This would require stringing wire across the town—something local officials did not want Parsons to do. As he recalled, "The city council just plain refused to grant us that franchise unless I could get on the power and light poles. Ma Bell absolutely refused to let us on the poles."[35] Pole attachment, as it was called, was an issue that would plague the cable industry for decades to come.

Parsons's solution was to work around AT&T and use the railroad poles instead. It worked, and news quickly spread of Parsons's community television system. "I was swamped with letters from thousands of people all over the world and in all languages," he recalled decades later.[36] Though widely popular, his experiment also exposed the central challenge that cable operators would face repeatedly over the next half century to bring the technology into homes of eager consumers: negotiating franchising terms with city governments and pole attachment arrangements with utility companies.

Similar scenarios played out across the country in the late forties and early fifties. In Pennsylvania's mountainous regions, for instance, customers on the peak of a ridge could access television signals, but those at the bottom could not. The solution? Run a wire from a receiver at the top of the mountain and hook it up to homes in the valley so they would buy television sets. "You couldn't hook them up fast enough," remembered Irene Gans, who launched some of these early cable systems in the state with her husband.[37] Over time, a community of

Leroy "Ed" Parsons, an electronics engineer, built one of
the first cable systems in the United States in 1948. He used
coaxial cable, amplifiers, and a community antenna to deliver
television signals from Seattle, Washington, to Astoria,
Oregon.
Photo Credit: Barco Library, The Cable Center.

CATV operators grew and they began sharing technical approaches
and business strategies to keep up with the demand.[38]

The FCC paid little attention to how CATV took root, focusing
instead on boosting the commercial broadcasting industry. The reform
impulses of the previous decade had faded as President Harry Truman and especially his Republican successor, Dwight Eisenhower,
appointed regulators who celebrated the importance of free enterprise and the civic role of corporate America.[39] Network executives

developed a cozy relationship with these regulators, one that frequently gave the agency a negative reputation. Bribes, payoffs, and personal favors created tremendous improprieties that shaped how the FCC granted licenses, leading one commissioner to call the 1950s "the whorehouse era."[40] In one high-profile case, FCC Commissioner Richard A. Mack owed money to a college friend, Thurman Whiteside. In lieu of payment, Whiteside asked him to grant a Miami license to a local broadcaster who promised to cut Whiteside in on the deal. The appearance that Mack used public property—a broadcasting license—to pay off a debt prompted a congressional investigation and undermined the credibility of the agency.[41]

Eventually, the search for social prestige and a desire to maintain the regulatory system that made them millions of dollars each year also motivated some network executives to rethink their approach to public affairs. Indeed, they recognized that such programming could be a way to curry even more favor with lawmakers. As one NBC executive, Sylvester "Pat" Weaver, constantly reminded his colleagues, educational, cultural, and public affairs programs could "enrich the common man" while also delivering social capital to the networks, protecting the licenses of its affiliates, and ensuring its status as a regulated monopoly.[42]

That was the crossroads that CBS's Sig Mickelson saw the industry facing at the end of the 1950s. While television news remained in its infancy, he argued that expanding it and teaching politicians how to use it could be good business and good politics. He stressed this message at a 1959 annual luncheon for radio and television executives. "The impact of television on our political life has come through its effect not on the voter but rather on the citizen."[43] Voter turnout had increased in 1952 and 1956, and Mickelson credited television.[44] But he noted there was a missed opportunity on television because elected officials "fail to recognize the day-to-day news coverage" possibilities, even though the political benefits were tremendous: it was a free opportunity for candidates to shape audience understanding of current events.[45] Such a strategy was also consequential as it connected the application of the public service rules to the self-interest of politicians.

At the time, over 80 percent of Americans owned a television set, but television news still had to prove itself to the political establishment.[46] National politicians thought of newspapers as the main conduit for the news, even sometimes scheduling two different press conferences for those reporters with a pen and paper and those with a microphone and camera. Mickelson wanted television news to gain respect and credibility. After all, he argued, "television can deliver some types of news with more impact, leading to a better retention on the part of the public than any other medium has ever been able to do." He urged broadcasters to find ways to "be of enormous assistance to the candidate in communicating to the potential voter" during the 1960 election and beyond. This work, he emphasized, should be persistent, something that "goes on 365 days a year—in election years and off-years alike."[47]

In short, Mickelson recognized that elected officials didn't instinctually know how to use television news as a political tool. Rather, those in the burgeoning industry needed to teach them how to do it. Over the next year, Mickelson led efforts to do just that, creating a symbiotic relationship between television and politics that tethered dominant campaign and governing strategies to broadcasting values and tactics. As television journalism expanded its operations, network newsrooms brought tremendous profits and publicity to all involved while motivating those excluded from television news programming—notably conservative and Black Americans—to build alternative media institutions to promote their ideas.[48]

Forging a relationship with the president became an easy way for network executives to build political goodwill while also fulfilling their FCC public affairs mandates.[49] They happily gave President Eisenhower television time to deliver speeches on issues that ranged from foreign policy to civil rights and even televised a cabinet proceeding in 1954.[50] Eisenhower hadn't come to television on his own; rather, a team of actors, advertisers, and television executives sold him on the importance of the medium and pushed him to take it seriously. When he did, his television appearances expanded the star power of the presidency and shaped the very definition of "news."[51]

But it was John F. Kennedy who really implemented the vision that Mickelson had for television—in part because he listened to Mickelson's advice with a groundbreaking presidential campaign that made visual media a priority. The son of a former Hollywood studio executive, Kennedy transformed himself into a celebrity on the campaign trail with a media-savvy operation designed to turn voters into "Jack Kennedy fans." He hired a private production company as part of his team and even used a personalized song from Frank Sinatra to raise enthusiasm and dollars for his candidacy. Kennedy also experimented with ways to attract favorable, and free, news coverage—going so far as to appear on popular entertainment programs like *Tonight Starring Jack Paar* to build a direct connection with viewers as media consumers first, voters second.[52]

That year, the "Great Debates" illuminated how broadcasting interests connected with political ambitions in the television age. Republican Party candidates Harold Stassen and Thomas Dewey had debated on the radio in their efforts to win the party nomination in 1948, and the idea of presidential debates was batted around in 1952 and 1956.[53] The Equal Time Rule made the networks reluctant to do this though, as it would have required them to give equal airtime to *all* candidates running for president, including those from outside the two-party system. It was easier to avoid debates altogether.[54]

In 1960, however, the networks were desperate to make debates happen so they could "show their best once their worst had made them rich," observed the journalist Theodore White, who chronicled the campaign that year.[55] The chase for profits over the previous decade had come at a cost. Journalists alleged that popular quiz shows like *The $64,000 Question* (CBS) and *Twenty-One* (NBC) were rigged. A congressional hearing looked into the question in the fall of 1959, and testimony exposed clear instances of abuse. Most famously, Charles Van Doren, a multiweek winner on *Twenty-One*, confessed to receiving questions in advance as the network sought to draw in viewers with heightened drama.[56] The scandal shocked the nation and propelled networks to do something big to regain the trust of the public and regulators.

Congress had also amended the Equal Time Rule. In 1959, it passed legislation that allowed for four exceptions in which legally qualified candidates could appear in newscasts, news interviews, news documentaries, or "on-the-spot coverage of bona fide news events" without broadcasters having to meet requests for equal time in these appearances. Worried that fringe candidates would try to take advantage of the requirement to disrupt campaign coverage and bolster radical ideas, Senator John Pastore, the bill's sponsor, urged its passage as an effort to avoid "a very chaotic situation come next election."[57] Even those who supported the bill had concerns as it generated debate about what constituted a "bona fide" news event, and politicians understood the growing power of network news executives who crafted such definitions.[58]

The rule change helped make the debates—and the extended coverage of the presidential race that year—possible, ultimately elevating the political prestige of television networks and bolstering the two-party system. The two candidates faced off in four debates that fall, but Richard Nixon's sweaty and haggard appearance in the first debate, complete with a gray suit that made him blend into the background, dominates historical memory of the broader election. Indeed, that first debate has since assumed a place of mythical proportion in media history, the moment when style, performance, and television seemingly overtook the political process overnight.[59] For decades, scholars have challenged the popular notion that the television debates delivered the election for Kennedy, who squeaked out a victory by just over one hundred thousand votes.[60] But in the minds of politicians, journalists, and campaign advisers, the lesson was clear: television performance and access to millions of viewers could be a path to political power for candidates and networks alike—just as Sig Mickelson had predicted.[61]

Kennedy certainly believed in the power of television. As president, he launched a variety of new television initiatives that connected the White House to the networks in ways that tipped the balance of power dramatically away from Congress and toward the executive branch, while bolstering the authority of the new television journalism profession. He introduced the first live televised press conference, something networks enthusiastically covered, for free, even though such events "preempted millions of dollars in commercial time," observed Kennedy's press secretary, Pierre Salinger.[62] Regular "reports to the nation" as well as "conversations" with network news anchors like Walter Cronkite gave the American public "an intimate glimpse of a President: his personality, his mind at work, his sense of history—and his sense of humor," remarked Salinger. It also allowed Kennedy and his team to remain in control of the information discussed and to "manage" the news in a way that bolstered his agenda.[63] Kennedy recognized the central role that the medium played. "We couldn't survive without television," he admitted to an aide while reviewing a recording of a recently televised interview.[64]

Members of Congress looked to the growing spotlight on the White House with concern and envy. Soon, they sought to emulate it. By the early 1960s, many representatives and senators had come to understand how important it was to "make news" because "publicity is his lifeblood," explained one congressional guide.[65] The previous decade, House Speaker Sam Rayburn had distinguished between "showhorses" and "workhorses" in Congress.[66] The former, whom he disdained, only wanted attention, while the latter followed the rules of secrecy and seniority. Television had begun to change these dynamics, and creating a show became part of the work itself. However, with only three networks and limited coverage dedicated to public affairs, members of Congress struggled to find national airtime.

Televised congressional hearings created an important exception. Indeed, one political scientist observed in 1962, the "post-WWII upsurge in congressional investigations primarily reflects an attempt on the part of the legislature to restore a balance of power in the area of publicity."[67] As Richard Nixon (R-CA) learned in 1948 during the House Un-American Activities Committee hearings investigating Alger Hiss, and as Estes Kefauver (D-TN) discovered following his 1950–1951 Senate investigation into organized crime, television could provide a path to national recognition that allowed both men to climb the party ladder and secure their respective vice-presidential nominations.[68] And yet, journalists like Douglass Cater warned about the distraction embedded within such "publicity brouhahas," which he feared could open the door "for the demagogue who is prepared to oversimplify the grave issues of our time and to regard publicity as an end rather than a means in the drive for power."[69]

That certainly was the case with Joseph McCarthy as the postwar anticommunist environment intensified and the Wisconsin senator adroitly manipulated television to become a household name by viciously smearing opponents with accusations of communist loyalties. But McCarthy's widely televised 1954 investigation into alleged communist activities in the Army demonstrated that the spotlight could also expose such fearmongering tactics. After voting to censor the Wisconsin senator, Congress then began discussing a code of fair practices to shape future hearings on television.[70]

More so than nationally televised hearings—which only raised the profile of those few individuals involved—local television news quickly became an even more powerful tool that members of Congress could use to connect to their constituents and shape the news agenda. Initially, local television news consisted mostly of fifteen-minute wire service headlines and short summaries taken directly from newspapers. During the 1960s, stations began to invest more time and money into local news programming—fostering a close and productive relationship with members of Congress in the process.[71]

Both the House and the Senate built expensive television studios for members to record regular radio or television programs for hometown stations.[72] There, members of Congress could create short clips explaining the news from their perspective, which would then be sent to local stations. With a selection of backgrounds to choose from—a shot of the Capitol, bookshelves, or a congressional desk—representatives could deliver affordable weekly briefings to connect more intimately to constituents at home while they lived in Washington, D.C., and worked on Capitol Hill. The studio also offered other production assets to enhance the professional quality of these clips, including a teleprompter and postproduction editing.[73]

Following similar protocols that had been established with local newspapers (which frequently reprinted speeches and press releases verbatim from these same representatives), such footage allowed local broadcasters to avoid the time and expense of sending a reporter to Washington to cover national political events.[74] This was a tremendous benefit to members of Congress, of course, as their perspectives became defined as the news itself. The result: on Capitol Hill and in the White House, making news became a political priority and success increasingly became defined by publicity itself.[75]

———

Elected officials also had an economic stake in the regulated broadcast system. By 1969, fourteen members of Congress had substantial investments in their own radio and television stations.[76] Republican Congressman Alvin O'Konski from Wisconsin, for example, owned a radio and then a television station in his home district of Rhinelander. While representing this rural northern district filled with woods, lakes, paper mills, and iron mines, O'Konski also worked as president of the television station and even used it as his district office, asserting proudly that his "office in the station is the most modern and well-equipped home office of any congressman."[77]

The smooth-talking O'Konski took advantage of the government payroll, using his congressional secretaries—paid by tax dollars—also as assistant managers for the television station. At home, his critics raised questions about whether, ethically, a member of Congress should be allowed to make money off a federally regulated business. And yet, for thirty years he easily won reelection, and his career exposed a truth about politics: "the art of being successful at whatever you can get away with," as the authors of his profile for Ralph Nader's Congress Project put it.[78]

Such arrangements revealed how the entanglement of politics and television did more than make elected officials local media celebrities. It could make them wealthy as well, even if clear conflicts of interest emerged as members of Congress cast votes each year for the FCC operational budget—sometimes even when the agency was reviewing their own license renewal request.

No one demonstrated the economic and political power embedded in this relationship among Congress, the FCC, and broadcasting quite like Lyndon Johnson, a Texas Democrat who won his first House race in 1937 and then moved to the Senate in 1949 before quickly climbing the party ladder as majority whip in 1951, minority leader in 1953, and then finally majority leader in 1955. It was an impressive political ascent—aided by a media empire he had built that also generated substantial personal wealth. To avoid the kind of criticism O'Konski faced about conflicts of interest, Johnson repeatedly emphasized that his wife Claudia Alta "Lady Bird" Johnson owned and operated the business, calling himself a "broadcaster-in-law."[79] However, records show the significant role he played in acquiring the KTBC station and turning it into such a profitable venture.[80] Investigations into these holdings repeatedly showed that Johnson did not violate any laws.[81] Rather, his family business exposed ways in which public officials could legally reap financial rewards, especially when it came to federally regulated media industries.

The broadcasting business brought tremendous financial returns for the Johnsons. In 1943, Lady Bird purchased an Austin radio station, and then four years later, merged the station into a company she named Texas Broadcasting Corporation—later to be called the LBJ Company once it ventured into television—with a value of $488,000.[82] In 1952, she acquired the license to build a VHF television station at KTBC, just as other radio stations looking to enter the TV business across the country did as well. Knowledge of FCC operations paid off—a freeze on new licenses had just ended, and the Johnsons jumped in quickly when it did.[83] By 1959, the company's value had skyrocketed to over $2.5 million, aided in part by Johnson's political stature.[84] As *Broadcasting* magazine noted, Lyndon Johnson "used to sell time on the sly," and companies eager to curry favor with the congressman bought advertising time on the air.[85]

Johnson's looming political presence played another role as Lady Bird Johnson's application for a VHF channel in Austin had no competition. "Lyndon Johnson was in a favorable position to get that station even if someone contested it. Politics is politics," wrote one applicant who refused to even try to battle Johnson for a VHF license and instead applied for the less desirable UHF one.[86] His political clout in Congress and at the FCC also helped to ensure that KTBC-TV remained a monopoly in Austin. The numbers speak for themselves: in Dallas-Fort Worth, five VHF stations had licenses to operate; in Houston four did; and in Corpus Christi, with a population of 108,000, two stations operated.[87] In Austin, with a population of over 132,000 in 1950, the FCC granted only one license, and it quickly became known as LBJ-TV. As the only local station, KTBC (its official call letters) then crafted a lucrative arrangement to affiliate with all three networks, ensuring viewers access to the most popular programs, but only one at a time.

Broadcasting was the pillar of his family's fortunes, but Johnson also saw the opportunities embedded in cable. As cable operators across the country were quickly learning, economic survival depended on advancing the bottom line of broadcasters rather than competing with them. Nothing made this clearer than the process of bringing cable television to "LBJ Country."[88]

By the 1960s, cable started entering cities that already had broadcasting with a promise of providing subscribers a clearer picture and even more channels on the dial—and in doing so, operators began to conflict with local broadcasters and federal regulators. In Santa Maria, California, for example, a cable operator offered access to all seven of Los Angeles's broadcasting stations, along with the local signals. The FCC worried that this extra competition for the local Santa Maria broadcaster infringed on the station's economic viability, and so it attempted to develop new regulations to protect local broadcasters as part of its regulatory commitment to promoting "localism."[89]

Legally, the FCC did not have explicit authority to regulate cable television, as it simply didn't exist in 1934 when Congress passed the Communications Act. But it could regulate one essential part of most companies' operations: signal importation. The majority of cable operators brought in the signals wirelessly via a microwave system,

An example of an antenna tower that brought in signals to cable operators to then disseminate via wired connections. This is from Meadville Master Antenna, Inc., circa 1965.
Photo Credit: Barco Library, The Cable Center.

and then fed these distant signals through cable to subscribers. And so, the FCC implemented a "blackout clause," also called nonduplication, which mandated that cable operators using microwave could not show the same programming as the local broadcaster for a designated period. This limited the types of programs that cable operators could offer on the extended dial it provided subscribers.

The merits and problems of this regulatory approach captured national attention in Austin when one of the most powerful families in the country stood to make millions of dollars from ownership of a cable franchise. Initially, Johnson's broadcasting station in Austin had made the city "one of the most promising markets in the nation for delivery of out-of-town TV programs," observed *Wall Street Journal* reporter Louis M. Kohlmeier in the spring of 1964.[90] Since viewers only had access to one station, controlled by LBJ-TV, cable could provide significantly more viewing options, and, as a result, competition to the Johnson media monopoly.

The Johnson family recognized this early on and took part in the discussions with the municipal government about bringing cable to Austin. They weren't alone, however. In 1957 when the town launched a conversation about a potential cable television initiative, many applicants expressed interest; LBJ-TV was one of two especially promising applicants. The other was Midwest Video Corp. from Little Rock, Arkansas, with a record of building successful cable systems operating in towns across Texas, Mississippi, and New Mexico.

Given Johnson's political clout, Mayor Thomas Miller proposed a solution to C. Hamilton Moses, the president of Midwest: a business arrangement with the LBJ Company, which Kohlmeier described as "remarkably favorable to the Johnson Broadcasting Company."[91] They formed the Capital Cable Company, which was fully financed by Midwest but offered an option for the Johnson company to acquire 50 percent ownership at any time for three years after building the franchise. It also created a lucrative arrangement to erect an antenna on the roof of the Johnson television station to bring in the signals for a fee of $1,000 a month.

Over the next five years, the Austin City Council sat on the application from the newly formed Capital Cable Company, with the Johnson Broadcasting Company enjoying its monopoly control of the market (even if it had a stake in the competition). Soon after Lyndon Johnson became the country's vice president, local pressure for cable to provide an alternative on the television dial grew.[92] In a raucous January 1963 city council meeting, Austin citizens, likely encouraged by a local journalist keen on starting his own cable company, pushed the city council to reconsider franchise applications from three other companies alongside Capital Cable.

Johnson kept his eye on the situation, meeting with his lawyers on the issue of "Capital Cable" five times between November 28,

1962, and February 4, 1963.[93] Capital Cable had a clear plan on how it would deliver television programs to the public via the LBJ-TV tower and an agreement already in place with Southwestern Bell to use telephone poles to string its cable lines. And so, the company emerged as the frontrunner in the renewed franchise debate. The council voted 4–0 to award it a contract with the city. It was a huge financial win for the Johnson family, which stood to make $5 million if Capital Cable succeeded and the Johnsons cashed in on ownership options.

The companies that struck out cried foul. Accusations of misconduct and manipulation abounded during what the local newspaper called a "stormy call session" that included participants "heckling and booing when the decision was announced."[94] The connection between Capital Cable and LBJ-TV made the cable company appear to be just an extension of the broadcasting empire that the Johnson family already had, and other applicants argued that the television market desperately needed more local competition to ensure a diversity of voices. While the FCC had raised concerns about broadcast ownership of cable systems, it had not formalized its policy yet. And so, the proposal itself didn't violate any regulations, even if it did undermine the spirit of existing duopoly rules, which restricted cross-media ownership in the same marketplace.[95]

Hoping to appease all parties, even as the council voted to give the franchise to Capital Cable, it also opened the market to competing companies. This departed from the general treatment of cable as a natural monopoly. Since operations required stringing lines on telephone poles or other utility poles, city governments usually reviewed applications by potential companies and then selected one to provide the service to avoid cluttering the poles. But in Austin, the city council decided to allow any company that followed twenty-one specific local regulations to set up a potential cable service for residents.[96]

Several cable operators outside Austin followed the controversy, and once the council opened the city up to all applicants, one person thought, "Well, let's just give it a try."[97] John Campbell, who had successfully brought cable television to Mineral Wells, Texas, sent a one-page letter to the council outlining his qualifications and a proposal for the city. After its quick approval, he got to work with a plan to bring in distant signals via microwave from San Antonio so that cable subscribers could have access to all three networks simultaneously for only $4.95 a month.

While Capital Cable had local connections and political leverage, Campbell's TV Cable had wires stored in a South Austin warehouse ready to go and the technical knowledge to build and operate a system. Campbell faced an uphill battle, however. First, he had to convince Southwestern Bell—which already had an agreement with Capital Cable—to run his lines. Initially Southwestern Bell explained it didn't have enough room for both companies to string wire from their poles. According to the *New York Times*, "public uproar" persuaded it otherwise.[98] By March, TV Cable started construction, eager to be the first company to chart out a grid for laying cable in Austin and the first to get its cables on the poles. Cable television lines, Campbell noted, had to be installed "12 inches above the telephone plant, which didn't leave any room for the second cable company without very expensive pole replacements to be borne by the cable company requesting additional space."[99]

FCC regulations quickly halted TV Cable's head start. As it began construction, TV Cable had also submitted a request to bring in microwave signals from San Antonio. It took until July for the FCC to approve the request, and when it did, it had a condition: nonduplication, mandating that TV Cable must wait fifteen days to show a program also shown on the local broadcast station.[100] Because LBJ-TV affiliated with all three networks, this meant that it could effectively "black out" the most popular network programming across NBC, ABC, and CBS, leaving TV Cable fewer options to offer viewers. By contrast, Capital Cable could skirt such rules because of its arrangement with LBJ-TV to receive distant signals from its tower. Because of this deal, the company did not have to use microwave to import the signals like its competitor, which meant that the FCC could not regulate its programming.

TV Cable quickly asked the FCC to rescind the nonduplication rule. It argued that Johnson's station "cannot openly aid and abet a cable television system in which it has an interest and at the same time reasonably expect the commission to impose substantial restrictions upon the operator of a competitor cable system."[101] The FCC had to make what one commissioner called a "be damned if you do and be damned if you don't" decision.[102]

As it almost always did, the FCC sided with the local broadcaster—in this case, it was the Johnson family—to uphold the noncompetition ruling, something that smelled fishy to the nation's top newspaper outlets. TV Cable protested the decision. The lawyer for TV Cable argued that Johnson's broadcasting monopoly, and then its agreement with Capital Cable, squashed any potential competitor.[103] "Capital Cable literally and figuratively has been placed in a corporate strait jacket for the benefit of KTBC-TV," wrote John P. Cole Jr. in a letter disputing the FCC rulings. "Every provision in the agreement is designed and intended for the benefit of KTBC-TV."[104] TV Cable, the lawyer contended, offered the only real alternative for consumers.

Back in Austin, both TV Cable and Capital Cable built their cable systems and signed up subscribers. Capital Cable advertised to cable subscribers with promises of "total television . . . no delays!"[105] As required by the FCC, TV Cable featured frequent blackouts, when instead of airing a popular program, it aired the statement: "Delayed telecast. Write or wire your opinion to the FCC, Washington, D.C."[106] The company also used resentment toward the Johnson media monopoly to fuel sales, frequently featuring ads that asked viewers if they were "chained to one channel."[107]

When he assumed the presidency following John F. Kennedy's assassination that November, Lyndon and Lady Bird Johnson put their media and other business holdings into a blind trust. And yet, this did not prevent further scrutiny on how the new president had acquired his private wealth and his cable connections. In a series of articles in the *Wall Street Journal*, Louis Kohlmeier shone light on the Capital Cable saga once again and repeatedly raised questions about the fact that the "presidential family had its wealth concentrated in a Government-regulated industry with the full knowledge of the regulators," all of whom would be up for re-appointment by the end of President Johnson's first term.[108]

In relentless coverage of the issue, Kohlmeier studied FCC files, the *Congressional Record*, land deeds, and stockholder lists. He interviewed FCC commissioners, staffers, elected officials, and a range of Johnson confidants in a quest to understand how Lyndon Johnson acquired his broadcasting empire, and the political and economic ramifications of this prized government-regulated possession. He found that the blind trust itself did not guarantee that Johnson would not use his position to influence regulatory decisions that directly impacted his family's pocketbook. Overseen by two old friends from Texas, with whom Johnson remained in contact, the trust created only a "halfway measure that does not divorce the family from the stations," an FCC member told Kohlmeier.[109]

One of the trustees, J. Waddy Bullion, disagreed. He maintained that the Johnsons didn't have any knowledge of or influence over business decisions, including when the Texas Broadcasting Company may decide to exercise its option to purchase 50 percent of Capital Cable.[110] Bullion explained in an oral history that it would have been easier to sell the stock of the cable company to alleviate the political suspicions surfacing. But, as a trustee committed to pursuing the "best interests" of the business, Bullion kept the Johnsons' stock option in Capital Cable until 1967, when changes in FCC ownership policies forced him to choose between the local broadcasting station and the cable system.

TV Cable's John Campbell repeatedly alleged political pressures, applied by Johnson and Senator John L. McClellan (a partner in the law firm that represented Midwest Video Corp.), as the reason the FCC refused to rescind the nonduplication order throughout the entire franchise debate.[111] When Capital Cable initially declined to give the FCC details as to the agreement it had with the LBJ Co., it only fueled media interest in the topic and generated questions of potential presidential misconduct.[112] In the end, TV Cable accepted Capital Cable's offer to buy it out in June 1964, which also came with the stipulation that information surrounding the sale would not be announced until after the presidential election.

The controversy over cable did bring negative publicity to Lyndon Johnson, though, in part because Louis Kohlmeier refused to let the issue die. The thirty-nine-year-old graduate of the University of Missouri would ultimately win a Pulitzer Prize for "his enterprise in reporting the growth of the fortune of President Lyndon B. Johnson and his family."[113] He wasn't alone. During the summer of 1964, journalists became obsessed with Johnson's media empire. The headline in *Life* magazine directly asked: how did President Lyndon Johnson become such a wealthy man, with holdings that totaled almost $14 million? The article then explained the very operations of the broadcasting industry, which *Life* called the "cornerstone of the Johnson holdings."[114]

The *Life* story portrayed Lyndon and Lady Bird Johnson as media entrepreneurs who transformed a struggling radio station into an Austin television powerhouse with both FCC favor and lucrative monopoly status that allowed the station to command higher than normal advertising rates. It introduced cable television as "another potentially rich television harvest" that "looms for the Texas Broadcasting Co." by adding value to the family's estate and preserving "KTBC's Austin-area monopoly." The article made clear that Johnson had not violated any laws in his pursuit of "free enterprise," but it did raise the question of how related the "two different planes" that Johnson pursued were: "He did become a millionaire; he did become President of the United States. The planes are different, but are they unrelated?"

The answer, of course, is no. The relationship between elected officials and the very broadcasting industry they shaped with legislation and FCC appointments tightened during the 1960s, with mutual benefits for all involved. In 1964, cable television fit into this system merely by bolstering the broadcasting industry's reach. Cable operators competed with one another and battled with city governments and telephone companies as they crafted franchise plans. They faced off against FCC regulators as they sought to deliver timely programming.

But in the early days, broadcasters and cable operators were allies, not enemies.

Yet there were signs that cable could do something more, something that would bring cable and broadcast into direct competition: fulfill a consumer demand for more choice on the dial and charge viewers directly for this luxury. Indeed, a battle over pay television that same year was the beginning of a decades-long war between different forms of television.

2

A Business Rivalry Forms

"One fine morning last February, a tall man with gray hair and the casual grace of a six-figure income, but also with the jug ears, freckles and glorious optimism of eternal American youth, went ringing doorbells in a hilly section of western Los Angeles." So began the 1964 *Saturday Evening Post* profile of former NBC executive Sylvester "Pat" Weaver, who was now basking in the sunlight of Southern California and the spotlight his new position as president of Subscription Television (STV) cast on him.[1]

As Weaver walked door to door, the charismatic man who still held such high hopes for television's future tapped into the growing frustrations about the limits of commercial television. When housewives answered the door, he asked them if they felt fulfilled and satisfied with their television programming. Overwhelmingly, they answered no. One woman complained to him, "You know that program *Outer Limits*? It starts with this statement that 'we have complete control over your television set.' Well, that's just what I feel that someone controls my set." Another told Weaver she wanted self-improvement and educational programming during the day. Many more just wanted something other than nonstop children's programming that numbed their minds and threatened to turn them "into a blob." The fast-talking executive had the solution to all these woes: subscription television.

This form of pay television used the same wired infrastructure as CATV systems, but it promised to do more than merely extend the reach of broadcasting signals. While community television systems relied on subscriber fees to pay for connectivity costs, pay television boldly introduced the concept of subscriber fees to pay for television programming itself.

This alternative approach to television, Weaver promised them, could provide sports for their husbands, a movie for the family on Friday night, a Broadway play for date night, or an educational lecture while the children napped in the afternoon. Subscribers could have quality content delivered with vivid reception, and in color, something only a small minority of television sets delivered at the time. Drawing on a vision of television he couldn't get support for at the ratings-driven NBC, Weaver proclaimed to isolated housewives and luncheon crowds alike that subscription television will "make us Athenians all." It only cost fifteen dollars to sign up—which included the installation of a selector box to record which specialty programs were watched each month—and then each day viewers could tune into the information channel for that day's offerings or turn on the premium channels for six minutes to sample a more exclusive program. If they stayed longer, they would be charged around $1.50 per program.

With Weaver at its helm, the company pitched pay television as a vehicle for personal empowerment and social change. And he found investors—sporting teams, electronics companies, and wealthy individuals—who contributed $7 million to launch the splashiest pay television venture yet. He then got the public to buy stock to raise $16 million more.

Despite such financial backing, technical support, and public demand, Weaver soon encountered a tremendous obstacle: the political mobilization of theater owners and broadcasters. In California, powerful people and institutions worked tirelessly to undermine the business potential of pay television. And it worked. "Citizens for Free TV" convinced the majority of the state's voters that fall to outlaw pay television.

The 1964 "free television" campaign was a culmination of an extensive lobbying effort against the very concept of pay television. Such an economic model challenged the advertising-based structure of television that allowed anyone to access programs, but at a cost of their time during commercial advertising breaks that underwrote the programming expenses. Over the previous decade, network executives and the National Association of Radio and Television Broadcasters (NARTB, renamed the National Association of Broadcasters in 1958) had issued dire warnings of the "gilded curtain" that would descend on the country if pay TV became a reality, dividing the nation into households who could afford television and those who could not.[2] The Cold War imagery of this public relations campaign reflected the ways in which consumption had emerged as central to American citizenship in the postwar era. Television, what NBC called a "selling machine in every living room," fueled the power and prominence of Madison Avenue advertising firms and padded the pocketbooks of network executives.[3] Pay television, or what the NARTB classified as "toll television," would result in "an agonizing rejuggling of the family budget," and it would "have an undemocratic and divisive effect," the lobbying organization argued, by depriving viewers of their right to consume television.[4]

With a massive political campaign, broadcasters and especially movie theater owners, who worried about losing even more audiences to television, did everything they could to strangle the nascent pay television industry. Their efforts exposed the power that entrenched media industries had, and the lengths to which they would go to preserve it. At the time, the concept of pay television divided the cable industry—some believed it offered potential for new revenue streams while others saw it as distracting from the original mission of disseminating broadcasting signals. All agreed, however, that the battle over subscription television in 1964 impacted the industry's future. As *CATV Weekly* editor Stanley Searle fretted on the eve of the election, "If California outlaws subscription TV by cable, what lies in store there, and in other states for other forms of free enterprise . . . such as CATV?"[5]

He was right to worry. The pay television fight in California that year set the stage for a war that would soon unfold between broadcasters and cable television operators. At its core, it raised regulatory questions that impacted both of their business operations, notably whether state governments, Congress, the courts, and the FCC could and should protect the interests of broadcasters by limiting competition from other forms of television. Yet the debates also helped to usher in a foundational shift in television's perceived political and economic role. Pay television advocates argued that individual choice and market competition could empower citizens by expanding viewing options.[6] While they lost the battle that year as Lyndon Johnson's Great Society vision swept the nation, this argument would gain traction in the cable industry and in Washington, eventually instilling doubt that a government-regulated monopoly served the public interest.

———

STV offered Pat Weaver a chance to start over in television. A philosophy major at Dartmouth College who saw the medium as a "miracle" with tremendous potential to "upgrade humanity across a broad base," Weaver had joined NBC in 1949 and quickly climbed the corporate ladder.[7] Through a cultural enrichment program called Operation Frontal Lobes and a range of live programming, Weaver cultivated a record of public service within the company.[8] He also launched the lucrative *Today Show* and then later *The Tonight Show*, two programs that would make television history.

Significantly, Weaver also reshaped the role of advertising in television programming. He urged NBC to abandon the model of having advertising companies produce shows featuring their products and instead to adopt a "magazine format" in which the networks controlled the programming and sold slots during commercial breaks to advertisers. The shift of content control from advertisers to networks changed power dynamics and corporate calculations. Viewers became more

Sylvester "Pat" Weaver in his NBC office.
Photo Credit: Wisconsin Historical Society,
WHI- 10798.

loyal to individual networks and the shows they produced, which ultimately gave networks tremendous social and cultural capital.

Weaver's New York City office got bigger and bigger as he moved from vice president of television programming to the network's president in September 1953.[9] Soon, stories about Weaver's success (as well as his appreciation for lobster, use of a bongo board for exercise, and his swanky private pool) appeared on the front page of *Newsweek* and in a *Life* magazine spread.[10] He expanded the length of the daily television programming schedule, frequently with television "spectaculars"—live special event theatrical performances (like a 1955 telecast of Broadway's *Peter Pan*) that *Life* called "almost as marvelous as the technical marvel of television."[11] Such cultural programs gained acclaim from TV critics, eager to improve the stature of the very medium they frequently denounced for its crass commercialism. These shows also elevated Weaver's reputation as a television visionary.[12] But, the cost often caused tensions with advertisers, who cared more about audience size than program quality.[13]

During his storied career at NBC, Weaver also clashed frequently with General David Sarnoff, the president of NBC's parent company, RCA. Sarnoff, a Russian Jewish immigrant who lacked Weaver's penchant for publicity, was angered by Weaver's flair for the limelight and expensive programming—especially given that most Americans did not have color television sets and that CBS was sailing ahead in the ratings. In 1956, "The General," as he was popularly called following his celebrated service in World War II, had his son, Robert W. Sarnoff, break the news to Weaver in his office.[14] He would become the new president of NBC and Weaver would be promoted to chairman of the board, a move that stripped him of his authority. In September, Weaver left NBC.

While Weaver first focused his attention on developing independent programming, by 1957 he was studying the landscape of pay television. He followed the well-publicized introduction of pay TV into the affluent community of Bartlesville, Oklahoma.[15] Spearheaded by Milton Shapp, the Pennsylvania entrepreneur whose electronics company Jerrold provided the essential infrastructure for early cable operators, the venture charged subscribers a monthly fee to access three channels that featured movies, musical performances, the news, and weather reports, alongside standard network television fare.[16] Despite tremendous fanfare and a significant cost, the experiment lasted only a year, undone in part because of the prices AT&T charged the company to put wires on their telephone poles.[17]

Undeterred, Weaver eyed Honolulu, Hawaii, and Southern California as potential places to launch a new subscription television business.[18] His legal team noted the challenges. In Honolulu, "no one at this moment knows anything about the cost or what the returns might be or when."[19] His advisers observed that the telephone companies had posed the biggest challenge in Bartlesville because of a refusal to allow the use of their poles "for any closed circuit wire television operation and then charged exorbitant amounts."[20] A potential production partner, Skiatron, worried about the cost of distribution to lay new wires and the "political fights that would be involved."[21]

Such concerns were on point. Just a few months later, Weaver's former NBC rival traveled to Washington, D.C., to testify before the House Interstate and Foreign Commerce Committee about the issue of pay television.[22] Robert Sarnoff joined CBS's Frank Stanton and Leonard Goldenson, the president of ABC, to issue dire warnings of a future in which pay television would bring about the end of the "American system of free radio and free TV" that they argued the people demanded and democracy needed.[23]

Here's the scenario they painted for legislators: pay television would start "siphoning" the talent from the airwaves. Soon, the best stars and most exciting programming—notably sports and movies—would seek the higher paychecks made possible by pay television. This would leave broadcasters with smaller audiences, so they would not be able to command high advertising rates to pay for their programs. Slowly, the quality of entertainment would decrease, and out of sheer necessity, the networks would have to enter the business of pay television simply to survive. This would then divide Americans "along economic lines" between those who could afford television and those who could not. Goldenson likened a pay television experiment to "starting an epidemic to test a new vaccine," then reminded members of Congress that "once the epidemic has started, it cannot be controlled."[24]

Such warnings exposed a fundamental contradiction, of course.[25] First, the network executives contended that the public did not want to—or could not—pay for a television subscription. But then, they argued that if pay television were allowed to compete, it would be so successful that it would destroy free television.

The hearings exposed the ways in which broadcasters used their political power to shape their business environment. During their testimonies, the executives also warned that the free coverage of news and public affairs would end. Congressional investigations, presidential speeches, election and convention coverage, and "discussion of public issues in interview and panel programs on which so many members of the House and Senate and officials of the executive branch so frequently appear" would cease to exist because they are not "revenue-producing services."[26] The message was clear: allowing pay television to compete would undermine the very communications industry that elected officials were becoming more and more dependent on to win elections and govern.

While legislation introduced to limit or outlaw pay television following the congressional hearings never gained any muster, the FCC soon issued a report that severely hamstrung the pay television industry by setting a three-year trial period in which it would only permit a pay television station in a single market. Then, it would be subject to FCC approval on whether the system could exist on a more permanent basis. While restrictive, this still left an opening for experiments to take place.[27]

The 1958 hearings skirted around the issue of wired television services as it focused on over-the-air pay television, but soon the controversy entangled cable operators. Many of them wanted to keep their distance, expressing concern about the idea of cable television functioning as an alternative to broadcasting, not simply a retransmission or extension of it.[28] The more entrepreneurial operators, however, understood pay TV as an opportunity for cable television to offer something different from the network broadcasting fare that currently filled the cable dial. Indeed, pay television opened up new possibilities for Hollywood studios and sports teams to sell their products directly to the people—bypassing the networks in the process.[29]

The key distinction between the two industries lay in the classification of service. According to one cable operator, "Pay TV offers specially selected programs for a price. Community antenna television, better known as CATV, does not discriminate between programs. It serves as a convenient pipe-line for all broadcast matter coming from stations it is designed to receive. For this service, subscribers pay a monthly fee, rather than erect their own towers and antennas."[30] But, there was potential for synergy between the two, something that cable pioneer Milton Shapp recognized. In an unpublished autobiography, he recalled how he traveled to regional and state meetings of theater operators to first clarify that cable television and pay TV were not the same during the mid-1950s. In the future, however, he predicted that movies, sports, and "other great attractions" would be shown on television for a fee, and that cable television would make pay television a reality.[31] So Shapp asked broadcasters and theater owners to join the cable industry, not fight it. His company, Jerrold Electronics, would happily provide the necessary equipment, which also came with advice on how to secure local franchises. Like arrangements the company made with other cable operators (which ultimately sparked an antitrust lawsuit in 1957), Shapp promised to design and install the system and teach them how to make money off it.

He repeatedly emphasized the ways media industries could grow by working together. In an open letter published in *Broadcasting*, the industry's trade magazine, he called attention to the public's "insatiable appetite for a greater diversity of programming and for higher quality services," and he warned that "if our industries fight each other, both will be hurt and the public will be denied extra services."[32] He also emphasized that the idea that cable television would swoop in to steal audiences and force local broadcasters out of business was rooted in fear, not facts. If no evidence existed, he asked, "why . . . all the fussin' and feuding?"

Many broadcasters were swayed and sought to diversify their media holdings and purchase a cable system. By the end of 1964, *Broadcasting* magazine estimated that broadcasters submitted at least one out of every five applications for a CATV franchise (although such systems soon would have to be outside their broadcast markets per FCC ownership policies).[33] Nevertheless, Pat Weaver was about to find out how such "fussin' and feuding" could derail a wired television experiment that offered a fundamentally different approach to the business of news and entertainment.[34]

———

In June 1963, the California state legislature unanimously passed a resolution to amend the Revenue and Taxation code to allow companies to offer wired subscription television services at the local level.[35] Soon after, the news of STV's official launch and Weaver's hire broke, and it seemed that pay television would soon become a reality in the state.

For Weaver, the new company allowed him to pursue the ideas about subscription television that had intrigued him over the previous years. Having partnered with the San Francisco Giants and the Los Angeles Dodgers to bring home games directly to viewers, STV promised to combine innovative programming with unprecedented technological advances to transform homes into a stadium, movie theater, or opera house. Finally, Weaver could develop the expensive cultural programming that he had so adamantly pushed at NBC. Weaver's leadership at STV brought credibility and respectability to an industry that had struggled to compete in the television marketplace. He also brought contacts in the entertainment world that the company needed to supply the first-rate programming necessary to convince Californians to pay for their television each month.[36]

Theater owners quickly led the charge against STV, but they also attracted support from a range of civic organizations that saw pay television as exacerbating inequality by making information accessible to only those who could afford it.[37] By October 1963, STV's opponents were ready. Led by the Southern California Theatre Owners Association, the campaign for "Free TV" launched with the familiar warnings about the dangers of "pay TV." Since the state legislature had already passed a law making STV operations legal, its opponents decided to use the California ballot initiative process to change the law by putting the question before voters in the 1964 election. Under the mantle of the "California Crusade for Free TV," theater owners vowed to collect the 468,259 signatures necessary to put a measure on the ballot that would outlaw the pay television industry from operating in the state.[38]

In December, STV struck back, filing a lawsuit against the theater owners for an antitrust "conspiracy" that prevented the company from competing in the marketplace.[39] The lawsuit just stoked the fire, however. Theater owners across the country sent money to the Citizens Committee for Free TV, seeing STV as the gateway to unleashing pay television, the villain they and broadcasters had spoken out against for over a decade.

Flush with cash and led by advertising executive Don Belding and Gerri Teasley, a leader in the California Federation of Women's Clubs, the Citizens Committee unleashed a massive advertising campaign. It spent over a million dollars on direct mail, radio and television broadcasts, newspaper advertisements, billboards, and a flood of brochures, bombarding California voters with messages about the dangers of pay television.[40] (By contrast, scholars estimate that President Johnson spent around $4 million on his entire presidential advertising campaign that year.)[41] One flyer featured a devastated young boy with a football helmet, apparently eager to watch the game, only to be prevented from doing so with the ominous "PAY TV" box that kept the television screen blank. "Darn that Pay TV! Pop says he don't have any more dollar and a halfs for me to watch each ball game," read the caption.[42] Another one featured a television with a gun pointing at viewers demanding them to "pay me." Yet other ads warned that "this could be the last World Series on Free TV"—a statement the Los Angeles Better Business Bureau asked the committee to remove because of its inaccuracy.[43]

On January 14, 1964, in a room packed with over three hundred people, a battle over television's future took shape, with theater owners and their hired consultants on one side, and STV executives on the other. Weaver envisioned the community conversation as an opportunity to share his vision for STV—but he quickly realized that he would be playing defense in a conversation centered on how pay television would hurt Americans. The "Free TV" advocates emphasized the "hardship" that pay television would bring to "senior citizens and shut-ins," the very people who "are the most dependent on TV for their entertainment and in many cases the least able to pay for it."

Although no broadcasters took part on the panel discussion, the panelists invoked the network executives' 1958 congressional testimony on pay television to validate their argument that free TV and pay TV could not coexist. Subscription television, panelists contended, was nothing short of "piracy." Pay television would "steal" a "great mass medium" that brought entertainment, sports, and news to "the rich and poor alike."[44] Such arguments resonated with organizations across the country representing veterans, senior citizens, and African Americans as they too joined the fight against pay television, emphasizing the importance of freely accessible television to educating and entertaining the poor and those on fixed incomes.[45]

Weaver and his colleagues disagreed. STV vice president Robert F. MacLeod called such attacks "curiously distorted," "unconstitutional," and "directly opposed to the concept of free enterprise."[46] MacLeod continued to defend his company against persecution from the "rich and frightened broadcast media" and "political bombardments by office seeking and office holding opportunists." He and his partners also highlighted how "Free TV" was not free but funded by advertisers—which meant a cost to viewers' time and aggravation. These men, all affiliated with STV, posited that they would "gladly plunk down any amount of money to rid my living room of the white tornado, the woman with the headache that is cured by Excedrin and those little monsters with 20% fewer cavities." Building off Newton Minow's famed critique of television, they called the medium a "vast land of advertising trivia" and "garbage."[47] Pay TV, they argued, would rescue viewers, and they likened their service to the ones that Red Cross trucks provided to disaster victims.[48]

Rather than attacking "Free TV," Weaver argued that Americans' love of television meant that both industries could make tremendous profits. Stimulating production in the "creative community" would expand television as a broader business, which would be good for both broadcasters and wired service providers.[49] Like other advocates of pay television—which also included organizations like the liberal Americans for Democratic Action (ADA)—he emphasized the democratic possibilities of a market that catered to audience demands for more programming.[50]

The "Free TV" campaign relentlessly vilified pay television as "greedy" and "profit-driven," highlighting the dangers of an unregulated television marketplace. Then, it simultaneously portrayed the network television system as proof of a "growing, prosperous, and well-regulated free enterprise telecasting industry."[51] Such arguments revealed the different definitions of "free enterprise" circulating during the time as the term was used to both support and critique the expanding administrative state.[52] On one hand, those with a stake in the current economic and political system saw regulations that gave the Big Three networks an oligopoly as advancing commercial and public interests, which they believed reinforced one another. On the other hand, the pay television debate called attention to the failure of a monopolistic television system to meet consumer demands and pushed the idea of choice as a hallmark of democratic progress (something that would soon unite conservatives *and* liberals, both of whom were growing disgruntled with New Deal liberalism for different reasons).[53]

STV's initial success seemingly exposed this consumer demand as many California residents decided to give subscription television a chance. STV debuted its services on August 14 and hooked up over forty thousand homes over the next ninety days.[54] The Citizens Committee disparaged the idea that STV would actually offer any new programming, arguing that it would simply siphon away the best entertainment and sports already available on commercial television. But in fact, the three pay television channels available via STV did offer original programs—lectures by academics; career programs on how to become a publisher, pilot, or clergyman; educational sessions teaching math, foreign languages, and bridge; and a range of cultural programs with stage plays and opera performances.

In an effort to demonstrate its ability to also cover public affairs in an innovative way, STV even produced a news program in Washington, D.C., featuring columnist Drew Pearson, journalist Alistair Cooke, conservative intellectual William F. Buckley, White House correspondent Russell Baker, journalist Richard Rovere, editorialist William S. White, commentator Murray Kempton, Pulitzer Prize winner Clark Mollenhoff, Congressman Robert Kastenmeier (D-WI), and cartoonist Jules Feiffer.[55] The tagline: "STV . . . to enlighten, to entertain, and to engage the mind. All showings complete with no interruptions from commercials." Weaver credited buzz generated by early subscribers as then fueling demand for service across northern and southern California.[56]

Nevertheless, while tens of thousands signed up for STV, even more signed a petition to outlaw pay TV, ultimately succeeding in getting the measure—now known as Proposition 15—on the ballot for voters that fall.[57] Each side formed lobbying groups and worked with the political consultants who had helped to put California on the national map for its ability to stage media-driven political contests.[58] In a direct mail campaign, STV heralded the discounts early subscribers could receive, including a year of free programming and reduced installation rates. It distributed fact sheets to dismantle what Weaver called the "false, misinformed and malicious statements about STV" being "recklessly" advanced by the Citizens Committee.[59]

Nevertheless, STV was fighting an uphill battle against a well-organized opposition. Gerri Teasley mobilized over seventy thousand women in the Federated Clubs to speak out for the need to "protect the family pocketbook from pay television charges."[60] She encouraged senior citizens and church groups to get involved in the fight by signing petitions, writing letters to editors, and calling into radio programs. Despite the appearance of grassroots mobilization, the letter encouraging such local activism revealed the extent to which commercial networks set the parameters of the debate. Promotional material constantly referenced their recent statements affirming that "television, now a democratic unifying force, will be divisive" and "Free TV as we know it, cannot survive alongside of Pay-TV."

In a clear violation of the FCC's Fairness Doctrine, which required broadcasters to air both sides of political debates, all three of the network-affiliated San Francisco television stations refused to air STV's commercials, citing the ads' controversial nature.[61] Weaver asked the FCC to investigate, and an attorney and opponent of Proposition 15 alleged that such actions were "a conspiracy under the law and under the moral codes that television, radio, and newspapers share—to offer both sides in any issue the opportunity to be heard."[62]

The California initiative brought the public into the conversation about television's economic structure and civic responsibilities—and increasingly it ensnared cable television and severed the love affair between the cable and broadcast industries. In February, the Board of Trustees for the National Association of Broadcasters (NAB) had released a policy opposing any form of pay television for the home.[63] The NAB emphasized that this policy covered not just the question of STV in California but "any community antenna system which originates programs for its subscribers."[64] The NAB also opposed all local origination cable programs—music services, weather updates, local civic programs, and education initiatives—that could present an alternative to broadcast programming. The following month the industry's trade magazine went even more directly to the question of CATV and asked: "What to do with community television?"[65] The *Broadcasting* article noted the transformation the industry had undergone from "mom and pop operations of strictly local influence" into a "significant force that is commanding the attention of the federal government."

By May, however, the NAB had pulled back from its initial stance opposing pay television after many of its members expressed concern that supporting the California initiative meant that broadcasters were "fighting government regulation on one hand and advocating it on the other."[66] Stanley Searle, the editor of the cable industry's trade publication *TV & Communications*, urged broadcasters to have "good judgement" and "to exercise considerable restraint in pushing for restrictive CATV legislation that could easily backfire with more controls for broadcast television," especially when a number of broadcasters, CBS included, were trying to get in on cable television operations themselves.[67] In the end, most broadcasters shared a goal articulated by NAB Vice President William Carlisle: to "ensure that CATV does not become a vehicle for the emergence of a nationwide interconnected web of wired pay television systems."[68] In short, they wanted CATV to grow only as an extension of broadcasting. If it offered alternative programs that competed with local broadcasters—even by importing distant signals—then it needed to be highly regulated.

A report issued by the NAB in the fall of 1964 seemed to show that this competition was already happening, and it raised red flags about cable for the FCC. Calling it the "first definitive economic study of the impact of community antenna television systems on local TV stations," the NAB concluded that in systems where CATV subscribers had access to the local broadcasting station and other distant stations, the local broadcasters' revenues went down. CATV, this study showed, did not simply extend broadcasters' reach, it directly competed against them.[69] Cable advocates quickly pointed out biases and misrepresentations of their industry in the study.[70] Still, it deepened the divide between broadcasters and cable operators by pitting them against one another economically and soon such research became a standard line that the FCC would use to justify regulation of cable. This was what broadcasters really wanted: control and influence over cable's development in ways that put their financial interests first.

––––––

"The eyes of the nation are upon us, for what is decided in California sets the scene for the entire United States," declared the Citizens Committee for Free TV.[71] This dramatically overstated the importance of the issue during a presidential election year in which the campaign centered on questions of Barry Goldwater's fitness for office and Lyndon Johnson's Great Society—but not its significance to the broadcasting and cable industry, as their bottom lines depended on the issues raised in California.

As the vote neared, Weaver deployed the star power of STV programming with a "Phonathon" that featured Hollywood stars answering questions about pay television.[72] Such performative efforts were not enough to overcome the fear that the Citizens Committee instilled in voters. In the end, it came down to both money and messaging, and Proposition 15 advocates dominated both. The Citizens Committee had a budget of nearly $1.2 million. By comparison, STV only spent $180,000.[73] Despite their financial advantages, the Free TV activists tried to turn the tables on STV's biggest asset, Pat Weaver himself. They pointed to his salary (at $85,000 a year with a "bonus agreement providing up to $165,000 more") as an example of pay television's willingness to buy influence.[74]

On Election Day, California voters had to weigh in on seventeen different ballot measures, which included Proposition 14, an initiative that would overturn recently passed legislation barring housing discrimination. While Weaver attempted to use star power to sell pay television, celebrity activists were much more focused on defeating Proposition 14 to keep fair housing enshrined in state law.[75]

Both campaigns failed, however. A majority of voters supported Proposition 15 to outlaw pay television on the premise that "the public shall have the right to view any television program on a home television set free of charge regardless of how such program is transmitted."[76] They also overwhelmingly voted for Proposition 14, which a highly organized network of real estate brokers and developers had framed as necessary to allow "freedom of choice" in the housing market.[77] While the initiative had been introduced in 1911 as a reform tool to give voters more of a voice in shaping legislation, the overloaded ballot that year and the prominent role of professional media consultants driving conversations around these initiatives made outside observers question the entire system. The battle, it seemed to a *Wall Street Journal* journalist, came down to the size of war chests, not necessarily public demand.[78]

The results of the election reverberated across the country, slowing plans to develop pay television in Georgia, Florida, and Texas.[79] Weaver was bitter, claiming that voters "have, unfortunately, been duped into defeating their own best interests by a powerful and wealthy lobby of theater owners aided by some broadcasters, through a most fraudulent campaign."[80] STV suspended its service as it took to the California court system to challenge the new law on the grounds that outlawing a business was unconstitutional.[81] In the legal appeal, Weaver emphasized how the new law violated First Amendment rights and discriminated against paying for content in the home versus in theaters. And he won. The California Supreme Court eventually overturned the referendum on the grounds that it "violates the free speech and press guarantees" of the First Amendment.[82]

The business of STV, however, did not survive. Pat Weaver would later emphasize that the early number of STV subscribers, over forty thousand, showed proof of its potential for success.[83] A 1965 survey revealed that 80 percent of former STV customers said they would have continued to subscribe to the service.[84] But the political challenges made the business model—which incurred high startup costs for laying wires—too difficult to sustain during the two-year legal battle.

Despite its failure, STV showed that a market existed for targeting narrow audiences with niche and original programming, if only entrepreneurs in the industry could overcome the resistance by broadcasters, theater owners, the FCC, and policymakers. NCTA Chairman Bruce Merrill hammered home the importance of political organizing to his colleagues. Frustrated by the smoke created by "those who would harangue and maim the CATV industry," he reminded his colleagues of the one asset that they had that no lobbying campaign could take away from them. "Do not the stokers realize that the CATV industry has thrived and will continue to survive for one reason? . . . It is the will of the public. The simple truth is, the cable systems are giving the public something they want. Something broadcasting is not giving them."[85]

While the public voted to outlaw pay television in California, many in the industry saw this as a manipulation of the public will by a better-funded and more organized political campaign. The solution was clear: public relations and some organizing of their own. The expanding National Community Television Association was up for the job.

3

Distinguishing Cable Television

He lived in Atlanta, but J. Leonard Reinsch was well known in Washington, as Newton Minow found out when he arrived. According to one journalist, "Little of interest to the broadcasting industry goes through the Washington sieve without his knowledge, if not involvement."[1] Reinsch drew authority from his profession (president of Cox Broadcasting Corporation), his extracurricular activities (famed Democratic radio and television presidential adviser), and his reputation in both realms as an innovative "dynamo" who refused to "be caught in the buggy-whip business when automobiles are in vogue." Although news teams such as "Huntley-Brinkley have become public bywords in the world of broadcasting," wrote the *New York Times* in a 1964 profile, "in the considerably more private corporate worlds there is another formidable radio-television team—Cox-Reinsch."

Just as Reinsch offered sage advice to Minow in 1961, he had long helped members of the Democratic Party navigate the world of television. For a party that had traditionally relied on urban bosses and labor unions to mobilize voters with patronage promises, turning to showmanship came with growing pains.[2] During the Democratic National Committee's first experiment with television at the 1948 convention, viewers witnessed live pigeons—meant to symbolize "doves of peace"—escaping from crates and attacking

J. Leonard Reinsch presents President John F. Kennedy with a medal from the
Radio and Television Executives Society to honor Kennedy's innovation of
holding live, televised press conferences.
Photo Credit: Abbie Rowe, National Park Service / John F. Kennedy Presidential Library and Museum.

Speaker Sam Rayburn's sweaty, bald head. Reinsch recalled how
one of the most powerful politicians in the country appeared on
television waving his arms wildly and yelling angrily, "Get those
goddamned pigeons out of here!" The broadcaster certainly had
his work cut out for him.

Over the next fifteen years, Reinsch wore hats in both the political and broadcasting worlds. He climbed the ranks of Cox Broadcasting, and learned about Democratic politics from Cox Sr., who
had pursued an unsuccessful presidential bid in 1920 with Franklin
Roosevelt as his running mate. Eventually, Reinsch assumed a leadership role in orchestrating the Democratic National Convention television operations and helped John F. Kennedy prepare for the 1960
debates to great acclaim.[3] He agreed with Sig Mickelson about the

importance of radio, and then television, in the news industry itself and changed the name of "press conferences" first to "press-radio conferences" and then simply to "news conferences" during his time volunteering in the White House media operations.[4]

Reinsch's career highlighted how media insiders shaped the assumptions, attitudes, and uses of television by elected officials, and vice versa. His experiences as a broadcaster influenced the strategies politicians used to communicate via radio and then television—and his insights and prestige as a presidential media adviser, in turn, affected operations in the television world. For example, in a 1968 article for the *Journal of Broadcasting & Electronic Media,* Reinsch stressed that broadcast media must "continue to present complete news and comment on public affairs," including comprehensive coverage of party conventions every four years.[5]

In 1957, James Cox Sr. passed away, and his son, James Cox Jr., took over as chairman of Cox Broadcasting Corp. According to the *Times,* what made this new Cox Jr. and Reinsch partnership so powerful was the vision they shared for the future. "They think the period of industry growth is by no means over. In particular, they foresee a great potential for community antenna systems, which, incidentally have been opposed by many station owners."[6] After telling Newton Minow that the future of television lay in wired television, Reinsch put his time and money behind such a prediction.

The following year, Reinsch entered the cable industry, bringing his political connections and his reputation for innovation—both in business and politics—with him. He helped teach cable operators how to play the game that broadcasters had dominated for so long. By distinguishing their new technology from broadcasting, cable operators could secure political recognition, which, Reinsch repeatedly emphasized, had long brought the networks tremendous power and profits.

———

Reinsch, over the doubts of some colleagues at Cox Broadcasting, saw cable as an industry brimming with possibilities. "Most other

TV station owners are fighting CATV," he explained during a 1965 interview.[7] "I see CATV as a new form of communications and service to the listener." He envisioned a time when every room had its own television, some of them the size of walls. He imagined devices to record television shows and play them back. He even believed that eventually everyone would have a small mobile television that they could carry around. After he worked with Bill Daniels to purchase two cable systems in 1962, the Denver businessman was pleased, seeing it as an incredibly important moment for the cable industry. "When other broadcasters with Leonard's fine reputation saw what Leonard was doing, it got their attention," Daniels later recalled.[8]

Perhaps. But the lessons Reinsch taught cable operators about political maneuvering behind the scenes were what really made waves. As a newcomer at the National Community Television Association convention in the summer of 1964, he emphasized the "urgent need for a good image for CATV." Perplexed by the "strange inferiority complex" he witnessed in the industry over the course of the Proposition 15 fight, he warned his new colleagues that such posturing had dangerous consequences. He also called attention to the "appalling barrage of negative propaganda, speculation, half-truth, half-fiction, emotionally charged misstatements of facts pouring from many strange places."[9] The industry had a bad reputation, made worse by the 1964 debate about pay television, and he pushed his colleagues to make fixing it a priority.

Reinsch had a specific solution, which he knew worked: cultivating relationships with politicians. Citing his experiences with Democratic presidential administrations, he emphasized the importance of selling cable's potential to elected officials and showing them how a different form of television could eliminate the vexing limitations of network television—notably the expense of using it and the limited airtime. Rather than just replicating broadcasting, he pushed his colleagues in the field to do something different on the cable dial, which had the capacity for twelve stations rather than just the three broadcasting stations that most viewers could access through the airwaves. "Throughout all of our image building effort, we should talk in simple terms of user benefits," Reinsch emphasized.[10] "We can do more for you; We can save money for you; We can free you from dependence on unreliable fringe television stations. So let's start now, full confidence and respect for our industry, to project the good side of CATV into the national conscience."

Another Washington insider agreed with Reinsch on the need for cable to differentiate itself from broadcasting: FCC Commissioner Frederick W. Ford. At that same convention, Ford openly admitted that he was confused about what cable actually was. Wired television took on so many different forms, he observed: pay TV, which required the public to pay for individual programs; STV, which charged a fee for new types of local origination programming; CATV, which distributed broadcast signals via wire; and finally cablecasting, distribution of programming produced by the cable industry. All served the same purpose, he argued, in that they met a public demand for more and better television and bolstered his belief in a wired television future.[11] Nevertheless, he saw cable television at a crossroads, one that hinged on answering a basic question of self-definition: would cable television continue to supplement broadcasting or would it offer something new?

A Republican from Clarksburg, West Virginia, Ford had almost two decades of experience working in administrative law, and he knew that such definitions mattered. Though he later stressed that he was "not a New Dealer," he, like many other Republicans at the time, supported many programs launched by Franklin Roosevelt and believed in the benefits of regulatory agencies stacked with experts shaping business practices to curb excesses of the marketplace.[12] He worked on antitrust cases as an FCC staffer and eventually moved to the Department of Justice before returning to the FCC as a commissioner appointed by Dwight Eisenhower in 1957. Following the resignation of John C. Doerfer for allegations of corruption, Ford briefly became commission chairman, and he stayed on the FCC after Kennedy's election tipped the balance of power and the chairmanship to the Democratic Party and Newton Minow.[13]

The commercial possibilities of a post-regulatory career also drew Ford to the agency, as he anticipated how legal expertise and government contacts could propel private-sector opportunities.

Frederick Ford at his desk as president of the National Cable Television Association, 1968.
Photo Credit: Barco Library, The Cable Center.

For him, it did. At the end of 1964, Ford resigned from the FCC to assume the reins of the NCTA as its next president, where it then became his job to define and then defend the cable industry.[14]

Ford pushed the organization to lay to rest the passive antenna argument and offer something innovative on the cable dial. If some cable operators were initially reluctant to embrace Ford's agenda, FCC rule changes over the next year made clear the economic stakes of crafting a more positive image and strengthening relationships in Washington. Notably, the FCC made official the practice it had pursued in places like Austin, in which it restricted how and when CATV systems could import distant signals via microwave. It mandated that the operator prioritize the local broadcasters' signals (those within sixty miles), which included the blackout of any distant signal that carried the same program in the name of ensuring larger audiences for the local broadcast airing of that program. While in its 1965 First Report and Order on CATV, the FCC noted that it lacked the evidence to show that cable television caused economic harm to broadcasters, it enacted this policy anyway under the pretense that protecting broadcasters took a priority.[15]

As Milton Shapp studied the situation, it became clear to him that, "The FCC is supporting the private interests of the networks and broadcasters at this time. They make no bones about it."[16] In response, he then proposed a bold shift for government's political priorities when it came to television: the need to encourage market competition that empowered individuals as viewers. He refuted the central premise of the 1965 FCC decision about cable potentially fracturing audiences to the detriment of local broadcasters. "Fractionalizing takes place only when the public exercises its own choice and when people view programs they want to see at a given time," he wrote. People should be allowed to make this choice, he emphasized. The FCC fanned the fears of fractionalization for what it would do to broadcasters. But, he argued, if this happened in the future, it would merely constitute a "manifestation of the free enterprise system in proper operation."

Less than a year after the California pay television debate, Shapp, a Pennsylvania Democrat who would win the state's governorship five years later and secure it for two terms, connected the argument about the need to expand viewers' right to choose to the cable television regulatory debate. Such a philosophy exposed the ways in which liberals had long relied on cultivating consumption and forging partnerships with private businesses.[17] And yet, such an argument also reverberated with the growing antistatist criticism championed by the expanding conservative movement. Indeed, just three years earlier, economist Milton Friedman published his groundbreaking 1962 book, *Capitalism and Freedom*, in which he argued that "economic freedom is also an indispensable means toward the achievement of political freedom."[18] Barry Goldwater made this economic philosophy central to his unsuccessful bid for the presidency two years later. Shapp's response to FCC regulations revealed that such ideas favoring market choice transcended ideological and party lines—as would become clear a decade later when both parties advocated for deregulation.[19]

In the short term, however, things got worse for the cable industry. In February 1966, the FCC released its Second Report and Order on CATV systems, transforming the commission from a frustrating bureaucracy to a villain in the eyes of cable operators. First, the report openly stated that the FCC had the authority to regulate CATV systems—something the National Association of Broadcasters applauded while the NCTA lamented as a clear violation of the 1934 Communications Act.[20] The real dagger came from what the FCC wanted to do with this power: freeze the cable industry's expansion in the top one hundred markets. Commissioners justified the ruling because it gave broadcasters an opportunity to develop UHF programming so that offerings on "free television" could be expanded in the future.

Ford called the new rules "highly discriminatory," and the president of Shapp's company, Jerrold Electronics, classified it as an "unprecedented attempt to restrict the freedom of TV reception."[21] At its core, the ruling showed two things: FCC political priorities and the power of the broadcasting industry's research. The commission recognized the limitations of the current broadcasting system but decided to encourage investments in UHF, not cable, as the solution. Moreover, findings from the NAB 1964 study, which showed cable television doing economic harm to local broadcasters, shaped the basic assumptions undergirding the decision. Ignoring other data provided by the NCTA that refuted this study, the FCC report extended broadcasters' protection from cable competition in the lucrative urban markets, forcing the cable industry to turn to the less profitable smaller markets across the country if it wanted to build systems.

The FCC ruling sparked controversy in Congress. Broadcasters told their Capitol Hill allies that it didn't go far enough to protect the industry. Other members of Congress were angry that they weren't consulted in advance of the ruling. More broadly, the legislative debate centered on the question of regulatory authority and who had it—Congress or the FCC. While the House Commerce Committee held hearings on the issue and ultimately proposed a bill that reinforced the FCC ruling, it died in the Rules Committee. Without enough political drive in Congress to rethink communications policy, the FCC ruling stood, and the outlook for the cable industry looked dismal.[22]

The 1966 order made it clear in the minds of cable operators that they were David battling a Goliath of telephone companies, broadcasters, and the federal government. During a rainy annual convention in Miami Beach that summer, NCTA leaders declared to members that a sunny future for cable television depended on its adaptation of an aggressive public relations strategy to counter the "unusually virulent publicity and lobbying campaign" waged by CATV opponents to undermine the "health of CATV."[23] The convention's chairman, Benjamin J. Conroy Jr., also emphasized the importance of the cable industry asserting itself and not becoming a subsidiary of the broadcasting or telephone corporations. Members of the NCTA, he argued, needed to have cable's interests in mind. While recognizing that the NCTA saw welcoming "members of other industries to our ranks as a blessing," Conroy made it very clear that split loyalties were no longer accepted. "You're either with us or against us."[24] The war had begun.

———

Frederick Ford saw a silver lining to the 1966 FCC ruling: it inspired a national conversation about cable television—what it was and how it should function.[25] And so, NCTA members finally listened to what he and Leonard Reinsch had said for over two years: they needed to defend against misinformation and sell the possibilities of cable to politicians, regulators, and potential subscribers.

The NCTA organized a public relations committee to study the current state of the industry and its image, and its findings showed just how much work needed to be done. The public "is confused, indifferent, or suspicious," concluded the committee.[26] This confusion heightened divides between operators within the industry and left legislators and regulators uncertain about how to treat the industry. Moreover, it created an opening for anti-CATV broadcasters and Ma Bell to advance their own interests, to cable's detriment. The very survival of the industry depended on addressing three questions: "where are we going . . . where we should go . . . and how we ought to get there."

While operators had previously dabbled in public relations, the 1967 promotional push that came out of the committee's study was different. It combined education, research, sales, and networking to celebrate cable's achievements and to inspire faith in its future potential. This was not a reactive campaign but a proactive one seeking to "open doors in new <u>markets</u>" while also "adding subscribers and expanding coverage <u>in the unsaturated systems</u>," explained the committee.[27] Their goal was to encourage the "untrammeled growth and development of CATV" by convincing the businesses, politicians, and viewers that the economic expansion of cable television would benefit everyone.[28]

Working with a public relations firm and an advertising agency, the NCTA launched the first "National Cable Week" to generate national news coverage of its activities.[29] It prepared advertising packages for local operators to use, including radio scripts and monthly mailing material to promote cable's services to the public. The theme made clear its goals: "Promote to Protect . . . Your Industry and Its Future."[30]

The NCTA also developed and distributed a "Wonderful World of Cable TV" brochure to counter the negative image of the greedy and parasitic industry that had developed over the previous decade.[31] The cover depicted a television dial with twelve colorful screens that viewers could choose—sports, dancing, movies, the symphony, and even an educational science experiment. "CATV is a superior way of receiving television pictures," the brochure explained in the sixteen-page booklet. It emphasized that cable did not threaten the local broadcaster or "free TV," distinguishing CATV from pay TV to avoid the criticisms that arose two years earlier. And yet, the last page highlighted the additional programs cable operators offered outside of transmitting broadcast signals, including weather, news, music, public service announcements, and even public access programming that would allow political candidates to reach new audiences.

The NCTA sent the brochure to newly elected members of Congress and encouraged cable operators to contact their representatives to make them aware of cable's existence. It worked. Officials wrote back to Ford, expressing their appreciation for the information

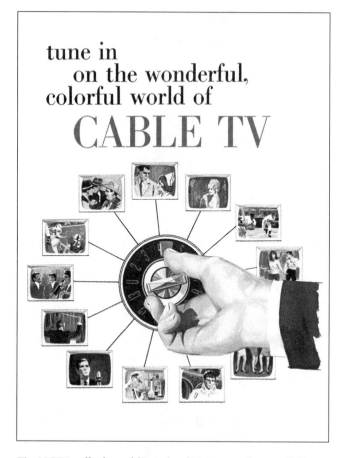

The NCTA sells the public and politicians on the possibilities of cable television in its *Wonderful World of Cable TV* brochure.
Photo Credit: Barco Library, The Cable Center.

and best wishes for the launch of the first National Cable Week at the end of January.[32] A letter from Robert Everett, a Democratic representative from Tennessee, underscored the importance of a personal connection to cable in advancing its interests. "I am one of your biggest boosters," wrote Everett, because "we have it in Union City, Tennessee, my hometown."[33]

As the brochure's fleeting discussion of program origination showed, exclusive cable programming (or local origination as the industry called it) was only in its infancy. Frederick Ford hammered home the message that developing this aspect of the business was essential for the industry's growth and expansion. The 1966 FCC rule hinged on the premise that broadcasting allowed for local self-expression, but cable television did not.[34] In an effort to fight this policy, Ford urged all stations to embrace local origination. "Your opponents do not want YOU to cablecast the discussion of public issues. They do not want YOU to cablecast the local public service programs."[35] Adding this programming could transform the media landscape, Ford proclaimed, "Our industry was born in public service. This industry will be reborn because of an even greater need for its public service programs." He called on operators to reserve a channel for public affairs, arguing that the upfront costs would be justified in the long term through goodwill cultivated from subscribers and regulators.[36]

In short, Ford argued, local cable programming was both good business and good politics. Some companies, like Cox Cable, already understood this and had encouraged local operators to reach out to city councils and high school football teams to discuss televising their meetings and games, respectively.[37] Others experimented with a weather channel—initially just a camera scanning a clock, thermometer, and other weather devices—films, programmed music, or a news wire channel, which conveyed the text of the latest Associated Press wire dispatches.[38] Creative operators noted an opportunity to broadcast local election returns or feature interviews with congresspeople and senators, ultimately providing television experiences and "exposure that would have been impossible without CATV"—and a chance to recruit allies in their state legislatures or on Capitol Hill.[39]

The 1966 election emerged as an opportunity to do just that, something that another NCTA member, William Adler, pushed when he introduced the idea of expanding political broadcasts on cable systems.[40] The West Virginia native first experienced the power of television as a student at Princeton when he and his college friends would gather in the evenings to watch programs like the fifteen-minute *Camel News Caravan* that aired on NBC. Over the next few years, as television took the country by storm, Adler returned home and was shocked to discover that cable television could bring those same signals to his rural hometown. By 1953, he had come up with enough money to launch his own system as an operator. The key to his success was showing the concrete ways cable actually worked. He remembered the excitement that came after he brought cable to a local beer garden and demonstrated the clear pictures on the television screen that the wired technology could deliver.[41]

Adler kept these lessons in mind as he worked with the NCTA and its newly formed Community Service Committee to launch a different type of lobbying strategy, one that hinged on the premise of raising awareness of CATV by carrying candidates' speeches on their systems. Operators could also open up local origination facilities for local, state, and even national candidates, Adler encouraged. In short, the West Virginian firmly believed that the industry's financial health depended on showing elected officials how cable could compete with broadcasting to facilitate political communication. While he acknowledged that this plan offered a "drastic departure from the established concepts of our industry," he emphasized that no other strategy "could have a more beneficial effect on our relations with state and federal legislatures in the coming year."[42]

Anecdotal stories later that year from the 1966 elections emerged to validate Adler's ideas. In places like Springfield, Illinois, cable offered local programming about sports, news, and religious organizations to subscribers, becoming an "impartial Town Hall" and the "talk of Springfield," according to the local operator who reported that "more people have wanted to be on this channel than we have been able to schedule."[43] There was a concrete economic payoff, too. The push for more local programming resulted in over one thousand subscribers in less than thirty days—all of whom also had access to broadcast signals but chose to pay for a cable subscription.

Original programming did not just generate positive relationships with city officials and viewers; it also made a powerful statement to FCC regulators. Having just joined the FCC in the summer of 1966, Nicholas Johnson, a young lawyer inspired to public service by Newton Minow, began to criticize loudly how corporate networks had failed to serve the public interest.[44] He lamented the FCC's role in facilitating such complacency by allowing the networks to maximize corporate profits through oligopoly behavior, what he called "imitation, restricted choice, elaborate corporate strategies, and reliance on the 'tried and true'" at the expense of seriously considering "what the public wants."[45] These corporate "media barons" had tremendous power shaping public knowledge about current affairs, which served as an important check on government institutions. But, he asked, who had a check on them, especially if their monopoly status made them immune to viewer demands and pressures?[46]

Cable television could, and Johnson urged cable operators to shake things up with diverse programming, which he argued would then force the FCC to take the industry seriously as a media business. As the FCC reevaluated cable policy, which Johnson called the most "vexing" issue he confronted at the agency, he also urged operators to take action and "use your imagination to seek out new kinds of markets and new sources of program supply for the potential channel capacity of your cables."[47]

Johnson wasn't the only one studying the cable issue. The 1966 ruling created a task force dedicated to researching the industry's regulatory future, and luckily for the cable industry, Sol Schildhause took the reins.[48] Raised in New York City, Schildhause grew up with dreams of playing major league baseball.[49] His family pushed him toward law school instead and during the 1950s, he landed a staff job at the FCC. Schildhause claimed he was initially placed at the head of the CATV task force to "move papers around and not accomplish anything of note." But he took his job seriously and began studying the cable television industry, attending its annual conventions, and getting to know its operators and operations. Stanley Searle called Schildhause a "man of determination, energy and action" who sincerely "believes in the future of cable television."[50]

Schildhause joined a growing coalition of policymakers, researchers, journalists, activists, and regulators across the political spectrum who increasingly saw cable as the solution to network television's social and political failures. In 1964, Leonard Reinsch had pleaded with cable operators to revamp the industry's image, and Frederick Ford had pushed them to embrace cable as an alternative to broadcasting. Such public relations efforts gained support within an industry frustrated by FCC red tape and they also laid the rhetorical groundwork for the cable craze about to reverberate across the country as frustrations with commercial broadcast television mounted. In 1967, the NCTA officially cast off the label of community television, changing its name to the National Cable Television Association. Such a move symbolized the organization's commitment to advancing a new narrative of the industry.[51] The story of Ed Parsons finding ways to extend broadcasting signals from the top of mountains or hotels faded, and a new futuristic vision for cable television emerged, one in which the medium would revolutionize American society.

———

According to Ralph Lee Smith, a progressive writer who penned a 1970 visionary article in *The Nation* called "The Wired Nation," cable television would end the broadcasting network "oligarchy" and produce a form of television "far more flexible, far more democratic, far more diversified in content, and far more responsive to the full range of pressing needs in today's cities, neighborhoods, towns and communities."[52] Smith imagined a world where cable provided "newspapers, mail service, banking and shopping facilities, data from libraries and other storage centers, school curricula and other forms of information too numerous to specify. In short, every home and office will contain a communications center of a breadth and flexibility to influence every aspect of life." Known as a vision for "Blue Skies," the industry's future captivated public attention and inspired think tanks and foundations to study ways to unlock cable television's potential.[53]

New communications media had long inspired utopian dreams and an optimistic belief that technology would bring radical social change. Indeed, similar ideas and rhetoric emerged during the development of the printing press, the telegraph, the telephone, radio, motion pictures, and of course, television.[54] Now it was cable's turn, as grassroots activists, researchers, and policymakers grappled with the growing political and economic power of network television and the clear bias and limitations it had in terms of the few voices it elevated and limited programs it offered.[55]

Nothing exposed both the power and problem of broadcasting more clearly than coverage of the Black freedom movement during the 1960s. After television cameras captured the horrific scenes of white authorities brutally beating activists marching for the right to vote in Selma, Alabama, in March 1965, Martin Luther King Jr. powerfully declared, "We are here to say to the white men that we will no longer let them use clubs on us in the dark corners. We're going to make them do it in the glaring light of television."[56]

Overall, white network television reporters covered desegregation efforts in a favorable light.[57] But these news programs overwhelmingly celebrated stories of white moderation and focused on racism as an individual problem, not a systemic and institutional one. As racial tensions escalated over the next few years and uprisings broke out in places like Watts, Detroit, and Newark, television journalists frequently portrayed activists as angry extremists. Discussion of "looting" and senseless violent behavior overlooked any conversation about the rationale underpinning these activities—notably seething frustration over police brutality, housing discrimination, and economic inequality.[58] Moreover, there were only a handful of Black television reporters and no minority-owned television stations.[59] And so, while civil rights activists took advantage of television to draw attention to their cause, they also understood it as a technology that served white supremacy, and the adherence to "balance" meant the elevation of segregationist voices on news programs as well.[60]

Media ownership and control over production emerged as key goals for many civil rights activists, and cable franchising debates opened opportunities to demand more representation on television.[61] For example, in Boston, community organizer Mel King had watched violence play out in places like Birmingham, Alabama, where Commissioner of Public Safety Eugene "Bull" Connor attacked peaceful civil rights demonstrators with dogs and firehoses, and saw the powerful role television could play in advancing the movement for racial equality.[62] A decade later, when local city officials began debating the introduction of cable television into the city, King and other Black Bostonians pushed the local city council to implement franchising requirements that allowed minority communities to shape local cable productions while also generating economic opportunities for the Black community to be involved in cable operations.[63]

Civil rights activists weren't the only ones frustrated with broadcast television and looking to cable as a solution. So too were their segregationist opponents. While white-owned stations in places like Jackson, Mississippi, gave voice to segregationists on the local news and ignored the perspective of African Americans pushing for racial equality—a violation of the FCC's Fairness Doctrine that required the presentation of both sides on controversial issues—southern conservatives were still unhappy with the network news programs that they felt were too sympathetic to civil rights.[64] Mississippi congressman John Bell Williams requested the networks to more fairly cover segregationists' points of view, lamenting in 1963 that he had "yet to see a network documentary designed, planned, and programmed for the purpose of giving the prosegregation side of the race problem, yet we are continuously bombarded with the other."[65]

These disgruntled white southern Democrats alleged "liberal media bias," bringing them closer to the Republican Party and the growing cadre of conservatives who were developing alternative media institutions—magazines like *National Review*, publishing houses like Regnery, radio programs hosted by Clarence Manion and Dan Smoot, and later an independent news program with a conservative agenda called TVN that helped launch the television career of the future Fox News head Roger Ailes.[66]

In short, activists on the left and the right agreed on the problems with network television: the bias in newsrooms where white male liberal elites made decisions about public affairs programming and the economic concentration of a monopolistic network system.[67]

Television critics like Jack Gould at the *New York Times* and politicians across the political spectrum had long raised concern about networks eschewing their public interest responsibilities. The civil rights movement—and massive resistance by segregationists to it—forged a crisis in television newsrooms and intensified criticisms about the limitations of a medium that increasingly demonstrated its power to propel, or thwart, substantive social change.[68]

Three different solutions emerged in efforts to diversify the dial and expand access: UHF, public television, and eventually, cable. Newton Minow had worked with Congress to pass the All-Channel Receiver Act of 1962, which mandated that television manufacturers include tuners to receive UHF signals. The 1966 FCC ruling that so infuriated the cable industry aimed to boost the chances of struggling UHF stations even more by limiting competition from cable operators, and it seemed to work. Between 1961 and 1967, the number of UHF stations increased by almost 50 percent (from 76 stations to 118) and about 42 percent of all television sets could access these signals by 1967.[69] Initially, cable operators also benefited from this expansion of the UHF dial as they could offer more channels to potential subscribers.

Minow had envisioned that educational programming would fill this channel space, and also in 1962, had pushed for the passage of the ETV Facilities Act to subsidize the growth of new educational television stations.[70] By the mid-1960s, the National Educational Television network—an outgrowth of a decades-long campaign to advance educational television funded by organizations like the Ford Foundation—developed to expand the distribution of noncommercial programming on the UHF dial, and especially in the realm of public affairs during the 1960s.[71]

Several programs were designed to expand political conversations by bringing in perspectives from conservatives and civil rights activists, both groups that had expressed frustrations with the limits of commercial television programming.[72] Famously, in 1965, founder of the *National Review* William Buckley Jr. debated the author and activist James Baldwin on the question: "The American Dream: Is it at the expense of the American Negro?" With a standing ovation, the latter won the debate as he detailed the history of white supremacy and an economic, political, and social system that depended on racial discrimination.[73]

And yet, neither educational television nor UHF lived up to its hype. Noncommercial television struggled to find funding while UHF station managers failed to produce any original programming, opting instead to air network reruns.[74] And so, the federal government soon took action to support educational television, which it then renamed public television.[75] Working with the Carnegie Foundation's Commission on Educational TV, the Johnson administration developed a legislative proposal for public broadcasting that garnered bipartisan support. Such efforts culminated in the 1967 Public Broadcasting Act, which established the Corporation for Public Broadcasting (CPB). A private, nongovernmental organization with a board appointed by the president, the CPB received money allocated by Congress each year to support local public broadcast operations. Since the newly passed legislation prohibited the CPB from operating a network, CPB worked with the Ford Foundation to launch a different organization to create and distribute noncommercial programming (later formalized into the Public Broadcasting Service network for public television and the National Public Radio network for public radio).[76]

The obstacles embedded in this approach became clear quickly. Across the political spectrum, people worried that annual federal appropriations politicized public broadcasting (which is why the Carnegie Commission had recommended funding public television through an excise tax in its report).[77] On the left, activists also saw white supremacy and patriarchy still shaping programming decisions, notably on the issues of racial inequality, the Vietnam War, and feminism.[78] On the right, conservatives worried that a government-funded network would soon become a vehicle for government propaganda and further perpetuate an "East Coast cultural elitism" embedded in the federal bureaucracy (even though the CPB did not have control over programming).[79] Cable operators saw all of this frustration as evidence of an untapped market and a way to pad their pocketbooks, if only they could fight through the cumbersome federal regulations holding them back.

————

In 1968, Supreme Court decisions and new FCC rulings rocked the industry once again. In *United States v. Southwestern Cable Co.*, the court confirmed that the FCC had authority to regulate cable television, a decision that disappointed many in the cable industry who were unhappy with the restrictions imposed on them two years earlier. A week later, the court ruled in *Fortnightly Corp. v. United Artists Television* that cable operators had not infringed on copyright laws when disseminating network programming. While a short-term victory for the industry, the court based its decision on the view that cable television was merely a passive antenna, not a different form of television. Clearly, the court paid little attention to the Blue Skies rhetoric permeating the country, and the decision exposed exactly why some CATV operators wanted to merely retransmit signals from broadcasters. It was less of a legal hassle and allowed them to skirt the copyright issue, even as it fueled accusations that cable operators were pirates and thieves who stole network programming to make a quick buck.[80]

Despite this ruling, Blue Skies thinking had taken over at the FCC, and the commissioners—with newly codified legal authority over the industry—set out to establish rules to cultivate cable's democratic potential. While the agency continued the freeze on cable's development in the top one hundred markets, it also pushed the industry to develop original content and required educational and civic programming for systems with over thirty-five hundred subscribers.[81] The 1969 local origination rule also required that systems make available production studios for the creation and presentation of such programs by community members.[82] Three years later, Commissioner Nicholas Johnson successfully pushed for an expansion of these local origination requirements by requiring operators in the largest one hundred television markets to set aside three channels for noncommercial use—what became known as the PEG stations as one was for **P**ublic access, another for **E**ducational purposes, and finally one for local **G**overnment use.[83]

Some operators grumbled and saw the requirement as just more FCC interference into their business operations. Several also worried about having the staff to produce programs that did more than automatically rotate a camera to show a clock and most recent weather data.[84] Others argued that providing PEG channels would not be a problem, but they anticipated that getting people to use and then watch these channels would be.[85]

And yet, the NCTA recognized how public access and locally produced programs more broadly fit into its public relations strategy to integrate cable systems into communities. It also anticipated that such initiatives could pave the way for cable operators to enter urban markets in the future, which it did.[86] This calculation revealed two aspects of NCTA's lobbying approach: stirring up grassroots demand for different types of programming (and opportunities for ordinary Americans to appear on camera) and cultivating relationships at the local and national levels by demonstrating the political potential of the cable dial.

Over the next few years, a diverse coalition of individuals and organizations bought into the idea that cable television could unleash a communications revolution.[87] Engineers at Rand Corporation and researchers at the Ford Foundation produced studies that envisioned how cable television could provide meaningful social change and help combat economic inequality and racial injustice. Soon, minority activists, consumer groups, Americans for Democratic Action, and the ACLU all became champions of cable. A range of nonprofit media centers and volunteer collectives popped up as activists saw access to television studios and screens as a right of citizenship.[88] Significantly, the introduction of mobile and affordable technology, notably portapaks, gave ordinary Americans the technical capacity to record their own video productions. Cable, along with public television, then provided a way to distribute it.

Such experimentation flourished in the counterculture.[89] Just as writers like Hunter S. Thompson and Tom Wolfe worked to redefine journalism by replacing the notions of balance, fairness, and objectivity with emotion, authenticity, and shock, video guerrillas, as they were called, wanted to shake up the television world. Like those in the world of "New Journalism," avant-garde art circles, and even independent producers making edgy Hollywood productions, they worked to decentralize media productions and push the boundaries of acceptable content, something they saw as a direct contrast to network television, which just conditioned audiences to accept the status quo.[90] To them, "narrowcasting" emerged as a way to challenge and change mainstream institutions that stifled democracy and creativity. They believed that encouraging the latter was essential to preserving the former.

"Guerrilla TV," as it became known, was part of a broader effort to use art and radical performances to criticize the racial discrimination, capitalism, and imperialism embedded within a white- and male-dominated political and media establishment.[91] Michael Shamberg coined the term in his 1971 manifesto, *Guerrilla Television*. The following year, he launched Top Value Television, or TVTV, to directly challenge the ethics, values, and voices included in network television boardrooms and newsrooms.[92] These radical leftists believed that it wasn't enough to produce new types of content; meaningful political and cultural changes required building alternative media institutions to distribute it.[93] Both the public access channels and local origination rules pushed so vocally by Nicholas Johnson helped them do it.[94]

Liberals also saw the potential of cable television, focusing instead on how it could help deliver Lyndon Johnson's Great Society agenda that was increasingly facing turmoil amidst growing racial unrest in cities at home and a controversial war abroad. For example, New York City mayor John Lindsay captured national attention in his efforts to wire the nation's largest city. In 1967, Lindsay created an "Advisory Task Force on CATV and Telecommunications" to "recommend to the Mayor policies and programs to ensure that modern telecommunications in New York City is fully exploited to further the City's economic activity and its social well-being."[95] With its density and signal-blocking skyscrapers, many potential viewers were unable to access broadcast television; the report concluded that cable offered "glittering" possibilities.

But the state of wired television in the city told a different story and foreshadowed the challenges cable expansion faced, especially in urban areas. Since 1965, three cable companies had secured temporary franchise agreements with the city to start wiring sections of Manhattan and the Bronx.[96] In addition to familiar challenges—including franchise contracts stipulating that cable was not to compete with broadcasters and offer original programming—the city presented unique troubles. Wiring was costly and cumbersome. Cable crews needed to install wires in the underground duct system, which required negotiating with recalcitrant Empire City, a subsidiary of AT&T that saw the cable industry as a potential competitor. In a city with a crumbling infrastructure and dense traffic, cable companies had to constantly reroute installation plans due to construction and frequently found parking tickets on their vehicles. One of the companies, TelePrompTer, estimated the installation costs totaled about $125,000 per mile (almost $1.1 million in 2022 dollars).[97] Uncooperative landlords also limited business opportunities in apartment buildings, as the law required their permission to enter a building. Increasingly, landlords allowed companies to wire their building only after receiving a cut of the profit, typically a percentage of the building's monthly subscriber fees and free cable for themselves.[98]

And yet, the 1967 task force envisioned a different way for cable television to function, notably by providing original programming. A wired city, it imagined, could provide more educational opportunities, communications services for "all the ethnic communities that make up the City," and allow political candidates to connect with voters in a more direct and affordable manner.[99] Of course, it was not surprising that the push for locally originating programming became central to the franchising process under John Lindsay's watch. A media-savvy politician who had just started his own weekly half-hour local television show, the handsome mayor was always looking for creative ways to elevate his public profile.[100]

Cable also presented a significant opportunity to raise funds the city desperately needed through both tax revenue and franchise fees. The task force encouraged a trial for pay television, which the city would then tax at a rate of 25 percent of the gross receipts of each program.[101] Theoretically, it was a win-win-win: local government and businesses would cooperate, both would make money, and viewers would get more programming choices.[102]

Over the next few years, cable companies secured franchising agreements in places like Philadelphia and Newark by pitching the same idea: that cable television could solve the political and economic challenges cities faced with shrinking budgets and escalating demands for media access. And yet, even from the beginning, the New York State public service commissioner observed that many companies made these deals with a plan to "get rich quick," not to actually fulfill their promises. "In too many instances," he argued, "applications have sought franchise not with a view to building a system but with a view to selling the franchise to some other operator at some future date."[103] Desperate for new revenues, cities agreed to such terms because officials wanted to make money—for the city and for themselves.

This tension among profits, politics, and public responsibilities continued to shape the cable industry and political attitudes toward it. By the end of the 1960s, visions for cable television's "panaceatic" possibilities abounded, wrote a University of California law professor and former member of the Sloan Commission on cable television, Dr. Monroe Price.[104] After all, "one was either in favor of the wired nation, or against progress." Yet in less than five years, all of the hopes for the "wired nation" had come crashing down. Someone, wrote Price, "pricked the bubble." That prick came from local frustrations when cable operators overpromised and underdelivered services to consumers and elected officials. And it also came from a new occupant in the White House.

4

Revenge Politics

In 1962, bitter after losing the California governor's race, Richard Nixon lashed out at reporters in what he called his "last press conference."[1] There, in the Beverly Hilton Hotel, the man who also had lost an agonizingly close presidential race two years earlier uttered words that would become infamous when he later revived his political career: "You won't have Nixon to kick around anymore."

His statement revealed his anger toward the press and toward media coverage he felt had undermined his political career. During the fifteen-minute rant, he also complained about lack of coverage. If the press was against a candidate, grumbled Nixon, they still needed to at least put "one lonely reporter on the campaign who will report what the candidate says now and then." His tirade urged journalists to recognize their responsibilities to report "all the news" and not just a narrow version of it.

Ten years later, Nixon stood on top of the political world having scored a landslide victory for a second term as president. But over these years, his obsession with media bias and access intensified, something evident in another scathing speech delivered by his director of the newly established Office of Telecommunications Policy (OTP) on December 17, 1972. On that afternoon in Indianapolis, Clay "Tom" Whitehead shocked members of Sigma Delta Chi, a professional journalism organization, with a diatribe against network newsrooms for failing the American people because reporters advanced "ideological plugola" that stressed or suppressed "information in accordance with their own beliefs." Newscasters confused "sensationalism with sense" and dispensed "elitist gossip in the guise of news analysis," he contended. The message was clear: local broadcasters needed to stand up to network executives and demand less bias in the news if they wanted to keep their licenses.[2] The speech was designed to inflame, and it did. Whitehead left behind stunned broadcasters and journalists, many of whom feared what was coming next from the Nixon White House.

They were right to worry. Nixon actively used the most powerful office in the country to wage war on the press and network television. He had help not just from his cronies willing to indulge his darker impulses, but also from respected policymakers like Whitehead. And yet, as OTP director, Whitehead was not simply a pawn in the president's ever-intensifying campaign against the media. Rather, he sensed an opportunity: the president hated the national broadcasting networks for deeply personal and political reasons, and Whitehead understood that this resentment could be channeled into meaningful legislative changes, particularly in the field of television.

During what Whitehead later called an "uneasy alliance," the two men transformed the media landscape in a way that elevated the visibility of cable television and reshaped its political trajectory.[3] For Nixon, cable became a tool to undermine the authority of the television networks he despised. For Whitehead, favorable policies for cable countered a media monopoly he saw as inefficient and generated a path for more media competition and choice for consumers. While they had different motives, both saw a deregulated cable industry as a tool to dismantle the political, economic, and social power that networks had amassed. With a legislative approach that blended their political and economic agendas, they promoted market-based solutions at the expense of publicly funded options in their efforts to reform the television landscape, and such a policy approach persisted long after Nixon was ousted from office.[4]

Nixon's attitude toward cable television exposed the extent to which personal biases can shape the policymaking process and the very operation of government and media institutions. Indeed, his hatred of the liberal establishment led him down a cunning and manipulative legislative path on issues like environmentalism, fair housing, affirmative action, and the National Endowment for the Arts.[5] He frequently supported popular liberal initiatives—but did so in ways that divided Democratic coalitions and shifted resources and authority away from the federal government and to the states.

When it came to communications, "Tricky Dick" was open about his desire to dismantle the power of the media and to bypass the authority of journalists and television reporters. In fact, he saw his political success as dependent on it, even as these efforts brought out the worst in Nixon and paved the way for his downfall. While cable operators had long contended that both broadcasting and cable could coexist and flourish, Nixon latched on to the very idea that broadcasters had popularized about how the latter could destroy the former. His administration pitted network executives and cable operators against one another, pushing cable to develop as a form of television committed to demonizing gatekeeping and glorifying competition.

———

In his memoir *Six Crises*, Richard Nixon wrote of the major mistake that cost him the 1960 election. He thought that if he conveyed to television audiences his "knowledge," "sincerity," and "confidence" as a political leader, then "my image would take care of itself."[6] He firmly believed that his television strategy that year (which included boring advertisements that featured just him sitting on a desk talking about specific issues) cost him the presidency, and as he resurrected his political career, he did so by emulating John F. Kennedy's use of "showbiz politics."[7]

Convinced that media games determined political success, Nixon appeared on entertainment shows like *The Jack Paar Program* where he played the piano, and *Rowan & Martin's Laugh-In* where he awkwardly asked the audience to "Sock it to me!"[8] He brought together a powerful team of media advisers—Harry Treleaven, an advertiser who had just crafted a successful congressional bid for George H. W. Bush in Texas; Ray Price, a former editorial writer for the *New York Herald Tribune*; Frank Shakespeare, a CBS executive; and Roger Ailes, a producer for the daytime entertainment program *The Mike Douglas Show*. All these men reinforced the same message—Nixon didn't lose in the 1960 election, his "tinker-toy" television operation did—and electoral success demanded the skills of advertisers, entertainers, and pollsters who would help make people "like him."[9]

During the 1968 campaign, with the largest cable system in the country located in his home state of California, Nixon eyed cable television as a way to expand and control his campaign message.[10] Republicans worked with eager cable operators on their political cablecasting strategy to distribute election materials that year. The United Citizens for Nixon-Agnew set up a Nixon-Agnew Television Network run by Jay Baraff, a communications lawyer.[11] The amateur cable network produced half-hour features and compiled clips of Nixon and his running mate Spiro Agnew speaking on the campaign trail. Baraff then encouraged cable operators around the country to play these tapes for free on their systems, highlighting the "favorable publicity" such efforts would generate for them and Nixon.[12] While he stressed that cable systems should give ample time to other candidates, in keeping with the NCTA's Code of Ethics encouraging equal time, the lawyer also made clear that cable operators did not have to uphold the FCC equal time requirements and that "no sanctions are involved" if they didn't.

Cable operators enthusiastically complied, with Baraff boasting that he hoped to distribute between 300 and 350 tapes.[13] The initiative had a clear message for the Nixon campaign: cable placed "no limitations" in terms of time and cost—as expensive thirty-second advertisements on broadcast television did. And cable had the potential to reach over 3.5 million homes, which totaled about 11.5 million television viewers—numbers that could make a difference in a close election.[14]

Bill Daniels, left, shaking hands with President Richard
Nixon.
Photo Credit: Barco Library, The Cable Center.

Cable operators didn't discriminate based on party; they welcomed all comers willing to provide material. Notably, Eugene
McCarthy's bid for the Democratic nomination included a cable program in which his daughter, Mary McCarthy, answered questions on
an hour-long panel show in California. Of course, after Nixon won,
industry leaders wanted to call attention to their work on the new
president's behalf. Bill Daniels wrote a letter to the Nixon administration, extolling the economic potential of the industry to bring
in jobs, stimulate the economy, and pay taxes. He also noted that
during the 1968 campaign, "415 cable television systems showed an
average of three times during prime time, Nixon-Agnew spots to a
total audience of 5,000,000 people *at no charge* to the Republican
National Committee."[15]

Daniels and others wanted to use political cablecasting to win
"legislative friends," as Robert Searle, the editor for *TV & Communications,* put it.[16] Sure, Nixon likely appreciated the free airtime, but
what really drew him to cable television was the idea that it could
undermine the authority of the television networks, which he saw as

an enemy that he needed to take down by any means necessary. After all, the 1968 election taught Nixon and his top advisers a powerful lesson: the difference between Nixon the loser and Nixon the winner hinged on creating and controlling a compelling television image. In the eyes of the new president, when he could control the media narrative, he succeeded, but when the press controlled it, he faltered. Nixon repeatedly preached his belief that the "press is the enemy," and he encouraged members of his administration to treat them with hatred and vengeance. As his speechwriter William Safire observed, in the president's "indulgence of his most combative and abrasive instincts against what he saw to be an unelected and unrepresentative elite, lay Nixon's greatest personal and political weakness."[17]

Nixon turned to two men for advice on how to navigate a media environment he saw as hostile and biased: Herbert Klein and Charles Colson.[18] Klein, who had experience in the news business and had started his career as a reporter in California, was tapped as head of the newly established Office of Communications in the White House. While Press Secretary Ron Ziegler maintained the responsibility to deliver regular briefings to the press, Klein would develop a longer-term media strategy and coordinate communication within the White House.[19] Soft-spoken and with "an aura of sincerity," Klein was accepted by the national press as "one of the 'good guys,'" wrote a journalist in *The Nation.* Klein's job focused on responding immediately to any negative stories and providing reporters with information to help manipulate news coverage in ways that generated positive publicity for the administration. He also worked with administration officials to better navigate television and rehearse for television appearances—something Nixon made clear he wanted from his staff.[20]

Charles Colson took a different approach. In charge of the Office of Public Liaison, Colson's official job was to work with special interests outside the White House, bringing their ideas to the president and mobilizing them on the ground to support Nixon. Unofficially, Colson emerged as Nixon's most notorious "hatchet man." His White House colleague Jeb Stuart Magruder called him an "evil genius" who emboldened Nixon's darker impulses, notably his "instinct for the jugular."[21] He also built what became known to White House insiders as "the Department of Dirty Tricks"—a variety of illegal and unethical efforts to attack those on Nixon's "enemy list" by doing everything from staging fake campaign events to spying on opponents and even using the IRS to harass them.[22]

Particularly on matters of the media, Nixon was more likely to listen to Colson than Klein, making the latter's pledge that "truth will be the hallmark of the Nixon administration" a laughable assertion.[23] Working closely with his trusted Chief of Staff H. R. Haldeman, Nixon launched what one scholar has aptly called "a government offensive against the media."[24] Manipulating, targeting, and undermining the press—from the *New York Times* to the network television news—became a White House priority.[25] Such attacks created what journalist Harry Ashmore called an "atmosphere of fear" among journalists, reporters, publishers, and especially, broadcasters.[26]

While journalists could lay claim to their First Amendment rights, and even gain fame for being on the president's enemy list, broadcasters were in a more precarious situation: their business depended on a license granted by the federal government. Richard Nixon understood this and used this regulatory power to his advantage. According to *CBS News* anchor Walter Cronkite, Nixon pursued an "orchestrated, coordinated campaign" to bring direct and indirect pressure on television newsrooms.[27] It began, Cronkite argued, in 1969 with Vice President Agnew's speech in Des Moines when he classified network anchors like Cronkite as elitist, biased, and undemocratic. "A tiny, enclosed fraternity of privileged men elected by no one and enjoying a monopoly sanctioned and licensed by the Government," Agnew contended, had misinformed the American people, "slandered" political leaders, and abused the public interest.[28] The fiery vice president assailed not just news content, but television's very business structure. He warned that a "virtual monopoly of a whole medium of communication is not something that democratic people should blindly ignore." Rather than ignoring public affairs, as Newton Minow had lamented years earlier, the Nixon administration claimed that the networks had manipulated such coverage to advance their own liberal agenda at the expense of informing the people.

The speech made Spiro Agnew a hero among conservative media activists, who had been sounding the alarm of media bias for more than a decade.[29] In the aftermath, the Committee to Combat Bias in Broadcasting worked to capture examples of liberal bias by distributing Media Watch Monitoring cards to conservative organizations.[30] Identifying and documenting media bias also became an obsession of the Nixon administration. Jeb Stuart Magruder, Charles Colson, and even Herbert Klein found ways to draw attention to media bias: targeting individual newscasters with accusations of bias in an effort to tar the entire profession; holding televised seminars on "press objectivity" to draw attention to "the problem"; encouraging allies on Capitol Hill and appointees at the FCC to "express concern" about media bias; and even urging a massive letter-to-the-editor writing campaign at the grassroots level.[31]

As Nixon frequently did to punish perceived enemies, he also had the federal bureaucracy do his dirty work.[32] In 1970, the FCC implemented several policies that directly targeted the pocketbook of the three networks. It banned network ownership of cable television systems, forcing CBS and NBC to divest their holdings. (CBS had to sell off its cable holdings, giving birth to Viacom.)[33] It also introduced the Financial Interest and Syndication Rules and the Prime Time Access Rule.[34] Since Pat Weaver's pitch two decades earlier to shift from advertiser to network-created programming, the three networks had garnered tremendous profits and social prestige. The arrangement had limited opportunities for independent production companies, however. The new FCC rules restricted what programs the networks could develop and air, opening up prime-time television hours for independent producers and local programming (indeed, the "fin-syn" decision paved the way for *All in the Family* to explode in popularity the next year).[35]

When network executives appealed, delaying the implementation of the ruling, the administration stepped up political pressure. On April 14, 1972, the Department of Justice filed an antitrust lawsuit against the three networks. While there were legitimate antitrust

questions that the Justice Department and the FCC had been studying for years, Nixon saw a political opportunity to pressure networks
into more favorable news coverage during an election year.[36] "We
don't give a goddam about the economic gain," he told Colson privately. "Our game here is solely political."[37]

According to Robert Sarnoff of NBC, these efforts threatened to
undermine a network's balance sheets by raising its "costs, disrupting
its operations, and reducing its economic opportunities."[38] That was
the goal. And yet, the Nixon administration envisioned these rules
as mere short-term remedies that "could provide a counter-balance
to network power pending the full development of cable television,"
explained one memo following a meeting between Charles Colson
and Tom Whitehead.[39] The two White House advisers had made it
clear to their boss that cable television could provide the long-term
solution to the network monopoly, and Nixon was all ears.

———

Tom Whitehead was out of place in an administration where corruption abounded and personal loyalty mattered more than credentials.[40] He embodied the postwar image of a policy wonk and
technocrat—the type of establishment figure that Nixon hated. A
native of Neodesha, Kansas, Whitehead grew up as a Republican.
At eighteen he headed off to the East Coast for college, enrolling
at the Massachusetts Institute of Technology—an institution Nixon
despised and worked to exclude from any federal funds for allegedly undermining his foreign policy in Vietnam.[41] For Whitehead, an
MIT education launched his career. He first started working for Bell
Telephone Laboratories in an experimental cooperative program
that it had with the university. Eventually, Whitehead earned various
degrees from MIT—including a BS and MS in electrical engineering and a PhD in management—before joining the research team at
RAND to study spacecraft systems for NASA.

Whitehead joined Nixon's campaign in 1968 because, he would
later say, he saw a "historic opportunity to change the political directions of the country into more constructive directions."[42] He viewed

the use of government spending to solve public problems as inefficient and wanted to bring new ideas to Washington. During the campaign he focused on budget policies but quickly became the go-to person on communications issues after Nixon won the election. He recalled the transition process as unfolding haphazardly, with Haldeman "basically dealing cards" by handing out responsibilities for individuals to oversee certain agencies and allegedly saying something along the lines of, "Hell, Whitehead went to MIT, he knows all that shit, let him fix it."[43]

As the go-to communications policy person, Whitehead first had to deal with the Rostow Report. On August 14, 1967, President Johnson had sent a message to Congress that announced the formation of the Task Force on Communications Policy. The message highlighted the importance of developing a communications satellite system that "will meet the needs of a dynamic and ever expanding world."[44] It also signaled the need to seriously study telecommunications policy, concluding that "historians may write that the human race survived or faltered because of how well it mastered the technology of this age." He urged action, and as with so many policy issues during the Kennedy and Johnson administrations, he formed a team of experts to study the issue and recommend policy solutions.[45]

The commission took over a year to complete the final report, which it submitted to Johnson in December 1968, just weeks before the end of his presidency. The study had been contentious, frequently pitting economists, who wanted more competition in the marketplace, against engineers, who believed that consumers benefited from a regulated monopoly.[46] To distance himself from any changes in the communications field that could be seen as a conflict of interest with his own broadcasting holdings, Johnson did not take action on the recommendations. Instead, he instructed his staff to brief the incoming administration on them.

Whitehead decided to start with the issue of satellites and introduced an "Open Skies" policy to inject competition into the celestial business. The giants of telecommunications—AT&T and the three broadcasting networks—eagerly petitioned for an FCC satellite policy that would allow them to bring a system of regulated monopoly

Clay "Tom" Whitehead working as special assistant to the president in the Old Executive Office Building, 1969. The following year, Whitehead would become the inaugural director of the newly established Office of Telecommunications Policy.
Photo Credit: Richard M. Nixon Presidential Library and Museum.

to the skies. They argued for a bifurcated setup with a few dedicated satellites operated by one or two industries to establish a system that would provide "a degree of competition" and "obviate" a monopoly.[47] Whitehead disagreed. He noted that the industry-proposed plan "wasn't a great way to preserve private enterprise" and argued that if "we're ever going to have competition in the communications business, we have to start it with this new technology." He opened a bid for other companies to submit plans to build and operate satellite receivers.[48] New businesses—notably several cable companies—got involved.[49]

Whitehead's work on the Open Skies proposal coincided with implementation of the Executive Reorganization Plan in 1970 and its recommendation for a new executive agency: the Office of Telecommunications Policy (OTP). The day after being sworn in as the agency's first director, Whitehead held a press conference declaring that with satellites and cable television, the OTP would ensure that competition, not a regulated monopoly, would define the media landscape of the future. *Broadcasting* saw the message from Whitehead as clear: that the OTP had "considerable swinging power," with the weight of the president behind Whitehead's efforts to shake up a television landscape brimming with possibilities but stuck in corporate complacency.[50]

The idea of developing cable policy in a way that encouraged a diversity of perspectives and more television access thrilled many media activists and researchers. Indeed, Whitehead kept abreast of the progress of the Alfred P. Sloan Foundation's Commission on Cable Communications that had convened earlier in 1970, and even convinced President Nixon to publicly endorse the committee's research agenda. "For the first time in history," wrote Nixon in a letter to the Sloan Commission, "we are aware that the time to think about the consequences of a technology is before it has become so firmly fixed in places that it is very nearly beyond reconsideration."[51]

The Sloan Commission understood the importance of presidential leadership on the issue of cable, emphasizing that the medium's effectiveness and structure would ultimately depend on the skill and approach of those who shaped policies undergirding its formation. And yet, the Nixon administration's focus on prioritizing marketplace reforms and using cable as a political tool meant that it closed off other pathways for its development, notably nonprofit or government-funded solutions. The OTP's emphasis on market efficiency also ignored the warnings about the social and political consequences of a segmented approach to television that had surfaced in the commission's report as well.

Headed by two scholars, Paul L. Laskin and Monroe Price, the Sloan Commission eagerly shared its findings with the OTP.[52] The study highlighted the undemocratic consequences of broadcast television's structure, notably the growing expense of election campaigns and the rising barrier to entrance for candidates challenging incumbents. The report called attention to the whopping $68 million spent on television advertising in the 1968 election and the "attractiveness" and "enormous persuasive power" of television appearances that gave "unassailable advantages" to well-known candidates and those with "bulging coffers."[53] Ironically, Nixon's election had exacerbated the urgency of the issue by sparing no expenses when it came to television buys. The $27.9 million forked out for television and radio time by both sides in 1968 marked a 64 percent increase in media expenditures from four years earlier.[54] Then, campaigns also had to hire staff to test, craft, and promote these advertisements. The GOP set a record that year for money raised and reporting rules, whether formal or informal, disregarded.[55]

The Sloan Commission saw cable television's democratic potential hinging on its ability to solve these issues of escalating campaign costs and declining television access. It was cheap and offered a dozen potential channels without the programming limitations imposed on local broadcasters by affiliate contracts. With cable, political parties and civic organizations could use programming to raise money and educate the public about their work. Coverage of city council meetings or school board discussions could also "expose the political process" itself, bringing transparency and accountability and allowing local activists to participate in these conversations.[56]

Despite the "awesome" possibilities of narrowcasting to connect individuals with shared interests, the commission also noted a potential downfall: "the possible side effects of the fractionalization of the audience." The report concluded that "one could, if one wished, shape an entirely new political system around the ability of the individual citizen to make his views known at every moment. Our instincts lead us to believe this would be an extremely bad system."[57] It was a prescient warning that revealed how experts weren't blind to the potential downside of flooding the television market with choice and fragmentation. Instead, scholars raised such warnings, which policymakers then ignored, more than a decade before media critics sounded similar alarms as they watched the explosion of cable television.[58]

But at the time, the idea of more voices on the television dial unified a strange coalition of progressive visionaries seeking to upend the political establishment, liberals and moderate Republicans working to bolster the integrity of government, and antsy conservatives looking to remake political institutions and traditions.

———

In June 1971, Nixon established a special cabinet committee to explore the status, potential, and policy implications surrounding cable television. Appointing Whitehead as chair, Nixon then asked Leonard Garment (one of his media advisers during the 1968 campaign and current legal counsel) and Herbert Klein to join Secretary of Health, Education and Welfare Elliot Richardson, Secretary of Housing and Urban Development George Romney, and Secretary of Commerce Maurice Stans to form a committee. Their mission? To "take full account of the wide range of social, economic, and political considerations involved" in cable television's development and how White House action could influence policies surrounding its future.[59] The cabinet committee worked hard to understand what it called a "whole business [that] crackles with crisis," studying the range of regulatory issues confronting the cable industry: copyright, distant signal importation, and ownership.

Under the leadership of conservative Dean Burch, the FCC also took action. On February 3, 1972, it released a report that rescinded the 1966 freeze that had closed off cable's entry into the top one hundred markets, firmly rejecting the idea of cable as a passive antenna.[60] It opened these markets, required cable companies to make copyright payments to program producers, permitted the importation of some distant signals, set mandates for public service channels, and required larger systems to have locally originated programming. The order also notably capped local franchise fees, in hopes of avoiding the corruption and exploitative practices that had emerged during franchising negotiations. It was not an entire win for cable operators—as the public service mandates and copyright payments indicated—and it still protected local broadcasters from competition. It was more a messy collection of compromises, and Whitehead pledged that the cabinet committee, which was still investigating long-term policy recommendations, would work to rectify these inconsistencies.[61]

As the committee slowly began its work, the OTP launched a new initiative following Nixon's stunning electoral success that November. With Project BUN (Break Up Networks), OTP policymaking mixed directly with Nixon's antimedia politics.[62] Penned by Bruce Owen, an OTP economist who loved to scatter policy booklets around the office, the project explicitly connected cable television to Nixon's media vendetta and offered a clear political analysis of television's structural problems and solutions. The "network triopoly was created by technology, demographics, and policy," explained Owen, and thus, this trifecta could also be used to combat the networks' power, notably in two areas: "cable television and encouraging new networks."[63]

Thirty years later, as Whitehead prepared to write a book about his time at the OTP, Project BUN stood out as some of the "politically damaging stuff" that OTP critics during later administrations saw as undermining the agency's credibility.[64] The report made the connection between Nixon's media war and communications policy explicit, and this mission helped cable deregulation get support from Nixon himself. "I think cable hurts all the networks," Nixon privately told Colson that same month. "When we go out for cable that will really stir them up." Colson responded with glee, "We'll really screw these guys."[65]

The report identified broadcasting's regulated monopoly as the central problem in modern communications.[66] Viewers had only three options to hear the news. Advertisers and program producers had only three choices to sell their products on television. This economic power yielded "high profits for the networks, as well as freedom to make what are essentially political and social decisions without market discipline," the report observed.

The networks' political power also raised concerns because the broadcasters had "the ability to control the flow of information and of ideas to the people." Moreover, they "can significantly mold public opinion" and quash diversity and freedom of expression. This power, wrote Owen, "is unacceptable in the United States, whether it is viewed from antitrust or First Amendment perspectives." "Politically, economically, and philosophically," concluded the Project BUN report, the concentration of power in network television constituted the central barrier to the Nixon administration's pursuit of objectivity in news programming and its effort to reverse "the growth of regulatory intervention in the private enterprise broadcasting system."[67]

The solution? Cable television. Even though it would likely take a decade for cable to begin to effectively dismantle network television's authority, Owen emphasized that the promotion of favorable regulatory policies for cable was essential now. The deregulation of cable television promised to show the merits of the marketplace in promoting technological innovation, diversity in programming, and a true freedom of speech upon which network dominance currently infringed. Playing into the antimedia outlook of the president, Owen's program pledged that "if properly structured," cable television would bring perspectives that current news programs—which had become "cliquish, if not incestuous"—failed to provide.

Project BUN and Whitehead's subsequent formal report to the president about integrating these OTP initiatives into Nixon's governing agenda clearly connected combating network power with the expansion of cable television through deregulatory policies that advanced the free market. It also urged an intensive publicity campaign to derail the authority and credibility of the networks as a harbinger of the public good. Whitehead pitched the ideas to the president as a win-win. Economically, they promoted Nixon's effort to restructure government to "let the private sector play its role."[68] Politically, they afforded Nixon the opportunity to bring a "more competitive free enterprise framework" to the information age.

That's why Whitehead traveled to Indianapolis to deliver his incendiary speech on December 17, 1972. Whitehead had worked on multiple drafts of the address that would define his political career, getting feedback from Charles Colson and clearing the final version with the president himself. His bold criticism of the "ideological plugola" embedded in network news generated the attention the administration wanted. Reporters claimed that he waged an "attack on the TV industry" by threatening licenses of local stations who aired "biased" network news programs.[69] Charging "onto the playing fields last week with all the sis-boom-bah of a linebacker kept too long on the bench," wrote the conservative columnist James Kilpatrick, Whitehead "had come to replace Vice President Agnew, who has turned demure in recent months, in the Administration's great body contact game with badgering the TV networks."[70] In a *Firing Line* television appearance, the conservative television host William Buckley Jr. congratulated Whitehead for coming up with the term "ideological plugola," which he professed to love.[71]

But while he railed against the bias, elitism, and inefficiency of network news, Whitehead also actively pushed the administration to move forward on policy initiatives. "The Administration's image on communications matters has been colored by the network news battle," the OTP director wrote John Ehrlichman. "We need a more statesman like record of policy development and advocacy to stand on."[72]

Two months later, Whitehead met with Nixon to talk about messaging and policies. Nixon expressed admiration for how Whitehead "had been handling his job, particularly with respect to the problem of the networks and broadcasting," and he urged Whitehead to continue pursuing the battle "vigorously."[73] Moreover, if any staff in the White House did not share this view of the network problem, Nixon would "reorder" them. As the Oval Office conversation turned to specific policies, the president announced support for recommendations about using cable television to solve "many of the problems brought by the current network dominance of broadcasting." He also endorsed Whitehead's proposal to provide a carrot along with this stick by promising broadcasters that if they improved network news, then the administration would push to extend the licensing renewal agreements from three to five years.

Whitehead's strategy—engaging in public attacks on the news to curry the favor of the president—seemed to be working as it opened avenues for him to shape policy. And yet, although he, Owen, and other OTP staffers prided themselves on the economic rationales

Members of the Cabinet Committee on Cable Communications discussing
policy recommendations for cable television's growth. Released on January 14,
1974, the report encouraged the deregulation of the cable industry.
Photo Credit: Richard M. Nixon Presidential Library and Museum.

shaping their policy recommendations, their pages and pages of
graphs, charts, and statistical research were not unbiased.[74] Deeply
entangled with Nixon's antimedia campaign from the beginning,
such research had an agenda: to illustrate that media bias stemmed
from a regulatory flaw (the policies granting the three networks
monopoly status) and that only a narrow economic solution of marketplace competition could solve the problem.

All the while, Whitehead kept working on the cabinet committee report. It was almost complete when the Watergate hearings
captured the attention of the nation. The investigation into White
House corruption, broadcast each day on the television networks
during the summer of 1973 and on public television in the evenings,
threatened to undo all the work the OTP had done. Antimedia language had become a liability, and the cabinet committee decided to
wait to release its report on cable.[75]

Finally, on January 14, 1974, Whitehead submitted the 117-page
report to Nixon. The report highlighted how cable was not a "modern

day Rosetta stone capable of unravelling the complex problems facing this society."[76] Rather, it emphasized that the medium "has much to offer and it should be given an opportunity to prove its worth to the American people." The underlying message: let cable television compete with broadcasting television and see what it might do. The report reflected the belief that permeated OTP discussions over the previous three years: cable development began with the assumption of First Amendment rights, similar to the printed press. These rights—as Bruce Owen emphasized—were tied not to the Constitution, but to the marketplace.[77] The government would not force any station to produce political news and commentary but would ensure that diversity, as defined by marketplace success, triumphed. Consumers, acting with their wallets and eyeballs, would determine which ideas, perspectives, biases, and content they wanted. Gone would be the "elitist view" of what broadcasters thought constituted news and entertainment.

While the report pushed for the deregulation of the industry, it also warned about the dangers of consolidation and emphasized the need to separate ownership of operating systems from program producers, a recommendation that filled the bigger cable players with dread because it had the potential to limit the income stream that could come from developing (and selling) programming. Such nuanced policy recommendations, however, helped the report gain credibility as a serious look at the future of the cable industry, rather than a Nixonian vendetta to attack the networks.[78] Once again, this was by design. Indeed, Whitehead worked diligently to encourage such substantive discussions around the report. He coordinated its release with a collaborative session on its findings held at the Brookings Institution with the very people who would shape the future of cable policy. Sponsored by the Aspen Institute, eighty-five people, including FCC commissioners, OTP policymakers, journalists, academics, think tank scholars, foundation representatives, Senate staffers, lobbyists, and cable industry leaders, came together to discuss the report, refusing to cede interpretation of it to members of the press, whom Whitehead knew distrusted him.[79]

During the discussion, cable's critics raised many concerns—ones that would plague legislative efforts to deregulate the industry over the next decades. As Kenneth Cox, a former FCC commissioner, noted, "I am troubled by the assumption that all you need to do is unleash cable and you're going to get all the wonders people talk about."[80] He was right. Over the next few years cable television did grow, but not only because of major regulatory shifts. Rather, it was because of satellite. Once cable operators found ways to distribute signals celestially, the programming floodgates opened, and then came new urban markets.

Jack Valenti, the president of the Motion Picture Association of America, used the moment to hammer home the message about copyright payments, arguing the "blight on cable" would persist until operators paid a copyright fee to retransmit programming. He was also correct. Overwhelmingly, cable operators relied on programming that originated on network broadcasting, including old movies. Legislative debates about cable television during the 1970s were frequently torpedoed by the argument that operators needed to pay for this content if they were charging subscribers for it. It took the landmark Copyright Act of 1976 to establish a royalty system in which operators agreed to pay in hopes that they would then shed their reputation as pirates and thieves.[81]

At its core, however, the discussion showed how much the intellectual ground about cable television had shifted during the Nixon administration. Through the OTP, Nixon and Whitehead, albeit for very different reasons, used the White House to promote a political narrative of cable television that challenged the basic regulatory principles undergirding network television's power. The mavericks of Nixon's White House were not the secretive men in the White House shadows who plotted their revenge on the president's enemies. They were the smart staffers of the OTP—men like Tom Whitehead who threw caution to the wind, scoffed at the network executives and their allies in Congress, and embraced new communications policies out of principle, pragmatism, and political opportunity. Whitehead had entered public service eager to influence policy from his White House perch, and in the realm of communications, he did.

But such an opportunity had a price. In a 1977 interview with *Cablevision*, Tom Whitehead opened up about this trade-off. When asked, "did Nixon understand or care anything about communications policy development," Whitehead firmly answered yes.[82] The former "television czar" argued that he witnessed firsthand how the president would privately lament the "sad state of nationally controlled television around the country," which is why Nixon wanted to inject competition into the television landscape. His political vendettas even went beyond hurting the networks, Whitehead explained. Nixon "realized very explicitly that governmental controls over the media would be used much more effectively by a liberal president who followed him in office than could be done by him or a conservative." And so, Whitehead argued, the president "seemed to have a schizophrenic personality on the subject." He wanted to loosen government regulations over the media, but yet he also very actively attempted to censor the press by pursuing lawsuits, bullying reporters with IRS audits, and threatening to revoke broadcast licenses linked to critical newspapers like the *Washington Post*.[83]

These contradictions illuminated two mutually reinforcing things: first, that Nixon studied television and its business structures, from licensing requirements to affiliate relationships to the power and profits of hit entertainment shows like *All in the Family*; second, that Nixon believed television was central to political power, and his governing strategy was inextricably linked to his quest to shape it.[84] Rather than seeing network television as an ally, as his predecessors had, he understood it as an enemy that had long thwarted his political career. As president, he was determined to fundamentally remake television in ways that would benefit him personally, undermine the economic power and political authority of network executives, and allow new perspectives to appear on the television dial in the future.

Such convictions about the political importance of television only intensified over the next decade. That's why the policy initiatives Nixon and the OTP initiated persisted long after the president resigned and the OTP folded under Jimmy Carter's administration. In fact, because of Nixon, politicians across the political spectrum firmly believed that they needed more access to television. The cable industry astutely came up with a solution, thanks to another OTP staffer who turned a political cablecasting experiment into a cable network that showed the democratic potential and political utility of a new approach to television.

Coming of Age

Before he became one of the most well-respected and well-known figures in the cable television industry as the founder and CEO of Cable Satellite Public Affairs Network (C-SPAN), Brian Lamb was just a kid from Lafayette, Indiana, who loved listening to the radio and playing the drums. At the age of seventeen, he became a DJ at the local radio station, which he continued through his college years at Purdue University, located just a few miles from his childhood home.[1] His music career never took off, but his work in radio and television soon did.

After spending four years in the Navy, Lamb did a two-year stint as a public relations officer at the Department of Defense. There, he had an epiphany that would drive his career and transform the media landscape: the curated nature of television news.

The lightbulb went off while Lamb was watching coverage of an anti–Vietnam War protest. Activists were laid out quietly and peacefully on the floor of the Pentagon entryway—but when an ABC correspondent began to interview them on camera, their demeanor changed; they transformed into raucous protesters yelling with anti-war placards. The moment left what he called an "indelible mark" on him: it showed the construction of a performative news story that entertained but misinformed about what actually was happening.

He thought there must be a better way to capture and convey the whole story around current events.

Over the next few years, as a staffer at the White House Office of Telecommunications Policy (OTP), he met others who shared his conviction: Tom Whitehead, Bruce Owen, and Antonin Scalia. He learned about a range of policies shaping new technologies—from satellites to copyright negotiations, and of course, cable television. And he saw the political process at work: negotiating policy terms with Congress and the FCC while also navigating the dynamics of a presidential administration run by corrupt and power-hungry men. Despite the inroads he and his OTP colleagues made in reshaping public conversations around media policy, Nixon's downfall cast suspicion on the office's work, especially regarding cable television. During the new Ford administration, an assessment of the OTP concluded that the "Watergate calamity" gave even more credibility to the notion that cable television would destroy the broadcasting industry by design.[2]

Lamb disagreed with such a damning conclusion, and he left the White House determined to bring more clarity and less vindictiveness to conversations about the television landscape. He started chronicling the relationship between government and the media through a newsletter, *The Media Report*, and as a columnist for cable industry trade magazines. As he consistently called out the behind-the-scenes political maneuvering that gave government and broadcasting networks so much power, he underscored the toll of these tactics on American television viewers—as both consumers and citizens.

There was another challenge. By the mid-1970s, even as cable suffered from Nixon-era notoriety, it continued to face the challenge of obscurity and the same bad press that had plagued the industry for decades. While all members of Congress had cultivated relationships with local broadcasters that they deemed essential to their reelection, only a handful of them really understood cable television. Mainstream journalists also frequently maligned cable.[3] James Reston, a *New York Times* columnist, saw cable operators as "small town used car dealers," in direct contrast to the television networks, which he characterized as "more urban," "responsible," and trustworthy in guarding the public interest.[4] His colleague at the *Times*, Les Brown, agreed, writing that when dealing with cable, he felt that "everyone was on the make," and "it's hard to get a religious feeling about an industry that gives you that feeling."[5]

While the broadcast networks had long championed their civic role to gain political favor and maintain high profits, cable operators had overwhelmingly focused on simply making money, eschewing any substantive commitment to the public interest despite the flourishing of Blue Skies dreams over the past few years. Lamb pushed his cable colleagues to change this and make good on the industry's democratic potential. The regulatory future for cable television was incredibly malleable in this post-Watergate moment, he observed. "Atmosphere, perception, mood, feeling and power to help in the re-election process will make a substantial difference in reaching long-range government decisions," Lamb argued.[6]

The public and politicians alike looked to the rapidly changing technological environment of the 1970s with both excitement and anxiety: computers that could process data at unprecedented speeds, two-way communication that would allow electronic conversations, and, more significantly for those in the cable television industry, satellite technology that could bring programming to cable operators instantly through the sky. Activists on the left envisioned cable television as a medium to upend "the establishment" by decentralizing information structures. Hoping to tap into its revolutionary potential, they worked to connect wired systems with community-centered organizations—frequently funded by individual donations, foundations, or advocacy groups.[7]

Cable television business leaders and lobbyists embraced such language of media democracy and empowerment percolating during the 1970s, but they also learned how giving elected officials a concrete stake in cable systems could advance their bottom line. In the end, a corporate vision for cable overshadowed the progressive one in part because operators finally agreed to fund an initiative that made members of Congress think about cable television differently: C-SPAN. Lamb later recalled he had a simple pitch for his cable colleagues. "If you want to be taken seriously in Washington or in the country you will have to build a base of doing something other

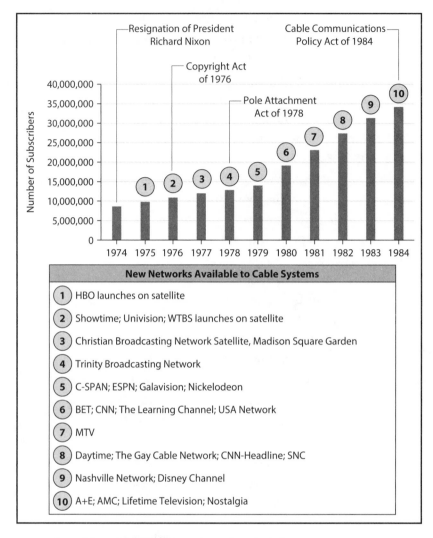

A snapshot of the cable television industry's growth from 1974 to 1984.
Sources: Television & Cable Factbook; SNL Kagan; Larry Satkowiak, *The Cable Industry: A Short History through Three Generations*, Barco Library, The Cable Center.

than entertainment and sports. The way that CBS, NBC, and ABC became powerful and important was through the news."[8] The path to prominence and prosperity for cable television, Lamb contended, was rooted in covering public affairs.

He was right.

5

The Watergate Hangover

Peter Rodino Jr., the Democratic representative from New Jersey, read carefully scripted remarks before television cameras on May 9, 1974. He understood the stakes of this historic moment. "For some time," he began, "we have known that the real security of this nation lies in the integrity of its institutions and the trust and informed competence of its people." He then pledged to conduct the forthcoming public deliberations by the House Judiciary Committee, weighing the possible impeachment of President Nixon, "in that spirit."[1]

Rodino's opening statement was the latest chapter of the Watergate drama that had engrossed the public for the past year. The previous summer, Senate investigatory hearings had played on network television for hours a day, and then again on public television in the evening.[2] Televised hearings were not new, but the gravity of the charges—break-ins, bribery, and corruption at the highest level— elevated the stakes. The captivating stories—including details about dirty tricks on the campaign trail and demonstrations of how to bug a phone—kept viewers glued to their television sets.

Such drama did more than entertain. It also gave the public a stake in the political process as people engaged in a national conversation about public affairs that went beyond the thirty or sixty minutes traditionally allocated for news programming each day.[3] After the House Judiciary Committee televised its impeachment vote that May, a *New York Times* journalist applauded the opportunity for elected officials to be able to "explain themselves" to constituents. The stakes were high, perhaps just as "profound as [television's] impact on presidential politics since 1960." The result? "Through a means the Founding Fathers never dreamed of, the Representative could truly become the Federal office-holder closest to the people."[4]

Like earlier televised hearings, the Senate and House events also gave Congress a taste of the limelight, something members refused to give up in the aftermath. After Nixon's resignation, a Joint Committee on Congressional Operations studied different possibilities for regular television coverage to improve "the clarity and completeness of the message sent to the people by the Congress."[5] It concluded that "better communication between Congress and the people it represents is required for our representative democracy to remain viable." The solution also seemed clear: "Broadcasting of House and Senate floor proceedings seems to be the most practical, immediate, and direct way to enhance public understanding of congressional activities."

Conversations over how to do this became intertwined with another issue made visible by the power, reach, and appeal of the televised hearings: the regulatory structure of the communications industry itself. Increasingly, regulators and legislators could no longer ignore a pressing question: Did a network television monopoly serve the interests of the public that increasingly demanded more transparency in the political process?[6]

Perhaps more significantly, the hearings themselves generated research that helped cable television emerge as the answer. In a deeply ironic twist, the media event that brought down Richard Nixon and elevated the social prestige of the broadcast networks he hated also helped to transform Nixon's personal war against liberal bias on television into a bipartisan congressional effort to revamp the very regulatory landscape that had given broadcasting its authority. The debate over television that intensified during and after Watergate paved the path for new policies, people, and programming to emerge, with far-reaching consequences for Congress and cable.

————

Three years before the Watergate hearings, Senator J. William Fulbright (D-AR) worried about how "television, because of its peculiar capacity and power, threatens to distort and to destroy" the American constitutional system that had increasingly become unbalanced in favor of the executive branch over the past two decades.[7] He highlighted how the president enjoyed prominent events like the televised State of the Union address to lay out a policy agenda to the country, while Congress—the actual legislative body of government—struggled to challenge the media narrative the president crafted. Fulbright had experienced this firsthand several years earlier when he worked with network executives to televise hearings on Vietnam. President Lyndon Johnson, furious that the networks had agreed, simultaneously staged a televised meeting in Hawaii with General William Westmoreland, a top American general in Vietnam, and the prime minister of South Vietnam.[8] The president also pressured CBS to stop live coverage of the hearings, and the network ended up airing reruns of *I Love Lucy* instead.[9]

The cable industry astutely exploited these congressional frustrations with network television and the growing authority of the televised bully pulpit. In January 1969, Bill Daniels, now serving as the chairman of the NCTA's public relations committee, moved forward on his idea for a "Congressional television series for the C.A.T.V. industry."[10] He had Thom Keith and Tony Acone of Internet Productions Inc. travel to Washington for the ceremonies and pomp surrounding Nixon's inauguration and meet with members of Congress to gauge interest in an idea for a national cable television program called *Congressional Report*. For two weeks, Keith and Acone talked with members of Congress about how political cablecasting could advance legislators' agendas and self-interests. Although pitched on Capitol Hill as a way to expand civic education, correspondence among the three men made clear the project's priority was to make friends with people in high places so that they could then advance policies more favorable to the industry's bottom line. Profits and politicians' personal interests took priority—not necessarily a commitment to the public good.

Per the request of Daniels, Keith and Acone crafted a plan to build a studio on Capitol Hill, complete with a limousine service, at which to interview elected officials on pressing issues of the day. As Acone later recalled, "the format of the show was already done. The guy's interviewed, the show is done, you move him into an edit room and they look at the show, maybe make a few changes, and the limo takes him back to wherever."[11] The proof of concept would be baked into the show, as a member of Congress could talk directly to constituents, notably bypassing a "reporter sticking a microphone in his mouth." Then, the program's host would read constituent letters to him for the last ten minutes of the interview to show the "immediate evidence of what cable is doing for them because their constituents will be right there asking questions."[12]

In the end, the project never manifested. It was too costly, and, even more importantly, most cable stations simply didn't have channels set aside for local programming (notably the first FCC "Public, Educational, Governmental" [PEG] channel requirement for systems with over thirty-five hundred subscribers came later that year). Nevertheless, Daniels continued to push his fellow NCTA members to develop creative ways to offer free time to elected officials.[13] That summer, he wrote an urgent letter to his NCTA colleagues to take unified action to capitalize on an exciting "public-relations opportunity to the Cable Industry" by offering "more time to political candidates at less cost, or perhaps preferably free time, to qualified candidates in substantial quantities."[14]

Across the country, imaginative cable operators did just that. For example, at the end of 1969, operators from Easton, Pennsylvania, traveled to Washington, D.C., in a "mobile cablecasting studio" to interview Pennsylvania Senator Hugh Scott, the Senate minority leader and the ranking Republican on the Communications Subcommittee of the Committee on Commerce.[15] Such innovations revealed how the future of cable depended on meeting the growing demand for political communication on the tube and showing the ease and accessibility of alternatives to broadcast television.

Increasingly, think tank studies also showed that cablecasting could help win campaigns. In 1970, RAND researchers Herbert S. Dordick and Jack Lyle found a perfect case study for testing cable's electoral impact in the Honolulu suburb of Waianae. They worked with the manager of the local Cablevision system, Gene Piety, to make free time and local studio production resources available to candidates running in the local city council and state legislature elections. Then they monitored their cable usage and conducted a range of postelection interviews with the candidates and cable subscribers.

Their experiment showed that viewers liked what they saw on cable television. Each program had a call-in option, which many viewers used to ask the candidates questions in real time. They estimated that about 28 percent of cable subscribers tuned in to one of the ten political programs that aired. The surveys also overwhelmingly demonstrated that viewers used the programs to select candidates, with roughly 60 percent of viewers saying that the programs "helped them make up their minds as to voting."[16] This alone, argued Dordick and Lyle, indicated that "the programs were a positive force in the electoral process."

The trial highlighted how using a mix of audience research and cable appearances could empower a candidate to score an upset.[17] One Republican candidate used cable programs to get more comfortable around the camera. He had more control over interviews, during which his campaign manager fed him questions derived from polling surveys about which issues mattered most to constituents. His campaign staff then undertook a massive effort to promote these interviews, placing advertisements about them in local newspapers and on placards along a busy highway. In the end, the campaign manager told researchers that cable television "was a contributing factor" in his victory.

In the end, the handicaps—poor equipment, noisy studios, and inexperienced candidates—limited the effectiveness of political cablecasting in the early 1970s. Perhaps the biggest obstacle was the concern that nobody was watching. The NCTA worked diligently to change that, however. The organization understood how the shifting political scene in the 1970s offered tremendous opportunity to shake up both the political and media establishments, and it pounced on opportunities to do so during the 1972 election.

After the disastrous Democratic National Convention in Chicago in 1968, the McGovern-Fraser Commission (named for Senator George McGovern, who initially chaired it, and Representative Donald Fraser, who took over when the former launched a presidential bid) reformed the presidential nominating process to put the selection of presidential candidates in the hands of primary voters rather than state party insiders.[18] The result was a wide open 1972 primary, with over a dozen candidates contending for the nomination.

It quickly became clear that electoral success demanded grassroots organizing and an effective media strategy. The mayor of New York, John Lindsay, knew this, and that is why he recruited Carroll O'Connor, star of the most popular show on television, *All in the Family*, to campaign for him.[19] For a little-known antiwar senator from South Dakota, George McGovern, finding ways to play "media games" helped him to rack up delegates (as did his intimate knowledge of the new rules for delegate selection he helped to write and popularize as "honest" and "responsive").[20] The campaign had a "strategic rule which we took as gospel," explained one staffer who helped to coordinate the California primary campaign: "anytime you appear on radio or television you automatically have more listeners than at any scheduled appearance at an event at the same hour."[21] Such a political strategy opened the doors for candidates to rethink television appearances and accept offers to appear on cable television programs, even if they only had a small audience.

Desperate for media coverage and short on cash, Democratic candidates had little to lose in experimenting with cable, and the cable industry mobilized because it had everything to gain. The NCTA launched its "National Cable TV Week" in mid-February with the theme of "Changing Time, Changing Communication," and it worked astutely to turn this idea into a reality on the campaign trail.[22] A range of Democratic candidates started to work with cable operators and "put their heads together to exploit the unique assets of the medium," explained the NCTA guide to cablecasting.[23] In an effort to demonstrate relevance and reach, the NCTA collected data on all the ways candidates used cable, stressing the creativity and accessibility of the medium—even if the lobbying organization ignored the reality that cable was a mere afterthought for both local newspapers and candidates.

Cable operators worked hard to shed light on cable's possibilities. The NCTA wrote letters to the McGovern campaign emphasizing the "substantial" impact that the 38,191 cable homes could make in the pivotal New Hampshire primary. It also referenced how other candidates had already taken up its offer of free airtime on cable systems, perhaps in an effort to spark competition and make the McGovern campaign return its calls.[24] The New England Cable TV Association set up a videotaping studio in Concord where it invited candidates from both parties to sit for thirty-minute interviews. (Notably Nixon's Republican primary challengers—Ohio's conservative representative John Ashbrook and California's more liberal representative Pete McCloskey—took advantage of the opportunity, but as the incumbent expecting the nomination, Nixon refused.) Operators then compiled all of these interviews into one longer program and, exposing the low-tech moment of how cable operated, physically drove the tape to one another.[25]

Orange Cablevision in Florida offered the same opportunity to Democratic contenders canvassing the state: Lindsay, Senator Edmund Muskie, and Alabama Governor George Wallace. In California, a state known for its reliance on performative politics, thirty-two cable systems formed a "California Cable Network" to facilitate the transfer of similar videos. The network even endured after the campaign to provide California residents with "regular political information programming," including a weekly distribution of Governor Ronald Reagan's press conferences.

Even more dynamic possibilities for a new approach to cable television emerged that year from the very counterculture that Reagan loved to bash. TVTV founders—Allen Rucker, Michael Shamberg, Megan Williams, and Tom Weinberg—pitched an idea to several cable companies of creating two one-hour documentaries about the

Democratic and Republican conventions that could then air on their cable systems.[26] Having just received press credentials to attend the conventions, TVTV's media activists convinced these cable systems to pay a portion of the expenses in exchange for a copy of a documentary they could then disseminate to fulfill local origination requirements.[27] The start-up production team noted the "timidity" on part of the cable operators, who only covered a fraction of the cost, but also highlighted the important "precedent" set by any type of investment into cable programming.[28]

TVTV featured young upstarts, like Maureen Orth, who asked different types of questions. In fact, with her television training, journalistic chops, and countercultural credentials, Orth was an ideal person to join the TVTV convention experiments. She had studied political science at University of California Berkeley during the early 1960s. Like the hundreds of young Americans who had pushed John F. Kennedy to follow through on his promise to create the Peace Corps, she joined the new diplomatic program that fought the Cold War by building schools rather than dropping bombs.[29] After returning home from Colombia, she took a graduate class in documentary film and journalism at University of California Los Angeles on a whim and quickly became fascinated by the power of storytelling. After getting her master's degree in the field, she soon became a prominent chronicler of the counterculture for *The Village Voice* and *Rolling Stone*, where she published a story in the summer of 1972 on TVTV's plans for the upcoming convention. Impressed with the story and eager to have a reporter with some professional training, Shamberg invited Orth to join their hippie-clad convoy to the conventions that year.

Orth and other TVTV chroniclers captured political perspectives and experiences ignored by network news anchors. While Walter Cronkite sat in a studio far away from the raucous convention happenings, Orth went into the middle of heated Democratic delegate disputes, notably interviewing Willie Brown, the head of the McGovern delegation from California who battled Chicago Mayor Richard Daley and the "Stop McGovern" coalition over the new procedures for counting delegates.[30] It was contentious and the TVTV cameras captured the fight as it played out in real time. The coverage helped to shed a light on the complicated political process, and also on the media—highlighting how reporters operated and pointing out what they ignored.

At the Republican Convention, TVTV profiled anti-Vietnam protesters, even giving a press pass to a paraplegic member of Vietnam Veterans Against the War, Ron Kovic. Then, on the convention floor, he yelled, "Stop the bombing! Stop the war!" directly challenging the chants of "four more years" that permeated the well-choreographed convention show. The scene later became famous in the 1989 movie *Born on the Fourth of July*, but it was made possible by TVTV's willingness to give voice to people and stories overlooked by network television coverage.

Orth's interview with Henry Kissinger also showed how the new television journalists played by rules they made themselves. After asking him about the Vietnam War, she then threw a curveball. With a smile that showed knowledge of Kissinger's playboy reputation, "How are the girls?" she asked. The question posed by an attractive young woman visibly threw off the powerful national security advisor. "Fine," he said with a smirk.[31]

The "video scrapbook," as the *New York Times* called it, first aired on cable systems to a limited viewership. The New York TelePrompTer system wrote the NCTA with pride that the *Times* characterized these programs as "a brilliant tapestry of cable journalism," and it celebrated the human stories that came to light with such an unconventional approach.[32]

Soon after, the cable experiment commanded the attention of the mainstream media and broader public.[33] Westinghouse Broadcast asked TVTV to combine the two hour-long cablecasts into one ninety-minute production, which the company paid $4,000 to broadcast on their stations in Boston, Baltimore, Pittsburgh, Philadelphia, and San Francisco to tremendous acclaim and viewer interest.[34] "It was like a breath of fresh air to have someone give the feeling of the event instead of the canned-programmed prepackaged

Maureen Orth interviewing National Security Advisor
Henry Kissinger for TVTV at the Republican National
Convention, August 1972.
Photo Credit: University of California, Berkeley, Art
Museum and Pacific Film Archive.

version we were spoon fed at the time of the convention," wrote one
grateful viewer. Indeed, even the networks noticed the success of
TVTV, and the limited budget on which they operated. One CBS
executive drew attention to the fact that they had spent more on
coffee than "the kids" did on their entire operation and conceded
that TVTV did a better job too.[35]

Such comprehensive interviews and more candid conversations
with candidates became a cable calling card during the campaign
in ways that garnered attention from leading politicians across the
country. Systems in Decatur, Illinois; Melbourne, Florida; and Harrisburg, Pennsylvania, highlighted the contrast between political
cable programs and the shorter and more cursory coverage of public
affairs by broadcast television. The Harrisburg program *Dialog* had
cable entrepreneur-turned-governor Milton Shapp appear regularly
to discuss legislative activities and the "political climate." It proved
so successful with subscribers that the operator shared tapes of the
program with other systems and the Pennsylvania Department of
Education for public distribution.[36]

In the end, 258 cable systems featured some type of campaign coverage; some of it involved paid political advertisements while other systems featured free "public service political programming." Wired communities across the country also tuned in to their local cable stations for election returns and commentary, with over 230 Senate and House races featured on cable television.[37]

Far from a simply altruistic civic initiative, the NCTA used this campaign coverage to demonstrate to elected officials why they should encourage, rather than limit, the growth of cable television.[38] Over the next few years, the NCTA published a breakdown of cable-casting facilities in congressional districts across the country—and increasingly members of Congress integrated such an affordable communication tool into their media plans.[39] Between 1974 and 1975, over 130 representatives and senators worked with their local cable operators to use the new medium to promote their campaigns or to connect with their constituents.[40]

For example, Tim Shuey, a cable operator in Junction City, Kansas, wanted to build on the state's successful political cablecasting network that had emerged during the 1972 election and to create new programs for senators. James B. Pearson (R-KS) jumped at the idea: "Yes, yes, yes, let's find a way to do it," he responded.[41] Collaboration among different cable studios and operators in Kansas resulted in an innovative fifteen-minute program series filmed in Washington, D.C., and then distributed to seventeen systems with over thirty-five thousand subscribers. One of these programs in 1974 even featured Vice President Gerald Ford in conversation with Senator Pearson, who called the program "fantastic." Such shows featured students and other members of the community, casting a different lens on what constituted news on the cable dial. Shuey repeatedly emphasized the importance of cable in building and connecting different types of people and empowering individuals to become "an actual functioning part of the community."[42] It was also good for business. The advertisements for these programs made sure to note the number people could call "to get on the cable."[43]

Although the 1972 election saw the flowering of new possibilities for television production and coverage, over the next few years,

Promotional campaign for Salina Cable
TV Systems, *Salina Journal*, April 30,
1974, 15.

operators saw forging alliances with lawmakers as much more of a
priority than funding experiments like those proposed by TVTV.
Indeed, despite the success of their groundbreaking coverage of
the conventions, community and nonprofit media organizations
like TVTV struggled to find the funding necessary to sustain their
work. In part, this came from FCC regulatory shifts that loosened
PEG requirements. Legal challenges around public access channels
also played a role, leaving such public programming requirements
up to local governments during the franchise process.[44]

Significantly though, cable operators increasingly invested in different types of programming, which tapped into elected officials'
desire to win elections and cast Congress in the spotlight rather
than countercultural experiments to overturn the political establishment. Indeed, cable lobbyists wanted the industry to be part

of political institutions undergoing change, seeing this as the way to break through the regulatory red tape they saw as undermining their financial potential.

Such thinking was clearly on display during the 1972 political cable-casting experiment. As part of its promotional campaign, the NCTA published a prescient quote from a letter written by *New York Times* reporter John Finney to Senate Majority Leader Mike Mansfield. "There is a good possibility that cable television will be more inclined than commercial television in the past to turn to Congressional hearings for coverage. In this case Congress has a chance to be prepared for once for a technological development, and in the process enhance its power and prestige."[45] While the next year broadcasters eagerly stepped into this role as the Watergate investigation unfolded, in the scandal's aftermath, cable operators across the country found ways to convince Congress that their medium could bring the transparency the public wanted and the television access lawmakers craved.[46]

———

The Watergate hearings were a television sensation, and the high viewership they generated exposed a demand for political programming, even among daytime viewers. President Nixon and his defenders had argued that the decision to televise the Senate hearings constituted proof of the "political witch hunt" that the liberal media had pursued against him all his life.[47] Vice President Agnew criticized the "Perry Masonish impact" of the media event that "will paint both heroes and villains in lurid and indelible colors before the public's very eyes." He lamented that the hearings were "essentially what is known in politics as a 'beauty contest' and the attractiveness and presence of the participants may be more important than the content of the testimony."[48] A public process, which could foster poor information and an overly emotional reaction, would harm the system of law and order, he contended.

Majority Leader Mansfield disagreed. He saw television coverage as bolstering the integrity of the process.[49] And it did. One viewer complained of a "Watergate hangover" from staying up too late watching the reruns of the day's coverage, while another complained that watching such extensive coverage at night "was ruining my sex life." Significantly, another viewer openly acknowledged that the hearings had directly resulted in more civic engagement by stimulating a deep desire to understand "how my government worked."[50] The hearings validated the ideas advanced by OTP staffers like Bruce Owen and Brian Lamb about how news could work when the people themselves could decide what to believe, rather than having to rely on elite newscasters to interpret it.[51]

Scholars also paid attention. One study by economists Stanley M. Besen and Bridger M. Mitchell—in consultation with OTP's Bruce Owen—broke ground by arguing that "television viewing can be increased by the addition of new alternatives if they are sufficiently dissimilar to the programs presently being shown."[52] This study challenged the intellectual basis at the core of the 1964 NAB study that had guided broadcasting regulations: "the passive viewer theory," which argued that people had a set number of hours they would dedicate each day to watching television, and they would decide among the programs available at those times. Under this theory, the introduction of more channels (i.e., cable television) would splinter audiences instead of increasing overall viewing hours—indeed, this idea is exactly why Nixon became so enamored with cable because it could fundamentally hurt the bottom line of the networks. But, if Besen and Mitchell were right, cable could be good for the economy, not simply an antimedia political vendetta.[53]

Such research resonated with staffers in the new Ford administration who were committed to open communication and regulatory reform. When Vice President Gerald Ford took the oath of office on August 9, 1974, he pledged that "straight talk" would be a pillar of his administration.[54] To do this, his media advisers worked to return integrity to the executive branch by staging symbolic events like televised news conferences in the Rose Garden. Behind the scenes, a team of economists worked to bring public confidence to government regulations that activists on the left and right called out for serving entrenched interests at the expense of the public.[55] In these regulatory reform initiatives, Paul MacAvoy, a Yale-trained economist and head of Ford's Economic Advisory Council, led the way.

MacAvoy believed in the merits of deregulation, especially in the fraught arena of communications.[56] He also understood why it had not yet happened—because politicians were unwilling "to assault the television establishment and thus, conceivably, jeopardize the most important of individual objectives—reelection, reappointment, or future employment by the industry."[57] Whether this power was real or merely perceived, MacAvoy recognized that it gave broadcasters tremendous influence that had long stymied legislative proposals pushing for regulatory reform.[58] Undeterred and armed with research from the OTP and the cabinet committee report, MacAvoy started to tackle the issue of cable television legislation. By the fall of 1975, lobbyists, executives, and operators cycled in and out of the Roosevelt Room at the White House, some beaming with excitement and others brimming with anger.

The cable industry arrived first. Viacom president Ralph Baruch expressed his enthusiasm for the invitation, calling it "the first time in my recollection that the Executive has taken an interest in furthering competition between various media of communications."[59] During these meetings, cable executives and lobbyists emphasized the need to separate cable from the regulatory regime governing broadcasters, arguing that the new medium did not fall into the category of "public airwave" that necessitated the restrictions implemented by the Communications Act of 1934. They hammered home the need to rethink what constituted the "public interest" because under the current regulatory structure, the "broadcasters' interest" had overshadowed the true needs of the American public.[60]

During these meetings, cable leaders discovered they had allies in the Ford White House. Along with Paul MacAvoy, there was Jonathan Rose, a former Nixon adviser who now served as assistant attorney general in the Antitrust Division of the Justice Department. Rose repeatedly called out the fear and emotion undergirding broadcasters' economic arguments at the expense of hard facts.[61] Lynn May, the Domestic Policy Council's associate director for Housing, Community Affairs, and Communications, emerged as another advocate for cable. He had studied history at UCLA before joining the U.S. Department of Labor as a low-level staffer in 1972. Under the Ford administration, he gained greater responsibilities, dealing with issues that ranged from the postal system to privacy to drugs to minority business ownership.[62] May was eager to learn more about cable television and that November, he traveled with the acting director of the OTP, John Eger, to the Western Cable Television Show and Convention. They both pledged that their study of cable television would fit into the administration's broader regulatory reform initiatives that aimed to eliminate barriers for competition and increase programming for consumers. Claiming to speak directly for the president, May promised that Ford would "develop a long-range national policy for cable" as part of his efforts to reform other "unnecessary and inefficient government regulation affecting telecommunications and other aspects of the economy."[63]

This professed commitment to cable reform made for stormy meetings with broadcasters. Having already sent strongly worded letters to Whitehead and Eger over the past year warning the OTP to leave the issue of cable alone, CBS President Arthur Taylor arrived at the White House ready for battle.[64] Emotions ran high at an October 16th meeting, which turned into a ninety-minute shouting match. One White House aide called the session "very disturbing" because the broadcasters "basically stated . . . that we had no business bothering them. There was a sense of guarded threat to what they said—that they have a job in providing information sources to the public and are above questioning."[65] Rather than backing down, however, Paul MacAvoy stood his ground, simply offering his regrets that the meeting turned into a "confrontation," which he attributed to the fact that broadcasting executives had never before been challenged on technical questions by federal officials.[66] One participant labeled the donnybrook "not worthy of being called a White House meeting." When reports of the conflict circulated on Capitol Hill, one Democratic official told Brian Lamb that "it just reinforces the feeling the town has about the arrogance of the networks."[67]

Broadcasters felt they had been treated unfairly, and Taylor's "bull in a China shop" approach aimed to send a firm message to MacAvoy that pursuing cable legislation would unleash a "'hornet's nest' of opposition from the broadcast industry," explained an account of the incident in *Broadcasting*.[68] And that is exactly what happened. The National Association of Broadcasters quickly mobilized its grass-roots army to apply political pressure through a carefully orchestrated letter writing campaign.[69] The goal? To overwhelm the White House, Congress, and the FCC with mail that addressed two themes: that cable should only supplement broadcasting, and while it could be "encouraged to provide new, innovative services," the public should not have to pay for programs that it currently receives for free over the air. The broadcasters planned to hammer the point over and over again—understanding how potent it had proved in stifling cable previously.

Yet the economic charts that mattered more to people like Mac-Avoy told a different story. First, they saw that broadcasters made money under the current regulatory structure—a lot of it. "The television broadcasting industry is one of the nation's most profitable," a memo titled "Broadcasting Industry Profits" explained as it noted the industry's 16.5 percent rate of return on investments.[70] Perhaps more significantly, when Ford's staffers asked economists about the prevailing assumption that cable would bankrupt the broadcasting industry and undermine its ability to inform and educate the public, experts overwhelmingly disagreed with the research that the NAB had disseminated for years. In a "mini economic summit on cable" organized by Eger and MacAvoy, Bruce Owen and others presented the results of recent studies (including the Besen and Mitchell report on the Watergate hearings) to demonstrate that the "consuming public stands to gain substantially from the proposals put forward to deregulate cable television."[71]

In short, the policy conversation around cable had shifted. For the Ford team, it was about what would be best for the consumer rather than for broadcasters. Consumers, they believed, should be allowed to "vote with their dollars" as they did with almost all other commodities.[72] When broadcasters raised the alarms about the catastrophic impact of cable competition as the first step on a slippery slope toward pay television for all, Lynn May simply told them that he failed to see any "conclusive evidence" to support these "emotional" claims. Without this evidence, he would stay true to the administration's goal of "expanding the media choices available to the American consumer."[73]

Broadcasters vehemently disagreed. Arthur Taylor charged MacAvoy with being "anti-broadcast" like his boss's disgraced predecessor. "Ludicrous," exclaimed John Eger as he jumped to defend his colleague.[74] NBC also kept pushing, alleging that the administration's analysis of the industry was "oversimplified" and that it failed to understand the unique nuances of the communications system.[75] The NAB chairman publicly assailed MacAvoy for his willingness to "kill half of all stations," asking him to think carefully about the "implications of this attitude toward the survival of local television stations, the public's major source of news and information in the country."[76]

MacAvoy attempted to quell broadcasters' outrage by encouraging them to rise to the challenge and improve their product. He also reminded them that even if profits declined, their enormous profit margin ensured that they would still make money. But he insisted that since television was such an "important consumer service and present regulations have probably kept its full potential from being realized," the White House needed to move forward.[77]

The Domestic Policy Council, OTP, and the Department of Justice all had different ideas about the specific legislative path the Ford administration should take, but they all agreed on the importance of the research they had generated. Broadcasters and their allies had always shaped the contours of the policy conversation, and fear had always won: fear that Americans would lose their beloved television programs; and fear that broadcasters could politically sabotage reelection campaigns. In contrast, the research the administration had compiled used a more data-driven approach that prioritized consumer choice. Notably, such studies ignored the social justice implications that media activists had raised around television reform as they pushed the federal government to restructure license rules to encourage minority ownerships and force local stations to be more responsive to feminist audiences.[78]

These economists-turned-policymakers, rather, focused on television's market efficiency over moral and democratic imperatives surrounding questions of equity.[79]

And then everything stopped and at the end of March 1976, Ford's policy advisers made a formal recommendation not for deregulation, but for more research. The issue allegedly needed further analysis, and the Ford administration should wait for the "resolution of the current copyright legislation by the Congress" before moving forward.[80]

Cable advocates outside the White House immediately knew what happened, and the cover of *CATV Weekly* visually articulated their suspicions. Two talking bubbles over the White House conveyed an imagined conversation between MacAvoy and a senior White House adviser, with MacAvoy allegedly saying, "But what about my credibility as an economist—everyone knows cable has been studied to death?" The other figure exposes the truth: "Paul, it's an election year; the broadcasters are screaming—and we need THEM. We've got to save the President from himself. Just tell them we need more research—that should put the whole thing off."[81]

Brian Lamb had a name for these official reports about the need for "more research": "baloney." While officials would never admit they caved to broadcasting pressure, Lamb wrote that "off the record it's hard to find a Ford aide who can honestly look you in the eye and give you that 'research and analysis' nonsense."[82] That summer, another Washington columnist who worked for *Television Digest*, Irwin B. Arieff, crafted another description of the lobbying campaign that derailed the bill.[83] According to his account published that summer in *Videography*, top network lobbyists met with Robert Hartmann, counselor to the president, over an expensive dinner at a French restaurant and told him how angry broadcasters were over the issue of cable. They reminded Hartmann that he needed "whole-hearted broadcast support for the President during this upcoming campaign." The president's election team had established a "Rose Garden" campaign strategy to capitalize on the free media coverage and prestige from televised White House presidential addresses. Souring relationships with network executives was just not worth the legislative fight

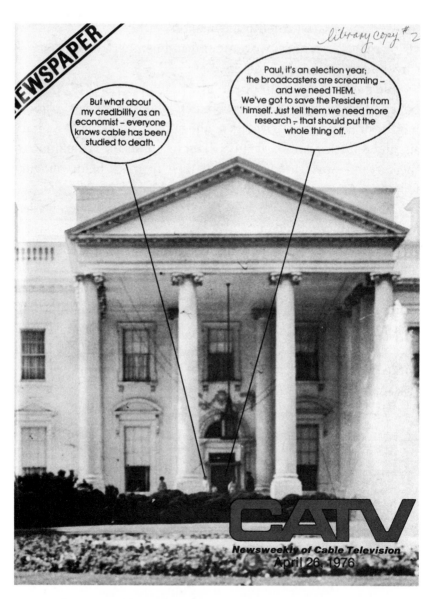

A cover of *CATV Weekly*, April 26, 1976, raises questions about what really happened with the call for "more research" in the Domestic Policy Council's cable television initiatives.

Photo Credit: *Multichannel News*/Barco Library, The Cable Center.

over an issue that could link him to his disgraced predecessor in the public eye.[84]

Such suspicions were dead-on. In a post-election memo, Lynn May explained that the cable initiative laid out by the Domestic Policy Council "was subjected to considerable criticism from senior White House Staff members as being inimical to television broadcasting interests and thus untenable in an election year."[85] And so, the president specifically told broadcasters that such legislation was not "in line with my views," despite the fact that he had earlier seen the issue as part of his regulatory reform agenda. While Jim Cannon, Ford's domestic policy adviser, considered revisiting the issue after the election, May warned him that doing so would "give credence to the charges that the Administration backed down in the face of broadcaster opposition in an election year," and it would contradict the president's public statements on the issue. Revisiting the topic would make Ford look like a weak leader who succumbed to the industry capture of regulatory agencies that he promised to eradicate.

While Ford ultimately did defer to broadcasting interests, the policy debate his administration led generated cracks in the protective armor broadcasting had long used to shape communications regulations. And new faces in Congress were more willing to take on this powerful broadcasting lobby, especially if they represented areas like Denver, Colorado, home to some of the largest cable companies.

———

Tim Wirth came to Washington, D.C., in January 1975 as one of the ninety-three men and women who made up the "Class of '74." He was part of a new breed of liberal Democrats, frequently called the "Watergate Babies." These men and women won congressional elections across the country with promises to bring meaningful reform and transparency to Washington, D.C., following Nixon's resignation. As a product of the "rights revolution," they framed their policy goals as moral obligations, and they cheerfully dismantled the seniority system that underwrote congressional activities.[86] They wanted to end the war in Vietnam and pursue racial and gender equality. They proudly pushed the Democratic Party to sever its historic connections with segregationist white Southerners, most of whom had left the party after Lyndon Johnson signed the Civil Rights Act and Voting Rights Act a decade earlier. Instead, they drew support from suburban neighborhoods. Because many represented white homeowners who disliked high taxes, these freshman Democrats advocated for good, but lean, government.[87]

Wirth had lived all across the United States. Born in Santa Fe but raised in Denver, the new congressman had attended a prep school in New Hampshire, Phillips Exeter Academy, before heading to Harvard University for his undergraduate education and then to Stanford for a PhD in economics.[88] From there, he joined the White House Fellowship Program, which Lyndon Johnson had established to "provide gifted and highly motivated emerging leaders with some first-hand experience in the process of governing the Nation and a sense of personal involvement in the leadership of society."[89]

When Wirth returned to Colorado from D.C., he became frustrated by the long-time incumbent congressman in his district, Donald Brotzman, who he felt "didn't have a clue about what was happening in the country in terms of Watergate, and Vietnam and Richard Nixon, and all of the turbulence in the early '70s."[90] And so he ran for office, and narrowly won. He traveled to Capitol Hill eager to change the status quo of how Congress operated.

Years later, Wirth admitted that when it came to telecommunications, the industry he would leave such a dramatic mark on over the next two decades, he "didn't know this cable television stuff from diddley." But he soon met with Bill Daniels—who lost a race for the Colorado governorship that same year—and the Denver businessman worked diligently to explain to the new representative the importance of the industry to Colorado.[91] Cable systems had arrived early in the state, thanks to demand for reception created by the Rocky Mountain terrain. Denver also became a financial hub for the industry. Bill Daniels set up his powerful brokerage firm in this booming metropolitan city that offered a fresh mountain breeze and beautiful views. More significant, of course, were the low taxes and the promise of a better "quality of life" for businesses and residents, which local policymakers defined as a political environment committed to advancing consumerism and market-based solutions to issues that ranged from education to environmentalism to economic and racial inequality.[92]

Wirth quickly met key players in the cable industry who had also built their business headquarters in Denver: along with Daniels there was Monroe "Monty" Rifkin, who had made the western city the headquarters for American Television and Communications Corporation (ATC); William "Billy" Thompson, a defensive back for the Broncos who had become a celebrity spokesman for cable; and Stanley Searle, the editor of the influential industry magazine *TVC*, which had its editorial offices in Englewood, a southern suburb of Denver. The freshman congressman then learned about the struggles the industry faced as he watched the efforts at reform fizzle during the Ford administration.

Congress seemed perplexed as to how to handle cable legislation, but Wirth soon realized that he might be able to do something about a specific issue: pole attachments. As a new member on the Communications Subcommittee of the House Committee on Energy & Commerce, he went to work, studying the topic and bringing cable operators to Capitol Hill to explain their concerns, and in some cases (like when he encountered his college friend and Army buddy Amos Hostetter), even facilitating their testimony.[93]

Cable operators had long complained about the control that the telephone monopoly had over their business. They had to negotiate with the utility companies about availability of space and the rate to hang cable wires. AT&T had a vested interest in keeping rates high: at the time broadcasters paid them over $65 million a year to transmit video on their wires, and they wanted to keep this major client happy.[94] When they did allow cable operators to hang wires, they would frequently hike up the rate unexpectedly, knowing operators had little choice but to pay. After receiving so many complaints about rate hikes, the FCC ordered the Bell companies to negotiate a compromise with the NCTA over how to resolve such disputes. Over the next six years, a lot of talk happened, but nothing changed.[95]

As a newly elected representative from Denver, Colorado, Tim Wirth
ushered in the first piece of cable television legislation with the Pole
Attachment Act of 1978. Here he sits in the hallway with Robert
Schmidt, president of the National Cable Television Association, and
Lionel Van Deerlin, the Democratic representative from California
who would later advocate for televising the House of Representatives
floor proceedings on cable television.
Photo Credit: Barco Library, The Cable Center.

In his oral history, Wirth summarized what made him take on the
pole attachment issue. "The communications industry . . . is all about
the haves keeping the have nots out. Those who are inside the industry want to keep the new voices out. The industry's full of that. . . .
Those who were inside try to control the Congress and control the
FCC and control who gets what."[96] The pole attachment debate captured this process, in Wirth's eyes. The telephone companies partnered with network television corporations to prevent—both physically and legally—cable companies from operating. Wirth wanted
to break up such monopolistic arrangements, especially because
it impacted businesses in his home district. So, he teamed up with
other newcomers in Congress to try to foster competition—in this

case by writing new rules lowering the rates telephone companies could charge to string wires—as the solution.

The NCTA cultivated support for Wirth's pole attachment bill by delivering to members of Congress a one-foot-long piece of cable wire that a rural telephone company had ripped from its poles during a dispute with a local cable company. One of its lobbyists, Tom Wheeler, explained that it became a powerful visual reminder of their argument: "This is what we are talking about here. Do you believe in competition? Do you believe in people's right to have this new information coming over the cable?"[97]

For people like Al Gore Jr., a representative from Tennessee, that argument proved compelling, and in 1978, Congress passed the pole attachment amendment to the Communications Act, which ended up being both Wirth and the cable industry's first piece of successful legislation. The NCTA commemorated the bill by sending a piece of a telephone pole to supporters in Congress with a plaque that celebrated the "first piece of cable television legislation ever enacted by the Congress—Pole Attachment Law."[98] While the industry constantly clamored for deregulation, this legislation showed how the right kind of federal regulation could produce economic benefits.[99]

Congress also tackled another issue that divided the cable industry at the time but became key to unshackling FCC regulations down the road. The 1976 Copyright Act forced cable to assume financial responsibility for the retransmission of broadcast programming and make royalty payments for the signals operators used.[100] Especially before satellite, cable operators relied on rebroadcasting old movies or television series, whose signals came from both local and distant broadcasters. Hollywood studios and production companies— whether financed independently or by the networks—had long cried foul, claiming that operators stole their programming in their efforts to lure new subscribers. The new law created a Copyright Royal Tribunal that developed a fee schedule to access programs over the airwaves and ensure payment to copyright holders (whether broadcasters, film studios, or sports teams that produced the programming).

While some operators were appalled by the idea, the NCTA recognized that the accusation that cable operators were "pirates" and "parasites" continued to hamper lobbying efforts. Indeed, the FCC had very firmly told the industry that its permission to import even more broadcasting signals would depend on developing a compromise with programmers (mostly in Hollywood and in sports organizations) on payments.[101] Burt Harris, the NCTA chairman, summed up the struggle adeptly: "I was always opposed to copyright for cable because I felt along with many others in the industry that it had already been paid. But then there were those who felt Congress didn't share that view and I think we realized that some form of copyright payment was inevitable."[102]

Rather than simply being pro- or anti-cable Congress was in the mood for change. Across the political spectrum, its members wanted to break up the regulated monopolies that controlled so much of American economic life, and increasingly, they agreed that ideas of market efficiency should reign supreme as they developed and evaluated legislative solutions.[103] Another issue that transcended ideological or partisan divides also boosted the political power of cable television: how to televise Congress.

———

As Brian Lamb chronicled the frustrating legislative obstacles the cable industry kept confronting, he also witnessed the debate about televising Congress intensify. House Majority Leader Tip O'Neill understood the benefits such coverage could bring to the House of Representatives: connecting constituents directly to their elected officials, fostering a more informed citizenry, and countering presidential power.[104] Opponents, however, feared that "show business" would undermine congressional operations, and they felt that "the proceedings are too complicated and boring to have any impact on the average American." While Watergate had demonstrated a proof of concept for congressional television, it was also a unique moment of constitutional crises. The question remained: Could viewers understand the complexity of daily House floor speeches and procedures? Would they even tune in?

Once he became the new speaker of the House, O'Neill wanted to give it a try. On March 15, 1977, he proudly announced that the House would begin "a historic 90-day House test of televising our proceedings."[105] It would not yet be open to the public; the closed-circuit system made viewing such coverage available only on the television sets that House members had in the Rayburn House Office Building. It was an experiment to evaluate the utility and quality of recorded proceedings.

Tensions quickly emerged between the networks and members of Congress over the purpose and goal of potentially translating this test into a broadcasting program. Network officials wanted a more "active camera" to make coverage "more interesting," while House members put an emphasis on the importance of "obtaining a complete, uninterrupted record of the official proceedings."[106] Some Republican members, notably Rep. John Anderson (R-IL), argued for network control of the cameras, emphasizing that those who made the news (televised members of Congress) should not influence coverage of it. Minority Leader John Rhodes (R-AZ) agreed. He distrusted the Democratic leadership more than the networks, claiming that he believed the "networks will be unfair in an absolutely fair way."

Many sided with the views of the new majority leader, Jim Wright (D-TX). The southern moderate congressman who balanced ideal-ism with a pragmatic, deal-making approach to politics emphasized that the House needed to control the cameras to protect the "integrity of the House" from the "circus of show business" and the bias of the networks.[107] Younger congresspeople challenging the white- and male-dominated institution agreed about the importance of House control but for different reasons. Rep. Ronald Dellums, a Black Democrat from California, reminded his colleagues how the networks consistently "screened out the remarks of a black liberal as too radical."[108] A different type of public affairs coverage, however, could change that.

The test ended on September 15, 1977, and by the end of October, the Rules Committee put forth H.Res. 866, "which provides for closed circuit TV coverage of the House and directs the Speaker to implement TV coverage of legislative proceedings for distribution to the public."[109] Rep. Trent Lott (R-MS), a younger congressman who recently had won election as one of the first conservative Republicans in the South, opened the debate by stressing the importance of the resolution to make the institution more relevant to Americans.[110] Anderson quickly jumped into the conversation, emphasizing that "the question is no longer whether we should go public with broadcast coverage," but what the terms and arrangement would be with broadcasters. When the conflict over camera control stymied negotiations with the networks, some representatives turned to public television. PBS refused, fearing a conflict of interest with the government institution that helped to fund public television.[111]

And then, Lionel Van Deerlin (D-CA)—whose district held one of the largest cable systems in the country—offered a different idea. What about cable television, he asked his colleagues, which could connect them to over two million subscribers "through the miracle of the satellite."[112] Earlier that day, Van Deerlin—chair of the House Subcommittee on Communications—had done an interview with Brian Lamb for *Cablevision*. Afterward, Lamb floated a concept he had discussed with John Evans, president of Arlington Cable Partners. What if cable television carried the House proceedings as a public service initiative? An enthusiastic Van Deerlin brought the idea to the well of the House and urged his colleagues to consider how cable could do something that broadcasting could not and would not do.[113] "Gavel-to-gavel coverage of the House and Senate proceedings, although they may create no new star competition among the performers, will be available at times and to an extent that no commercial station, certainly no network, could or would provide. It is not within their economic capacity," explained Van Deerlin.[114] Cable, he contended, would allow the House to take "a step forward toward restoring the Government of this land to its own people."

O'Neill was intrigued by the idea, and his office immediately reached out to Van Deerlin to find out "what the hell you were talking about yesterday."[115] The California representative connected him to the man behind the idea, and Brian Lamb explained how cable could make it happen. Soon after, the House finally decided to open its doors to television by a vote of 342–44.[116] In the next few months, Lamb and O'Neill hammered out the details. With a promise that the cable industry would fund the coverage as a public service initiative and an agreement that the House would retain control over the cameras, the two men shook hands during a January meeting. Lamb left Capitol Hill with political support for a groundbreaking political cablecasting idea, one that took the NCTA efforts to a new level and could finally break the hold that politicians believed broadcasters had on their reelection bids.

Lamb convinced cable operators that paying for this operation was good business because it was good politics.[117] That argument wasn't new, of course. But Lamb had the timing, contacts, and sheer persistence that made it happen. Having worked in Washington as a staffer and in the cable industry as a journalist, Lamb knew how to make the pitch to politicians *and* cable operators. With the launch of Cable-Satellite Public Affairs Network (C-SPAN), he blazed a new path for public affairs programming that eschewed the economic limitations and political assumptions that, to the frustration of members of Congress, had long shaped network news.[118] One viewer later called C-SPAN "one of the best things to happen to TV since the Watergate hearings," an observation that the cable network happily shared with Speaker O'Neill as proof of its success.[119]

But there was another secret to the success of C-SPAN: satellite technology. And thanks to the "Open Skies" policies that Lamb's OTP boss had initiated, the cable industry was primed to take advantage of a more affordable and accessible way to bring such diverse programming to viewers.

6

Exploding the Cable Dial

Irving Kahn was down, but not out. The nephew (and namesake) of famous composer Irving Berlin had gone to prison on March 1, 1973, after being found guilty of bribery, perjury, and conspiracy in TelePrompTer's franchising battle in Johnstown, Pennsylvania.[1] In court, he testified about a shady deal he had made with the incoming mayor, Kenneth Tompkins, to protect his company's franchise.[2] Kahn allegedly met with Tompkins and two other city councilors in a Holiday Inn hotel room and paid them $15,000 directly. After Kahn then secured the franchise for the next twenty years, Tompkins continued to collect additional money under the guise of paying for public relations work and office equipment.

During a contentious legal battle, Kahn claimed the money was extorted, with local officials threatening to revoke the franchise unless TelePrompTer provided this "payoff." The scandal ended poorly for all parties—Tompkins resigned and Kahn went to federal prison. It also confirmed to outside observers that local officials were cutting "suspicious" deals "behind closed doors."[3] In many ways, Kahn's experience—being sent to jail for such bribery—was exceptional. But it also exposed a truth about early cable operators' focus on turning a profit, often at the expense of the industry's public image and credibility.

After serving twenty months of his sentence, Kahn hit the speaking circuit to restore his reputation as an industry visionary rather than a corrupt convict. On February 27, 1975, at the Texas Cable TV Association, he took the stage. "Now, as I was saying before I was interrupted," he began a speech that would go down in cable history, "you have never had a speaker more pleased to be standing before you than the man you see here today."[4] Titled "Blue Sky through a Green Filter," the speech urged cable operators to invest in a satellite distribution network to expand programming on the cable dial.[5]

That fall, this dream became a reality, one that saved a struggling pay channel and transformed the cable television industry. Out of desperation, Home Box Office (HBO) forged a path in both satellite experimentation and direct market sales, transforming it from a financial liability for its parent company, Time Warner, to a profit machine. The next year, Ted Turner turned an independent broadcasting station in Atlanta into a "superstation" by using satellite to distribute old television reruns and Atlanta Braves baseball games to cable operators across the country. (As Turner owned the baseball team, it was a boost for both of his business ventures.) Not only did Turner bypass the commercial broadcasting networks and telephone companies to distribute his programming, he also introduced the idea of a 24-hour station, "bringing all-night television to many markets for the first time," observed a report in the *Washington Post*.[6]

By early 1977, 262 cable operators had receivers to grab the signals beamed from programmers like HBO and Turner through newly launched commercial satellites.[7] It transformed cable businesses by introducing new revenue streams. Now operators could charge more for a basic cable subscription because they offered programming that differed from broadcasting fare. They could also negotiate a portion of advertising revenue with these independent satellite programmers, or make money by offering pay channels like HBO and then splitting the higher fees that viewers would pay for such exclusive programming aired without advertisements.

The numbers alone tell a powerful story. In 1975, cable had 9.8 million subscribers; by 1977, 12.2 million; and by 1980, 17.5 million.

Income from pay television services like HBO grew from $29 million in 1975 to $769 million in 1980.[8]

And yet, as Irving Kahn repeatedly emphasized in his speeches before and after his time in prison, people didn't just naturally flock to the cable dial. The industry had to sell them on the concept, just as they had politicians. Effective marketing campaigns pushed consumers to think about their television differently and to expect new services and forms of community as cable subscribers. As Kahn told one audience of advertisers, "Instill in [subscribers] a desire to be linked to the future and you'll have a solid and lasting customer to your credit."[9]

It worked. Entrepreneurial approaches to programming—from HBO to C-SPAN and CNN—solidified the economic strength of corporate cable companies. In the process, the marketing tactics that helped such cable programs succeed also made civic engagement increasingly dependent on cable consumption.

———

On October 1, 1975, an event unfolded that one HBO employee called "just as important as the development of the birth control pill."[10] Gathering at a Holiday Inn in Vero Beach, Florida, HBO executives, along with cable subscribers in the area and in Jackson, Mississippi (home to the other cable system that purchased a satellite receiver), witnessed something only available live on cable television: a legendary fifteen-round boxing match between Joe Frazier and Muhammad Ali in the Philippines, soon to be known as the "Thrilla in Manila." Ali may have won the fight, but for HBO employees and customers, it was pay television that emerged as the real champion.[11]

It was a major victory for a channel on the verge of folding. Three years earlier, Sterling Manhattan had been looking for a way to sell cable subscriptions in New York City. Initially, the appeal of cable television in NYC hinged simply on the fact that wired television provided a clearer picture than signals brought in by broadcast, due to interference from high-rise buildings. To expand interest in it, Sterling Manhattan's president, Charles Dolan, wanted to offer something exciting on the dial. He envisioned an outlet that offered movies and live sporting events, and he hoped to charge an additional fee on top of monthly subscriptions for access to this "premium" channel. In 1972, he brought in Gerald Levin, a lawyer with great contacts in the entertainment and sports worlds, to try to make it happen.[12]

It was a disaster. Although HBO found ways to extend its signals via microwave to places like Mount Vernon, Babylon, and Ithaca, it simply didn't attract enough subscribers to cover costs. HBO's future looked especially dismal because it had an exceptionally high "churn rate"—subscribers who signed up eager for the promised additional services but who quickly became bored by the repetition or poor program quality.[13] After all, how many times could someone watch the same old "B" movie over and over again?

Then, Levin thought about the idea Kahn had been pushing so vociferously for years.[14] The satellite industry was brimming with possibilities. Thanks to the "Open Skies" policy that Tom Whitehead had initiated—which encouraged a range of potential companies to submit plans for commercial satellite service—Western Union, Irving Kahn's TelePrompTer, and a new company in Georgia, Scientific Atlanta, had crafted business proposals to jump into the industry. They discovered that satellites could offer stronger signals than broadcasting or microwave towers. While a company would need to pay money upfront to build and launch a commercial satellite, it was a one-time capital investment that paled in comparison to the cost that broadcasters paid to transmit signals via the pricey AT&T wires each year. Programmers could then purchase an earth satellite station to beam up a signal on space they leased on the satellite transponder. Then cable operators with receivers could access that signal and transfer it to their customers via the cable wire.

RCA had plans to launch a domestic-communications satellite in 1975, and it had open carriage space, raising the question: what if HBO used this new celestial technology to get more programs and subscribers? It could tap into cable markets across the country without having to deal with telephone companies or the commer-

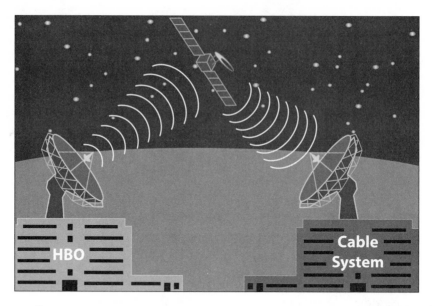

Satellite Transmission Demonstration. Image drawn from sources at the Barco Library, The Cable Center.

cial networks for distribution, and it could offer live events like the "Thrilla in Manila." The plan would not be cheap—the struggling company would have to invest in its own satellite system, work with RCA to lease space (a cost of $9.6 million for a six-year contract), and then convince cable operators across the country to purchase receiving dishes at a hefty price tag of $75,000 (HBO subsidized the cost to encourage such purchases and even loaned money as needed to operators).[15]

And the new technology was only the first step. As HBO employee Leslie Read recalled, "you've got to let the people know the signal is there." They needed to build relationships with local operators, programmers, and subscribers.[16] The strategies they used to do this— splitting revenue with operators and deploying cutting-edge direct marketing tools to enhance subscriber loyalty—would reshape the entire idea of what television could offer by promising a sense of community that accentuated differences rather than cultivated consensus.[17] Such a marketing approach forged the cultural basis of what the Cabletelevision Advertising Bureau would later call "Cable America," citizens with different viewing and consuming habits than those who just watched broadcast television.

By the 1970s, businesses across the country had embraced the idea of market segmentation, shifting advertising strategies from appealing to the "middle of the middle" to targeting key demographics defined by age, gender, race, region, and economic status.[18] Commercial networks invested substantial money into understanding audience demographics for individual shows so that they could sell expensive commercial slots to advertisers looking to appeal to particular groups. But even as they gambled on edgy shows like *Saturday Night Live* to tap into the much-sought-after younger demographic, their priority was always to generate the biggest audience possible.[19]

Satellite offered an opportunity for cable companies to develop an entirely different business model for television programming—narrowcasting—and this required a different advertising strategy.[20] Rather than worry about attracting corporate sponsors, operators relied on expanding subscriptions by offering niche programming on the basic cable dial and having people pay a premium for commercial-free movies or access to live sports. Success, then, demanded cultivating an individual relationship with viewers, one that celebrated and catered to their personal preferences.

To do this, HBO, in particular, used ideas and tactics taking the direct mail industry by storm in the 1970s. With powerful and affordable computers to process data, a small but growing field of direct marketers built extensive mailing lists and used them to study the purchasing habits of individual customers by encouraging survey responses about whether they had bought a product, and why.[21] Direct marketers deployed a variety of strategies—sweepstake competitions for example—to make consumers feel valued as individuals, not just as one of the masses. Likewise, HBO's marketing campaign pitched cable subscriptions, and the access to entertainment programming that came with it, as a form of empowerment.

With a shoestring budget, the campaign strategy itself reversed the dominant advertising model: rather than launching a national and polished campaign on network television, HBO salespeople

HBO presentation marketing slides selling the perks of pay
television.
Photo Credit: Barco Library, The Cable Center.

(and overwhelmingly they were men) started small and local as they
knocked on doors to pitch their services. Manuals taught them to
"identify and satisfy that customer's particular need for HBO."[22] It
was a grassroots, experimental approach, recalled John Billock, who
started working in HBO marketing in 1978. "We were a bunch of
merry pranksters running around America, launching HBO, moving
on to the next market. It was taking off."[23]

HBO marketing materials encouraged using the "bandwagon
technique," recruiting new subscribers by talking about all the
advanced services their neighbors already had. It also used research
on viewers from different income brackets to teach salespeople
about how to highlight certain features. According to sales manuals, they should pitch lower-income families on the value provided
by HBO, which would save them from needing to go to a movie
theater, whereas salespeople should hype the arts programming
of live operas and theater to higher-income households. Finally,
salespeople were taught to sell the "social value of HBO." Subscribers could be the center of social events if they had access to sports
and entertainment programs that all their neighbors would want
to see.

More significantly for the cable industry, salespeople focused on selling HBO to new cable customers first. After all, noted the manual, "it's easier to sell down to basic cable than to trade up to HBO." The sales pitch was always supposed to include a reminder to subscribers that they needed basic cable to also get HBO, so buying into the dream of HBO required becoming part of a broader cable community. It worked and a decade after California voters wanted to outlaw pay television, HBO convinced over 1.6 million subscribers to not just pay for a cable subscription but to pay extra for premium programming.[24]

The new technology at the root of it also allowed cable companies to skirt FCC restrictions. HBO and WTBS relied on distribution through satellite, circumventing FCC signal importation rules that focused on transmission of broadcasting signals. A 1977 court decision, *HBO v. FCC*, upheld cable's First Amendment rights, legally allowing cable companies to negotiate directly with film studios and sports teams for exclusive content.[25]

Boosted by this ruling, HBO led the way in pushing cable programming opportunities well beyond local origination programs and the retransmission of local broadcasting signals. Soon, HBO became one of Time Inc.'s most profitable assets alongside such magazine powerhouses as *Time, People,* and *Sports Illustrated.* Gerald Levin moved from head of HBO to executive vice president of Time Inc. by 1984.[26] Other companies developed competing premium stations like Showtime, which launched in 1978, and The Movie Channel, which launched in 1980. But none achieved the visibility and reach that HBO did in those early years, leading the company to proudly take credit for the cable mania of the next decade. "But the most notable thing HBO accomplished in its history—and the thing that probably gets most overlooked—is that it changed . . . *everything,*" wrote one employee in his account of the company's history.[27] Tele-Communications Inc. (TCI) executive John Malone agreed, noting that during the late 1970s and early 1980s, selling HBO became *the* way to sell cable.[28]

In part, HBO's success hinged on its willingness to experiment with new technology, both in distributing its programming via satellite

William Johnson, the president of KBLE in Columbus, Ohio, agreed to offer HBO to his subscribers only if the network increased programming of interest to Black communities. Here, Johnson stands at the NCTA trade show to announce an affiliation agreement with HBO alongside Judy Anderson, HBO regional manager, and Gloria Johnson, KBLE Ohio treasurer.
Photo Credit: Barco Library, The Cable Center.

and in selling it through a direct marketing campaign. The company also listened to its operators and their programming demands. For example, at KBLE in Columbus, Ohio, William Johnson made it clear that HBO would need to deliver "programming with a multi-cultural society in mind," if the company wanted to secure a channel on his dial. "We're not going to pay to see white motorcycle riders," the

Black cable operator told HBO executives. He noted that the company had to sign more Black entertainers to meet the demands of the Black community in Columbus and across the country.[29] Desperate to secure contracts with cable operators and aware of the growing urban market, HBO executives agreed to increase programming designed for Black audiences.[30]

HBO's ability to turn a profit from individual subscriptions rather than corporate advertising dollars made other media companies and market researchers rethink how to garner loyalty from individual consumers.[31] HBO did more than provide the "explosion of entertainment" it promised on the cable dial. It made the cable industry explode and showed to those inside and outside the industry that people would pay for TV more narrowly tied to their personal interests. It also revealed a growing public desire to find community connections through cable channels, which was exactly the sentiment HBO worked to cultivate.

Other attempts to capitalize on new technology and creative marketing were not as successful, but even they also exposed how the business of cable television had begun to reshape civic engagement, especially at the local level. Two years after HBO made headlines with its satellite experiment, Warner Cable excitedly announced a new cable system that it planned to test: QUBE. Launched in Columbus, Ohio, in December 1977, this interactive system empowered viewers to push buttons on a "magic box" (what was really a push-button control panel) to connect individual televisions with Warner's main cable television studio in the city.[32] This technology would open up myriad possibilities for viewers. They could select specific programs on demand (and for a fee), vote in local talent contests, or participate in a local referendum or poll. Celebrated as the "world's most sophisticated pay TV cable system," QUBE offered subscribers thirty channels of programming and the ability to "talk back" to the television. While ten channels required an additional fee per program, the other twenty channels featured local broadcasting fare, imported signals, and new programs created and produced by Warner Cable Corp.

Two programs in particular garnered attention: *Pinwheel* and *Columbus Alive.* The former provided children's programming without the "commercials for toys or sugared cereals," according to one marketing campaign.[33] *Columbus Alive* brought television viewers two hours of "chatter" that could include a cooking demonstration or a conversation with the local police. Unlike local programs on broadcast networks, however, the show was built around polling and interaction. A local version of the "The Gong Show" quickly emerged as a favorite part of the program. Viewers served as judges for this talent show and could even collectively vote to stop a poor act mid-performance.[34] The program also broached serious political debates. Following President Jimmy Carter's 1979 address to Americans on the crisis of confidence the nation faced, over seven thousand audience members responded to a poll asking them how the president's speech made them feel—61 percent responded "optimistic," 18 percent replied "pessimistic," and 21 percent conveyed that the speech left them "confused."[35] Another program featured former Nixon counsel and Watergate witness John Dean and asked audience members to vote on who they wanted to run against Jimmy Carter in 1980 (Ronald Reagan won).[36]

Warner Cable celebrated QUBE for its ability to inform and engage viewers in civic life, but it was a technical experiment designed to help the company win franchises (Warner regularly pointed to QUBE as something that the company could exclusively deliver to subscribers) and collect data on individual viewing habits. The latter aspect was a defining legacy of the experiment, which fizzled out within just a few years. QUBE gathered a tremendous amount of consumer information: what programs viewers watched and when, as well as the information they voluntarily gave through poll responses and purchases. Such specific data far surpassed information previously gleaned on television habits from Nielsen reports, arousing tremendous concern among journalists about privacy issues.[37] Similar to the growing direct marketing business, this data allowed programming services to get immediate feedback directly from consumers. As the president of the Direct Marketing Creative Guild Michael Slosberg observed, such data-driven research was

QUBE systems promised viewers a chance to talk back to television sets.
On this 1978 *Columbus Alive* program, viewers voted on potential
Republican nominees during a conversation with Watergate figure
John Dean, former counsel to Richard M. Nixon.
Photo Credit: Barco Library, The Cable Center.

effective because it was efficient. "You know exactly what every
media dollar spent has returned to you in sales," he explained.[38]

In the end, QUBE didn't survive. After American Express and
Warner merged in 1979, the consolidated corporation saw the main-
tenance costs as too high, and so it began canceling and selling off
QUBE programs.[39] Nevertheless, such an approach to collecting
data about viewers did persist, and over the next few years, cable
executives and lobbyists shared this information with political campaigns, urging them to think about constituents as not just different
demographics based on age, income, race, gender, and employment,
but based on television viewing habits.

Soon, identifying the purchasing and viewing habits of Cable
America increasingly became a political priority as lobbyists pointed

to the marketing data as evidence of how narrowcasting and micro-targeting could also make political campaigns more effective. Cable market researchers showed members of Congress convincing graphs about how cable viewers were more committed to the communities they found on the dial and more likely to be politically active. And then, they taught them the tried-and-true tactics of how to reach cable subscribers by "melt[ing] the minds" of television viewers with a more "intrusive media."[40] Transforming the business strategy of cable television—targeting specific demographics using market research and niche programming—into a political strategy created a society in which data and consumer demands reigned supreme.

———

If HBO propelled cable in the popular imagination and helped to spur subscriptions, C-SPAN transformed the idea of public access television from a fledgling local experiment into a national network with significant political clout. Public access channels had struggled to deliver programming that attracted an audience. Over ninety-four hundred communities across the country developed their public access operations as part of an effort by cable companies to fulfill earlier FCC requirements and sell themselves during the franchise process.[41] In some places, creativity did emerge. Community colleges and Ivy League universities alike used local cable systems to provide educational fare, while city councilors had televised meetings and high school students developed their own shows.[42] Senior citizens in Castro Valley, California, launched the "first in the nation television show, by and for senior citizens," which used cable television to connect adult learning programs and hospital initiatives with performers in their eighties and nineties.[43]

But, as TCI's John Malone observed, people wanted to watch sports and entertainment on cable, not city government debates, educational programs, or amateur productions. "The public access aspects are at best uncertain, generally overly ballyhooed and under-utilized," the executive explained in an interview.[44] And yet, the idea of public service continued to be an important sales tool for the industry as it worked to show that private companies could make money and serve democracy simultaneously.

C-SPAN was different because it had financial support for programming from cable companies and the prestige of covering national, rather than local, politics. In fact, the latter was central to securing the former. C-SPAN's first investor, Robert Rosencrans, explained why he decided to support Lamb's idea. "I was tired of knocking on congressmen's doors to explain what cable television was. . . . So if nothing else, I thought it would put cable on the map in Washington."[45] However, he also believed that cable had a responsibility, if it wanted to expand, to generate its own programming beyond sports and entertainment and highlight how "cable is the only medium which has the capacity to bring . . . such a highly regarded programming service to highly specialized groups, educational institutions and the general public."[46]

Funded by the cable industry and run as a nonprofit, C-SPAN officially launched in 1979 with a board of fifteen people that oversaw its activities, all of whom committed $25,000 or less to the venture. TelePrompTer executive and C-SPAN board member William Bresnan called C-SPAN a "delightful combination of sound business practice and a public service with broad social impact" that will ultimately "enhance our public image with cable communities, our subscribers, and the media."[47] Organizations advocating for political reform—Common Cause, Public Citizen, the League of Women Voters—and even both the Democratic and Republican National Committees welcomed the new cable network as one that would bring much needed transparency to the political process, especially after a decade marred by scandals and politicians caught in lies.[48]

The rules governing the television experiment went beyond the crucial agreement that the House would control the channel's cameras. They also dictated that the coverage would be free of advertisements, and C-SPAN video could not be used in political campaigns by incumbents or challengers.[49] The cable network encouraged operators to cooperate with local broadcasters who wanted to use up to three minutes of C-SPAN footage excerpts, but also emphasized that if they did so, they needed to credit the local cable TV system for this feed.

All of this would combine to demonstrate the public service of cable television and provide a novel opportunity for an unfiltered and unedited view of the federal government. As Brian Lamb emphasized, "it makes no difference whether the average viewer spends fifteen minutes a day or fifteen minutes a year watching C-SPAN. What is important is that it will decentralize the information structure in this country. C-SPAN will not rely on a highly paid network commentator to deliver his interpretation of events in the House. C-SPAN will provide the most balanced presentation of views anywhere. He [the viewer] will witness more debates on important issues facing this country than ever before."[50]

C-SPAN's funding depended on demonstrating its value to the cable industry, and as president of the network, Lamb took this responsibility seriously from the beginning. The C-SPAN launch kit reminded local operators of the channel's significance and of the need to carry it. "We believe that C-SPAN is one of the most important industry activities ever undertaken—an important plus in cable TV's legislative posture," the introductory memorandum made clear.[51] "Therefore it is important that we strive for as much local public relations mileage as possible." The launch kit emphasized that C-SPAN could help systems undergoing franchise negotiations or even help to justify a rate increase.

Just as citizens dreamed of being Walter Cronkite on their local access channels, House members also saw the very presence of the camera as a way to reimagine themselves as the stars of a television show.[52] In fact, even before the network launched, House members strategized on ways to leverage such television coverage for maximum political gain. Rep. Charles Rose (D-NC), who helped lead negotiations to bring television into the House chambers, immediately used his computerized mailing list to notify people in his district when he would be debating certain issues so they could tune in. "It doesn't take much imagination for me to notify all the cable subscribers in Fayetteville, North Carolina to watch the debate on abortion that is going to take place on Wednesday and call in to my office on the recording telephone or some other device and quickly get a response," Rose explained.[53]

His colleagues soon followed suit, and the summer of 1979 saw a surge in "special orders," short statements that members made at the end of the day to a usually empty chamber to address a pressing policy concern or to simply congratulate constituents on a golden wedding anniversary.[54] Speaker O'Neill grumbled about the uptick in what he called "grandstanding."[55] In fact, he and Rose attempted to convey to their colleagues that late evening "special orders are seldom carried out to the public" since C-SPAN initially shared transponder space with the Madison Square Garden Network, and so operators switched to covering sporting events in the evening. And yet, representatives across the political spectrum continued to take to the floor to make such speeches, notifying their constituents in advance in the hopes that they would tune in.[56] By August, less than five months after C-SPAN launched, the number of special orders speeches had increased by 25 percent.[57]

After only four months, Washington, D.C., newspapers began talking about C-SPAN's "cult following" and how it had become the "most popular daytime television talk show."[58] According to the *Washington Post*, many people "watch sporadically while doing this and that, and become quite familiar with its story lines and leading characters."[59] Representatives understood this, and just months after the channel launched, they celebrated it as a way to "boost their political stock" at home.[60]

C-SPAN also made a commitment to civic education with other types of partnerships. In December, it launched a collaboration with the Close-Up Foundation to televise election year programming that would put high school students into conversation with elected officials. The show would be a "real, live participatory democracy," explained Lamb, and it was just the beginning of the 24/7 "public-event tv" he envisioned by "letting the cameras loose throughout Washington's public-affairs happenings."[61] His experience on Capitol Hill paid off, as he knew that "every day, there are hearings, speeches, seminars and conventions in this city, involving the top government officials . . . that never see the light of day." In the process, C-SPAN programs also garnered the attention of those people who set the news agenda, and that mattered for elevating the prestige of the entire industry.

But could the public thirst for more public affairs also be a for-profit business venture? Ted Turner bet his entire savings on the idea that it could. An eccentric millionaire sailor, Turner hated the commercial television networks, which he frequently called out for being biased, elitist, and monopolistic. Initially, he dismissed news in favor of entertainment on his Atlanta "SuperStation" that used satellite to beam its programs across the country.[62] While at a cable television convention, however, he discussed with Reese Schonfeld, who ran a service providing news to independent broadcasters, the idea of a twenty-four-hour news station as a business entity that would make money both through advertisements and subscriptions. By naming it Cable News Network (CNN), Turner went all in on the cable industry and later emphasized how news programming that also promoted the cable industry helped him get carriage from cable operators and allowed him to make money on the expensive operation (something he finally did by 1985).[63]

The official launch had all the pomp, spectacle, and confidence of Turner himself. Indeed, Turner worked obsessively to turn June 1, 1980, into what a *New York Times* television critic called a "scintillating media fanfare that was unprecedented in cable television's history."[64] CNN officially began with a live press conference that allowed the flamboyant Turner to speak directly to one group in particular: local cable operators—on whose carriage decisions his success depended.[65]

On that hot summer day, three flags flew in the gentle Georgia breeze, symbolizing the promise of CNN. The state flag honored the location of the news organization that notably eschewed the network broadcast headquarters of New York City. The southern state also had the right-to-work laws that allowed Turner to avoid the union contracts that drove up the cost of labor.[66] The American flag symbolized Turner's promise to "serve [the country] with our cable news network." The United Nations flag embodied an even

Ted Turner at the podium at the launch of Cable News Network (CNN),
June 1, 1980.
Photo Credit: Barco Library, The Cable Center.

more ambitious hope. "Cable News Network with its international
coverage and greater depth coverage will bring both in the country
and in the world a better understanding of how people from different nations live and work together," pledged Turner.[67] After vow-
ing to make his network a force for "kindness and friendship and
peace," Turner stepped down from the podium and then placed his
hand over his heart as the national anthem played. On the television
screen, the iconic image of the stars and stripes on the American flag
soon faded as the camera focused on the large satellite dishes in the
back of the brick mansion—a former country club—that served as
CNN's headquarters. Turner yelled, "Awwright!"[68]

Just as it had gotten behind C-SPAN, the NCTA celebrated Ted
Turner's experiment for moving "cable off the back pages and into
the headlines" and encouraged operators to carry the channel. "If
cable systems throughout the country do not wholeheartedly support CNN, the cable industry's promise of performance may become
a promise lacking in performance," the lobbying organization told
members.[69] Tom Wheeler equated the significance of CNN's debut

to that of HBO's less than five years earlier. While HBO provided entertainment for television-hungry viewers, he noted that CNN provided "credibility with our legislators and regulators."[70] And it didn't take long for the NCTA to try to leverage the launch of C-SPAN and CNN. Pointing to both as proof that cable could be a force for enriching American democracy, the lobbying organization pushed both parties to include cable deregulation as part of their party platforms in 1980.[71]

Cablevision emphasized how C-SPAN and CNN finally allowed cable to "lay claim to the comprehensive kind of public service programming that until now had been the special purview of broadcast television."[72] And this, it noted, "reflected a cable industry that had finally come of age as a major communications medium in America." Brian Lamb had pitched the idea that public affairs programming would be a path to political power, and people across the industry bought into this idea, even as total subscriber numbers for *all* of basic cable, while growing, had just broken 17 million.[73] By comparison, the evening nightly news programs on the three networks regularly attracted an audience of over 52 million.[74]

As a for-profit news channel, CNN embraced the money-making potential of the news. Its business blended two types of revenue streams together. Turner charged cable operators fifteen cents per subscriber to carry CNN (if they also carried WTBS—twenty cents if not), and similar to the broadcasting networks, he also made money on advertising.[75] So too did local operators, and CNN held seminars for them on how to sell advertisements and even led efforts to revamp research on audience size and preferences.[76] Ratings gauged on broadcast programming by A.C. Nielsen—which relied on diaries families filled out each week about what they watched—didn't work, argued Robert Sieber, who led CNN's advertising campaign. "With 35 or more channels for a viewer to keep track of, the diary requires a lot more work, and may prove to be too demanding," Sieber explained.[77] Committed to integrating both national and local advertising into its channel (so both CNN and local operators could make money off of it), CNN pushed for an industry-wide collaboration on research about its subscribers.

Others agreed. Irving Kahn, always attuned to the importance of marketing, was also banging the drum for market research done by industry insiders, not "outsider observers."[78] In 1980, industry executives and operators raised $400,000 to launch a new Cabletelevision Advertising Bureau, which would collect research on cable consumers that it could then use to convince Madison Avenue that they could find "happiness on a coaxial cable."[79] To make up for having smaller audiences than network television, cable operators emphasized not just their cheap rates, but also that cable audiences were the "right" kind of viewers—a message that resonated with firms trying to find ways to target consumers more directly based not just on race and gender but also age, income, educational level, and marital status.[80]

————

By the end of the decade, the cable dial was filled with programs pledging to fill specific niches, made possible by satellite technology, innovative business approaches, and an awareness of the political need to demonstrate cable television's public service capability.

On April 1, 1979, Nickelodeon launched with programming exclusively for children. The demand for this channel came from cable operators: they needed proof of quality programming for children to offer when negotiating franchise agreements with local city councils.[81] Nickelodeon offered thirteen hours a day of children's programming with programs designed specifically for different youth demographics. On this network, shows like *Pinwheel* (which had originated on QUBE) aimed to educate preschoolers with puppets, while *Bananaz* generated a "talk disco series" for teenagers.[82] Advertisements encouraging operators to carry the station emphasized the public relations benefits. With the motto "It Makes You Look Good," Nickelodeon marketing emphasized that "educators, civic leaders, parents—they're all looking for an alternative to commercial 'kids' TV. The cable operator who can offer them that alternative will be their hero."[83]

That same year, Bill Rasmussen and his son Scott came up with the idea for the sports channel that would transform the athletic world over the next few decades.[84] The father-son team wanted to televise University of Connecticut sports in the Northeast. The cheapest option was via an RCA satellite, which charged either $1,250 for five hours in the evening or $35,000 a month for around-the-clock access. With a five-year lease for transmitting programming twenty-four hours a day, Entertainment and Sports Programming Network (ESPN) was born. While not the first sports cable network—Madison Square Garden Sports Network had launched on satellite in 1977—ESPN promoted its 24/7 "total sports network" programming as breaking new ground. When it secured an agreement to air NCAA men's and women's basketball, it lured in Anheuser-Busch as a sponsor, gaining the funding necessary to market the network and develop the programming to live up to its motto.[85]

A 1979 survey of attitudes toward cable television revealed just how far the industry had come. Commissioned by the NCTA, it showed that arguments against cable television—that it would force all television to become pay television; that it would hurt local broadcasters or the movie industry; and that it would do nothing more than replicate network fare but at a cost—no longer resonated with the public. While voters had flocked to the polls in 1964 to outlaw subscription television, by the end of the 1970s they surrounded cable trucks demanding services. In its analysis of the public perception of cable, Peter D. Hart Research Associates made clear "the most universal finding" in its survey: "television's appeal is no longer universal; for the medium to succeed in the eighties, it must become more varied and appeal to more diversified tastes within our society."[86]

That's exactly what the expansion of cable television did, and in the process, it brought about new ways of thinking about how television—and the marketplace—could function in American civic life. Deploying a range of direct marketing tools, cable companies promised citizens a personalized entertainment experience and membership into new communities based on shared interests. Simultaneously, they developed innovative public affairs programming—from C-SPAN to CNN—which showed elected officials how cable could strengthen democratic institutions and, more significantly, advance their own political agendas. It would take time to realize how this segmented marketplace distracted and divided Americans. At the moment, viewers bought into these promises, and so too did politicians. Indeed, the importance of a growing and more accessible television landscape certainly had the support of a media-savvy president committed to deregulation: Jimmy Carter.

7

Visions '79

Tom Wheeler became president of the NCTA in 1979 when he was only thirty-three. The Ohio State University graduate—known for starting every day with a three-mile run, a cheeseburger, and lots of iced tea—was the youngest person to assume the position.[1] Having worked directly with his predecessor Robert Schmidt since 1976, Wheeler had the experience and confidence to take the lobbying reins for the industry. Like Schmidt, Wheeler believed in the importance of government relations to advance the prospects of cable. The key, he argued, was to capitalize on the fact that "public policy makers and the public in general have a pent-up frustration with the existing television systems. They want to give some other ideas an opportunity to thrive. If we don't live up to the opportunity that others have given us, then it will be taken away from us."

Wheeler recognized that the cable industry had achieved some remarkable things over the previous few years, all of which were on display at the National Cable Television Association's annual convention in Las Vegas that summer.[2] With the theme "Visions '79," the event promised to offer attendees "FORESIGHT into the bright future of cable television . . . INSIGHT into new government policies from the men and women who are making them . . . IMAGINATION into making your system the medium of tomorrow . . . and

VISIONS of new services and technologies to help you plan in the rapidly changing world of television."[3] It delivered.

Attracting over six thousand participants, the May meeting featured two presidents, one Republican and one Democrat. The convention opened with rousing remarks from former President Gerald Ford. As a private citizen, Ford's tune about cable had changed.[4] His appearance at the NCTA convention reflected his embrace of the corporate world and the security and money it offered in his post-presidency.[5] While he had bowed to broadcaster opposition on cable issues as president, as a private citizen with new media investments (he had a contract with NBC, a book advance from Harper & Row, and an ownership stake in two Colorado radio stations), he spoke with confidence of the "big chips" that cable television had on the line, and he encouraged the industry to take bold action.[6]

Ford's keynote address was soon overshadowed by the very man who had ousted him from office. *A Conversation with Jimmy Carter* used a two-way satellite teleconference to beam the sitting president in from the White House to discuss the pressing political issues of the day—the Middle East, oil, and inflation—with convention participants and over five million cable subscribers across the country. *TVC* called the high-tech event "a mind-blower."[7] In another session, Speaker Tip O'Neill appeared via C-SPAN to introduce the FCC chairman, Charles Ferris, and lauded his work in expanding the "channels of communication available to the American people."[8] The convention put on display the various ways in which the industry's programming innovations had begun to generate political capital and new opportunities for political communication.

Cablevision called the convention "the most political (in the most positive sense) in history."[9] NCTA leaders celebrated how "politics is now a major part of our business," just as figures like Leonard Reinsch and Bill Daniels had long touted.[10] Cable clearly provided more than sports and entertainment; it had become a political tool embraced by people across the political spectrum. And policy shifts followed. Even as the OTP lost the political spotlight and authority Nixon had once shone on it—and even though Ronald Reagan and his FCC chairman Mark Fowler generally receive credit for deregulating television and radio—it was during the Carter administration that may of the embattled agency's economic ideas finally gained traction.

———

For Tom Dowden, Jimmy Carter's appearance at the NCTA convention was the culmination of years of political organizing. Born and raised in Tennessee, Dowden built his career in Atlanta under the mentorship of Leonard Reinsch. Having studied journalism and political science at the University of Georgia, he was deeply interested in the relationship between politics and media and wrote his thesis on the FCC's equal time clause. Dowden was working in broadcasting when Reinsch offered him a job in Cox Broadcasting's cable operations. Impressed by Reinsch's political connections and intrigued by his vision for cable television, Dowden accepted the offer, even though it meant a $5,000 salary cut.[11]

The 1966 FCC freeze on cable's growth made a mark on Dowden, and it also brought him to Washington, D.C. In an effort to encourage legislation overturning the rule, he worked "on loan" with the NCTA as Cox Cable paid his salary while he promoted the industry's political interests on Capitol Hill. While there were no significant policy changes during his time in Washington, Dowden claimed that even pushing for legislative hearings that had "favorable testimony for cable" made an impact as such efforts redirected conversations from concerns about cable's parasitic operations to a celebration of its achievements.[12]

In 1976, Dowden launched his own cable company, Dowden Communications. He soon set his eyes on a new project: Jimmy Carter's presidential campaign.[13] He told fellow cable operators that Carter's campaign organizers were "very much interested in the potential of cable" and wanted to work with cable operators to disseminate a taped program of the candidate.[14] Notably, Dowden explained, it would include Governor Carter "recognizing CATV for its contribution and expressing his thanks for being able to use cable to reach people who are not in primary television coverage areas." Thanks to Dowden's efforts as the Carter campaign's "CATV

Coordinator," the film was shown multiple times to over three million households, most of whom "would not normally be exposed to Jimmy Carter's campaign messages," he explained proudly.[15]

While only a blip on Carter's radar that year, Dowden's cablecasting effort forged a relationship between the cable television industry and the candidate.[16] Dowden then organized the "Electronic Town Hall" three years later at the 1979 cable convention to cash in on this work, urging the president to accept his invitation as "a way to acknowledge the contribution made by the CATV industry in 1976." Dowden explained that Carter's "support (or at least recognition)" of the growing industry—with tentacles all over America—would be "good politics for 1980."[17]

Carter did join the convention—but he ignored the talking points Dowden had prepared in a four-page letter outlining cable television's history, its growth, and its appeal to the millions of Americans who "are bored with Network TV and are willing to pay several dollars a month to get more choice and diversity of programming offered by cable."[18] Instead, Carter discussed the SALT Treaty, inflation, and the energy crisis. Even so, the technical aspects of the satellite operation intrigued the president, who "asked a lot of questions," according to observers.[19]

The event showed that while cable never became a priority or a passion for Carter, he did understand the importance of new media technology. Indeed, his mastery of media was central to his political success in 1976. He built relationships with local newspapers and focused attention on overlooked political events, like the Iowa caucuses, to generate a public narrative of momentum—winning delegates and securing much needed financial support in the process.[20] Such innovations on the campaign trail raised questions for cable insiders. Would Carter's appreciation for media translate into an interest in reforming telecommunications policy, as it had with Richard Nixon? Or would he ultimately cave to the broadcasting interests, as Gerald Ford had?

At first, nobody knew—in part, as Brian Lamb observed, because Carter frequently tried to "duck the issue."[21] In an interview with *TV Guide*, the Democratic candidate emphasized that he had not "studied the question" of cable television in particular, but broadly believed that "adequate competition should be encouraged."[22] On the California primary trail, he talked about how "new applications of telecommunications can do much more to improve our quality of life," and he articulated the importance of "greater variety and quality of educational and community-oriented programming through broadcast and cable television." Yet when his campaign prepared a policy briefing on the topic of telecommunications policy that fall, it focused solely on the telephone industry and the legal and legislative debate over the Bell system—with no mention of cable.

Still, Carter's approach to the AT&T monopoly excited cable operators and worried network executives.[23] Over the previous decade, the FCC, Congress, and even Tom Whitehead at the OTP began questioning the laws that had allowed the powerful company to monopolize the telephone business.[24] As the FCC attempted to encourage the growth of new industries and technologies, from computers to fax machines that threatened AT&T's dominance, the company retaliated to destroy potential competitors and undermine the commission's rulings. Such campaigns ultimately backfired as they provided evidence that lawyers at the Department of Justice used to build a case that Ma Bell had abused its monopoly.

The Carter-Mondale campaign supported this decision, calling the corporate monopoly "wasteful and expensive."[25] Policy briefs emphasized the need to pull back federal regulations to spur competition. And while Carter admitted that he wasn't familiar with the nuances of communications policy, he did support the break-up of AT&T because he had personally experienced the "telecommunications needs and problems" as a "businessman and as a candidate running a large campaign."[26] Such a statement was revealing and consequential for a cable industry eager to get on Carter's radar. It showed how a politician's experience with new technologies shaped regulatory attitudes about it. That was true of television too.

Barry Jagoda, Carter's television adviser, took the lead on shaping regulatory policies for the medium that he believed was too monopolistic and powerful. Jagoda, too, knew this from experience. A graduate of Columbia Journalism School, he had worked at both

NBC and CBS, where he learned what he later called the need for "alternatives for news and public affairs programming."[27] In 1975, he even began to make plans to launch a fourth network, American Television Alternative, but soon abandoned these efforts to help Carter capture headlines on the primary trail.

After Carter's election, Jagoda expressed interest in shaping media policy.[28] The new president initially agreed, instructing his TV man to help oversee the future of the OTP.[29] The agency had remained director-less since Tom Whitehead's departure, and the Carter team struggled with how to handle what it saw as the "unnecessary" controversy the office had provoked during the Nixon years. The problem was clear to the incoming administration: "Efforts to articulate new or alternative policy approaches have inevitably become highly controversial as the regulated industries perceived their interests being infringed on as the White House turned the policy studies toward its own political advantages."[30]

And so, Jagoda's early presence in the OTP aroused considerable controversy because it potentially placed a media strategist as a policy adviser on the industry.[31] It once again raised the question that had created so much tension during both Nixon's and Ford's time in office: Was communication policy driven by informed expertise or by efforts to placate or manipulate players in the media industry?[32] To evade such criticisms, Jagoda shifted his focus to working with the National Endowment for the Humanities, bolstering public radio and television and shaping news coverage of the Oval Office all while the directionless OTP continued to flounder.[33] Nevertheless, as President Carter embarked on fulfilling his campaign promise to reorganize the executive branch, debate about the proper place of communications policy in the executive branch intensified once again.[34]

The OTP saga exposed a fundamental truth: the seductive allure of airtime almost unavoidably affected media policy. Tom Whitehead emphasized this reality in a 1977 interview with *Cablevision*. Yes, Nixon attempted to use the power of his office and policies to shape media coverage of himself, Whitehead admitted. But "that instinct, I suspect, is natural in any politician," he explained, pointing out that congresspeople did the same to elevate their television coverage. "The alliance between politicians and their local television stations for mutual benefits is well known. And in those matters, Mr. Nixon was no better and no worse than any other office holder," the former OTP director concluded.[35] In the interview, Whitehead called out what politicians didn't want to admit: that, in practice, their own political calculations shaped their approach to regulating a communications industry that was theoretically supposed to serve the public interest.[36]

In 1978, Carter skirted the controversy by reassigning OTP's functions to a newly created National Telecommunications and Information Administration (NTIA)—housed in the Department of Commerce rather than directly in the White House. This new home in a less-than-glamorous cabinet department removed communications policy from the limelight, sending it to what one political scientist described as "an obscure corner of one of the least prestigious executive organizations in Washington."[37] While the newly established NTIA undoubtedly sacrificed influence by being so distant from the corridors of power at 1600 Pennsylvania Avenue, it actually *gained* credibility, as Congress began to see its policy recommendations as products of expertise and research, not politics.[38]

When President Carter appointed Charles Ferris to the FCC that same year, he made good on another campaign promise to encourage competition and choice, showing how the deregulation of television, which Nixon had previously made controversial, had become a bipartisan issue by the late 1970s.[39] Ferris quickly became the person to actually implement Carter's vision for change in communications policy by cutting bureaucratic red tape, promoting competition, and eliminating industry capture of the agencies designed to regulate them.[40]

————

Charlie Ferris grew up in a working-class Irish neighborhood on the south side of Boston. After serving in the Navy, he used benefits from the G.I. Bill to attend law school and dreamed of being the next Atticus Finch.[41] He ended up working in the Justice Department during the Kennedy administration, then for Senate majority leader Mike Mansfield and, in 1977, for Speaker Tip O'Neill. According to the notes Carter's Domestic Policy staff compiled on him, Ferris was "one of the shrewdest, most capable political staff persons to work on Capitol Hill during the last 10 years," and senators across party and region relied on his ability "to detect 'the mood' of the Senate floor" and know the optimal time to introduce certain amendments during the legislative debate.[42]

Ferris had also come to understand how much power television had to transform America. During the civil rights debates in the 1960s, southern Democrats once again used the filibuster to thwart the 1964 Civil Rights Act. Ferris watched as CBS correspondent Roger Mudd stood on the steps of Capitol Hill daily with reports and a running clock counting the hours of debate over the issue.[43] The impact of this coverage stuck with him years later. "The whole country followed these reports of the debate as if the proceedings were televised," Ferris recalled in an oral history. "It took away the possibilities of backroom compromise. Transparency had come to Capitol Hill because of coverage by the media."[44]

Ferris's reputation garnered him goodwill and support in the Senate for an administrative position in the Carter White House, and he was named FCC chairman.[45] Sol Taishoff, the publisher of *Broadcasting* and an industry leader who had long advised presidents about FCC appointments, took the news poorly. Carter had not consulted him on the selection, and he felt Ferris did not have the qualifications or knowledge of the broadcast industry needed to run such an important agency. Ferris recalled that he responded by emphasizing his experience as a consumer, just as Carter had on the campaign trail. "I've been using a telephone for 40 years, listening to a radio for about the same amount of time, and I've been watching television for about 30 years, so I'm going to bring to it the perspective of a user rather than someone who has a vested economic interest in one of the entities."[46]

As Ferris came to grips with basic questions about the regulatory issues his agency would be responsible for crafting, he turned to economists, rather than lawyers, for the answers. Historically, legal professionals had staffed and led regulatory agencies like the FCC (for example, Frederick Ford, Newton Minow, and Sol Schildhause all had legal backgrounds). Lawyers brought with them a conviction that the right administrative laws would serve the public interest (and of course, elevating the status of their profession in the process).[47] But economists increasingly influenced regulatory decisions in the 1970s, and they focused overwhelmingly on market performance as a measure of policy success.[48] Ferris saw the television marketplace as inefficient. The economic research made it clear to him that restrictive cable television rules "were just imposed by broadcasters who wanted to protect their markets," he later explained.[49]

And so, in the fall of 1977, Ferris used his perch at the head of the FCC to push the other commissioners to take swift action. In September, the FCC modified franchising standards to allow for revenue from pay cable and cap local franchising fees, even hinting that it would consider eliminating franchise fees entirely. In December it eased rules for satellite transmission to allow operators to add more programs without FCC authorization for each one. In line with Ferris's commitment to letting economic analysis, not a legal perspective, guide the FCC's operations, the agency launched a study into network television dominance, which ultimately concluded that the commission needed to promote alternatives to the commercial broadcasting model, not protect it from competition.[50]

Under Ferris's leadership, the FCC was finally moving forward on issues that had stalled in Congress and the White House for years because of political pressure from broadcasters. And then, on July 22, 1980, the commission released a report that dramatically altered the terrain in which cable television operated. It pulled back restrictions on what signals cable operators could import, opening the door for them to air any program they could access. With programs now available via satellites and independent superstations—like Ted Turner's WTBS—cable operators could offer subscribers an unprecedented selection. The programming rules that had hampered the cable business for two decades were gone, and cable companies started looking to expand in urban markets to see if they could capitalize on the economic possibilities such regulatory changes unleashed.[51]

Ferris firmly maintained that he made these decisions without pressure from President Carter. Having come from working on Capitol Hill, he had a firm understanding that regulatory agencies like the FCC were "a creature of the Congress and that is to whom we report."[52] And so, he made it clear from the beginning of his time as chairman that "we are not part of the executive branch" and that "we had an independent obligation to make decisions in an intellectually honest way." He emphasized that if Carter had wanted to provide input on a particular issue, then the NTIA could submit, through a formal process, ideas for the FCC to consider. With telecommunications low on Carter's radar, the president never got into a political fight over cable legislation, with his advisers warily recalling what had happened with Ford and Paul MacAvoy. One memo highlighted the "substantial political costs" that came with such a legislative battle, concluding that it might be good policy but it raised controversial political questions for the administration. And at the time, the cable industry itself had yet to gain political clout to push the issue.[53]

But one cable operator captured the interest of Jimmy Carter, in part because he was the exception in a white-dominated industry.

———

The cover of the October 9, 1978, *Cablevision* magazine exuded energy and excitement around an issue that had long been swept under the rug in the industry: racial diversity. It featured a picture of Carter's characteristic broad grin as he shook hands with William Johnson, a Black cable operator in Columbus, Ohio, who had clawed his way into the industry. Johnson's smile matched the glow of Carter's as he presented the president with a piece of his cable system framed on a plaque in the shape of the Buckeye state.[54]

Since the campaign, Carter had emphasized the importance of minority business ownership, and in conversations about broadcasting regulatory reform, this regularly surfaced.[55] In January 1978, the administration launched a concerted effort to use Small Business Administration loans to address the stark imbalance in radio and

The October 9, 1978, cover of *Cablevision*, which featured
Jimmy Carter meeting with William Johnson in an effort by
both men to draw attention to the importance of minority
media ownership.
Photo Credit: *Multichannel News*/Barco Library, The Cable
Center.

television station ownership: minorities only owned sixty-five stations total across the country, a mere 1 percent.[56]

A politically savvy Ohioan, Johnson saw an opportunity to connect the launch of his new business, KBLE, with Carter's civil
rights agenda. He pitched the administration on the idea that, as
the first Black-owned cable company to serve a major city, KBLE
could provide evidence that Carter's "campaign commitments to

encouraging and fostering minority economic development . . .
in inner cities has not been forgotten."[57] Johnson was angling for
a telegraph from the president to read at the company's dedication
ceremony. But he got something much better: Carter decided to
make an in-person appearance at the "turn on" festivities in Columbus to highlight how much he valued the issue of minority media
ownership.[58]

Johnson used the attention surrounding the event to draw attention to two things: the importance of Black television consumers and
his commitment to transforming KBLE into a "national outlet for
black programming" (and indeed he had already made inroads on
the latter issue with his negotiations with HBO).[59] The local Black
newspaper, *Call and Post*, understood the stakes of Johnson's venture and his promise to introduce new types of channels on his cable
system.[60] With a Black-owned business pledging to deliver Black
programming in a major market, "the eyes of the entire communications industry are watching closely to see if the venture succeeds
or fails." The *Call and Post* emphasized the responsibility the community had to make it a success: "We must invest in it, subscribe
to it, work for it and utilize its services to the max. If we fail to do
so, KBLE will not succeed. If KBLE does not succeed, we will all
be the losers."

KBLE seemingly emerged as proof that Carter's economic program and diversity initiatives worked.[61] But in fact, the history
behind Johnson's efforts to secure the franchise, and the consequences of Carter's deregulation initiatives told a different story,
one that made clear the limits of deploying policies that used market
metrics to solve structural issues of inequality. Indeed, the contradictions on display under the Carter administration's approach to
minority media ownership would also undermine his Democratic
successors' efforts to use market incentives to combat racism in
housing, education, healthcare, employment, and policing.[62]

Cable television came to Ohio in 1950. The first system served the
village of Glenmont (population 242), allowing its residents to access
the previously out-of-range broadcast signals. By the late 1960s, as
cable television emerged as an alternative to broadcast television

rather than merely an extension of it, Columbus city officials took the lead in delivering the benefits of a "wired city" to residents. On July 14, 1969, the city council granted the first franchise to Canterbury Cablevision Corporation, which Warner Cable eventually took over. Over the next few years, the city council divided Columbus into four sections and selected different companies to service each in the hopes that competition would enhance consumer experiences.[63]

Across the country Black media activists were working diligently to secure more control over television production and ownership and used grassroots pressure to win city mandates for minority-controlled franchises.[64] That included Columbus, where the city council required that one of its four areas of service must have a "minority controlled concern."[65] The minority-owned Advance Cable—which pledged to serve Black consumers in the urban area of Columbus—won the franchise, but it struggled to generate funding. Building a cable company required extensive up-front capital, and white-owned banks refused to loan the start-up company money. Loan managers questioned the profit projections that Advance provided, and they also expressed doubt that Black communities could and would subscribe to cable television.

In 1974, Advance hired a lawyer to help with the process: William Johnson. A graduate of Ohio State University, Johnson earned his JD from Capital University Law School and soon started his own practice. Even as a successful lawyer with a reputation for civic activism and strong connections in city government, Johnson couldn't help Advance clear the racial barriers to gain the capital needed. Frustrated by the process, he decided to stake his own money and reputation on making the dream of a minority-owned cable television operation a reality.[66]

Johnson formed a new company, KBLE, in 1977. He used his contacts in the mayor's office and the city council to secure a new franchise agreement. He spoke with the other cable companies, notably Warner Cable, about the technical design of the system so he too could offer interactive features to his customers. He quickly got a certificate of compliance from the FCC and began to design the system with some of QUBE's engineers. Notably, Johnson didn't apply for guaranteed government loans for minority businesses to pay for the construction costs. Instead, he opted for a public stock option. "This is important," he told *Cablevision*, "in that it provided an opportunity for our cable subscribers to become owners of KBLE."[67]

To get the final round of financing, however, he needed a loan from a commercial bank, where he confronted the same obstacles that had impeded so many Black entrepreneurs before him in dealing with the white-controlled financial industry.[68] As a Black man asking for a million-dollar loan, he was told flat out by one financier that "no banker in town would touch this loan." One bank said it would only consider his application if Johnson put 25 percent down and the SBA secured 90 percent of the loan—conditions Johnson called "lunacy." He finally found a bank that "was willing to look at the KBLE loan on its merits rather than as a minority loan" and ultimately made the "largest ever" loan by "an Ohio bank to a black group with no federal government involvement."[69]

This arduous process wasn't helped by the FCC's deregulation of cable television under Carter's watch. Even as the president promised to encourage Black media ownership, a report compiled by the Department of Justice highlighted how Carter's economic policies might do just the opposite. On October 2, 1980, Louis Martin, Carter's special assistant and liaison to the Black community, received a report that outlined cable television's capacity to address two crucial demands from Black Americans: the need for jobs and the ability of the Black community to control its own media images, something civil rights activists had long understood to be central to social justice.[70]

The report underscored a key contradiction embedded within Carter's administration, notably how cable's deregulatory trend had emerged as one of the "biggest stumbling blocks" toward "encouraging Black participation and ownership in all aspects." While recognizing initiatives advanced by Ferris's FCC stemmed from "the desire to allow greater growth and diversity in the communications industry," the report highlighted the historical reality: "de-regulation in and of itself has never been in the best interest of black people. It often reduces governmental ability to effectively protect our rights." The report ominously and presciently warned that corporate consolidation of the cable industry would push out Black entrepreneurs looking to stake an ownership claim but lacking the hefty bank accounts or credit lines needed to win and build franchises.

And that is exactly what happened. The Carter administration and Ferris's FCC advanced an agenda that celebrated the idea of minority ownership in cable, but in reality, bolstered the economic fortunes of the bigger players in a cable industry that continued to be dominated by white men. Indeed, by the 1980s, mom-and-pop operations had faded and cable conglomerates had started to form. As one *Cablevision* article noted, the intensifying franchising competitions in urban markets unleashed a wave of mergers, ultimately changing the "corporate profile of the cable television industry" from "ownership by entrepreneurs who got their feet wet in the business to ownership by well-heeled mega corporations, essentially outsiders with diversified holdings."[71]

ATC merged with Time Inc., while Warner Cable teamed up with American Express, becoming the Warner Amex Communications firm. Newspaper chains also eagerly joined the fray. Times Mirror—which owned the *Los Angeles Times*, *Newsday*, and four other dailies—bought Communications Properties in Austin, while the *New York Times* bought Irving Kahn's cable systems in New Jersey. In 1980, Westinghouse Broadcasting Company merged with TelePrompTer. Several years later, William Johnson sold KBLE to Telemedia, a Pittsburgh-area cable conglomerate, stating that "the economics of making it work are just not there" as he needed to grow and upgrade his operations to turn a profit. Without the resources or collateral to buy competing Warner systems, he decided to take the cash from Telemedia.[72]

The era of corporate media conglomerations had arrived. Under Ronald Reagan's watch, such mergers would accelerate the concentration of media ownership into the hands of a few, but the trend firmly began under Carter, who bought into the promise of deregulation, but neglected to grapple with consequences of corporate consolidation.

———

With the 1980 election on the horizon, *Cablevision* reported that "there is some historical justice in the fact that Jimmy Carter's campaign will be among the first campaigns benefitting from the special kind of attention cable television will provide, since deregulation occurring during his administration has been a major force in making cable a significant medium in America."[73] One industry lobbyist, whom *Cablevision* identified only as "nonpartisan," agreed that Carter deserved the "highest marks" in "turning loose the forces to deregulate cable," and even wondered if credit belonged to Tom Dowden's efforts in 1976 when "Carter was gotten to" by a handful of operators who pushed the possibilities of the cable dial. Dowden certainly wanted to believe that notion, and he refused to let the Carter administration forget cable's contributions to its success.[74] But it was another Georgian who upped the political stakes for cable television during Carter's bid for reelection: Ted Turner.

As the flamboyant and audacious entrepreneur prepared to launch CNN on June 1, 1980, Carter's advisers encouraged him to accept an interview invitation for that historic day since Turner "has been very helpful to us politically and financially."[75] They highlighted how such an appearance would support a more expansive notion of the "news" at a time when the press was hammering Carter's administration with stories about a "killer rabbit" attacking the president to the devastating count each night by Walter Cronkite and Ted Koppel on the number of days Iranian revolutionaries had held Americans hostage abroad.[76]

In the memo preparing Carter for the interview, press aide Ray Jenkins reminded him of the problematic limits of network news reports that spent only twenty-two minutes on the pressing issues of the day. Recalling Walter Lippmann's assessment of the role of the press as creating "a picture of reality in which men can act," Jenkins reminded Carter that "TV network news creates an exceedingly limited picture of that reality and hence does not provide a very good basis upon which men can act."[77] Such words likely resonated with a president feeling crippled by the ineffectiveness of his messaging—something he had mastered four years earlier to propel his dark horse candidacy to the White House.

Two television journalists whom CNN had poached from the networks, Daniel Schorr (formerly of CBS) and George Watson (formerly of ABC), conducted a friendly pre-taped interview in the Oval Office.[78] Carter began the forty-five-minute conversation by emphasizing that "there has long been a need in my judgement for a network which could cover the news in much more depth than has been the case with the very brief allotted time on the major networks."[79] Calling his fellow southerner "one of the finest and most competitive men I have ever known," Carter joked that he only hoped that Turner's performance with CNN "will be much more similar to the way he's performed in the America Cup Races where he's brought home the trophy of the year than he has been with the Atlanta Braves." In a collegial conversation, Carter discussed the upcoming election, the Camp David Accords, inflation, the hostage crisis, détente, and Soviet aggression in Afghanistan. He answered questions at length and spoke uninterrupted about the "nitty gritty" of complicated issues of energy and foreign policy.

While the Carter interview was celebrated by television observers as historic, it reflected an important reality: CNN did not change journalism, cable television, or politics overnight.[80] Despite this hyped-up interview, neither the Carter nor the Reagan campaign tapped into the political cablecasting strategies that had begun to percolate in local and state elections. One cable executive expressed frustration that both sides were "still hung up on the mass audience concept" and "don't understand cable as a medium."[81] But C-SPAN and CNN now provided the very tools that cable operators, programmers, executives, and advertisers needed to make this change happen: political programming.

8

Becoming a Household Name

On March 19, 1979, Speaker Tip O'Neill recognized the "gentleman from Tennessee," and Rep. Al Gore Jr. approached the podium. Dressed in a dark suit, light blue collared shirt, and a red tie, he spoke not to the few people milling on the House floor but directly into the camera. "Television," Gore declared, "will change this institution just as it has changed the executive branch." The "solution for the lack of confidence in government," he went on, "is more open government at all levels."[1] Scrolling across the bottom of the screen were the words "Live coverage of the U.S. House of Representatives is a service of C-SPAN."

The son of a prominent senator, the younger Gore had been thinking about the relationship between television and political power since his time at Harvard University when he wrote an undergraduate thesis, "The Impact of Television on the Conduct of the Presidency, 1947–1969."[2] He concluded in his research project that television had broadened the president's "legitimacy and power," placing the chief executive at the center of party politics and legislative debates. The result? The "President's opinion on almost everything" shaped news coverage, he observed.[3]

Launching a decade later, C-SPAN did something different by shining a spotlight on Congress. It did more than provide House members like Gore an opportunity for the limelight, however. Its programming fundamentally challenged, and then changed, how Americans consumed politics. The network's signature call-in program and its election coverage, which interviewed ordinary people on the primary campaign trail, gave average citizens—farmers in Iowa, union workers in New Hampshire, housewives in Nebraska, retired executives in New Jersey, and high school students across the country—an opportunity to be heard.

In the early 1980s, cable enabled alternative approaches to the news to flourish, and in the process, offered opportunities to break glass ceilings; challenge racial, gender, and sexual stereotypes; and bring more ideological diversity to political conversations. C-SPAN and CNN led the way, but they were not the only ones that capitalized on a growing demand by television viewers for different types of information about the world around them. Opportunities for experimentation abounded on the Christian Broadcasting Network (CBN), Spanish International Network (SIN), Black Entertainment Television (BET), and even through public access experiments like the Gay Cable Network (GCN) that launched in New York City in 1982.[4] Such programs frequently blurred the line between entertainment and news as a strategy to generate the attention, and then the loyalty, of a particular demographic. In this environment, the needs and interests of the viewer were scrutinized by market researchers who increasingly saw America as more socially divided and then catered to those divisions based not just on race, gender, and income but on other "lifestyle" factors.[5]

New forms of political media also openly challenged a foundational belief upholding the broadcasting television regulatory system since its inception: that news programs put networks in the red but demonstrated a corporate commitment to the public good. In reality, the news had always made money—something network executives purposely obscured.[6] But, cable television busted this myth and then later benefited economically from changing these basic assumptions about news, public interest, and civic duty that had previously underpinned the entire television regulatory system. Indeed, cable's success, especially in covering politics in a more expansive manner,

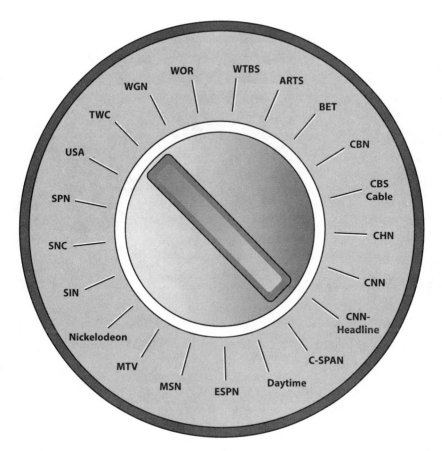

A sample of cable options from 1982.
Source: Cable TV Advertising, Paul Kagan Associates, 1983.

also became a justification for freeing networks from their civic obligations, especially amid the massive corporate consolidation of the media industry that happened under Ronald Reagan's administration.

———

The differences between C-SPAN and CNN were embodied in the contrast between the two men who launched the respective cable networks. Journalists always relayed colorful stories about Ted Turner, the Georgia entrepreneur with a capacity to both charm and

Ted Turner pictured in his office, smoking a cigar with his
wall of trophies in the background, 1986.
Photo Credit: Barco Library, The Cable Center.

offend. A front-page *New York Times* profile called Turner brash and
"utterly self-absorbed"—the kind of man who gave interviews chew-
ing tobacco and spitting its juice into a plastic cup.[7] Brian Lamb, the
modest Midwesterner, had a very different reputation, what one journalist called "the fervent enthusiasm and one-track mind of a political
science professor possessed."[8] Rather than pushing his employees to
the brink of their sanity with an explosive temper and often unreal-
istic expectations (a frequent complaint from CNN headquarters),
Lamb emphasized collaboration and motivated his loyal team with
the motto "You can accomplish anything as long as you don't mind
who takes the credit."

C-SPAN covered public affairs rather than creating the news, a
distinction Lamb emphasized in interviews. In contrast to the fast-
paced, nonstop news coverage from CNN's Atlanta headquarters,
C-SPAN took pride in televising events deemed boring. "We don't
have to be exciting every day," Lamb explained, and he said he would
willingly put "dead air" on television because it showed that the
political process could be dull.[9] C-SPAN was committed to "low
key" moderators and hosts, and Lamb did not tolerate his staffers

Brian Lamb poses for a picture for *Cablevision*, June 1982.
Photo Credit: *Multichannel News*/Barco Library, The Cable Center.

sharing their personal opinions on programs.[10] He led by example, saying that "no one cares about my views on world affairs." At a time when academics, journalists, and politicians alike increasingly saw the objectivity ideal as a myth, *Washington Post* reporter T. R. Reid conceded that "Lamb comes very close" to practicing it.[11]

And yet Turner and Lamb shared a mission: they both deeply disliked the elitism of network news operations and wanted to break the monopoly the networks had over the flow of information. The C-SPAN founder enthusiastically celebrated the launch of CNN, calling himself as "big as a booster as you could find" because he believed the country had long been deprived of the "news it could have gotten many years ago."[12] Both cable networks also had something to prove, as they faced skepticism that nonstop news and public affairs had an audience. Perhaps most significantly, they offered political consultants something to drool over: the possibility of getting their candidates on camera at any time of the day to talk for as long as they wanted. The only question was reach and whether anyone was really watching.

During the 1980 campaign, the cable industry celebrated its role as a "new force in election politics."[13] In reality, CNN and C-SPAN had limited carriage on a cable dial that reached just over nineteen million households. By contrast, 79.9 million households received broadcast signals.[14] Unsurprisingly, Reagan and Carter relied on a national broadcasting strategy. Nevertheless, C-SPAN and CNN made politics a priority, and the programming they created over the next few years would ultimately overthrow broadcasting's hold on the political process.

C-SPAN experimented by bringing a form of cinema verité to the campaign trail as its cameras followed the daily activities of Reagan and Carter. "Network television only offers about 45 seconds of coverage on the evening news," Lamb said. "Cable News Network will give more time to the political events and will occasionally go live. But C-SPAN will bring complete coverage during the day and in the evening."[15] C-SPAN didn't want to duplicate CNN or broadcast coverage, but rather worked to complement and expand on it. And people noticed. Jeff Greenfield of CBS wondered if maybe through cable television, "we'll find out what a campaign is all about."[16]

C-SPAN was proof of the effectiveness of narrowcasting—cable programmers' key programming innovation. Rather than thinking about Nielsen ratings and gross audience numbers, Lamb argued for the value of smaller niche audiences: the social science teacher who showed congressional proceedings to teach how government works or the professor who used a policy debate about foreign aid to El Salvador to explain to students the stakes of international economics. "It's not journalism, and it's not intended to be," emphasized Lamb.[17] The cable network aimed to deliver a civics education and to "introduce the public to the Washington players and show them in action," wrote a *Los Angeles Times* reporter.[18] Indeed, when commercial TV and radio stations rejected congressional requests to air specific policy debates, C-SPAN proudly covered them "in full on their regular schedule."[19] More got on the air, thanks to C-SPAN, even though congressional television would never come close to reaching audiences like it had a decade earlier during the Watergate hearings.

CNN president Reese Schonfeld had a different standard for determining success for the startup news business: credibility. Before joining CNN, Schonfeld had launched the Independent Television News Association (ITNA), which provided credible national and international news coverage to independent broadcasters eager to boost the prestige of their popular "tabloid-style" local news programs.[20] Speed and integrity were key to making money, and Schonfeld took this lesson to CNN. "Ever since the first 90 days, my goal has always been to get us quoted and recognized as an honorable and respected news organization," he explained in a *Cablevision* interview. "When the *New York Times* credits CNN on the front page of section one, it's very exciting for us. We're extremely proud."[21]

Like C-SPAN, CNN had a lean budget, and it showed. While network newsrooms had the latest technology, professionally staffed news bureaus, and budgets over $100 million a year, CNN launched its operations with a $20 million investment, which Turner came up with by selling his local broadcasting station in Charlotte, North Carolina.[22] Turner refused to pay celebrity anchors. Instead, correspondents like Bernard Shaw used long-form cable programs to develop relationships with viewers—a strategic move to generate a familiar connection that would keep people coming back.[23]

Shaw came to CNN after experience at both CBS and ABC, and the differences between the lush production sets of the network newsrooms and that of CNN stuck out to him. "It was a respectable rathole," he recalled.[24] When guests arrived, they entered a cold lobby with gusts of air sending chills through it during the winter. They didn't have a green room to prepare for their appearances and often tripped over the worn carpeting as they entered an interview room that Shaw categorized as "more a barroom than a newsroom." His former network colleagues derided his new employer as the Chicken News Network.

Yet, a slate of well-known activists, experts, and politicians from across the ideological spectrum still made time for appearances: feminist Bella Abzug, consumer advocate Ralph Nader, and conservative Arizona senator, Barry Goldwater. Eager for the media limelight to advance their own ideas and causes, commentators and politicians participated in discussions about current events at very little cost.

Political commentary quickly became a staple of how CNN covered the news, and the constant search for potential guests created openings for more obscure or fringe figures to appear on the network.[25] An evening talk show, *Prime News*, encouraged callers to dial in and ask their own questions of the guests.[26] One of the cable network's most popular shows, *Crossfire*, gave new life to a radio show by the same name which had been canceled for low ratings. Building on the liberal versus conservative debate made popular by public television shows like William Buckley's *Firing Line*, the revived program on CNN featured former Nixon staffer Pat Buchanan debating journalist Tom Braden about politics, and quickly became one of the network's most highly rated shows.[27] Controversy and conflict sold well, and conservative firebrands like Buchanan relished it.[28]

In its effort to "make the news the star," CNN emphasized its accessibility and adaptability. During the 1980 presidential campaign, while broadcast networks focused their attention on Carter and Reagan, CNN included coverage of Independent presidential candidate John Anderson. It offered live and round-the-clock reporting of events like the death of John Lennon and confirmation hearings for incoming Secretary of State Alexander Haig.[29]

It also emulated a successful strategy deployed by local news shows over the previous decade: a focus on softer news like weather and sports.[30] Journalists had railed against the infusion of show business into the news business, a critique made visible in the hit 1976 movie *Network*, in which a fictional network news anchor famously went off the rails, ranting, "I'm mad as hell, and I'm not gonna take this anymore!"[31] But local news stations across the country showed it could be profitable and CNN doubled down on this trend. It introduced segments—and then eventually entire programs like *Moneyline*, *Showbiz Today*, and *Larry King Live*—dedicated to business, sports, entertainment, and human-interest news.[32] In the process, CNN redefined the very idea of news: now, it could be whatever viewers wanted.

Network news executives expressed their dismay over Turner's bare-bones approach, but they also paid attention to the cash potential of cable. Due to FCC ownership rules revamped under the Nixon administration, networks could not own cable systems, but they could create programming.[33] In 1981, Turner even met with the head of CBS News, Bill Leonard, about possibly merging their two news operations. CNN had developed relationships with local affiliates who now had an option to integrate CNN's live coverage into their local news reports and not just rely on taped and carefully curated network news packages. A merger, Leonard thought, would help keep affiliates loyal. Turner considered the idea—he needed money to keep CNN afloat. But when Turner only entertained offering the network a minority stake, the deal fell apart.[34]

ABC took a different approach. Rather than co-opting CNN, it wanted to challenge its market dominance as the only 24/7 news channel. At the time, ABC News was flying high. In 1981, it had finally emerged as a serious competitor to CBS News in the ratings game—thanks to some huge gambles over the previous decade. In 1976, *ABC Evening News* recruited the star of NBC's *Today Show*, Barbara Walters, to bring celebrity appeal to its nightly news program. She blurred the lines between the entertainment and news divisions, which split her $1 million salary (a number so highly publicized she even referenced it during her debut appearance).[35] She worked as an anchor for the evening news, and also interviewed celebrities and other newsmakers during special features.[36] In 1977, ABC president Frederick Pierce made another risky move: hiring Roone Arledge to take over its news operations. Arledge had a successful programming track record—but in sports. (Turner would later point to Arledge's hiring as proof that the network prioritized ratings over professional journalism.[37]) Coming to a company that had long valued entertainment over news, Arledge aimed to revamp the ABC newsroom with new talent that would produce greater profitability.

Arledge immediately eyed cable as a tool for ABC to forge new frontiers, and in 1981, the network partnered with Group W Satellite

Communications, Westinghouse's new cable programming arm, to develop an all-news channel that could compete with CNN.[38] Enthusing how the new Satellite News Channel (SNC) would provide "new forms of coverage for those who feel unsatisfied by network news," Arledge highlighted the company's market research that showed a preponderance of "news junkies." He pledged to cater to their demand for even more news coverage.[39]

Furious and belligerent at the idea of a network competing with him for the cable news market, Turner pledged to do all he could to fight a channel he called a "second rate horseshit service."[40] As he prepared for battle, he reminded his cable colleagues how the networks had long underestimated all of them and knocked them down. He hoped that stirring such negative memories would make cable operators think twice about carrying the SNC. "It's pretty hard to be both for Israel and the PLO at the same time," as Turner put it.[41]

He also tried to take the wind out of SNC's sails by announcing the launch of CNN 2, a headline news program that would present blocks of short news programs similar to what SNC promised to do.[42] Then, to really stick it to ABC, he also proposed a syndication service to make CNN available to the network's local broadcasting affiliates.[43] To round out his offensive, Turner went to court, bringing an antitrust lawsuit alleging that Group W and SNC had colluded to keep CNN off Group W operating systems.

The NCTA convention that year featured Turner at his most bombastic, in a music video he'd commissioned for the event. To strumming guitars and against images of Turner tackling the elements in his sailboat, a country singer sang a catchy tune that captured Turner's version of recent history. The song, "He was cable, when cable wasn't cool," chronicled how Turner, the "good old boy," never got invited to elite Bel Air mansions "because he won't toe their line." It then narrated how the southern entrepreneur faced down the "network ivory towers" who thought "Captain Outrageous" was a fool. The video also reminded his cable colleagues how Turner took on "those jerks" NBC, CBS, and ABC because "their perspectives were bogged down in the past." At the end, Turner even appeared in a cameo to conclude "I must be doing something right," now that cable had become cool.[44]

Arrogant as the video was, the message deeply resonated with cable operators across the country who watched network executives—who had spent decades demonizing them for pirating programming—now try to enter the very business they had grown despite this opposition. To criticize SNC, Cox Cable's director of programming used the line that so many broadcasting executives once used against cable operators: "While we welcome the networks to the cable programming area, we hope that they will offer truly new and differentiated program services."[45] Marc Nathanson, the president of Falcon Communications and Valley Cable TV in California, reminded operators that "all those broadcast people who used to knock cable are jumping on the bandwagon. These are the same businessmen who used to turn red at the mere mention of cable. They lobbied in Congress and the FCC against any progressive development that benefitted cable."

Nevertheless, SNC had deep pockets and soon offered cable operators an initial fifty cents per subscriber to carry its programs, rather than charging them a fee per subscriber like CNN did.[46] Such a move went well beyond what other channels like MTV had previously done by providing a small per subscriber payout to help with marketing costs. SNC needed to secure subscribers upfront, however, to attract major advertisers. Initially, it seemed to work, as it announced deals with companies like Ford, Chevrolet, Kraft, Radio Shack, and the American fur industry before it launched in the summer of 1982. With a promise, "You Give Us 18 Minutes, We'll Give You the World," the fast-paced program included weather, sports, business, and news in a format that allowed people to jump in and out of the channel quickly, according to the programming and marketing director.[47] Rather than emphasizing depth—the goal of CNN that Carter had lauded two years earlier as so innovative—SNC wanted to take the existing segment-style model of network news and make it nonstop.

Determined to beat out SNC, Turner took one last drastic step. He offered a loyalty compensation incentive of three dollars per subscriber to be paid out over the course of three years, if cable operators

Basic Cable	Fee charged per month per subscriber
Cable Health Network	None
CNN, CNN Headline News	15 cents a month if WTBS taken as well; 20 cents a month for CNN alone. No fee for CNN Headline News
Daytime	None
ESPN	4 cents a month
MTV	None
Nickelodeon	15 cents a month
SNC, SNCII	None
Nashville Network	None
USA Network	7-11 cents a month
The Weather Channel	None (with exception that if put on a pay tier, operators would pay 5–25 cents a month)

A sample of cable network compensation plans from 1982.
Source: Cablevision, 1983.

continued to carry CNN, CNN2, and WTBS.[48] Such a promise subsidized the higher rates that Turner charged per subscriber at the time (fifteen cents a month per subscriber if the cable operator carried all his stations). Indeed, only Nickelodeon charged similar prices at fifteen cents a month per subscriber, and at the time ESPN only charged four cents a month per subscriber (by 2014, as the channel gained tremendous clout, the rate jumped to an average of $6.04, almost five dollars more per subscriber than any other channel).[49] Most basic cable networks, however, provided their content for free in hopes that gaining carriage would help them attract advertisers to underwrite costs, just as broadcasters had long done.

In the end, Turner's public relations campaign and financial gamble paid off. In a sly political critique, he declared victory by likening himself to Ho Chi Minh. "They pulled out like the U.S. did in Vietnam. . . . We fought like guerrillas and the flag is still flying."[50] He offered his competitors a $25 million buyout in the fall of 1983 and a promise to drop his lawsuit. Since SNC was losing about $35–$40 million a year, the deal helped the company recoup its losses, and Ted Turner once again became the king of 24/7 news, expanding CNN's subscriber base by seven million in the process.[51] "We may not have won the World Series," Turner noted, as his Atlanta Braves finished in a disappointing second place in the National League West to the Los Angeles Dodgers. "But we won the all-news war. Now it's time to call the troops back home."[52]

A message emerged loud and clear throughout this battle: the news could be profitable. Yes, launching a new venture could be costly, and both SNC and Turner lost money in the short term. But CNN then emerged in a stronger situation—and neither CBS nor NBC could come up with a viable cable news plan to compete with him.[53] At the end of 1983, Turner made a move to exercise the economic benefits of controlling the cable news market. He announced to cable operators that he would raise the rates to receive CNN, CNN2, and TBS, while also reminding them how much they needed a 24/7 news station to prove to elected officials that the cable dial provided true alternatives to broadcast television.[54] He pledged, in return, to expand coverage. With an election year coming up and Congress debating cable policy, he understood that operators needed him just as much as he needed them.

By contrast, C-SPAN didn't worry about ratings and advertising. It worried about relevance, which it measured by studying viewer loyalty. While originally C-SPAN shared satellite (and thus a channel) space with the USA Network (which had taken over Madison Square Garden Sports Network in 1980), in 1981 it announced that it would expand to a 16-hour-a-day channel. According to Brian Lamb, the "board was enthusiastic about making C-SPAN bigger and better and more relevant for the viewers. They felt strongly about our gearing-up to carry the Senate and they felt it was important to do whatever it takes to move into the prime-time hours in order to reach possibly ten times the audience most of our programming reaches during the day."[55] This meant the public affairs network had to acquire its own channel space, however. Cable systems paid the three cents per subscriber fee to help fund its operations, and some were reluctant to pay for a channel that didn't actually bring in advertising or other revenue. Four hundred systems stopped carrying the station.

That's when C-SPAN's philosophy of making the viewer the star quickly paid dividends. William Harris of Cherry Hill, New Jersey, founded a national nonprofit organization, Friends of C-SPAN, which encouraged other supporters of the channel to write letters and apply pressure on cable companies to keep C-SPAN.[56] The sixty-three-year-old retired executive from Prudential Insurance Co. soon found other C-SPAN lovers across the country. More than three hundred supporters across forty states pledged dollars and time to advocate for the station.[57] Shirley Rossi of Pueblo, Colorado, was one of them, and she became vice president of the new organization. "I got hooked on watching Congress and I won't be satisfied until we get the broadcasts back," she told her local newspaper.[58]

With its own channel, growing audience loyalty, and an expanding pool of subscribers, C-SPAN launched 24-hour programming in the fall of 1982. Tish Communications used the opportunity to celebrate the impact of C-SPAN. "Cable Keeps a Promise," it announced on the cover of its September 20 *Cablevision* publication. Thanks to C-SPAN, the cable industry had "immersed itself and its customers in the democratic process."[59] In this issue, cable executives hammered home the message to all cable operators: C-SPAN was an essential industry investment that was good business because it was good politics. C-SPAN chairman Ed Allen, the president of Western Communications, emphasized that C-SPAN didn't just carry the House proceedings, it offered a diverse range of public affairs programs, the "world's only 24-hour public affairs network." He urged the CEOs of all major cable companies to require C-SPAN be carried across all of their systems; its success was "too important to be left to the local manager."[60]

With a new tagline of "America's Network," C-SPAN launched what it openly called an "aggressive marketing campaign" to add a million new subscribers that fall under the motto "C-SPAN: Worth a Million." Viewer loyalty again aided the industry as it worked diligently to curry favor with local, state, and national politicians. "We're finding that the consumer accepts this product much more than the industry ever expected," explained Lamb.[61] What's more, he emphasized, "the quality of the people watching are the exact kind of people the politicians want to reach."[62]

Nothing showed the civic engagement of the C-SPAN audience quite like the call-in show, and with the advent of 24/7 programming, C-SPAN expanded this popular program to three times a day. Since the interactive show launched on October 7, 1980, thousands of callers had attempted to get through to chat with policymakers, journalists, or activists.[63] Both guests and callers alike celebrated the opportunity to talk to one another in an innovative television format.[64] Programs connected elected officials with not just their constituents, but voters across the country, raising their national profile. And the phone lines were always ringing. One program featuring Senator Warren Rudman (R-NH) had forty callers ask questions in just one hour.[65] Viewers and guests were eager for conversation, not the confrontation with one another that made politicians reluctant to take phone calls from outraged listeners on talk radio a decade later.[66]

Viewers also watched the congressional proceedings closely. They became more familiar with their own representatives and those in other states who spoke to them daily on C-SPAN. A housewife in Michigan, Jackie Rosenfield, saw Tip O'Neill with his gavel one day, and was drawn into watching the legislative proceedings. Soon, she called the "guys" in Congress "members of the family," even as she criticized one for wearing dentures that didn't quite fit.[67] In Sioux City, Iowa, a group of women who called themselves "Watch Dogs of Congress" met daily to watch C-SPAN, while in Moore, Oklahoma, the "Older Citizens of Moore" had regular club meetings to discuss what they saw on the cable channel. A viewer in Colonial Heights, Virginia, laughed at the popular "C-SPAN junkie" nickname that had emerged and argued that such a term "underestimates the audience of C-SPAN." It wasn't the spectacle that drew people in, she argued. It was the opportunity to see democracy at work. "I think that we will find out that C-SPAN is the most important thing that happened to democracy since the invention of moveable type."

To celebrate its five-year anniversary, C-SPAN cast the spotlight on its loyal viewers. In March 1984, it opened a competition that awarded a three-day, all-expenses-paid trip to Washington, D.C., which would include sitting in on a House session, visiting a C-SPAN studio for a live call-in program, and a tour of the Capitol and White House. Participants just had to submit a 500-word essay that completed the sentence, "I watch C-SPAN public affairs because . . ."[68]

Over one thousand people from forty-nine states, as well as the District of Columbia, Puerto Rico, and the Virgin Islands, submitted an essay that expressed their appreciation of the public affairs network. The winner came from San Diego. James Crosswhite wrote about how he got to know people from across the country. "A voice from Florida responds to a voice from Iowa; a voice from Oregon comments on the exchange. I heard voices raw, in dialect or regional accent. I descry [*sic*] the opinions of Americans in their fulness [*sic*]—the prejudice, the tolerance, the concrete perspective of a farmer, a secretary, a construction worker, a nun."[69] He expressed his gratitude for cameras that took him to the caucus debate in Iowa and the House floor where he could see beyond the "tidied *Congressional Record*, past the deletions of the daily press, behind the strangely attractive reporting of the network news, straight to the House and Senate floors, even into the subcommittees, where our elected representatives stand directly before us in all their eloquence and inarticulateness, their wisdom and foolishness, their openness and evasiveness, their glory and disarray."

Crosswhite, and hundreds of other viewers who submitted responses, turned on C-SPAN to participate in the democratic process and discuss politics with a community of strangers. Overwhelmingly, submissions referenced the call-in programs, which Dora McConnell of Arvada, Colorado, compared to "over-the-back-fence discussions with your neighbors on matters of common interest, but with such scope that the neighborhood extends to encompass all areas of the United States." Mary Ann Crary of Madisonville, Kentucky, loved how these programs gave "anyone a chance to speak on varied subjects and to express any viewpoint." Joyce Chippazzi of Erie, Pennsylvania, agreed. "C-SPAN's talk shows have broadened my exposure to the other person's perspective and deepened my understanding of fellow countrymen." It also motivated her to write to her representatives and donate time and money to political candidates running for office. "I can make a difference and as they say, 'move mountains.'"

Another thing became clear in all of these essays: the celebration of C-SPAN coincided with a critique of network news. One California man complained that "the networks have always treated the viewers as though they are morons."[70] C-SPAN stood out to him and hundreds of others because the channel's executives respected their viewers enough to let them make up their own minds. Viewers talked about the "fairness" and "impartiality" as a reason for tuning in. "What sets C-SPAN apart however, and makes it worthwhile is not just the format but the tone of your program," wrote Gay Boman from Pittsburgh, who called C-SPAN "America's network . . . and mine too."

Although the cable network never tracked ratings, a 1985 survey estimated that C-SPAN had a *potential* audience of 7.6 million households per day.[71] By comparison, network evening news programs had an *actual* average viewership of about 48 million households per night in the same year.[72] But as the viewer essay competition demonstrated, and as viewership surveys captured, C-SPAN's viewers were "extraordinarily politically interested and active" and looking for civic connections on the cable dial that they struggled to find through network television news programs or in defunded community centers or hollowed out Rotary clubs.[73]

The contest also became a way to highlight the contributions of the broader industry to the public good. C-SPAN shrewdly published the names and texts of the top essayists *and* the names of the cable operator and system that carried the channel in their areas. Its panel of judges included former congressional representatives from both parties, the NCTA board chairman, a cable executive, a journalist from the *Los Angeles Times,* and the organizers of Friends of C-SPAN. The contest celebrated the viewer, but it also reminded the cable industry and political insiders of its civic value. Its existence showed that private industry and the marketplace could advance the public interest—and with Congress debating whether to deregulate the industry, this proof of concept mattered.

———

While Ted Turner and Brian Lamb blazed the way in rethinking how the political media could operate, others capitalized on the expanding dial to pursue careers and ideas that network television had stifled and ignored. Public access offered opportunities for marginalized communities to use narrowcasting to assert control over media productions, build networks, and share information. The GCN embodied this approach. Its founder, Lou Maletta, a gay rights activist known for his love of leather chaps and cowboy hats, had aspirations of building a commercial channel dedicated to LGBTQ programming, but he struggled to convince advertisers and investors to fund it.[74] So, without the money to distribute via satellite, he sent videotapes to public access channels across the country.[75] Programs like *Pride and Progress* and *Gay USA* shared sources about the escalating AIDS crisis and grieved those who had died.[76] Maletta scored a press pass in 1984 to cover the national conventions, launching a decade-long effort to bring credibility to the organization and force both national parties to confront the gay community and the issue of AIDS.[77] More broadly, GCN offered an opportunity for LGBTQ activists and artists to make their own programming that eschewed the homophobia dominant in American life and relayed important information and empowering images to underserved television communities.

Public access experiments found their way into the commercial cable world as well, as Maureen Orth's career showed. In 1972, she had worked with TVTV and shocked the television networks by getting political scoops with a microphone, a portapak camera, and an eagerness to ask unconventional questions. During the 1972 conventions, she met Osborn Elliott, the editor-in-chief for *Newsweek*. Impressed by her political contacts, her pioneering reporting with TVTV, and her work with the *Village Voice*, he then helped her secure an editorial position for the magazine, which she almost didn't take because it felt "too establishment."[78]

Over the next five years, Orth pushed her way into a male-dominated journalism world by covering stories in the entertainment and lifestyle sections of *Newsweek*. She reported on music, art, and film—worlds that also increasingly connected with politics. In 1982, she joined other pioneering women in the news media—*Newsweek*'s senior editor Lynn Povich and NBC radio director of news Meredith Hollaus—to develop *Newsweek Woman*, which reported cable news stories that ranged from international issues to art to concerns about poverty.

Promoted as an "unprecedented concept" designed to explore news from "angles and developments that most affect women," the twenty-five-minute program aired three times a week on a new national cable network, Daytime.[79] Newsweek Video, the magazine's video arm, produced the program and then sold it to a recently launched Hearst-ABC venture, which was looking for innovative programs that would appeal to female viewers.[80] Mary Alice Dwyer, head of Daytime's programming, promised that the network's shows would not be "deadly dull and educational." Rather, she emphasized the importance of bringing entertainment into each segment to engage the audience. "They will be involving in the way that Phil Donahue is with his audience."[81] And yet, the cable network promised that such a personal touch wouldn't overshadow a substantive discussion. Rather it showed "the freedom of cable," remarked Daytime's president Jim Perkins. "You're not locked in."[82] Such freedom allowed women like Orth to interview new types of people, including working mothers on the challenge of balancing work and family life, the battle over the Equal Rights Amendment, and conservative women on their work in Republican politics.[83]

Newsweek Woman also reflected how the industry itself was changing. Newspapers and magazines looked for chances to buy cable systems, and many then partnered with cable companies or even broadcast networks to craft such magazine-style programs.[84] Tele-Communications Inc. (TCI), the fastest-growing cable company, even hosted a conference in 1981 for newspapers and cable operators to discuss collaborative business opportunities.[85]

Conservative activists also looked for ways to jump into the cable game. Indeed, evangelicals were early adopters of satellite. During the 1960s, Pat Robertson had built a small religious network, CBN, by physically circulating (i.e., bicycling) popular programs like *The 700 Club* to his own radio stations and by purchasing blocks of time on other stations to reach new viewers. When he saw Ted Turner use satellite to distribute TBS in 1976, he bought an uplink so that he could do the same.[86] Just as HBO subsidized this connection cost, Robertson bought the satellite reception disks for affiliates, and he soon found a way to connect with viewers through social commentary in real time as events unfolded. By the early 1980s, shows like the popular *Praise the Lord Club* on the CBN satellite station blended religion, entertainment, and politics to make a fundamentalist evangelical worldview more accessible and palatable to moderate Protestants across the country.[87]

Each year evangelicals came to the National Religious Broadcasters (NRB) convention with new ideas on how to expand the reach of religious programming on cable (along with CBN, the Trinity Broadcasting Network also launched using satellite in 1977 to provide 24/7 religious programming).[88] Alex Blomerth, president of the El Paso organization Satellite Technology for Christ, had a simple business proposition: "Buy an earth station from us, promise to run Christian programming . . . and we'll sell it to you for $6,000 to $12,000 less than you'll pay retail."[89] One attorney advised evangelicals during an NRB conference session to get involved in the franchising process, securing a "non-exclusive contract" with all potential bidders to ensure that whoever won, they would have guaranteed access to a channel.[90] Brian Lamb called attention to these innovations. "Christian folks have been pioneers when it comes to using the domestic satellite system," he observed. While the media had focused so much time analyzing their messages, they had overlooked "what they are doing with the 'medium,'" he wrote in a *Cablevision* column the year before he launched C-SPAN.[91]

What did this all mean for the future of politics? That's a question that Monroe Price asked in a 1984 piece in the *Wall Street Journal.*[92] As a member of the Sloan Commission ten years before, he had hoped that cable television would empower citizens, even as he had warned about the dangers of fractionalization for the polity. Now, he watched the success of "lifestyle" cable shows and networks, and he anticipated that a "new and disrupting marriage between television and politics may well be in the offing." Cable networks relied on appealing to particular demographics and providing entertainment and news through that lens. So, it seemed natural to Price that political parties would think about the messaging and fundraising power embedded in such a lifestyle approach for "collecting party regulators, preaching the true gospel to them, and gathering in a just reward."

Price imagined that in the near future, a partisan version of *Donahue*, *Good Morning America*, or a Jerry Lewis telethon could combine with specific types of entertainment (*All in the Family* for Democrats and *Death Valley Days* for Republicans) to have a "substantial" consequence for American politics. "The ability to marshal the inventive and magical power of carefully edited images to create intensity of emotion for a particular point of view will yield television propaganda of new heights or new depths," he predicted. The only things that had prevented such approaches to partisan television in the past were the Fairness Doctrine and the licensing process, both of which required adherence to the idea of fairness and balance in the presentation of public affairs. Cable's growth and the deregulatory approach of Mark Fowler, Ronald Reagan's appointee to head the FCC, had called these rules into question, however, making it clear that a new future for partisan television could be on the horizon.

Nevertheless, in 1984, even the prescient Price admitted that the "day of the 30-second commercial is clearly not over, as it is our painful privilege to observe during the current campaign." The frustration with the broadcasting landscape embedded in that observation was exactly the opening on which C-SPAN and CNN pounced.

————

The media landscape had changed substantially by time of the 1984 presidential campaign. At the beginning of the year, 31.4 million out of 85.5 million households were signed up for cable television, and three million more would do so over the next twelve months.[93] Having expanded their programming, operations, and subscriber bases, C-SPAN and CNN were determined to use the presidential election to generate credibility, respectability, and visibility. Their motivations were different—C-SPAN wanted to prove its value to the operators funding its operations whereas CNN wanted to make money. With all eyes on the electoral battle, both accomplished their goals.

Events like the Iowa caucus were perfect for C-SPAN. Since Carter realized its potential in 1976, this primary event had become an opportunity for presidential contenders to construct a media narrative of momentum—one that in turn attracted much needed publicity and dollars for candidates at the beginning of the long primary process.[94] C-SPAN turned the Iowa caucus into a political television experience, chronicling not just the results of the caucus, but the debate and conversation between candidates and Iowa voters—all while fostering relationships and goodwill that served its bottom line of being relevant and respected.

The network partnered with local cable operators across the state to offer an inside look at how a caucus formed and how individuals cast their votes. One live show featured voters debating candidates in a Des Moines school while another showed them coming together on a hog farm fifty miles away. According to one viewer, "C-SPAN cameras followed people into the candidate-group meetings and captured them counting heads and discussing whether to throw their support to one of the candidates who had amassed enough bodies to win representation at the country convention or whether to remain uncommitted." Such coverage, he argued, offered a "much better show than the second-guessing of journalists and the crowing or alibiing of politicians that dominated the coverage on the commercial networks."[95]

Brian Lamb was thrilled with the results and the "gushing comments" that came from viewers. "Without question it was the most reaction we've ever received out of anything we've ever done."[96] One Des Moines viewer highlighted how "C-SPAN gives a demonstration

C-SPAN coverage of the 1984 Democratic primary caucus in Iowa, featuring a meeting with rural Democratic voters in a private home in Jasper County. February 20, 1984. Copyright C-SPAN.

of the difference between real business and show business," and in the process, actually fulfilled the "original promise of television."[97] Rather than "reporting" on issues unfolding, C-SPAN brought in journalists and politicians and activists to comment on them. And most importantly to "America's Network," it gave viewers a voice.[98] "We can beat the polls to the punch just by listening to the viewers," explained Susan Swain, its public relations director (and future CEO).

In New Hampshire, C-SPAN programs offered local journalists an opportunity to shape the discussion of the day's national headlines. In one call-in show, Joel Blumenthal, a reporter for the local *Manchester Union Leader*, relished the opportunity to push back against the dominant portrayal of the New Hampshire primary as a "circus"—one painted by national reporters who "make more out of it than it is."[99]

Lamb called C-SPAN's campaign coverage "video verité" and emphasized that "we consider our responsibility to be capturing an event as if you were there and part of the audience."[100] And they did. Viewers from across the country eagerly called with questions and comments on the candidates, the primary process, and the issues of the campaign.

Viewers also wanted to discuss media coverage: how local newsrooms worked and how pollsters conducted their research, for example. Many call-in shows explicitly taught media literacy. The host would encourage viewers to look at their local newspaper and call in to discuss how stories were positioned and framed. During the New Hampshire primary, Swain took viewers on a journey through a day in the life of the conservative *Manchester Union Leader*. Later that year on Election Day, Lamb provided a tour of the production facilities of *USA Today*. "Our objective is to watch this newspaper being put out, not to bring you election results." He wanted to show the public how journalists gathered and reported information, demystifying the process of election coverage at the newly launched newspaper that controversially emulated the style of television news.[101]

Over the course of the campaign, C-SPAN continued to find ways to cultivate civic dialogue and build meaningful connections with both subscribers and cable operators. It launched a "Grassroots '84" program to shed light on local and state campaigns and featured local journalists and voters as the pundits on its shows.[102] Seven producers and a small production crew rode in a bus across the country to fourteen cities, creating a "video journey" that made grassroots politics the star of the show.[103] The week before the election, C-SPAN hosted five two-hour debates between "well known spokesmen on the left and the right," and then re-aired those debates on Election Day. It also opened phone lines, encouraging viewers to call in to ask questions or air their thoughts on the election. "We figured people had been listening to the commentators long enough and we wanted to give them a chance to reply," explained Lamb.[104]

CNN also raised its profile during the campaign with expanded coverage. Having won a legal battle to become part of the network news pool arrangement—where ABC, CBS, and NBC would share footage of White House events or trips that were too costly or difficult to duplicate—Turner declared that CNN had achieved "parity" with the three networks, and "by God we're going to use it."[105] Turner promised that CNN would be "the network of record for the whole campaign because we have the time and the manpower. All it takes is money." He pledged to use the necessary funds to make CNN the star of the election. He did, and political observers celebrated the ways that such alternative coverage boosted discussions of the candidates and issues at stake in the election.[106]

The chance for stardom really came at the Democratic and Republican national conventions that year, where the tensions between the networks and party officials created an opening for cable television. The three networks had long covered the conventions as part of their efforts to serve the public interest. Indeed, thanks to figures like Leonard Reinsch, such convention coverage had boosted the networks' political prestige and power. Since 1952, debates arose over what scenes the cameras showed viewers, what anchors told them about the proceedings, and who the networks interviewed. The 1968 Democratic National Convention revealed the stakes of these decisions as protesters outside in the streets played to the cameras and Black Power delegates inside the convention hall struggled to visually convey stances on issues like voting rights to viewers at home.[107] By 1976, however, the dramatic, contested convention became a thing of the past as selecting candidates now happened on the primary trail. In 1984, the networks decided to scale back coverage of the conventions, featuring only prime-time speeches and foregrounding coverage and analysis on a "need to know basis" by their anchors.[108]

The decision also reflected changes happening in network newsrooms. Corporate executives looked to cut what they saw as bloated budgets, and loosening FCC oversight no longer made them feel compelled to provide gavel-to-gavel coverage.[109] These changes then intensified media production efforts by the two parties as they crafted the schedule with potential prime-time coverage in mind. GOP consultant Roger Ailes blamed the broadcast networks for the fact that the conventions had become just another political show. Just as the networks went to Paramount and MGM to demand entertainment programming, Ailes complained how they had demanded of Republicans to "Give us a show to run between *Dallas* and *Nightline*." (Of course, he also relished how such increased production demands allowed him to climb the Republican Party ladder as a media adviser.)[110]

This shift in coverage, and the inability of public television to raise the necessary funds to cover the entire convention, created an opening for cable television to do something different. For CNN that meant introducing a technique that Maureen Orth and others with TVTV pioneered over a decade earlier: roving reporters to introduce the "human aspect" of delegates, many of whom had different perspectives on the events unfolding than those advanced by party leaders.[111] At C-SPAN, callers, not anchors, shaped conversation about what constituted convention news. "After Jesse Jackson's speech, we got real people calling up, not those in the business of making things exciting," Brian Lamb explained. "It's obvious that the networks are trying so hard to make things exciting here, telling a story that many times doesn't even exist."[112]

While famous anchors like Dan Rather and Walter Cronkite competed with politicos for celebrity attention on network programming, cable offered opportunities for politicians to expand their profile without having to share the spotlight. According to *Cablevision*, "For both CNN and C-SPAN, political coverage still has the air of a cottage industry. Employees continue to have that sense of the pioneering spirit, of the fact that, in many ways, both networks are moving in directions that American television had never gone before. They are redefining the uses of the media. And they're more than happy to tell the world about it. It's an effort of which the cable industry can be especially proud."[113]

Turner wanted CNN to become a "household name" on par with Ronald Reagan and Walter Mondale that election cycle, and while it never came close to achieving the publicity of the two presidential candidates, his marketing department did all it could to turn its campaign coverage into subscribers and carriage. "With this kind of public attention," stated one advertisement, "it seems to me like a perfect time for

CNN on location for the 1984 Republican National Convention.
Photo Credit: *Multichannel News*/Barco Library, The Cable Center.

a cable promotion." CNN thought so too and did the work by providing operators with newspaper, radio, and television advertisements,
bill stuffers, and posters all celebrating "the value of CNN's coverage
of the election on cable." Lamb saw a similar opportunity to inform
people about the candidates and issues while also "tell[ing] the story
to the cable industry about what we are doing." As he explained it,
"our broadcasting system got out of whack over the years, and the
cable industry is helping it get back in."[114]

The growth of the cable dial and the flourishing of new information and perspectives that came with it created both challenges and
opportunities for political parties and elected officials. As Al Gore
had anticipated in his undergraduate thesis, choices about how
to use new communications technology mattered. The messenger
shaped the medium and its message. "It is important to realize that the
President's dominance in television is accelerated by his awareness
and exploitation of his inherent advantages," wrote Gore. "It is not
simply a matter of the medium messaging the public subconscious,

the President uses television as the tremendous weapon that it is."[115] The cable industry knew this as well, as they had battled for recognition over the past decade only to always come up short, and second, to broadcast television. To improve their regulatory future, they needed to teach politicians that cable was an asset they needed.

The Triumph of Cable America

It was a simple yet potentially revolutionary idea: a cable network dedicated to electing an incumbent president.

Ronald Reagan's media team thoroughly studied the Presidential Reelection System (PRES) proposal that came from a persistent and passionate freelance producer and director named David Caldwell. Eager to join the president's reelection campaign, Caldwell wanted to launch a cable project that he believed would usher in the biggest transformation in political media since the 1960 televised presidential debates.[1]

PRES, Caldwell hyped, would compile daily campaign speeches and appearances to take viewers inside the campaign and expand media coverage of Reagan.[2] The week's coverage would culminate in a Saturday morning program with the look of a network news show but with an overtly partisan mission.[3] The long-form style of cable television was essential to the project's success, Caldwell explained, because it would allow viewers to "experience" the president's leadership qualities, creating an intimacy that would result in personal loyalty to him.[4]

The pitch dovetailed with the goals of Reagan's well-oiled media operations. The president had a talented team of speechwriters, advisers, and pollsters who worked diligently to stage presidential events that would enable the "Great Communicator" to dominate the expanding news cycle.[5] His crew had comprehensive strategies in place to drum up media interest in advance of televised addresses and then generate positive news coverage in the aftermath by deploying surrogates as radio guests and cable news commentators.[6] Caldwell's PRES plan, if they bit, would afford Reagan's team even more control over the dissemination of his message.

But they didn't bite. The Reagan team just didn't see the payoff of what they called "non-traditional projects" that year, preferring to focus on tried-and-true tactics like the powerful thirty- and sixty-second spot advertisements.[7] Instead, Reagan's reelection campaign relied on his "Tuesday Team," professional advertisers who crafted powerful and elaborate broadcast commercials that donned the American flag and a "God Bless America"–style soundtrack. Their goal? To turn voting for Reagan into an emotional, uplifting, and patriotic act.[8]

As a sitting president with strong relationships with both the dominant news and entertainment industries, Reagan lacked the incentive to experiment with long-form cable television and narrowcasting. His team's dismissal of the cable proposal reveals just how deeply ingrained broadcasting communications strategies—spot advertisements, mass appeals, and working with the Washington press corps—were in electoral politics. Indeed, the radio-announcer-turned-Hollywood-actor's rise in the Republican Party coincided with the growing authority of network newsrooms during the 1960s and their ability to shape political conversations and public opinion. The former movie star understood the centrality of performance to political success. "There have been times in this office when I've wondered how you could do the job if you hadn't been an actor," he famously admitted in an interview before leaving the White House.[9]

Broadcasting groomed him, particularly as he transitioned from an actor to a television spokesman for General Electric to a breakout political star during a prime-time television endorsement of Barry

Goldwater's presidential nomination in 1964.[10] It also served his central political goal: to build a consensus around conservatism itself. As an actor with a penchant for forging emotional connections with audiences, he had emerged as the conservative movement's most effective messenger. He exuded optimism and worked diligently to make his agenda popular, which—due to divided government—required flexibility, compromise, and appealing to common values rather than stoking division.[11]

That's not to say Reagan ignored cable television. He loved the industry. As governor of California, he had produced programs in which he would talk with voters about his agenda, and then have recordings bicycled around the state to local broadcasters and cable operators.[12] As president, he quickly became C-SPAN's "most famous viewer," regularly asking guests about their comments during daily call-in programs and even phoning into the program himself.[13]

He also regularly celebrated how the exploding cable dial crystallized the benefits of the marketplace as it provided sports, entertainment, and educational offerings to enrich the daily lives of Americans.[14] During his administration, as teenagers increasingly socialized at malls and connected with one another by watching MTV, they forged their relationships and community connections on the terrain of private businesses.[15] Cable television's dramatic expansion during the 1980s became another proof of concept for Reagan's deregulatory agenda, providing the political tools and cultural experiences that helped legislators and citizens alike buy into the free-market ideas pushed by both Republicans and Democrats.

And yet, this embrace of efficiency and effectiveness in campaign and governing strategies also emboldened and empowered Reagan's critics across the political spectrum. Indeed, cable television gave them a way to pierce holes in the power of the televised presidential bully pulpit. On the right, fringe members of the Republican Party turned to the growing medium as a way to advance ideological rigidity and an aggressive and combative approach to politics. They wanted to inflame viewers and polarize a small but impassioned electorate, whose loyalty they saw as key to gaining power. By contrast,

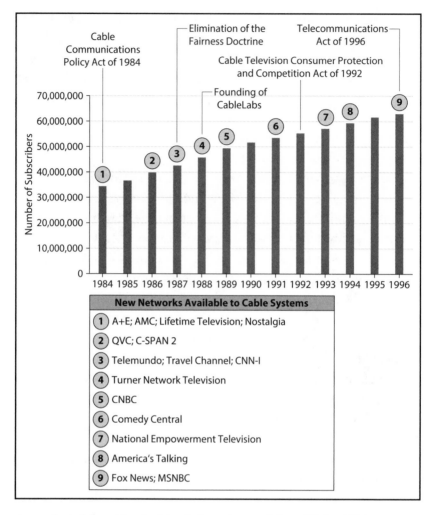

A snapshot of the cable television industry's growth from 1984 to 1996.
Sources: Television & Cable Factbook; SNL Kagan; Larry Satkowiak, *The Cable Industry: A Short History through Three Generations*, Barco Library, The Cable Center.

a younger generation of Democrats viewed cable as a way to remake and rebrand the party's crumbling New Deal coalition by embracing entertainment strategies that helped them engage new types of voters—albeit in more superficial ways.

Both approaches bolstered the fortunes of the industry while ingraining market incentives in the political process and nourishing anti-establishment political forces. Three decades later, Donald Trump would capitalize on these changes in politics and culture, doing so by bringing key aspects of Caldwell's PRES plan into the White House with his relationships with Fox News, a cable news channel that then helped to create a loyalty to the president by blending outrage and entertainment. While the strategy helped Trump win the presidency, it deeply divided the country and undermined democratic institutions, ultimately exposing the danger of connecting democracy itself to the metrics of the marketplace.

9

A Political Tool

Barney Frank was desperate. The fast-talking Massachusetts congressman with his trademark thick-rimmed glasses had won a congressional seat in 1980 with 52 percent of the vote. But two years later, the freshman Democrat found himself in an uphill battle for his political life. Massachusetts had lost a representative after the 1980 census, which forced Frank into a district against a veteran moderate Republican, Margaret Heckler, who had won her first term in 1966. The new district covered more of her voting base, and she emerged as a frontrunner in the race between two incumbents.

Frank was ready to embrace any idea that would boost his campaign and help him build a winning coalition by appealing to new voters in the redrawn district. "At that point," Frank recalled, "if someone told me matchbook covers were an underutilized campaign resource, I would have been doing that."[1] So he was all ears when the up-and-coming media consultant John Florescu pitched a low-cost but also untested strategy: cablecasting. Frank decided it was a "no lose situation" and "worth an effort even if it wasn't likely to be successful." And so he said yes.

Newt Gingrich, meanwhile, was frustrated. The history-professor-turned-conservative-firebrand had pledged to shake things up on Capitol Hill and in the Republican Party if he was elected to Congress in 1978. In one campaign speech to college Republicans in Atlanta, he pushed them to "be nasty" and voice oppositional opinions loudly.[2] "Fight, scrap, issue a press release, go make a speech," if they wanted to be taken seriously, he told them. When he arrived in Washington as a freshman congressman, he found several other young and aggressive allies—notably Robert "Bob" Walker from Pennsylvania and John Vincent "Vin" Weber from Minnesota—who also viewed politics as a media-driven field of battle, not a world of governance that required compromise.[3] As Gingrich scribbled on a strategy notepad, "this is a confrontation business."[4]

And yet, they were a radical fringe of the minority party in the House. How could they force the Republican Party to listen to their ideas? They were willing to experiment with anything that could give them a platform, including C-SPAN—if only they could figure out how to stand out during the televised legislative hearings and floor proceedings each day. Their solution? Using cable to build a national profile by flinging red meat rhetoric and seeding political discontent. They hoped this would engage and embolden a vocal sliver of the electorate craving a GOP with sharper elbows.

Frank and Gingrich turned to cable television out of necessity, but their different strategies exposed their contrasting goals and foreshadowed alternative paths for using cable television that their respective parties would later pursue. Frank, the Democrat, wanted to use cable to connect with populations he wasn't currently reaching by meeting people where they were: watching cable programs. As Florescu would later explain, voters increasingly felt "alienated from politics," and so they didn't automatically turn on political programming.[5] Campaigns had to go to them, he emphasized, with a tailored message and the toolbox of entertainment in hopes of engaging television viewers. The Republican representative from Atlanta had a different goal. He also recognized growing voter alienation from politics, but he wanted to turn it into smoldering outrage among cable subscribers to boost his national profile. It was not about selling specific policies or connecting with his own constituents. Rather, he believed that raising a ruckus would elevate the conservative fringe inside the Republican Party itself and help them secure enough power to force GOP leadership to pay attention and adopt similar tactics.[6]

Both approaches transformed cable into a political tool—one that notably muddied the waters among public affairs programming, entertainment, and partisan propaganda. By elevating their political status through cable television, members of Congress across the political spectrum also expanded the legitimacy of the cable business itself, even paving the way for its deregulation—something that finally happened in 1984 with overwhelming bipartisan support.

———

When John Florescu picked up the phone to pitch Barney Frank on a cablecasting strategy, he just knew the expanding cable dial was the future of politics. The son of a Romanian academic who wrote books about Vlad Dracula, the native Bostonian attended nearby Boston College where he studied history. He got his start in politics by joining Edward Kennedy's 1980 presidential campaign—while also making the celebrity gossip pages of newspapers across the country with reports that he dated the senator's daughter, Kara.[7] He pushed Kennedy to take advantage of the growing medium of cable television, which the senator did during the New York primary.[8]

In January 1982, Florescu penned an article for the *Boston Globe* to try to convince local politicians to "heed a virtual revolution at the front door."[9] He promised that cable would soon become the "new darling of campaign headquarters" because of three things: its ability to target specific demographics of voters, its affordability, and its flexibility. "In the years ahead," he predicted, "cable will change politicking as substantially as it has changed Madison Avenue, sports programmers, Hollywood studios, and porn kings. One can only hope tomorrow's voter will be better served than today's cable consumer."

That summer, hoping to drum up business for his new cable consulting and programming company, Florescu began telephoning Democratic candidates, urging them to use the medium in their midterm election campaigns.[10] When he called Barney Frank, he found a candidate open to his pitch. Frank had strong support already from the turf that had come from his old district: Brookline and Newton, two middle-class, liberal, and Jewish suburbs. Heckler was doing well in the wealthy and white outer suburbs of Wellesley and Dover. But there was a third section of the district up for grabs: Fall River and New Bedford. To win, Frank needed to get to know this fishing community home to many Portuguese Americans.

Cable, argued the young media consultant, was the solution.[11] It was in 56 percent of households in Fall River and would allow Frank to communicate directly with the Portuguese community on the issues they cared about—and ones that were notably different from what voters in the Boston suburbs prioritized. Florescu showed him how narrowcasting could help him target these key demographics. Notably, he bought super cheap time for three thirty-minute programs, billed as "town meetings," on the local Whaling City Cable TV station public access channels and ran them after popular local public affairs shows in the evening. Produced in the local cable studio, the program featured Frank answering questions from a panel of well-known citizens who doubled as promoters by encouraging their family and friends to watch the show. As Florescu reminded Frank, "it's not how many are watching that counts, it's who." Cable audiences, he noted, were more interested in politics and more likely to turn out to vote.

As Florescu made inroads with cable in New Bedford, the Democratic Speaker of the state house, Thomas W. McGee, took notice and encouraged colleagues facing reelection to reach out to Florescu in the last days of their campaigns. McGee explained that Florescu could help them take advantage of a "cost-effective media buy that could be important to your election race, enhancing the advertising effort you've already put into your campaign."[12]

A cable experiment was also happening in Connecticut where Governor William O'Neill "pretested" advertisements on cable to get feedback on their effectiveness before his campaign doled out bigger dollars for broadcast television time. The Democratic governor found this also functioned as a good party-building activity, as his campaign held fundraising parties in which supporters watched the cable commercials and offered feedback (and frequently then made donations).[13]

Even the Democratic National Committee explored ways to reach different demographics through targeted cable programming during the midterm elections.[14] In May, the DNC released a cable documentary called "Forget Not Old Friends" that told the story of Florence Sage, an eighty-two-year-old who had no support outside her monthly Social Security check. In June, the committee ran a two-hour cable program called *We Are the Democrats,"* which featured "commercials" urging viewers to donate to the party. Carried on over forty-one hundred cable systems via Ted Turner's WTBS channel, the program had a potential audience of around twenty-five million viewers.

Turner gave time to both parties that summer to connect with cable audiences, something that raised questions about whether this airtime constituted a "corporate contribution" that exceeded campaign finance limits. But this was uncharted waters. The FCC's policies governing political programs distributed by cable television were unclear and untested in court or through FCC cases. That left cable operators and party officials free to "gamble" that they weren't breaking the law.[15]

For the Democrats, the risk was worth it. The party added twenty-seven seats in the House of Representatives that year. Barney Frank's cable strategy not only helped him come from behind in Massachusetts—he crushed his Republican opponent by twenty points. Speaker of the House Tip O'Neill also credited C-SPAN as an asset that helped the Democrats outscore Republicans during the midterm elections.[16] Over the next year, O'Neill's party would continue to experiment with cable to counter the powerful White House messaging machine and its charismatic president. When it started to work, Republicans took notice.

———

On April 27, 1983, President Reagan arrived on Capitol Hill to deliver an address urging the legislative branch to approve $110 million in military aid for El Salvadorians fighting communism. The *Wall Street Journal* noted that calling together a joint session of Congress to push a foreign policy issue was "one of the most unusual and dramatic moves of his administration."[17] The speech—scheduled for 8:00 p.m. Eastern Standard Time and covered by network television—reflected the Reagan administration's effective media operation and his fondness for "going public" to bring Americans to his side on legislative issues, a tactic that many believed helped him pass his economic agenda in the first two years of his presidency.[18]

Democrats requested, and received, an opportunity to respond to the address on network television. Senator Christopher Dodd (D-CT) delivered the rebuttal, warning the public that Reagan's massive military buildup and his willingness to intervene militarily in other countries were leading the country down "a dark tunnel of endless intervention."[19]

Members of the House, however, also wanted a piece of the spotlight. So, in the aftermath of Reagan's speech, they took to the House floor to debate its merits—with C-SPAN capturing the discussion.[20] In the days that followed, the networks, local news programs, and radio broadcasts included these House perspectives in their reporting on the debate. As Chief Deputy Majority Whip William Alexander proudly declared, "The House of Representatives managed to hold its own in head-to-head media coverage with the most media-wise President in our history."[21]

With Reagan in the White House, Democrats had a partisan incentive to pursue a range of strategies to counter the Great Communicator. The Dodd response reflected one such strategy embedded in the broadcasting rules: invoking either "fairness doctrine" or "equal time" rules to request time for the "opposition" to reply to presidential addresses.[22] Traditionally, the networks had an inconsistent policy in terms of granting these requests—and frequently did so at off-peak hours. But during the Reagan administration, Democratic senators like Dodd as well as House leaders, especially Tip O'Neill, became more aggressive in demanding equal time. O'Neill astutely tapped into the media's desire for drama by creating a narrative of him versus Reagan—two Irishmen battling it out against one another in a saga that pit legislative versus executive and Republican versus Democrat.[23] A 163-page Congressional Research Service report released in 1984 noted that Democrats in Congress had achieved an "unprecedented success" with such an approach.[24]

And yet, O'Neill recognized that countering what he called Reagan's "superior access to television" required more than laying claim to equal time on network television, a medium that overwhelmingly favored the executive branch.[25] It demanded capitalizing on the television format unique to Congress, just as they did with the April rebuttal on C-SPAN. In the aftermath of that spring television success, William Alexander worked with John Florescu to develop a pilot program that coordinated televised special-order speeches—something Charles Rose had introduced in 1979 and more and more representatives began to use to take advantage of C-SPAN coverage—with local news coverage in hopes of turning what O'Neill had previously lamented as "grandstanding" into a way to boost the members' personal visibility in their own districts.[26]

Here's how it worked. Florescu notified local cable operators when the representatives planned to deliver their one-minute speeches during the special orders and encouraged the operators to tape the C-SPAN footage, which frequently aired later at night. Then, the cable operator would share this footage with local broadcasters—and both could replay it, with the line "Courtesy of C-SPAN" appearing on the bottom. And so, a speech to an empty chamber could then reach constituents through both the local public access channel and local broadcast news programs the following day. As Florescu noted, "at no cost, they are getting exposure in their district in a format . . . designed in part by the congressman himself because he knows what he is going to say on the House floor, and he is usually reacting to that day's news so it tends to be quite topical."[27]

Alexander encouraged his Democratic colleagues to expand this experiment and take advantage of C-SPAN's reach and affordability, underscoring how the free airtime "was worth well over $4,000 each time they spoke."[28] He even proposed to move the legislative schedule to prime-time hours to capitalize on the success of his cable experiment. In doing so, he called attention to the ways in which the conservative fringes of the Republican Party had also started to use these after-hours speeches to push their ideological agendas. The Democrats, he argued, needed to expand their counteroffensive.

Such thinking resonated with his colleagues who were growing frustrated with a handful of junior Republicans who had started to capture national attention for their aggressive, but engrossing, special-order speeches. While claiming to be inspired by the Democrats' pilot program, these conservatives used C-SPAN differently.[29] Their goal? To stir the outrage of viewers across the country in what the *Washington Post* called a "highly orchestrated symphony."[30] This was not about connecting with their districts on topical debates, but about pursuing "parliamentary guerrilla warfare" by crafting fiery speeches around arcane procedural rules to make viewers think that the Democratic leadership repressed debate on hot-topic issues like abortion and school prayer. These speeches frequently called out the Democratic opposition directly, daring them to respond. But nobody did because the legislative session had ended and everyone was gone (a situation the camera did not expose because it focused only on the speaker per House policy).

In short, it was a strategy designed to get viewers' blood boiling through a media spectacle.[31] And it seemed effective. At the time, C-SPAN reached over sixteen million homes, and while the network did not track audience numbers or ratings, Newt Gingrich estimated that 200,000 people could be watching at any moment, which he called "not a bad crowd" for a "nation-wide town hall meeting."[32] He and Bob Walker soon became C-SPAN stars as they led a minority of the House minority in a drama that won Congress the title of "Best Little Soap Opera on Cable" from the *Washington Post* in 1984.[33]

Democrats and Republicans alike watched such aggressive tactics with concern. David Obey (D-WI) circulated a memo to all members of the House calling out specific instances of this disturbing and "inappropriate language" used by these conservative members. He noted they were not debating the issues but questioning "people's motives or patriotism." He warned that if "it is allowed to continue unabated," such rhetoric "will poison national dialogue and cripple democratic debate, which is in the end the greatest safeguard to liberty in this nation."[34]

But that was the goal. Gingrich laid out his political philosophy of aggression and obstruction early in his career via handwritten strategy notes on yellow legal pads: "Bomb appropriate persons." "Run experiment in test media markets until something works." "Attack opponent." "Use freshman block to obstruct; swing or withhold votes to attract attention." "Generate disorder; form leadership takeover." "Make voting for Republican fun." "Have no shame."[35]

Indeed, Gingrich was open and direct with all of his colleagues about the need to revamp *both* the style and substance of the GOP to win "the battle for the understanding and loyalty of the American people."[36] In a strategy memo (one Democrats collected as part of their research on Gingrich), he argued that Republicans had separated "the art of winning elections" from the "art of managing systems once the election is won and power attained." He wanted to cultivate "the art of governing" and bring the competition long associated with the campaign trail into daily political operations. "Governing is the combination of politics and government to ensure that the American people understand it is in their common interest to rally to you and against your opponents," he wrote.

Gingrich saw politics as warfare, and television as both a battlefield and a weapon. "No matter how talented Republicans are, we cannot be effective if we do not train and do not practice" for television appearances, he emphasized.[37] "Until we are doing that, we shouldn't be surprised that our spokesmen perform on T.V. about as well as an amateur football team would perform in the Super Bowl." Traditionally, younger and newer members of Congress put their heads down and did the legislative work needed to climb the party ladder rather than lecturing the leadership on how to do their jobs. Gingrich saw a different path to power: confrontation with both senior and moderate Republicans as well as the Democratic Party.[38]

And yet, when William Alexander proposed in May 1984 to move legislative hours to prime time to take the wind out of their sails, people worried that it would only make things worse. The Democratic whip saw such opposition as reflective of a generational divide. "The younger guys basically got here using television," he observed. "They understand the power of this medium. Some of the older members are not comfortable with that power."[39]

But that wasn't the only issue. Tim Wirth, the young Democrat from Colorado, certainly understood the importance of expanding television access—which is one of the reasons he had pushed for cable-friendly policies like the pole rate legislation. And yet, he also expressed his concerns about television's potential to "skew" the legislative process by encouraging "those who are interested more in self-promotion or rhetorical flourishes than in the legislative process or product."[40] Wirth wrote a letter to Speaker O'Neill raising these questions, and he asked, "Can we, and should we, draw a line between legislative debate and political self-aggrandizement?" He worried that the flourishing of the latter would undermine the integrity of Congress, stall the legislative process, and sever working relationships between the two parties. That's exactly what happened with the chaos about to erupt in the House over what became known as "CamScam."

On May 10, 1984, Bob Walker donned patriotic colors—a navy three-piece suit, white shirt, and red tie—as he launched a speech on what might have been a boring topic: the handling of congressional records. However, Walker injected drama by alleging that the Democratic leadership had tampered with public records to cover up their own political misconduct.[41] He directly challenged the integrity of Tip O'Neill—a tried-and-true tactic deployed by these "guerrilla warriors." While initially, the Democratic strategy had been to dismiss such "obnoxious" tactics as "silly," "pointless," and indeed an "embarrassment," that day, O'Neill had had enough.[42] Still furious over the special orders from two days earlier, when Gingrich and Walker had personally attacked fifty Democrats over foreign policy issues, O'Neill ordered the cameras to pan the empty chamber.[43] Per the agreement with C-SPAN, the House controlled the cameras, and O'Neill had previously emphasized the importance of keeping the camera focused on the person speaking. But now, the Speaker felt it was more important to expose Walker as a phony performer.

Walker's Republican colleagues slipped him a note explaining what had happened, and he exploded. "It is my understanding that as I deliver this special order this evening, the cameras are panning this chamber demonstrating that there is no one here listening to these remarks." Seething and gesturing angrily, Walker called this "procedural change with no warning" just "one more example of the arrogance of power" by the Democratic leadership.[44]

House Minority Leader Robert Michel—who had previously warned Walker, Gingrich, and their crew against being "cast in the role of being obstructionists or hell-raising types"—came immediately to their defense.[45] In an angry letter to O'Neill, he wrote, "This was an act of dictatorial retribution against a Member of the United States Congress. It was deplorable, not so much because of the act itself, but because of what it represented and the motivation behind it."[46]

Speaker O'Neill defended his actions, explaining that he had made the decision to change the camera's focus earlier that day and that it was mere coincidence that Bob Walker happened to be the one on camera when it began.[47] Yet he also drew attention to the extensive requests made by Gingrich, Walker, and Weber for an hour's time at the end of daily sessions in the previous thirty days—making it clear he understood that one of them would likely be on camera when the panning started. While he admitted that he should have informed Minority Leader Michel in advance, he defended his decision by emphasizing the need to tame the incendiary rhetoric spewed by these conservatives, which O'Neill called "one of the meanest things I have ever heard of."[48] Showing the camera angle didn't infringe on freedom of speech, argued O'Neill. Rather it showed "the American people that this man is speaking for home consumption and is not in a debate." Even Michel concluded in his letter to O'Neill that a discussion about leaving the wide-angle camera coverage for the future was a "good idea."[49]

The conflict between Gingrich and O'Neill escalated on May 15, however. On the House floor, Gingrich refused to apologize for any personal or political attacks he and his colleagues had waged against Democrats during their special-order rants. In response, the

Speaker came to the well of the House and didn't mince any words. "You deliberately stood in that well before an empty House, and you challenged these people and you challenged their Americanism, and it's the lowest thing that I have ever seen in my 32 years in Congress."[50]

Before Gingrich could respond, his conservative ally, Republican Whip Trent Lott, jumped up and requested that O'Neill's words be taken down from the record—a major penalty in the House. The floor quickly became a flurry of activity. Visibly animated, Walker paced back and forth between Gingrich, still standing at the podium, and the Speaker pro tem, Joseph Moakley, another Democrat from Massachusetts. After several tense minutes of discussion, Moakley decided that because O'Neill had personally attacked Gingrich during a debate between the two, he had no choice but to rule the Speaker out of order, making him the first Speaker to have his words taken down since 1797, which also banned the Speaker from further participation in debate that day.[51]

The conflict captured headlines across the country, and the C-SPAN footage of O'Neill and Gingrich's fiery exchange appeared on network news programs.[52] According to the *Washington Post*, "the House of Representatives show" on C-SPAN had become "more turbulent than a 'Dynasty' cliffhanger, more riveting than the evening news, and at times funnier than anything on 'Foul Ups, Bleeps and Blunders.'"[53] O'Neill's press assistant acknowledged that "we've got a regular range war going on over here" over special orders and the rules of the camera. As one journalist observed, "House members are embroiled in a power play for what is a relatively new and not completely understood, kind of power."[54]

A flood of editorials across the country criticized both Gingrich and O'Neill, with C-SPAN emerging as the real winner in the televised battle. Brian Lamb called the incident a "terrific boost for the whole concept" because it got people talking across the country about Congress and cable television.[55] "Forget about right or wrong," exclaimed the C-SPAN founder. "It can't hurt us if you're talking about what gets people's attention."

Political cartoon drawn by Mike Morgan in the *Macon Telegraph &*
News capturing the "CamScam" controversy between Speaker of the
House Tip O'Neill and Representative Newt Gingrich.
Courtesy of Mike Morgan.

He was right. Editorials from Oregon to Texas, and from Iowa
to Maine, weighed in on the debate. Some disparaged "tricky Tom
O'Neill" for trying to be "Cecil B. DeMille," while others called attention to the deceptive tactics of Republicans, reminding them that
"those who live by the tube die by the tube."[56] The majority of the
editorials, however, dismissed both sides as "plain silly," "sopho-
moric," and "foolish," focusing instead on the specifics of how
C-SPAN actually worked (including the fact that it was funded by
cable companies themselves) and the growing power of television
in politics.[57]

The publicity surrounding CamScam showed that people
watched and valued the public affairs channel. Indeed, it helped to
further popularize a term for the network's loyal fan base: "C-SPAN
junkies." According to one newspaper in Boulder, Colorado, "When
this service started five years ago, cynics figured that the only viewers would be desperate people stuck at home who had seen all
the reruns on other channels. But what's this? Thousands, maybe

millions of voters are watching, and sending letters to their representatives about what they have seen."[58] The editorial page at the *Dallas Morning News* agreed: "Anything—anything—that goes on television on a national scale at whatever hour, on whatever subject, draws audiences of a size that most politicians would kill for. New fact of life: The politician who speaks to the camera whether he is in an empty House or atop Mount Everest at midnight, speaks to the multitudes."[59]

For Gingrich, this attention defined success. The Georgia congressman basked in the media glow of his battle with O'Neill and used it to articulate his vision for a new style of politics. "This is the beginning of the post-Rayburn House," he said excitedly in one of the many interviews following the incident. "It's like the transition from vaudeville to television, like going from being a Broadway actor to being a television star. O'Neill and others are pre-TV, pre-confrontational."[60] He proudly was the opposite and wanted to use cable television to usher in his art of governing.

Over the next four years, as cable expanded into more homes across the country, Gingrich and Walker—who never would have otherwise secured national broadcast airtime—used C-SPAN as a vehicle to make news and reshape party politics and the very operations of the House of Representatives.

In the short term, CamScam may have given some senators pause as they debated Brian Lamb's newest brainchild: introducing cameras into the upper chamber. "The Senate is not able to get its work done now," noted Senator Russell Long (D-LA). "It would be even worse if the Senate were on television."[61] Republican Senator John Danforth of Missouri agreed, calling it a "terrible idea" that would make people take to dramatic activities, like the filibuster, to generate media attention, particularly because "half of the Senate floor is running for President," noted Senator Don Nickles (R-OK).

And yet, many senators also thought that C-SPAN had allowed the House to overshadow the Senate in the public eye. Senator Robert Byrd (D-WV) introduced a resolution the following January to bring "selected broadcast coverage of the Senate" to cable, and in 1986, C-SPAN 2 launched to do just this.[62] Senator James McClure, a

Republican from Idaho, called televising the Senate "long overdue" and pushed his colleagues to move the institution out of its "horse and buggy days."[63] But McClure had already embarked on another experiment to do just that, even without the C-SPAN cameras. His secret weapon? Satellite.

———

While Gingrich proved that cultivating outrage could generate cable ratings and national publicity, James McClure wanted to find ways to promote the broader Republican Party and ride Ronald Reagan's television coattails. The head of the Republican Senate Conference had compiled newsletters, held media training sessions and op-ed workshops, disseminated public service announcements and graphics, and even hosted lunch sessions for news secretaries with tips on how to "groom" senators for television appearances, all efforts to inundate the American people with positive information about Republican senators.[64]

Radio actualities—short bits of recorded audio—had worked wonders for connecting senators to their constituents.[65] Senators themselves voiced these news updates from Washington, which let them shape the evening's local broadcast with statements like "today, I have written the President." The Senate Republican Actuality Network offered Republican senators the opportunity to create two of these each week, which it would then send out to at least forty radio stations. It was part of the GOP's "earned media strategy," which went beyond simple press releases about governing activities and plotted ways to snag appearances on news programs. One GOP media adviser likened the strategy to Chinese water torture. "It's the steady drip, drip, drip of news and information reaching the voters of your state that creates an impact on election day."[66]

Timeliness and speed were essential to the effectiveness and reach of these radio actualities. "Nothing will get less use than a dated actuality. Radio news 'eats' news stories faster than the 'Alien' eats people. An actuality that is news in the morning may be dated in the afternoon," explained one manual.[67] That was the central

challenge that television posed: how could the GOP distribute videotapes quickly enough to capitalize on the news cycle? And then
McClure had an idea. What if GOP senators used a satellite connection to send television actualities to cable operators instantly?

Over two dozen of his Republican senate colleagues were willing
to give it a try. Following Reagan's first State of the Union on January 26, 1982, twenty-seven GOP senators recorded short forty-five-
second responses. Then they rented time on the satellite and sent the
programming to over four thousand cable operators and two hundred
local broadcasters with satellites, who could then "downlink" their
responses and include them in the late local news that evening.[68]
For an entire cost of $1,200, over two dozen senators became part
of the story about the State of the Union for constituents back home.
Indeed, some cable operators ran all of these comments back-to-
back without interruption.[69]

Carter Clews, the director of communications for the Republican Senate Conference, sent out surveys to broadcasters and cable
operators to gauge their response to the experiment. He ultimately
concluded that it offered a "revolutionary change" for direct political
communication between elected officials and their constituents.[70]
And so, McClure and Clews launched "Operation Uplink": the production of programming using the Senate television recording studio
and then satellite and cable for distribution.

The project involved two types of programs. The first featured
"video actualities"—two-minute statements by individual senators
or a question and answer with a journalist from their home state. The
clip then would be uplinked to the satellite and then downlinked by
cable operators and local broadcasters in the senator's home state for
inclusion on the nightly news or public access channel. The second
program, *Conference Roundtable*, featured elected officials discussing public affairs with journalists.[71] Designed to emulate *Meet the
Press*, it looked like a traditional news talk show produced by the
commercial broadcast networks. On Saturday afternoons, senators and representatives sat around a table with two journalists—
generally one from print and one from television—to discuss issues
that ranged from foreign policy to tax cuts to prayer in school.

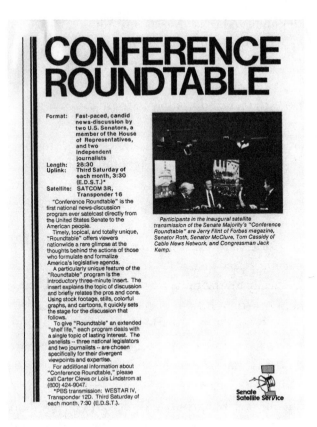

CONFERENCE ROUNDTABLE

Format: Fast-paced, candid news-discussion by two U.S. Senators, a member of the House of Representatives, and two independent journalists

Length: 28:30

Uplink: Third Saturday of each month, 3:30 (E.D.S.T.)*

Satellite: SATCOM 3R, Transponder 16

"Conference Roundtable" is the first national news-discussion program ever satelcast directly from the United States Senate to the American people.

Timely, topical, and totally unique, "Roundtable" offers viewers nationwide a rare glimpse at the thoughts behind the actions of those who formulate and formalize America's legislative agenda.

A particularly unique feature of the "Roundtable" program is the introductory three-minute insert. The insert explains the topic of discussion and briefly relates the pros and cons. Using stock footage, stills, colorful graphs, and cartoons, it quickly sets the stage for the discussion that follows.

To give "Roundtable" an extended "shelf life," each program deals with a single topic of lasting interest. The panelists -- three national legislators and two journalists -- are chosen specifically for their divergent viewpoints and expertise.

For additional information about "Conference Roundtable," please call Carter Clews or Lois Lindstrom at (800) 424-9047.

*PBS transmission: WESTAR IV, Transponder 12D. Third Saturday of each month, 7:30 (E.D.S.T.).

Participants in the inaugural satellite transmission of the Senate Majority's "Conference Roundtable" are Jerry Flint of Forbes magazine, Senator Roth, Senator McClure, Tom Cassidy of Cable News Network, and Congressman Jack Kemp.

Senate Satellite Service

An advertisement for the *Conference Roundtable* distributed to cable operators and local broadcasters by the Republican Senate Conference in 1982.

Clews highlighted the historic nature of Operation Uplink when encouraging cable operators and broadcasters to feature it on their television schedules. "On May 23, 1844, the U.S. Capitol was the scene of a communications revolution," he wrote broadcasters and cable operators in reference to the first telegraph sent from the Senate (which actually occurred the next day).[72] "This May 28, 138 years almost to the day after Samuel Morse's epochal transmission—the U.S. Senate is again on the frontier of communications technology." Along with thirteen two-minute video actualities delivered each week, Operation Uplink would provide *Conference Roundtable*, designed "to fuel a public dialogue that can't help but bring us ever nearer the enduring goal of a truly participatory democracy."[73]

Clews emphasized that Operation Uplink had been "designed with the needs of the local programmer in mind," and he even sold it as the "first news-discussion program ever satelcast directly from the United States Senate to the American people."[74] But it had a clear mission: to feature Republican messaging under the guise of a news format.[75]

Programs featured Republicans and the GOP footed the bill— something only alluded to in the credit line that identified the program as a production of the "Senate Conference of the Majority."[76] Advertisements called it "timely, topical and totally unique" because it "offers viewers a rare glimpse at the thoughts behind the actions of those who formulate and formalize America's legislative agenda." Promotional material consistently highlighted how participants "are chosen specifically for their divergent viewpoints and expertise," but it always kept the focus on showing what James McClure called the "breadth of thinking within the Republican Party."[77] While a House Democrat from Illinois, Paul Simon, did join one program discussing tuition tax credits, the slate of guests remained focused on giving a platform to Republicans in Congress.[78]

Beth Higgins, a cable program director in Seattle, did question why it only featured Republicans. Nevertheless, despite the limited perspectives presented, Higgins distributed it on her company's cable system, revealing how the desire to populate the cable dial trumped concerns about the ethics underlining the programming itself. "It's good technically and the show does deal with controversial subjects," she explained. But disagreement among Republicans still left something out, explained Higgins. "I'm concerned that the picture isn't as complete as it might be."[79]

For the GOP, that was the point. The combination of satellite and cable television allowed the party to get its message directly to voters at an affordable rate. Cable operators were eager for free programming that helped them fulfill their franchising promises to create and disseminate public affairs programming (and the GOP's promotional materials astutely reminded operators about these obligations).[80] Some even integrated the programming into their news broadcasts, as they had with recordings sent from the Senate television studios since the 1960s. Now, however, thanks to satellite, they could play these programs immediately. As a result, elected officials in Washington had a new tool to shape the interpretation of political news and debates instantly, and all without leaving Capitol Hill.

By replicating network news programs, these shows blurred the line between news and partisan propaganda, and both cable operators and the GOP reaped the benefits. Clews celebrated the news show for being "as entertaining as it is incisive" and emphasized its interactivity.[81] He proudly shared how a Wisconsin programmer used an episode to launch a local debate about a potential nuclear freeze, while a Colorado one used it as part of a League of Women Voters public affairs presentation.[82] But at the end of the day, as the direct mail expert Richard Armstrong observed, these programs were "a grand-slam home run" for public relations consultants because they bypassed the scrutiny of network newsrooms and the Washington press corps. "While network-affiliated and large independent stations look disdainfully on actualities, small broadcast and cable stations gobble them up," he observed.[83] A special report in *Cablevision* made it clear why. The cable industry saw such shows as proof of "cable keeping its promise" to provide expanded viewing options and to stimulate "awareness of the cable industry and of politics in general."[84]

Eventually, the Democratic Party would learn these lessons and a decade later, Bill Clinton deployed a similar playbook to win the presidency. But in the early 1980s, the party had a much smaller and less sophisticated cable operation than the Republican one.[85] Linda Peek, the Democratic Policy Committee's communications director, explained to *Cablevision* that she oversaw a smaller Democratic staff, working in a studio housed in the Capitol basement, and focused on providing "news" clips featuring the senators to commercial broadcast stations, rather than cable television systems. Broadcasting also made sense for the communications purposes of a Democratic Party struggling to find common ground among aging New Dealers, younger centrists, and progressive activists.[86]

As the Democratic Party moved forward with its cable television initiatives, it eventually accepted the lessons John Florescu had introduced about using narrowcasting to build its "big tent" electronic coalition. The media adviser had repeatedly emphasized how cable allowed candidates to test the appeal of specific policies to different demographics. It didn't mean that candidates needed to lie or say "different things to different people" about their stances on certain issues, Florescu explained as he pitched (unsuccessfully) a cable plan to Senator Gary Hart's 1984 presidential campaign. Rather, campaigns needed to understand what issues voters in a particular media market cared about, and then connect with voters on those issues. That was the beauty of cable. It allowed candidates to connect personally with the lives and concerns of local communities—student aid in college markets, Social Security in elderly communities, and farm subsidies in rural areas.[87]

Republicans—especially more ideologically conservative ones like Gingrich who were climbing the party ladder by stoking division—increasingly deployed a different approach to cable television, one shaped more by direct mail innovations designed to mobilize a passionate and dedicated minority of voters.[88] After all, many of them had gotten to Washington by listening to figures like Richard Viguerie, the direct mail pioneer who built an electronic mailing list of small donors to grow the conservative movement with emotional messaging specifically crafted to tap into outrage.[89] Using market research into voting patterns, Viguerie developed a "psychographic profile" for individuals who felt political and geographical isolation. "Are you as sick and tired of liberal politicians as I am? Force children to be bused; appoint judges who turn murderers and rapists loose on the public," began one tirade that then encouraged direct mail recipients to channel frustrations with the status quo into support for the conservative movement.[90] In his 1988 account of the communications changes in American politics, Richard Armstrong observed that cable provided the affordability and flexibility for experimentation, just as direct mail had, and he anticipated the convergence of the two. "Imagine how much fun it will be to turn on the TV and see someone call a U.S. senator a 'baby killer' or accuse the Democratic Party of promoting 'cannibalism' and 'wife-swapping.'"[91]

Of course, Gingrich didn't go that far in his C-SPAN diatribes . . . yet. Nevertheless, his aggressive efforts to ignite controversy illuminated how a direct mail style could also attract eyeballs on cable television by stirring conflict. Such an approach stood in stark contrast to the GOP's *Conference Roundtable*, which used a *Meet the Press* style conversation to hide partisanship undergirding the "news" program. However, by the twenty-first century, these two styles— Republican messaging cloaked in the guise of news and stoking discontent—would come together in Fox News as it eventually discarded the norms of professional journalism and broke ratings records in the process. But for that to happen, cable television needed to expand its operations, and in 1984, it finally got the legislative boost it needed to do so.

10

Regulatory Consequences

By the 1980s, many "Watergate Babies" had grown up into "Atari Democrats." Coined by Chris Matthews, an aide to Speaker Tip O'Neill who would later become a prominent cable news host, the phrase referenced the popular video gaming system owned by Warner-Amex, which also owned one of the largest cable companies.[1] The term stuck, as it captured the outlook of younger centrist Democrats who saw new technology as bringing opportunities for economic growth and social justice. Figures like Tim Wirth and Al Gore led an effort to revamp New Deal liberalism with a mantra that others like Colorado's Gary Hart and Massachusetts's Paul Tsongas also used: "The problems of the 1980s demand more than the solutions of the 1930s."[2] They wanted to push the Democratic Party away from its New Deal and Great Society traditions of robust social welfare programs and support of labor unions and into the information age with tax incentives and government funding for research and development in high-tech sectors.[3]

In 1984, the growing popularity of market-based policy solutions combined with the expanding appeal of cable television inside and outside Congress to bring significant changes to the cable television industry. Finally, Senator Barry Goldwater and Representative Tim Wirth had the momentum they needed to push forward bipartisan legislation unshackling cable businesses from the last vestiges of regulations limiting their operations. Conservative Republicans and New Democrats alike celebrated this policy for "liberating" the telecommunications system from the entrenched interests of the Big Three broadcasting networks.[4]

Ronald Reagan and his FCC chairman Mark Fowler loom large in accounts of the 1984 Cable Communications Policy Act, and certainly, the deregulatory atmosphere they cultivated helped generate support for the bill, which, along with their encouragement of corporate consolidation, boosted the fortunes of the cable industry.[5] Fowler famously called television just a "toaster with pictures," showing just how much the FCC had changed since Newton Minow lamented the commercialism that had overtaken the democratic potential of the television dial.[6] By contrast, Reagan's chairman saw the marketplace as the great arbitrator of democracy. "The public's interest then, defines the public interest," he wrote in a landmark article in the *Texas Law Review* in 1982.[7] Professing a commitment to the "marketplace magic," Fowler cut 89 percent of the agency's rules for mass media, and the Justice Department approved hundreds of mergers for media businesses under Reagan and George H. W. Bush, including a whopping 414 deals in 1989, all pivotal legal and regulatory changes for cable's growth that have been well documented.[8]

And yet, across the political spectrum, elected officials, lobbyists, and citizens also shaped the 1984 landmark legislation. The policy battle over cable television engulfed local city councils and a range of congresspeople as they debated deregulation and navigated the privatization that followed.[9] In the aftermath, the growth of cable television brought greater scrutiny over the business practices and political deals that made the industry's rapid expansion possible. These national debates about the opportunities and pitfalls of a free market legislative agenda also openly underscored its consequences—the flourishing of economic inequality and political selfishness—years before neoliberalism became a controversial word.[10]

———

Nothing quite exposed the controversy surrounding government's experimentation with privatization quite like the franchise wars of the late 1970s and early 1980s, many of which captured the attention of journalists, the FBI, and eventually Congress. The FCC's deregulatory turn combined with the new programming possibilities made possible by satellite to allow cable companies to finally pursue lucrative, but costly, franchises in urban markets. The financial stakes intensified for competing cable companies and so too did consumer demand for cable—just as local officials looked for partnerships with private companies to subsidize their shrinking budgets.[11] It was a perfect storm to show what happened when government relied on private businesses to serve the public interest.

Consider the case of the cable franchising wars in Houston, which produced sensational headlines and a very real FBI investigation. As *Cablevision* observed, "a whopping lawsuit and grand jury investigation into alleged antitrust activity filled the Houston papers with wheeling and dealing, politics, and cable television lore for months. By the time it was all over, every person on the street who could read fancied himself a cable expert."[12]

It all began quietly. In 1972, a few cable companies started looking into the booming multicultural metropolitan city and asking about the franchising process.[13] The city council voted 7–1 to give the franchise to Greater Houston CATV, headed by Lester Kamin, a close friend of Mayor Louie Welch.[14] Alleging a conflict of interest, the losing company, Gulf Coast Cable Television, joined citizens groups across Houston to demand a referendum to overturn the decision.

Gayle Greer—who would later rise through the ranks of the cable company American Television and Communications (ATC) and become known as the "mother of Black cable"—got her start in cable during this franchising fight.[15] Having grown up in Tulsa, Oklahoma, Greer attended Oklahoma State University and the University of

Gayle Greer at her desk as VP of Central Opera-
tions for ATC.
Photo Credit: *Multichannel News*/Barco Library,
The Cable Center.

Houston and graduated with a master's degree in social work. As
part of her work with the Urban League in Houston, she became
involved in the push to open up the franchising process. She saw
how cable corporations, looking to expand, took advantage of the
convoluted process to secure lucrative contracts, which didn't necessarily represent the interests of the local community. Joined by
members of the NAACP, the ACLU, the Houston Jaycees, and the
Harris County Women's Political Caucus, Greer and other activists
demanded transparency and competition.[16] They went on television
and spoke in churches calling attention to the dangers of having one
company control all of the city's cable operations.

Cable companies didn't always respond kindly to such pushback.
Greer recalled that she would leave the local city council meeting
and find her tires slashed. To her, operators were "a bunch of gangsters."[17]

But the public pressure she and other activists applied worked, at first. Voters mandated that the city offer franchises to competing firms. The city council divided Houston into different areas and opened bids for companies to compete for each of them. Jim McConn, the new mayor, emphasized the importance of awarding the franchise to "people who lived in Houston, people who had been a part of building Houston."[18] Rather than follow a public and orderly process, however, court records documented how the city evaluated proposals based on political relationships, not proposed services for constituents.

McConn ended up handing the process over to the competing applicants.[19] In a preview of what would happen two decades later following the 1996 Telecommunications Act, the companies sliced and diced the city into segments that would allow all of them to make the most money. The final division of the franchises looked as if "the city had been cut like a demographic pie," noted *Cablevision*.[20] When a sixth company, Affiliated Capital Corporation, run by the former chair of the state Democratic Party Billy Goldberg, attempted to get in on the bidding, they were allegedly told "the pie had been cut."[21] Protesting a process he called a "conspiracy" to violate antitrust laws, Goldberg turned the tables on Gulf Coast (which had won the southwest Houston franchise), suing the company, the city, and the mayor for excluding him from participating in the process.[22] A federal jury found all three guilty, a decision ultimately upheld by the U.S. Court of Appeals for the Fifth Circuit.

In the end, Gulf Coast retained its franchise, but Mayor McConn lost reelection. And yet, McConn continued to defend his decision to award local partners the franchise. "Houstonians should share in Houston's goodies, and cable TV is a goodie," he contended. "We have a large black population in Houston and they pay taxes and all of those things and to eliminate them would have been a mistake in my opinion. That's what I meant by politics."[23]

There were several problems with this approach, however. First, McConn neglected to address the interests of the Latino and Asian Americans who also lived in segregated and subjugated neighborhoods.[24] More broadly, his reference to cable television as a "goodie" highlighted how he understood cable franchises as a way to make a quick buck, not to expand democratic participation by creating media access for community members or to cultivate long-term business opportunities for them. In fact, none of these local groups had experience in television that proved they could deliver on their promises. When a cable consultant's analysis of the applications pointed this out, he was fired and his report altered.[25]

And indeed, the newly established Houston cable companies were not in it for the long haul. After securing their respective franchises, they soon sold out to one of the big out-of-state cable corporations, notably Warner-Amex and Storer, both of whom were eager to add new systems to their holdings. According to a report in *Longview News-Journal*, "documents contained in a City Council Report disclosed last month that about 40 local investors accepted at least $9 million in cash and securities."[26] The mayor may have wanted local Houstonians to help build the cable operations, but local entrepreneurs just saw it as an opportunity to pocket some cash.

What happened in Houston went to one extreme, but it was not an exception. Across the country, the urban franchise wars quickly escalated in complicated and costly ways, which overwhelmingly tipped the competitive scale toward corporate cable companies with the resources to win lucrative contracts. When considering franchise applications, city councils received "flashy multimedia displays" alongside multiple binders full of hundreds of pages of cable television jargon that one study called out for being "at best inadvertently complex and at worst deliberately misleading."[27] Like in Houston, cable consultants offered advice and research for city council members as they navigated all this information. And they made no small sum doing so, with fees ranging from the $49,000 that Baltimore paid to Telecommunications Management to the $250,000 that the Cable Television Information Center made for consulting in Chicago.[28] Cable companies then complained that consultants forced them to "play to two audiences": the city and the consultant. Indeed, Tom Wheeler blamed consultants for escalating tensions between the cities and cable companies.[29] Rather than brokering a compromise, they whet the appetite of cities to demand more from the bidders.

Promises by cable companies that they would fund libraries, firehouses, and sewer systems helped to convince city councilors to choose one cable company over another, but so too did cold hard cash. In San Antonio, Storer and UA-Columbia got into a bidding war with each offering a "franchise fee agreement" of $1 million.[30] In other negotiations, the line between bribery and lobbying was also quite thin, something Tele-Communications Inc.'s (TCI) John Malone admitted. "If you take your corporate jet and fly the entire city council to see one of your systems in California, and you happen to stop in Las Vegas, I mean, is that bribery?" he asked. "I don't think it is; but on the other hand, I don't think it's proper either. And there is a lot of that going on, a lot of back scratching."[31]

The notorious "Rent-a-Citizen" strategy—in which companies offered prominent community members equity in the system if chosen—became one widely publicized tactic that cast suspicion on the entire franchising process.[32] The ethical question was tricky. Cable companies needed to bring in local businesses and investors to prove that there was an element of local ownership. ATC didn't apologize for using this strategy. Rather the company saw it as a way to encourage community involvement and to give people a stake in the company's success.[33] But, as in Houston, local stakeholders frequently sold their interests to cable corporations after securing the franchise, getting a short-term payout and relinquishing any long-term opportunity to influence the trajectory of the operation. So, in reality, it functioned more as a bribe for their support.

Warner Cable used another strategy dubbed by critics as "Rent-an-Institution."[34] It beat out ATC and TelePrompTer in the bid for Pittsburgh's cable franchise by crafting a partnership agreement that provided seventeen minority organizations with a 20 percent ownership in the system. In Warner's eyes, this demonstrated their investment in the local community and minority ownership opportunities.[35] ATC disagreed, seeing such an arrangement as a kickback, or in legal terms, creating "a preconceived and unlawful preference" for one company over the other.[36] And so, it sued the city, the mayor, the city council, and Warner-Amex.[37] The two cable companies eventually settled out of court, and *Cablevision* anticipated the legal fees alone could reach up to $450,000.[38]

And yet, in the end, it was Pittsburgh that lost. Warner had pledged to provide the city with QUBE programming and an interactive "community communications complex."[39] But such promises were costly, and by 1984, Warner (which had now merged with American Express) sold the system to TCI. Once John Malone's company had ownership of the wired infrastructure, it then forced Pittsburgh to accept its terms, which axed the idea for the community center and eliminated QUBE and other interactive services. Cities like Pittsburgh began to realize that the earlier franchise promises would never come to fruition, and so frustrated local officials accepted the terms TCI offered, seeing such basic cable systems without the bells and whistles as their only option. Tom Wheeler worried about the consequences of such overselling and under delivering. Franchising, he told NCTA members, was "at once a great promise as well as a great threat to the industry."[40] Wheeler stressed, "Government will invite itself in the moment we step on our skirts."

Nevertheless, the franchising wars dramatically expanded cable's reach. Between 1980 and 1982, cable went from 13.7 million homes wired to potentially over twenty million with new franchise contracts signed in cities like Kansas City, Phoenix, Nashville, Minneapolis, Dallas, and Cincinnati. Cable had transitioned from a "passionate affair" to a "long term relationship" with Wall Street investors, noted *Cablevision*, and it was fueled by "high yield lending," or risky junk bonds that allowed corporations to grow by leveraging credit and growing corporate debt.[41]

With this growth came the merger wave civil rights activists had feared.[42] Newspaper chains and magazines like *Newsweek* also eagerly joined the fray, either by purchasing systems or launching programming services like *Newsweek Woman*. By 1984, most of the top media corporations—Westinghouse, Capital Cities, the Tribune Company, Cox Communications, Viacom, and the Times Mirror Co. to name a few—also had investments in both broadcasting and cable. "If there were two better businesses to be in, I haven't heard about them," remarked Westinghouse CEO Daniel Ritchie.[43]

And so, broadcasters were no longer enemy number one for cable operators. Rather, as Wheeler anticipated, they now faced off against local city officials bitter over broken franchise promises, failed interactive services, and unbuilt community centers, like in Pittsburgh. And that's where the Cable Act came in.

———

On March 4, 1982, Senator Barry Goldwater introduced S.2172: the Cable Telecommunications Act.[44] The bill offered favorable terms to the cable industry, notably prohibiting telephone companies from entry into cable operations, providing a procedure for automatic franchise renewals, and eliminating local rules to set rates on pay or premium channel services.[45] It allowed cities the authority to regulate basic cable rates, while also mandating that operators set aside 10 percent of the dial for local programming and another 10 percent for programs not under a cable corporate umbrella. Such a proposed rule addressed a frustration by local officials and consumers over the growth of vertical integration in the cable industry as corporations increasingly owned the wired system and had a financial stake in the cable channels they offered. Unsurprisingly, this arrangement introduced the potential for cable companies to only disseminate channels owned by their parent companies, and discriminate against others, something that city officials and media critics alike called out.[46]

Goldwater hoped that his bill, which offered economic incentives to cable operators, expanded programming choice for consumers, and ensured more local channels and even the possibility of municipal ownership of systems for local city officials, would appease everyone by giving everyone something and nobody everything. He was wrong.

Cynthia Pols, the lobbyist for the National League of Cities (NLC), remarked that "we've never had an issue take off, in terms of interest from our membership, the way this one has, where everyone feels exactly the same about the issue regardless of their party affiliation or ideological bent."[47] They overwhelmingly opposed the jurisdictional issues at stake and how the federal government set regulatory terms.[48] City officials argued that cable constituted a "natural mono- poly," which, like telephony, meant that local governments had the right to determine rules of operations. They worried that streamlining the franchising process would slow the cash flow to local government coffers and that getting rid of rate caps on popular channels would allow cable companies to charge whatever they wanted. (They were right on both accounts.) With a grassroots army of mayors and local city officials, NLC effectively killed the legislation.[49]

Cable operators fought back, desperate to address efforts by local government to keep franchise fees high and subscription rates low. For years, Tom Wheeler and the NCTA had worked with NLC to develop seminars, share information and concerns about the fran- chising process, and develop a mutual "code of franchising prac- tices."[50] But such efforts had repeatedly failed to garner support and agreement from both sides, so Wheeler understood the importance of pushing for federal legislation.

In the wake of the failed S.2172, Wheeler focused on mobilizing the NCTA's own grassroots army: operators and subscribers. The NCTA also reframed its argument by classifying cable operations as being similar to newspapers (many of which now owned cable operations across the country) and thus called efforts to regulate programming and rates a violation of First Amendment rights.

Both strategies worked. Over twenty-five hundred telegrams arrived on Capitol Hill supporting the next round of cable legislation, S.66: the Cable Communications Policy Act of 1984.[51] Along with Goldwater, Robert "Bob" Packwood emerged as a vocal advocate for the new legislation. Since the 1970s, he had been pushing for what he called a "rational framework in which cable could develop to its fullest potential."[52] The two Republicans could not have been further apart ideologically: the Arizona senator was dubbed Mr. Conservative and committed to deregulation, while Packwood was an Oregon mod- erate more concerned about First Amendment rights. Packwood's argument about the need to pull back government regulation on media content also gained the support of the Freedom of Expression Foundation, with representatives from NCTA, NAB, MPAA, Time Inc., Gannett, AT&T, and more.[53] This organization did something

Tom Wheeler making a presentation at the Goldwater Senate bill hearing, 1984.
Photo Credit: Barco Library, The Cable Center.

significant: it brought media corporations—newspaper, magazine, broadcast, cable, and motion picture—together to support the bill.

In response to criticism from the NLC, Packwood warned them that "they're killing the goose" and needed to work with cable companies, on whom they depended to make the private investment to lay the wires local citizens wanted.[54] The NCTA agreed. Chairman of the NCTA Board of Directors Douglas Dittrick emphasized that the franchising wars had gone too far as cities tried to force cable companies to pay excessive fees or build community production studios. "The cable business is not a panacea for government budgetary problems or social injustices. When cities and other parties extract more services than the market can support, both consumers and cable must absorb the costs."[55]

Consumer advocate Ralph Nader lambasted the proposed bill, calling it a "bail out" for cable operators who "made promises to get franchises" and "want to renege on legally binding commitments."[56] Nader had aligned with cable operators a decade earlier in their efforts to break up the networks and use cable television as a vehicle to empower consumers.[57] By the 1980s, however, cable companies were no longer the scrappy underdogs. The industry now had deep pockets and powerful allies in Congress, and the bill moved forward despite such criticisms.

On October 6, Tim Wirth introduced a House version of the bill by emphasizing the pressing need to address the "confusing and often counter-productive array of current franchising practices." He also stressed the importance of expanding cable to ensure people have access to the "wide diversity of services and sources" and to "establish a national diversity policy" for the industry, in both employment and programming.[58]

Negotiations continued during the winter and into the spring but by the summer had come to a standstill, thanks to NLC's opposition. Packwood wrote letters to mayors across the country warning them that waiting until the next year to resolve the differences "may be too late" as it would allow the FCC and the courts to set the rules, without their input.[59] Barry Goldwater took another approach, writing a letter to FCC Chairman Mark Fowler urging him that "if we don't get legislation out of the House, I want you to throw the whole damn book at the cities and give cable everything you can under your power." Frustrated by what he called the "double-crossing, double-talk, and downright lying" that he had witnessed from the city officials on the issue, Goldwater wanted to "get the word across to them."[60] In the final days and even hours, legislators worked to find a compromise among the NLC, the U.S. Conference of Mayors, and the NCTA, with Wirth warning his cable constituents to get on board or risk "los[ing] credibility."[61] Finally, on October 11, 1984, the bill passed by a voice vote in both the House and the Senate.

Packwood celebrated it as a win for consumers eager for cable's unique services.[62] Goldwater agreed, calling the bill "pro-consumer, pro-city, and pro-cable."[63] After President Reagan signed the bill into law on October 30, Tim Wirth declared it a "milestone in communications policy." America, he pronounced, "stands on the threshold of an information revolution which promises to enrich and enhance the life of every citizen. Cable television, perhaps more than any other medium, has the potential to deliver the benefits of the information age in the homes of our citizens."[64]

The legislation limited the rates local governments could charge companies and also the services they could demand from operators. Cable companies had complained about spending millions building cable systems only to face "arbitrary" political decisions at the local level that could interfere with their investments. The bill thus attempted to standardize the franchising process to ensure that franchises could not be taken away from a "company that is doing a good job."[65] After two years, the bill stipulated, companies could raise rates without local approval. Finally, the bill also required that cable companies meet Equal Employment Opportunity standards, on which they had fallen behind other media industries.

On the whole, cable operators, the trade press, and the NCTA celebrated the passage of the bill. Of course, the NCTA highlighted the value of its own lobbying work. But it also emphasized the benefits of corporate cooperation, rather than the competition that had fueled franchise wars just a few years earlier. As industry members gathered at the Atlantic Cable Show, they cheered the economic opportunities the bill created for them. ATC Chairman and CEO Trygve Myhren hammered this lesson home to his colleagues by emphasizing how collaboration—coordinating marketing promotions, clustering programming offerings, and sharing training workshops—worked to advance the industry's bottom line.[66] There was plenty of money to go around, he emphasized, especially if the industry continued to produce programming that consumers would refuse to part with, regardless of price.[67]

That soon became the problem, however. The public wanted cable, and increasingly, saw it as an essential part of their lives. When operators raised rates, subscribers felt trapped, so they voiced their frustrations to their congressional representatives, turning cable regulation into a new type of political football.

———

"Happy Deregulated New Year!" wrote James Mooney to NCTA members on Christmas Eve in 1986.[68] Five days later, controls officially came off cable rates.[69] Cable executives and operators across the country celebrated—and then promptly made a major miscalculation. Over the next few years, basic cable rates skyrocketed, increasing by an average of 90 percent.[70] Cable companies framed the rising rates as a consequence of market demand, not a monopolistic tactic they used to squeeze out more profits. "We're governed by our consumers. With deregulation, the temptation is there to raise rates, but in reality, the marketplace dictates what you get. Once we exceed the perceived value of cable you can still get into trouble," explained a marketing director at Columbia Cable.[71] Such a remark certainly distorted how the cable market actually worked—most franchises allowed only one operator to serve the local community—even as it also alluded to the public backlash that cable companies anticipated from raising the rates.

And that's exactly what happened. Rate hikes infuriated the public. So too did the lagging customer service and the long waits for service fixes. The negative image of "the cable guy" who missed appointments and overcharged for services became fodder for late night comedians and stirred the anger of subscribers.[72] Even operators acknowledged their customer service was "crummy."[73] Still, expanding their customer service simply wasn't a priority for most companies and people like Gayle Greer called this out. ATC had recruited her after watching her impressive community relations skills fighting cable companies in Houston and then later Fort Wayne. By 1985, she had broken through gender and racial barriers to become vice president of central operations at the company. And yet, she continued to draw attention to the promises made and broken by cable operators, whom she felt were too focused on internal operations and less concerned about subscriber and community needs. "We still talk about service, but you can't just talk about it," she told her colleagues. "You have to do something about it."[74]

Rural Americans had other grievances. Many of them had purchased their own satellite dishes to pick up the exciting new cable channels transmitted celestially without paying for a cable subscription. Cable companies now felt like their programming was being pirated. Networks like HBO began scrambling their signals to keep programming from independent satellite dish owners. Unless, that is, those owners paid for a descrambling set-top box that would allow them to subscribe to individual cable networks for a fee.[75]

Finally, local broadcasters started airing their frustrations as well. In 1965, the FCC had enacted a "must carry" rule. Reflecting the view of cable television as merely an extension of broadcast, the rule forced cable operators to carry all local broadcast channels. By the 1980s, such a rule became a business liability for operators who now had a diverse range of niche programming available via satellite and not enough channel slots. Carrying all the local broadcasting channels, particularly the smaller independent ones, took up valuable space on a dial that was certainly more expansive but still limited to only a couple dozen channels.

Ted Turner hated these must-carry requirements that benefited local broadcasters at the expense of programmers like him. And so, he led a lawsuit to challenge the rule's constitutionality. Initially, he was successful. In 1985, the U.S. Court of Appeals for the District of Columbia Circuit agreed that these must-carry rules violated operators' First Amendment rights. The NCTA called the decision "a strong confirmation of cable's status as a First Amendment editor" and a "victory for our consumers." The NAB expressed deep disappointment, warning that small local television stations would struggle to survive without must-carry provisions.[76] With the FCC unwilling to rewrite must-carry rules, broadcasters pushed for action from their allies on Capitol Hill.[77]

With rate caps eliminated, prices rising, and consumer demand intensifying, the issue of cable television was once again ripe for political debate, particularly for someone like Al Gore, now a senator with White House aspirations. Like Wirth, Gore was passionate about tapping into the potential of new technology. He organized a monthly brown bag seminar called "Congressional Clearing House on the Future" to discuss issues like computer networking, and he even put on a workshop for his congressional colleagues on how to use computers.[78] He traveled to computer industry conferences and wanted computer scientists to explain to him the newest technological developments, showing Gore's respect and appreciation of Silicon Valley as a partner and ally.[79]

And yet, his relationship with the cable industry was much more tumultuous. Gore had supported pole rate regulation, lauded the introduction of C-SPAN onto the House floor, and even voted for the industry's deregulation in 1984. But he watched the rapid growth of a corporate Cable America—and the conflicts these companies generated with local politicians and citizens—with politically calculated concern. He soon found a corporate villain on whom to unleash his frustrations and elevate his national profile: TCI's John Malone.

The TCI executive had become one of the most powerful and respected businessmen in cable television, and he embodied its rugged and entrepreneurial spirit. His roots were firmly in the East Coast establishment: raised in Milford, Connecticut, he studied economics and electrical engineering at Yale, where he received his bachelor's degree, and Johns Hopkins, where he received his doctorate.[80] He started his career working at the Bell Labs on computer science and video telephony, while also developing an economic analysis of how corporations responded to regulations.

Malone brought all those experiences with him to the cable industry when he accepted a job at Jerrold, the cable electronics company, and then later the cable division of General Instrument Corporation. In 1972, a Denver cable executive, Bob Magness, offered him a job running a struggling cable company called TCI. The job interested him because it offered tremendous autonomy, potential for growth, and it allowed him to move his family to Denver, a relaxed western city that appealed to him because of its stark contrast to Connecticut.[81]

TCI was in financial trouble when Malone arrived, but over the next decade, he built it into the largest cable operation in the country. Rather than engaging in the franchise wars directly, he grew the company by hunting for bargains, and ruthlessly looking for acquisition opportunities among companies that had overpaid in franchising fees and promises and were deeply in debt and looking for an out.[82] During the early 1980s, Malone approximated that the company made an acquisition almost once a week.[83] Such deals helped to advance the largest private construction project in recent history: cable companies invested over $15 billion into wiring American homes for cable from 1984 through 1992. TCI had become the biggest player in the industry during this process. In 1983, the company had over 2.5 million subscribers, the most in the country.[84] By 1989, it had almost eight million.[85]

TCI also strategically invested in new niche programming networks (something that Tom Whitehead had warned against in the cabinet report a decade earlier when he pushed for a policy mandating separation between hardware and software), which grew from twenty-eight in 1980 to over seventy-four by 1989. TCI had a stake in thirty-three of these cable networks.[86] For the past decade, Malone had crafted deals with entrepreneurs like Robert Johnson, the founder of Black Entertainment Television (BET). TCI took a 20 percent stake in the new cable network and helped secure carriage on its systems. For Johnson, the deal was an incredible opportunity to launch a new media business, one that tapped into the market of Black consumers by "mirroring the black community" on the screen.[87] Later he even recalled that if Malone had wanted 80 percent of the company, he would have agreed.

Such programming was notable because it broke the mold of what broadcast had done—something Malone constantly emphasized as central to the industry's success. It allowed for experimentation, even as it put pressure on cable networks to do something unique that was "edgier, more clever, and more outrageous than anything you'd see on broadest television," noted one programmer.[88] It also generated loyalty from subscribers, and even as rates increased, they stayed on.

In an age of corporate raiders, John Malone embodied the mantra made popular by Michael Douglas's character Gordon Gekko in the 1987 film *Wall Street*: "Greed, for the lack of a better word, is good." In fact, the legislative debate that brought Malone to Washington in November 1989 became a referendum on that very issue: is greed good?

Malone arrived on Capitol Hill ready to defend his reputation, his company, and his industry. Televised by C-SPAN, the very network that TCI helped to fund, the congressional hearings played out like a courtroom drama. At stake was the 1984 Cable Communications

John Malone seated with the TCI logo
in background, circa 1990.
Photo Credit: Barco Library, The Cable
Center.

Act, which had propelled both new programming and rate increases.
Malone was intent on celebrating the former—whereas Al Gore, who
was leading the hearing, was fixated on the latter.

For Gore, John Malone was the perfect anti-hero, someone who
stood in contrast to New Democrats' belief of "doing well by doing
good" by putting the pursuit of profit above all else. Listing the rate
hikes and coercive business practices that allowed cable operators
to function as a monopoly, Gore quickly homed in on TCI, which
he declared was "hell bent on total domination of the marketplace."
The senator was just getting started. "In another Senate committee there was considerable concern about the Super Bowl possibly
moving to pay per view," he added. "I think they're focusing on the
wrong danger. I think the real concern might be whether or not TCI
will own the NFL outright."[89]

For the man who would later proudly declare to have "cable industry tattooed on one of my rear-end cheeks and T.C.I. on the other," Gore's attacks were both personal and professional insults.[90] Malone saw cable as allowing "niche businesses"—like BET, C-SPAN, Discovery, and the Vision Interfaith Network—to survive and serve communities overlooked on the broadcast dial. When Gore called him "Darth Vader" running a modern day "Cosa Nostra," Malone countered that he was more like the "Wizard of Oz . . . credited with a lot more power and influence than I really yield."[91] While such a statement made Gore chuckle, it did little to calm the tensions between the crusading senator and the unrelenting businessman. "Do you believe your size and power have made your company arrogant and heavy handed?" Senator Gore asked the TCI chairman, who refused to apologize for making money as he defended his industry and his business practices.[92]

After listing rate hikes pursued by other cable companies in his home state of Tennessee—99 percent in Crossville, 113 percent in Nashville, 115 percent in Chattanooga, 117 percent in Murfreesboro—Gore then turned his attention to his gripe with TCI: the company's refusal to make its popular programming (which it used to motivate people to sign up for cable subscriptions) available to rural satellite owners in his own state.[93] Malone didn't back down. What Gore called unfair to rural satellite owners, he considered a shrewd business strategy that cultivated demand for cable programming, which "our subscribers wanted and desired."[94]

Gore then brought up an incident in Jefferson City, Missouri, when TCI allegedly threatened a cable consultant during the franchising process. "We know where you live, where your office is, and who you owe money to," an employee reportedly told him. "We are having your house watched. We are going to use this information to destroy you. You made a big mistake messing around with TCI." Malone didn't deny the allegations; he admitted that he "lost a lot of sleep" over the incident and had fired the employee when he heard about it.[95] The civil antitrust case that followed cost the company $10.8 million in damages. Nevertheless, Malone forcefully argued that such practices were an aberration, not the standard.

The Tennessee senator then turned to another issue of concern: TCI's ability to make or break a new cable network by controlling whether a huge swath of the country could see it. Such carriage decisions, Gore contended, meant that TCI also exerted unfair control over cable content. In particular, Gore accused the company of using such leverage to prevent NBC from developing a 24/7 news channel that would compete with CNN, in which Malone owned a stake. Malone denied the allegations and once again defended his vertical integration strategy of owning both cable operating systems and programs as simply good business—which benefited the consumer and the shareholder. It allowed the company to compete against other media giants while also letting it gamble on experimental programming. What Gore saw as manipulating the market and limiting competition, Malone understood as encouraging diverse approaches to television.

Gore concluded the hearings by bringing in a variety of witnesses to show how marketplace competition between operators could ameliorate cable's malpractices. A mayor testified about the story of Multivision, the cable operator in West Tennessee that raised rates by 40 percent in 1988. He claimed that when he tried to contact the company to discuss the rate hike, he was ignored. As citizens—many of whom relied on cable because of the poor broadcast signal in the area—became angry, the mayor developed a plan for the city to purchase the cable system from Multivision so the city could run it. The price tag—$3.7 million—was significantly higher than the assessed value of the system, which ran at only $1 million. Eventually, the local city board decided to award another franchise to a second cable company, which then motivated Multivision to lower its rates and return telephone messages.

For Gore, the lesson was clear: competition worked with the right government intervention. This was not New Deal liberalism with government rules regulating market conduct and providing a safety net for those it didn't benefit. Nor was it Reagan's celebration of market forces as determining outputs. Rather, it reflected the New Democrats' approach to policy: helping the market function better for all, in theory.[96] Over the next three years, Gore pushed forward legislation based on this idea, which he emphasized at the end of the hearing had bipartisan support in Congress. In the process, the young, ambitious senator—who had already run for president once—found a politically popular national issue: fighting cable corporations, even those like TCI that had less to do with the cable issues in his state.

By the end of 1989, the industry trade press reported what it saw as the writing on the wall given the "fiery rhetoric" and the intensity of "anticable bashing" on Capitol Hill: reregulation was coming.[97] But the growing clamor for regulation faced two significant obstacles: a new Republican president eager to demonstrate his conservative credentials and another Atari Democrat willing to go to bat for an industry in his home state.

11

Winning at Any Cost

In 1974, Tim Wirth was bright-eyed and eager to bring new ideas to Congress. "The old way doesn't work anymore," he proclaimed during his successful campaign to unseat a Republican incumbent that year.[1] Almost two decades of political battle had drained such optimism, however, and on April 8, 1992, he made a stunning announcement. Despite being only fifty-three years old and in his first term in the Senate, Wirth declared that he would not seek reelection.

In a khaki jacket and light blue shirt with a white and red speckled tie, the Coloradoan held a press conference denouncing the current political climate he saw as ripping Americans apart and threatening democratic institutions.[2] "Personal ambition and partisan bickering set too much of our agenda," he lamented. "Our rules are too weak to keep these divisive forces in check and the egos too strong to submerge in a common defense of the institution itself."[3] Campaigns, he said, are "increasingly shrill, negative, and devoid of content"; he did not want to be a "participant in such a destructive exercise."

Wirth's poignant critique, however, overlooked his own role in unintentionally ushering in such an environment. The flowering of cable television, which he had helped make happen, allowed for more substantive political discourse, in theory. And yet, in practice, a more salacious approach had triumphed due to a combination of business incentives, changing journalistic practices, loosening FCC regulations, and growing consumer demand.

During the 1980s, "soft news" began to overwhelm the national media environment as new publications like *USA Today* showed the profit potential of infusing the news with entertainment and colorful graphics.[4] Searching to unearth the next major political scandal in the wake of Watergate, journalists also began asking more personal questions, including the one about marital infidelity that torpedoed Wirth's fellow New Democrat Gary Hart's presidential aspirations in 1987.[5] That same year also saw the end of the Fairness Doctrine, one of the remaining controversial and consequential rules on the books that shaped broadcasting's civic conduct (and a rule that notably didn't explicitly apply to cable). Mark Fowler called the requirement on broadcasters to cover fairly issues of public importance a "misguided government policy" that chilled speech.[6] With the growth of cable television, Fowler's FCC contended that the expanded television marketplace ensured a diversity of perspectives—with no regulations necessary.[7] Not everyone agreed and a strange coalition of liberals and conservatives came together to attempt to enshrine the doctrine into law via bipartisan legislation.[8] But Ronald Reagan had the last say. Once again, he promised Americans that the marketplace competition could serve "freedom" while also safeguarding First Amendment rights that had long been denied under such regulations. He vetoed the bill, relegating the Fairness Doctrine to merely a relic of the broadcasting past.[9]

The presidential election the next year exposed the type of political behavior that would triumph in a cable future, much to the dismay of figures like Wirth. Attack ads had circulated on television for over two decades, but that year, the infamous "Willie Horton" advertisement took negative campaigning to a new level that allowed both racism and gullibility to surface.[10] As communications scholar Kathleen Hall Jamieson wrote in the aftermath of the election in her book *Dirty Politics*, the Horton advertisement "exploited the psychological quirks that characterize humans," notably a pack-rat-like mentality formed by appealing to fears over facts and personalizing political coverage for viewers by connecting it to "true crime" entertainment narratives.[11] And cable television made it all possible. Indeed, the election revealed what an effective tool cable could be for appealing to darker impulses of hate and racism. It may have worked, but it repulsed millions of Americans who turned off the news and decided to stay home from the polls that year, which featured the lowest voter turnout since 1924.[12]

Wirth made a powerful protest statement by dropping out of the race four years later. And yet, his congressional career made clear the political and economic stakes and the consequences, both good and ill, of cable television's privatized public sphere. In different ways, the 1988 election and the battle for cable's reregulation that soon followed elevated the political profile of the cable industry, launching experiments to fuel anger and build new types of community networks that would soon become standard political practices in Cable America.

———

The campaign that lifted Vice President George H. W. Bush to the White House by sinking American political discourse into the mud began in the spring of 1988. Bush struggled to inspire both the broader public and New Right activists, who saw him as too moderate and distrusted that he would be a true conservative heir to the Reagan legacy.[13] That left him floundering in general election polls even as he inched closer to winning the Republican nomination.

An independent expenditure committee, the National Security Political Action Committee (NSPAC), wanted to boost Bush's campaign and it reached out to Republican political consultant Tony Fabrizio for ideas.[14] Changes to campaign finance laws in the 1970s and the 1976 *Buckley v. Valeo* Supreme Court decision allowed "independent expenditures" from organizations like NSPAC to advocate for issues and candidates independent from the campaign itself. According to the Supreme Court, such advocacy fell under the protections of the First Amendment, which meant that these groups could spend an unlimited amount of funds. In 1980, Ronald Reagan and the Republican Party had reaped the benefits of this loophole in the new campaign finance rules. Organizations like the National Conservative Political Action Committee and the Fund for a Conservative Majority spent millions to support Reagan and a handful of Republican Senate candidates by using fear, distortion, and fabrication to tar, and then unseat, incumbent Democrats.[15] The NSPAC learned a powerful lesson from the "Tuesday night massacre" that delivered the Senate and the White House to the Republican Party that year: attack advertisements that tapped into the emotions of "politically passive" voters could boost the GOP electoral chances all while allowing the candidates to distance themselves from mudslinging.[16]

Eight years later, as the NSPAC looked for ways to help the fledgling Bush campaign, Fabrizio—the president of Multi Media Services, which helped Republican candidates place media advertisements—urged them to develop ads that would change the narrative around Bush. They collaborated on a "direct response ad" that compiled clips of Bush's career—from his plane being shot down during World War II to his diplomatic leadership roles to his work as Reagan's VP. Fabrizio stressed how the ad's targeted distribution, not its content, mattered most. It aired during the *Morton Downey Jr. Show*, a conservative tabloid talk show with a host who cultivated the kinds of confrontations and angry outbursts that would make Jerry Springer and Rush Limbaugh famous and wealthy in the upcoming years.[17]

The response shocked even Fabrizio. After running the ad only ten times during the program, thirty-two thousand people called the campaign eager to donate money to support Bush. Thousands more tried to call the phone bank but couldn't get through. It was a valuable lesson about the importance of advertising placement.

As Election Day neared, Fabrizio and the NSPAC set a strategy for the upcoming months: shift to attack ads after Labor Day, target specific demographics in battleground states likely to decide the election, and experiment with running the ads in new media.[18] The question was just what line of attack to pursue.

Like Bush's campaign, Fabrizio's team paid attention to a July *Reader's Digest* article about Massachusetts's furlough program, begun by Francis Sargent, the Republican gubernatorial predecessor to Bush's Democratic opponent and current governor, Michael Dukakis.[19] During Dukakis's administration, however, William Horton, a Black man convicted as an accessory to felony murder and given a life sentence, violated his furlough by going to Maryland, where he held a young white couple hostage, assaulting the man and raping the woman. Led by campaign manager Lee Atwood and media consultant Roger Ailes, Bush's campaign had focus group research that showed attacks on Dukakis's record on crime appealed to southern and blue-collar white voters, which the Republican Party had worked hard to flip from the Democratic Party.[20] And so, they hammered home criticism of the furlough program and the danger posed by a man they now simply called "Willie" and classified as a "convicted murderer." During stump speeches, Bush even incorrectly stated that he had "murdered again."[21]

The embellished and incorrect narrative began to take hold. That's when Fabrizio and the NSPAC stepped in to transform it into one of the most infamous, but effective, political advertisements in American history.

The NSPAC only had a $1 million budget for its media buys, so Fabrizio urged his clients to spend it on cable television "to get the biggest bang for the buck."[22] The bang came from the shock value it generated. It featured a mug shot of Horton as well as a picture of his arrest before highlighting the words "kidnapping, stabbing, raping" to show the difference between "Bush and Dukakis on crime."[23] The ad appalled many in the mainstream media because it used the harmful racist trope of a Black man assaulting a white woman to reach the very voters who had left the Democratic Party because of its embrace of civil rights two decades earlier. It advanced white supremacist ideas about Black criminality, stoking both fear and division.

That was the point. Fabrizio understood that cable allowed the team to target southern white conservative voters and at a much cheaper price than network television. That's why he placed advertisements on the Christian Broadcasting Network and Nashville Network. He also ran the advertisement on Lifetime, hoping that its overwhelmingly female audience would be moved by the issue of rape.

While he later denied that racial politics drove the efforts—claiming that he would have done the same thing if the criminal had been white—both the NSPAC and the official Bush campaign certainly accepted the votes that such racist fearmongering inspired.

The response was immediate. "We started getting deluged with phone calls from media outlets across the country," explained Fabrizio.[24] The controversy sparked by the ad then generated free media time. The broadcast networks ran clips of the ad and pundits discussed it on talk shows that had proliferated thanks to the 24/7 nature of cable programs.[25] Fabrizio took pride in this fact. "I love when I speak today and say how many people saw the Willie Horton spot and everyone raises their hand."[26] But he gleefully noted, "We never paid to put the Willie Horton spot on broadcast TV at all." Even Michael Dukakis's campaign advertising manager, Fran Albin, acknowledged the "incredible return" the NSPAC got on its investment.[27] "It got a devastating message out," she explained, because "even if people didn't have cable, they were made aware of the spot because it was picked up."

Because the NSPAC created it, Bush could distance himself from the controversial ad, even as his campaign capitalized on the growing attention and the white backlash the ad ignited.[28] The campaign soon released its own advertisement attacking Dukakis as "soft on crime," which didn't have the Horton mug shot but made the same argument about the Massachusetts governor's parole program.[29] And, following Fabrizio's lead, it also purchased advertisements on cable, even though it didn't make the medium a priority in the way the NSPAC did. In the end, the Bush campaign spent about $1.3 million or 5 percent of its advertising budget on cable buys.[30]

The Dukakis campaign struggled to effectively respond. His team attempted to tap into growing critiques of negative campaigning itself, with Dukakis speaking to the camera in an ad to say "I'm fed up with it. Haven't seen anything like it in the 25 years of public life, George Bush's negative T.V. ads: distorting my record, full of lies, and he knows it."[31] Dukakis also tried to get this message out on cable, with the campaign spending $800,000, or 3 percent of its total TV advertising budget, on major national cable networks: CNN, ESPN,

Turner Broadcasting, and USA Network.[32] It was certainly affordable. A thirty-second cable buy in Boston ran about $300 whereas
a broadcasting spot had an average price tag of $3,000. And yet, the
campaign quickly learned that *how* cable was used (both the message
and its placement) mattered.[33]

Indeed, the Massachusetts governor had a fundamentally different
approach to new communications technology and instead relied on
the dynamic duo of satellite and cable television to build electronic
coalitions and bypass the mainstream press. In the fall of 1987, with
his eye on the Democratic nomination, Dukakis had worked with
the Collect Satellite Network to develop a program for college campuses across the country. For under $8,000, Dukakis's presidential
campaign produced an event at the University of Texas-Austin where
the candidate delivered short remarks and then answered questions
from students on campus *and* from students at universities across
the country who, thanks to satellite technology, could watch the
speech in real time and call in with questions. The event made a bold
statement about Dukakis's commitment to collaborating with the
growing tech industry, something that had lifted his own state's economic fortunes under his watch and transformed its reputation from
"Taxachusetts" into the "Massachusetts Miracle."[34] It also allowed
him to connect with voters directly and affordably during the early
days of the primary.

Dukakis continued to deploy this strategy to win the nomination.
On January 12, 1988, the governor arranged an event in which cable
operators (and some local broadcasters with satellites) could bring
a live one-hour program to elderly viewers in Iowa, South Dakota,
Minnesota, and Illinois—all for a total cost of $7,882.[35] Two months
later, Dukakis set up a conversation with high school students called
"Mike Dukakis Talks to America's Next Generation." Local party
officials in states like Maryland, Florida, and Minnesota organized
groups of students with access to cable television so that they could
ask questions of Dukakis from afar.[36]

The satellite strategy allowed him to be in many places at once—
and the novel communication efforts themselves garnered media
attention. "Even on the rare occasions when Massachusetts Gov.

Michael Dukakis isn't campaigning in Iowa these days," wrote a journalist from St. Paul, Minnesota, "he's campaigning in Iowa . . . with the help of a satellite television link."[37] The campaign looked for new ways to promote its events, including on weather station crawls and cable channel guides.[38]

Of course, the bare-bones approach to production had its downsides. After one satellite appearance on a national network news program, Gregory Harney, an executive producer at Boston's public television program, wrote Dukakis a personal letter expressing concern about "lighting, video and background" that made him "look pasty, haggard, and sinister." Worrying that "our next president must not in the future appear under anything but the best circumstances," Harney observed that "it was not the usual good quality you get when the network engineers and technicians do the job."[39]

Nevertheless, the benefits outweighed the negatives, notably the instantaneous connection to multiple communities and the connections forged with specific demographics on the very issues that might motivate them to vote for the Democratic ticket. After winning the nomination, the presidential campaign expanded its satellite strategy. It immediately worked to install two dishes on the top of the campaign headquarters building in Boston and secure a cable connection with Cablevision, the cable company that served the area.[40]

The Dukakis team also built a network of cable operators willing to air its programs and crafted a plan for advertisement buys on cable systems that was attentive to the demographics of each community and the issues that might resonate with local voters. In Oyster Bay, Long Island, for example, the team highlighted the importance of issues like "crime, drugs, healthcare, childcare, family issues."[41] Most cable operators eagerly worked with the campaign on political programming offered directly to their viewers; some (like Ann Arbor's Columbia Cablevision) even provided television time on public access programs for free.[42]

Even as he took to the campaign trail, Dukakis continued to participate in events that used satellite to build an electronic coalition.

On October 19, he traveled to Hull, Illinois, and held a live "Rural Cable Teleconference."[43] Farmers gathered on a nine-hundred-acre farm to ask Dukakis questions, but so too did satellite viewers in over twenty states across the country. The campaign billed it as "the first-ever such satellite event in a general election Presidential campaign."[44] Press releases and campaign talking points emphasized the personal connection Dukakis forged with individual voters, in person and via satellite, and his willingness to "talk about the issues that matter to real people."[45]

The teleconference was carefully orchestrated, however, allowing the campaign to control the structure and content of the discussion. For example, campaign workers had reached out to state Democratic leaders to encourage them to host local viewing parties at "a home, school, community center, church—any place that has cable television."[46] The national team then provided the Massachusetts governor with information about each specific watch party, noting the details of the event locations, the participants, the questioners (identified in advance), and the specifics of the questions.[47]

The local press eagerly covered these events and highlighted their engagement factor. "Area Folks Get Answers from Dukakis," read one headline from the *Lansing State Journal* after a satellite town hall meeting that connected voters in Iowa, Michigan, and Minnesota with the candidate.[48] This too was thanks to behind-the-scenes work from the Dukakis campaign, which pushed state party officials to invite the local press to watch parties and other events—knowing that compared to national journalists, local reporters would be less jaded and less critical of staged political productions.[49]

Satellite events also allowed the campaign to build an image of Dukakis sitting down with citizens "in their living room," in direct contrast to Bush, who focused only on "phony issues" and "negative personal attacks." In the final weeks of the election, the campaign expanded this innovative media strategy even further. It hosted five satellite "Town Hall" meetings, arranged for the governor to appear on live interviews with CNN's Larry King, and sent his family members to be guests on the syndicated *Donahue* talk show. These appearances aimed to signal Dukakis's willingness to meet voters where they were, in contrast to Bush.[50] He even took C-SPAN appearances seriously, seeing the potential "41 million subscribers" as viewership with "tremendous growth potential."[51]

Cablecasting fit perfectly into the key message of the Dukakis campaign: that he was about substance and vision for the future, while the Bush campaign simply wanted to use negative advertisements and superficial sound bites to derail political discussions and distract from his past record. "Dan Quayle thinks sound bites are enough to get his thoughts out," explained one press release, which then pointed to an upcoming satellite town hall meeting as an example of "Dukakis' resolve to take the issue to the voters."[52] Cable and satellite also helped the Democratic campaign expand party operations and sell a message of individual empowerment, tapping into earlier blue-sky ideas that imagined cable as an electronic town hall. At a time when scholars and journalists debated what exactly "teledemocracy" looked like and whether it strengthened or weakened civic engagement and voter knowledge, the Dukakis team spun these publicity efforts as both technologically savvy and populist.[53]

Such a strategy also fulfilled practical needs confronting the campaign, of course. Satellite appearances were cheap and allowed Dukakis to control the parameters of the conversation. He could answer pre-scripted questions from town hall viewers, not hard-hitting questions from the Washington press corps, which had gained tremendous influence in shaping election discourse over the previous two decades.[54] It let him appear open and responsive, while reducing the risk of getting tripped up by a tough question.

Despite Dukakis's efforts to use technology to stimulate political participation and shape the media narrative around the campaign, he couldn't escape the negativity unleashed by the Bush campaign, the NSPAC, and the cable dial. The effectiveness of GOP messaging revealed something that Newt Gingrich knew well: confrontation attracted eyeballs. As Bush's media adviser, Roger Ailes hammered home this message as he delighted in the nonstop media debate about the campaign's effective use of negative advertising. "Let's face it," he explained in a postelection conversation with other consultants and journalists, "there are three things that the media are interested in: pictures, mistakes, and attacks. . . . And if you need coverage, you attack and you will get coverage."[55]

Consumer demand also seemed to play a role. One *New York Times* article traced the dissemination of anti-Semitic, racist, and false information to voters by PACs and even extremist groups through videotapes and direct mail, and it highlighted how "negative campaigning, once started at the national level, has spread as state party officials apply national themes to their own efforts."[56] According to *Chicago Tribune* columnist Mike Royko, journalists, academics, and pundits may have lamented the 1988 campaign as the "most disgusting in history," but it appealed to a public that preferred watching brawls on *Geraldo Rivera* over *Masterpiece Theatre*.[57] "The majority of Americans, deep in their souls, prefer a dirty, shin-kicking, nasty, uncomplicated campaign," he wrote following the election. "All in all, it was a worthwhile, constructive campaign because it brought out a profound truth about millions of Americans: they hate each other's guts."

This wasn't surprising to those familiar with targeting technology, however. As direct mail expert Richard Armstrong explained that year, cable had a "democratizing effect on the use of television in politics, making its power accessible to candidates who never would have had an opportunity before."[58] Yes, it allowed for elected officials to speak more extensively and directly on specific issues—but he noted that, just as with the direct mailing industry, it resulted in "more emotion[al], more divisive, and more polarizing" presentation of the issues.[59]

And that was by design. Armstrong watched Republicans and Democrats use new media very differently. "Democrats have lots of registered voters and no money. Republicans have lots of money and comparatively few registered voters," he observed. "As a result, the GOP has both the means and the motivation for trying new technology." Dukakis and the Democratic Party saw satellite and cable television as a way to broaden its coalition and address the different policy concerns of its various voting blocs.[60] Republicans, especially the more right-leaning ones, worked to knit together a smaller but more active and ideologically rigid network of conservative voters.[61] The 1988 election showed that the GOP strategy of targeted mudslinging captured the attention of these demographics, exactly in the way that Fabrizio had planned. He later explained that he and the NSPAC jumped on the Horton issue because they saw it as something that would "define Dukakis as not one of us."[62] As Fabrizio would go on to emphasize when advising conservatives on how they could win at the ballot box, they should use new technology to control their message—and in a way that fractured the public. "Elections are all about polarization," he told an audience gathered at a Conservative Summit hosted by the National Review Institute in 1994. "You polarize based on ideological lines, not on partisan lines and when we are able to do that, we are successful."[63]

Cutting-edge research from the advertising industry backed up Fabrizio's claims. Marketers at the time emphasized the importance of "relationship marketing"—studying consumer data to find the "right customer" and building a brand that emphasized shared values in a narrowly defined community in direct contrast to others.[64] Such branding emphasized personal empowerment and individual needs while also encouraging consumers to ignore those who didn't share their interests. Advertisers understood that bestowing privilege and entitlements on some at the expense of others could generate tremendous social divides—but they embraced such strategies anyway because they were good for business.

Deploying such tactics in campaigns brought tremendous profits for media consultants like Fabrizio and Ailes—who increasingly saw themselves as central to the political process—and for the cable networks and operatives who began to rake in political advertising dollars. Following the 1988 election, *Cablevision* ran an article highlighting the Horton spot as "a cable exclusive," one that had firmly pushed the medium from "barely a player in the national political ad game four short years ago" to becoming "a recognized big shot."[65] Such a boost to business came with a cost to civic life, though. That year, many voters chose to tune out from politics entirely because of the campaign's mean-spirited nature.[66]

The changing dynamics on display during the 1988 election reverberated beyond presidential politics. As Tim Wirth soon learned, such negativity also pervaded senatorial campaigns, and perhaps more distressing to the Coloradoan, the policymaking process as the debate over cable legislation escalated.

———

Tim Wirth took criticism waged by figures like Al Gore about the 1984 cable bill personally. He had helped craft the legislation that allowed the industry to flourish and proudly watched cable executives expand corporate operations in his home state. He certainly understood the need for what he called "fine-tuning" of the 1984 act, particularly to address the customer service problems and those who had taken advantage of deregulation to maximize short-term profits. But when the Commerce Committee brought up a bill in 1990 to reregulate cable television, Wirth argued that it simply went "well beyond the scope of basic rates and customer service" and would serve as a "devastating blow to the cable television industry."[67] Echoing John Malone, he contended that such an approach would discourage investments into new programming.

And so, on September 28, 1990, when Senate Majority Leader George J. Mitchell (D-ME) brought the bill up for debate, Wirth—with the support of Republicans Bob Packwood and Malcolm Wallop—blocked the legislation by objecting to a time limit on debate.[68] Without sixty senators to vote for cloture to cut off debate, this tactic effectively killed the bill. Gore and Republican John Danforth, one of the bill's other sponsors, were frustrated and initially refused to sit down with Wirth to discuss a compromise. Danforth promised Congress would revisit the issue but reiterated his commitment to a "tough" policy that reregulated cable.[69]

Wirth's move drew scrutiny from journalists, who asked questions about the financial connections between the senator and the cable industry. The *Washington Post* ran a story reminding readers that the "industry has been a major source of campaign funds for Wirth, raising more than $80,000 in April at a dinner."[70] The *Washington Times* dug deeper into this connection, highlighting Tele-Communications Inc.'s (TCI) $12,300 donation to Wirth's campaign and $25,000 donation to the Colorado Democratic Party in 1986 to help Wirth win his Senate seat—as well as a $2,000 honorarium he had received for delivering a speech to Viacom executives.[71]

Wirth firmly denied any wrongdoing and doubled down on his commitment to an industry that provided jobs in his home state of Colorado. "I get contributions from the ski industry and I defend them too," he explained. "This particular industry [cable] has its major headquarters in a state I represent." He wrote a detailed letter to the *Rocky Mountain News* editor to express how "flabbergasted" he was by "the negative tone of yesterday's story and the headlines' hints that there is something out of the ordinary in my support for a strong cable television industry."[72] Would the *Detroit News* take "Congressman John Dingell to task for his support of the auto industry" or would the *Dallas Times Herald* criticize "Senator Lloyd Bentsen's advocacy of a strong domestic oil industry?" he asked. No, because "those members of Congress are simply doing their jobs by representing their districts and states as best they can."

A political cartoon captured the poignancy of the growing critiques as journalists called attention to the "quid pro quo" between Wirth's support for the cable industry and the donations he had received from people like John Malone and Bill Daniels.[73] Surrounded by cash flowing from the television, a man and woman jump up gleefully. "We've done it, Edith! We're hooked up to the Tim Wirth channel!" read the caption.[74]

As someone who came to Congress on the heels of Watergate with a message of transparency and reform, Wirth was indignant over these allegations of corruption as he saw his staunch commitment to defending the business interests of his home state as completely ethical. And yes, it may have been legal and commonplace, but such an approach did have consequences, which is what political journalists called out with bold headlines. Indeed, since Wirth had arrived on Capitol Hill almost two decades earlier, reporters had expanded coverage of scandals as they saw pursuing stories about improprieties as the path to fame and fortune.[75] Their readers

Ed Stein's political cartoon, published in the *Rocky Mountain News*, raised questions about the financial issues between Senator Tim Wirth and the cable television industry.
Courtesy of Ed Stein. Photo Credit: The Denver Public Library, Western History Collection [Call #WH2352].

had become more cynical (in part because of this coverage) and increasingly saw politics as transactional, both for themselves in their demands for services from the state and also in how they thought about the motives of their elected leaders.[76] Self-interest, it seemed, had triumphed.[77] In the case of cable television, this also meant that the marketplace won out as Wirth crafted legislation that equated the public interest with Colorado's corporate interests.

With the 1990 midterm elections on the horizon, the controversial S.1880 never came up for a vote, but Wirth remained under scrutiny.[78] More stories ran highlighting Wirth's relationship with the cable industry, and Wirth continued to defend himself and his support of the industry. "There were people who were trying to hurt the cable industry," he explained in an interview. "Why should I sit back and watch someone attempt to destroy an industry important to my state? I wasn't about to let that happen."[79]

Bill Daniels speaking at podium during a 1988 Republican
Party fundraiser held at Cableland for President
George H. W. Bush.
Photo Credit: Barco Library, The Cable Center.

That winter, Wirth even accepted an invitation as the guest of
honor at a dinner at the industry's most opulent showpiece: Cableland, Bill Daniels's 14,000-square-foot home at 4150 Shangri-La
Drive. Daniels had combined eight residential lots to build a place
to woo investors—and the eighty-eight television sets, two pools, an
aquarium, and heated birdbaths scattered throughout the mansion
reminded visitors of the wealth that cable television could generate.
The interior featured blush and mauve tones and even a pink baby
grand piano designed to make women attendees feel welcome.[80]
The house quickly gained a reputation for extravagant fundraisers,
including one for President George H. W. Bush during the 1988 campaign, and social parties attended by the likes of former President
Gerald Ford.[81] Cableland embodied the success of the industry, its
corporate philanthropic style, and more broadly what the *New York
Times* called the "'80s master of the universe sensibility."[82]

Tim Wirth arrived to meet with all the major players in the industry on December 6 in an evening explicitly characterized as "not a money event."[83] At Cableland, Wirth celebrated the attendees' accomplishments and "entrepreneurial spirit," which helped make cable available to 90 percent of homes.[84] He lauded their investment in the cable infrastructure—from plants and equipment to researching new technologies that will "keep you the vanguard of the communications industry"—as well as the diversity of programming on cable networks. Regarding the "very real political problems" the industry faced, he proposed a solution: "keep giving consumers what they want" by investing in "new technologies, new services, and new programming."

Wirth concluded by also encouraging the industry to stop "shooting itself in the foot" with poor customer service and rate hikes, both of which, he highlighted, could be used as ammunition for ushering in reregulation.[85] He also urged them to tell a more positive story of cable television and its achievements. But that became harder over the next two years, thanks to Al Gore's unrelenting legislative crusade.

———

Although Gore had thrown his hat into the ring for the Democratic nomination in 1988, he sat out the presidential primaries four years later. His six-year-old son had been hit by a car in 1989, and Gore announced in 1991 that he wanted to focus his time and energy on his family.[86] The following January, however, he led a fiery debate on the floor of the Senate that garnered national attention on the issue of cable regulation, once again. Introducing another round of legislation, Gore criticized the exploitative and corrupt practices of the cable industry, as he had repeatedly over the past several years. In a dramatic performance before C-SPAN audiences, the senator highlighted the various ways that the "cable industry just cavalierly dismisses public concern" with a variety of "schemes" to cheat the consumers and pad their pocketbooks.[87] Congress needed to act, Gore emphasized, to avoid "getting rolled by the cable industry."

"This is not a partisan bill," claimed Gore. And he was right. While cable debates frequently pit arguments about "competition" against "consumer protections," Republicans and Democrats across the ideological spectrum felt pressure to address rate hikes and poor customer service.[88] However, Gore predicted that the issue "could have partisan overtones." If the president vetoed it, Gore argued, he would be making a statement that he sided with monopolies over the average consumer. (Over the next year, Gore would use this issue to help differentiate New Democrats from a Republican administration that actually shared many economic philosophies and ideas.)[89]

The speech sent Tim Wirth over the edge. He took to the Senate floor and urgently pushed for a "modicum of control in the rhetoric that is floating around on this important issue." Such blustering language, he argued, overlooked how cable television expanded choice on the dial and broke down the "real monopoly" that had previously existed: network television. He cited Nickelodeon and Discovery for providing entertainment and educational programming for children and highlighted the contributions of C-SPAN and CNN in expanding awareness of public affairs at home and abroad.

He then brought up the point that people like Bill Daniels had long espoused about the public demand driving cable's expansion. "If this is something that was so bad for the American public," Wirth went on, "if this is something that—to use the words earlier—is a product of the Cosa Nostra, a monopolistic shakedown, rolling, gag practices, why did 30 million more Americans subscribe to cable television? Obviously, there is a service and a product there that people want. Otherwise, they would not subscribe." Wirth emphasized the need to focus on the substantive issues and not launch "attacks on the cable television industry" using "pejorative" language that distracted from efforts to find solutions that would work for both the industry and consumers.

Over the next year, Wirth would continue to call out the "anecdotal reports about coercion and shakedowns" that Gore and other sponsors of S.12—the Cable Television Consumer Protection and Competition Act of 1992—used to build support for reregulation. Wirth's stance remained consistent: he supported reregulation over issues of basic cable rates, customer service, and signal quality, but saw the extra provisions of S.12, notably must-carry and retransmission consent—the former guaranteed carriage of local independent broadcasters and the latter required cable operators to reimburse the networks for carrying their programs—as "punitive" and "destructive." These provisions promised to benefit the broadcast networks and stations at the expense of the cable business. (He was right.)[90]

Even C-SPAN weighed in on the debate, releasing a statement reminding legislators that the channel that brought them closer to constituents "is a creation of a de-regulated telecommunications marketplace."[91] C-SPAN, noted the organization in a press release, "would not exist today were it not for the private cable operators" who believed in "applying free market, private sector values to public affairs television" and now delivered C-SPAN to over fifty-six million households. Finally, the nonprofit company concluded, the legislative proposal "appears to be directly at odds with S.12's statement of policy, which says at Section 3: 'It is the policy of the congress in this Act to . . . promote the availability to the public of a diversity of views and information . . . [and to] *rely on the marketplace, to the maximum extent feasible, to achieve that availability* . . . [emphasis supplied].' C-SPAN's success has proved that the marketplace is already working to achieve the legislation's goals. Why change it?"

So, when Wirth announced his decision not to seek reelection amid this intense policy debate, top cable executives mourned openly.[92] He pledged to work hard for the next six months—which he called "months to cause mischief."[93] But then presidential politics threw a wrinkle into Wirth's plans. That summer, Arkansas Governor Bill Clinton selected Al Gore as his running mate. That made it clear that if Wirth wanted to stay in the good graces of a future administration and see his party capture the White House, he would have to balance his criticism of S.12 against the damage it might do to the party.

While he stayed the course as a vocal critic of Gore's bill—even siding with President Bush on it that fall—Wirth was ready for a change. "I decided that . . . I'd done enough for communications," he explained in an oral history. "God hadn't put me on Earth to spend my life doing communications."[94] After he left the Senate, he joined the Clinton administration as the Undersecretary for Global Affairs in the Department of State. In 1997, he accepted a position with the United Nations Foundation, reuniting with the man who made him chuckle during a 1984 congressional hearing when he called out the elitism and arrogance of television networks in their election coverage: Ted Turner.

Meanwhile, Al Gore rode attacks on John Malone and the cable companies all the way to a presidential ticket. And the battle would only intensify as the national campaign heated up. Cable executives looked for other potential allies in Congress and "were giving until it hurts," noted a *Cablevision* article.[95] Lobbyists took out television advertisements to urge cable subscribers to tell their representatives to vote against regulation. After all, noted commentator Chris Nolan, this "quintessential Washington trade association battle" took place "outside the Beltway to television viewers—who in this election year were also voters."[96]

Gore and Clinton also understood this. In another ironic twist, one of the biggest assets for their campaign emerged from a cable initiative designed to revamp the industry's battered image: MTV's "Choose or Lose" campaign. The 1992 presidential election revealed not only how cable programming was transforming electoral politics, but how the regulatory environment itself shaped programming initiatives. It also emerged as a reminder that the industry would mobilize to serve the public good when its pocketbook was at stake.

12

The MTV Presidency

An unlikely duo, twenty-four-year-old Tabitha Soren and twenty-five-year-old Alison Stewart arrived in New Hampshire to cover the Democratic primary in February 1992. They looked like opposites—Soren tall and red-headed, Stewart dark-haired and short—and frequently conflicted with one another off the camera. But they shared a mission: to inject excitement into political media that would get MTV viewers, overwhelmingly white, middle-class, and suburban youth, involved in politics.[1]

The all-music channel had launched on August 1, 1981, with an audacious and memorable comparison to the moon landing. It also had played a key role in cultivating demand for cable television by using its celebrity power to encourage youth to demand that their parents sign up for services. Mick Jagger, David Bowie, and Pete Townshend appeared in advertising spots telling their fans, "Call your cable operator and say, 'I want my MTV.'"[2] As with HBO several years earlier, such creative marketing with specialized appeals to particular demographics worked, forcing cable operators to take seriously the new music television channel and carry it on their systems.

Now it was bringing that same strategy to politics. In 1985, Viacom bought MTV from Warner Amex, and that same year, the channel launched MTV News, developing what one executive called a "lean and mean" approach to the news.[3] Initially, the program just featured interviews with musicians about their upcoming albums, a reflection of a network deeply intertwined with the corporate music industry whose records it helped to sell. In 1992, however, program director Dave Sirulnick saw serious news coverage as a way to elevate the network's profile and open new advertising opportunities with sponsors outside the music industry.[4] His small team at MTV News started with a simple idea: what if they made election coverage fun and entertaining? What if they made the political process more like a music concert?

Soren certainly had the right experiences and credentials to bridge MTV and electoral politics.[5] While attending college at New York University, she had worked at ABC News, CNN, and the local NBC affiliate.[6] She later recalled how she would then change out of her suit, put on jeans, and head to her other part-time job at MTV. She had even made an appearance as an extra in the Beastie Boys' music video, "(You Gotta) Fight for Your Right (to Party)."[7] After graduation she got a job as a television reporter covering the local politics beat in Burlington, Vermont, which included chronicling Bernie Sanders' successful effort to unseat an incumbent Republican congressman as an independent and socialist candidate. Soren professed that she didn't want to be a "little Katie Couric," but she did want respect. "Just because I know about Axl Rose," she said in a *New York Times* interview, "doesn't mean I don't read Arthur Schlesinger."[8]

Soren believed that younger voters who shunned the polls in 1988 weren't apathetic and unintelligent. Rather, they were "uninspired."[9] Sirulnick agreed and encouraged her and Stewart to develop a different approach in their campaign coverage. "We are going to give them MTV, which isn't the mainstream way of looking at things," he explained.[10] Called "Choose or Lose," the MTV initiative aimed to educate, entertain, and empower viewers by turning them into voters. As Soren explained, voting was "one of the most important opportunities they have to have a voice in their country; that's why we say you either choose a candidate or you lose that opportunity."[11]

While many reporters made fun of the small team when they arrived in New Hampshire, some politicians took them seriously.[12] The presidential hopeful from California, Jerry Brown, changed from a suit into a flannel shirt for an interview, and then answered a question from Soren about how people could get their first job—not the kind of question posed by a traditional journalist—before telling MTV viewers directly that if they turned out to vote that year, they could "turn the country around."[13] Brown, Soren said later, was the only candidate during the New Hampshire primary who could "talk in an MTV speak and simplify things in a way that young people could understand."[14]

"Choose or Lose" certainly did capture the attention and enthusiasm of young voters as it "made the political process hip again," in the words of one MTV executive.[15] Expanding on the unconventional political coverage that TVTV had pioneered two decades earlier, it brought diverse voices, new issues, and a bit of disruption to political journalism. But, at its core, it was a corporate project designed to bolster the business of cable television. And it worked. In the aftermath of the election, cablecasting became firmly engrained in party politics and governing operations on the Hill and in the White House. And, as cable operators had long hoped, favorable legislation soon followed with the Telecommunications Act of 1996, which paved the way for corporate consolidation across *all* media industries. Although celebrated as a "win-win" for politicians, business, and subscribers, the reliance on consumer demand and market metrics to advance democracy had visible winners and losers.[16]

———

"Choose or Lose" reflected something made very clear during the debates over cable reregulation: the industry had an image problem. This was not a new obstacle. During the 1960s the NCTA fought against popular perceptions that cable was a parasite feeding off the hard work of the broadcasting industry. The following decade, Tom Whitehead likened cable's reputation to a "used car salesman," as operators frequently peddled promises during franchise negotiations that they never intended to fulfill.

By 1992, cable had become known as the "big bad monopoly" eager to rip off its customers and ignore even the most basic requests for service repairs, observed Craig Leddy, the editor of *Cablevision*.[17] Cable operators, the NCTA, and trade press made clear the consequences of such a negative reputation: reregulation and the possible entrance of telephone companies into the cable business. The 1984 Cable Act had excluded telephone companies from the cable business to avoid smothering the burgeoning industry. Such a philosophy didn't quite hold up in 1990 as cable now reached over fifty-one million subscribers out of the ninety-one million households with television sets, a jump from just nineteen million a decade earlier.[18]

Despite the consensus over cable's image problem, debates emerged on how to solve it. The NCTA took one approach: a national advertising campaign called "Cable Contributes to Life."[19] After convincing members to pay double their dues, the trade organization launched a two-year, $14 million campaign to celebrate the industry's achievements. Some ads reminded viewers of the sheer number of choices they had, thanks to cable. "Not every cable channel is everyone's cup of tea. That's the whole point," explained one ad. Another targeted the pending cable reregulation bill, featuring a man with a leaking umbrella and the line, "If the cable TV legislation is supposed to protect you, how come you'll end up getting soaked?" One even extolled the growing news environment, reminding that "news happens when it happens," and CNN made it so the world didn't have to wait to be informed.

Indeed, the previous year, CNN had become must-watch international news. Since the mid-1980s, Ted Turner focused on growing the channel's global reach, even fostering arrangements with communist countries to open bureaus in places like Moscow and Havana.[20] By 1988, an internationally focused news channel, CNN-International (CNN-I), expanded to over fifty-eight countries, capturing historical moments on camera and without interruption, including the prodemocracy demonstrations in China's Tiananmen Square and the fall of the Berlin Wall in 1989.[21] Turner spared no expense in sending his international team to cover the escalating tensions in the Middle East the following year. Connections from CNN-I programming then helped the cable news team secure access from the Iraqi government to use a portable uplink so they could provide live reports from Baghdad as tensions escalated between the United Nations and Iraqi dictator Saddam Hussein.[22]

When war broke out on January 17, 1991, a small team, which included the well-known anchor Bernard Shaw and foreign correspondent Peter Arnett, stayed in a hotel room, reporting live on the bombs hitting the city of Baghdad. Over the next weeks, CNN continued to provide a look at the war on the ground, even as many stories had to pass through Iraqi officials who facilitated such access. Overall, the reporting from the Persian Gulf was incredibly censored by both the American and Iraqi governments, as both understood that optics and storytelling mattered in modern warfare. And yet, CNN's ability to provide around-the-clock coverage gave viewers a *sense* of immediacy while bolstering the cable network's journalistic reputation.[23]

Such news coverage demonstrated the value of experimentation and of a television schedule not bound solely by the demands of advertisers. It also was a reminder that programming could forge key political relationships (for example with the Iraqi government) that might pay off in anticipated and unanticipated ways. That's certainly what public relations consultants and lobbyists had hammered home time and time again for the past two decades: do more showing and less telling about cable's political power.[24]

Despite C-SPAN's success in cultivating legislative goodwill, industry leaders realized that more needed to be done, and so they formed the Cable Television Public Affairs Association (CTPAA) to teach local operators basic public relations skills and develop a "proactive approach to industry issues."[25] As the debate around cable reregulation heightened by the 1990s with angry customers voicing frustration over rate hikes and shoddy customer service, the CTPAA tried to change the narrative and show the concrete benefits of cable television to subscribers, journalists, local city officials, and members of Congress.[26]

The organization pointed to the 1992 election as a "highly visible opportunity" to provide programming that showed cable's social value.[27] And cable networks stepped up. The Disney Channel hosted live awards shows honoring teachers, and the *ESPN Outdoors* Saturday morning show ran *Team Up to Clean Up* to promote environmental awareness. Lifetime launched a "Women and Politics" initiative to tap into the growing attention to gender inequality and sexism in politics. Its executives worked with local affiliates and organizations like the National Women's Political Caucus and League of Women Voters to register voters, raise awareness on women's issues, launch an essay contest, and of course, sell advertisements to companies eager to be associated with the campaign.[28]

"Choose or Lose" grew out of these broader cable projects and focused on encouraging youth voter engagement. As *Cablevision* observed, the "operators seemed to agree that timing, purpose, and MTV's awesome marketing machine combined to strengthen cable's reach into the community, an important accomplishment in the cable bill age."[29] MTV distributed kits to local cable operators that included T-shirts, banners, and public service announcement videos to play as advertisements. It worked with the League of Women Voters and the Rock the Vote organization (founded in 1990 to empower younger voters against the crusade to censor music led by Tipper Gore, the wife of the vice-presidential candidate) to register voters in malls, and during summer food fairs and music performances.[30]

In Minneapolis, for example, Paragon Cable had thirty-six "Choose or Lose" voter registration drives in only twenty-nine days, resulting in two thousand newly registered voters. Paragon made it clear that growing its business mattered more than stimulating civic engagement, though. "MTV provided critical national focus, raising awareness for our target audience," explained Debra Cottone, the company's VP of programming and marketing.[31] A market research company specializing in the college market also documented how "Choose or Lose" had such a positive reception on college campuses because over 70 percent of college towns had cable access. MTV campus events then added hype, which made other students sign up for cable. The "bandwagon" sales tactic that HBO introduced almost two decades earlier clearly worked.

Such public service initiatives boosted the visibility and demand for cable television by tethering it to electoral politics. But its success also hinged on the fact that a handful of presidential candidates turned to cable programming that year to bypass the Washington press corps and even shake up the two-party system. This included the industry's loudest critic: Al Gore.

———

The 1992 presidential race had only gotten started when an eccentric billionaire from Texas made a provocative statement on CNN's *Larry King Live*: "If you, the people, will on your own . . . register me in 50 states," H. Ross Perot pledged, then he would take their wishes *and* hard work seriously and run for president.[32] Having made a fortune on a start-up computer business that could process Medicaid and Medicare information, Perot soon turned into a critic of the big government programs that had made him filthy rich.[33] Like the real estate mogul Donald Trump, he became a celebrity CEO during the 1980s, and soon after, he began appearing on *Larry King Live* to rail against what he saw as a stagnant political establishment.[34] Perot celebrated the CNN program as democracy in action, especially when viewers called in to ask him questions. After his February appearance, his name appeared on ballots across the country, seemingly proof that such "electronic town halls" worked.[35]

Perot's announcement exposed how cable's political journalism could empower candidates who flouted traditional rules embedded within mainstream media and political institutions.[36] For Perot, CNN took the place of a political party, allowing him to turn viewers into activists working for his candidacy across the country. For Bill Clinton, talk shows, cable programs, and even local news helped him evade hard-hitting and intrusive questions from journalists about his record and past indiscretions.[37] It also allowed him to play up his strength: forging empathetic and human connections with individual voters.

Since the New Hampshire primary, the Arkansas governor had navigated constant allegations of scandal—infidelities, dodging the Vietnam War, real estate improprieties—that dominated mainstream media coverage of his candidacy. Unlike Gary Hart, however, Clinton was prepared. He had a team of media strategists ready to respond to scandals by deflecting attention and challenging the very credibility of such reports.[38] His campaign set up a "War Room" staffed with master "spin doctors" like James Carville, Paul Begala, George Stephanopoulos, and Madeleine "Mandy" Grunwald. When filmmakers Chris Hegedus and D. A. Pennebaker decided to chronicle the 1992 campaign, they quickly found the real action was in tracing how this behind-the-scenes media operation engaged in a battle to shape the nonstop news cycle by a combination of deflection, diversion, and distortion.[39]

Clinton had another weapon in his effort to avoid a scandal-hungry press and curry public favor: "BCTV: Bill Clinton TV" launched with the help of a satellite dish atop the candidate's Arkansas headquarters.[40] Like Dukakis, this technology allowed him to host electronic town halls with voters across the country, controlling the media narrative and avoiding what one media adviser had called "sound bite politics."[41] He even experimented with talk radio, appearing on the Don Imus radio show and a teleconference with talk show hosts (also televised on C-SPAN).[42]

While he continued his appearances on cable news programs like *Larry King Live*, the governor also turned to unconventional shows on network broadcasting, like *Donahue* and *The Arsenio Hall Show*. The image of Arsenio Hall smiling and pointing as Clinton donned sunglasses and played renditions of Elvis Presley's "Heartbreak Hotel" has become just as iconic as when Richard Nixon appeared on *Rowan & Martin's Laugh-In* or shook hands with Presley himself. Like Nixon before him, Clinton wanted to tap into entertainment to connect to younger voters, and with new programs eager to foreground political news that year, he had even more opportunities to do so. And yet, there was an important difference that underscored how dramatically the media and political landscapes had changed since the 1960s. While Nixon appeared for just seconds on *Laugh-In* so that millions of broadcast viewers might briefly see a humorous side of him (and like him more), Clinton appeared on programs that reached only a sliver of those viewers, but he dominated the conversation around election "issues" at length.

This was especially the case on cable television, and the Clinton campaign recognized what a *Los Angeles Times* article observed that spring: CNN and C-SPAN "are only the tip of the cable iceberg."[43] Low-cost television alternatives on the cable dial offered a "revolutionary, if obvious, development that is inevitably democratizing." It certainly brought new voices and topics to political conversations as cable shows explored stories beyond what Walter Cronkite and elite white men cared about by foregrounding the concerns of women, youth, Hispanics, and Blacks on issues like sex, jobs, the environment, and racial inequality.[44] Politicians turned to cable for more selfish and pragmatic reasons, however. It afforded them tremendous control over political discussions.

That's why on June 16, Governor Clinton appeared on MTV during a ninety-minute interview with Tabitha Soren and CNN's Catherine Crier, where he also took questions directly from audience members about topics that ranged from racism in America to his public service student loan program. In what a journalist called the "highlight of the campaign so far," the event emerged as an "alliance of high-tech entertainment and earnest political inquiry [that] shows that a true democratic conscience can emerge in the most unexpected of places."[45]

It may have just saved his presidential bid. According to *The Economist*, the Clinton campaign looked "Dukakissed" in early June—disorganized and hemorrhaging cash by the day. On MTV, however, Clinton was back: "Quick, not slick; sympathetic, not condescending; imaginative, not wordy."[46] The show, observed the British magazine, "was a tonic that lifted his whole campaign," and it happened "not on the networks or in the editorial boardrooms of the pompous old broadsheets, but on a channel best known hitherto for soft-core rock videos."

Clinton's campaign certainly believed it was a winning formula. He returned to MTV repeatedly during the campaign, and Al Gore

Arkansas governor Bill Clinton and MTV news reporter Tabitha Soren at the taping of an MTV "Choose or Lose" special, "Facing the Future with Bill Clinton," 1992.
Photo Credit: *Multichannel News*/Barco Library, The Cable Center.

Democratic presidential nominee Bill Clinton talks with audience members during the "Facing the Future with Bill Clinton" program, 1992.
Photo Credit: *Multichannel News*/Barco Library, The Cable Center.

also appeared to do an interview with Soren—where he received a warm welcome but was grilled over his wife Tipper's drive to label explicit records.[47]

MTV also secured access to the Democratic convention that year, with unconventional reporters asking new questions of participants inside and activists gathered outside the convention halls, just as TVTV had done years earlier. Megadeth star Dave Mustaine attempted to interview politicians—and they replied.[48] "Don't you think that the real politics happen out here in the street rather than inside there?" the musician asked Senator Bob Kerrey while wearing a sleeveless denim shirt, long unkempt hair, and aviator glasses. "Yeah, that's right," replied Kerrey, who stood in contrast to the singer in a white collared shirt and tie. MTV urged Mustaine to "treat it like a concert," turning the convention coverage into a very "sexy thing for our viewers," contended Soren. This also included interviewing people on the street. One Black man told Mustaine that "if you want to be completely unified in this country, then you have to share everything, and that includes power," as he then called attention to problems of systemic racism frequently overlooked in presidential campaigns.

Committed to the journalistic notion of fairness, MTV had a standing invitation for both President Bush and Ross Perot to appear on the program. Soren defended MTV news against accusations of liberal bias by sharing a recent poll done with viewers in which Barbara Bush emerged as the highest-rated "political role model."[49] The team also covered the Republican National Convention in Houston, where conservative rocker Ted Nugent and Treach, a rapper with Naughty by Nature, served as "political commentators."[50] Nugent walked through the convention with a sleeveless flannel shirt and a microphone as he sought to "Tedify" the proceedings, while Soren interviewed Newt Gingrich about smoking pot—something he admitted to doing and said others shouldn't.[51] President Bush, however, repeatedly turned down MTV's interview invitations. "I'm not going to be out there trying to be a teenybopper at 68," he remarked, attempting to turn Clinton's strategy into a political critique.[52]

While Bush did reluctantly agree to a prerecorded interview on *Larry King Live*, the only new media he took seriously was Rush Limbaugh's talk radio show. While MTV brought the lifestyle approach of cable networks to the political process, the brash conservative radio host embedded his shock DJ style in GOP politics—and did so to a large audience, with millions of listeners tuning in to his entertaining screeds each day. After witnessing how Limbaugh's endorsement of Pat Buchanan had helped the fringe candidate secure 37.5 percent of the primary vote in the New Hampshire primary earlier that year, Bush decided to court the controversial but popular talk radio host, even famously carrying Limbaugh's bags to the Lincoln bedroom during an invited stay at the White House.[53] Such efforts paid off. In the fall, Limbaugh invited both Bush and Vice President Dan Quayle as guests on his program (an exception to his normal format that traditionally just featured Limbaugh ranting and responding to callers).[54]

Nevertheless, Bush struggled in the new media environment, as he saw such entertainment appearances as beneath the dignity of the presidency.[55] For him, cable television was important not primarily as a campaign tool but as a policy issue that illuminated the substantive differences between the Democratic and Republican tickets that year. Unfortunately for him, many of his GOP colleagues disagreed.

———

The *New York Times* made an astute observation in the final month of the presidential election. "The debate over cable television prices has become subordinated to the broader theater of the election."[56] That was exactly what Al Gore had in mind. As a cosponsor of the S.12 cable bill, Gore, now the Democratic nominee for vice president, used the fall legislative debate as a warning about the dangers of being "Bush-wacked," a common message of the broader campaign. "George Bush is hunkered down there in the White House, in a state of political panic," he told North Carolina voters after the Senate passed the bill in September with the support of fifty Democrats and twenty-four Republicans.[57] "I'm going to direct this to the president," the vice-presidential hopeful dramatically announced. "If you veto the cable bill, you would have sided with the monopolists and against the American people. And the American people may just veto your desire for another four years."[58]

Bush, on the other hand, used the issue to cast Democrats as antibusiness, favoring regulation over competition. He repeatedly said that the bill would "hurt Americans by imposing a wide array of costly, burdensome, and unnecessary requirements on the cable industry and the government agencies that regulate it."[59] He tried to rally his party around his stance by reminding Republicans that the legislation would also undermine his "vision for the future of the communications industry," which hinged on "the principles of greater competition, entrepreneurship, and less economic regulation."[60] He also called attention to the bill's rate caps and the programming mandates—specifically must-carry and retransmission consent—as unnecessary and excessive government interference.[61]

On October 3, Bush fulfilled his promise to veto the bill. He did so with a firm message that it reflected "good intentions gone wrong" because it would discourage investments in the telecommunications industry and would produce an "undeniable result: higher rates for cable viewers."[62] The veto put Republicans in Congress in a bind, noted *New York Times* reporter Edmund Andrews, who had been covering the issue. The political posturing by Gore and Bush during the campaign ignored the bipartisan support for (and also against) the actual legislation, leaving "many Republican legislators in the uncomfortable position of being on the wrong side of an issue that many consumers are angry about."

Bush invited a handful of Republican senators to the White House for a Sunday breakfast, hoping to win over enough to sustain his veto.[63] The president had a perfect record on veto fights—not one of his thirty-five vetoes in office had been overturned. Minority Leader Robert Dole understood the stakes. "For heaven's sake," a staffer penned in a handwritten note. "This is the last of the big votes for the President. To lose it would be a major blow to the campaign—'even the GOPS are running from the sinking ship.' Morale will plummet— yet again!"[64]

He had no luck. John Danforth, one of the Republican sponsors of the bill, expressed his support for Bush even as he reaffirmed his backing for the bill, which he called simply a "difference of opinion" about how to handle "unregulated monopolies." The senator from Missouri laid claim to the trust-busting tradition of Theodore Roosevelt, rather than the new conservative deregulatory ideas espoused by Reagan and his White House successor. In the end, not a single Republican defected to support the president's veto. It was an ominous sign for the incumbent president's reelection bid a month before Election Day.[65]

The Clinton campaign immediately pounced. After casting a vote to override Bush's veto, Al Gore joined his running mate on *Larry King Live* where he proudly shared the news that seventy-three of his colleagues, including those twenty-four Republicans, had joined him in voting to override the president.[66] "It's a bellwether," he told King.[67] "It's an indication of the winds of change that are blowing across the country. And when President Bush sided with the cable monopolies, the majority in the House and Senate sided with the people of this country."

Clinton jumped in and emphasized how the "cable bill symbolizes a lot of the differences between our ticket and the Bush/Quayle ticket." The presidential hopeful contended that Gore had fought for the legislation to advocate for the "middle-class people who want cable, who like its benefits, but who are basically subject to a monopoly." Working-class people, he explained, "depend on cable TV for a major portion of their entertainment," and many "literally can't even afford to take their families out to dinner and to a movie very often anymore and they need cable TV and they need it to be reasonable."

News of the veto's override broke in the middle of the interview. "I'm Candy Crowley, reporting live from Capitol Hill," interrupted the Washington, D.C., correspondent. "The House has just joined the Senate in overriding the President's veto of a cable TV bill. This means the bill, which regulates cable TV rates and services, now goes into law, despite the President's objections. This is the first time the Bush White House has lost a veto fight with the Democrat-controlled Senate." Clinton and Gore cheered, with the Tennessee senator reminding CNN viewers that he had led this policy fight for years. "We're not going to protect the monopolies anymore. We're going to side with the people."

It was an illuminating moment: Clinton and Gore voicing support for cable reregulation on the very cable network that John Malone and Tele-Communications Inc., had helped to salvage just years before. Gore used his attacks on cable companies like TCI and figures like Malone to raise his national profile, and it became a frequent, and popular, theme of the Democratic campaign that year. But their appearance on CNN also was a reminder that the Democratic ticket desperately needed cable television's cheap and accessible programs to circumvent the press and speak directly to the people in an unfiltered and unedited conversation.

In the short term, the cable industry lost the 1992 legislative battle as the bill gave the FCC authority to require specific customer service operations and local government the ability to regulate rates. Cable programmers came out as other major losers in the legislation as it included must carry and retransmission consent mandates, ultimately opening unprecedented space for broadcasting networks and local independent broadcasting channels to take over valuable space on the cable dial.[68] Brain Lamb lamented these rules, which he argued made C-SPAN and other cable networks "second class citizens in the world of television."[69] And yet, at the same time, the industry's unique political programming initiatives—from "Choose or Lose" to *Larry King Live*—showed the value and power of cablecasting in ways that would provide the industry tremendous political influence in the long run.

The final days of the campaign foreshadowed the changes on the horizon. All three candidates, Bush included, sprinted to MTV, *Larry King Live*, and any other talk show in which they could forge a human connection with television viewers to overcome voter cynicism.[70] Bush's last-minute appearance on MTV came off as a desperate move to salvage his campaign, not a serious embrace of youths and the issues that concerned them, however. Soren called Bush "snarky and dismissive," and when she asked a question about his tax returns, his campaign team immediately stepped in to end the interview after only ten minutes.[71] By contrast, Clinton excelled in this changing media environment. Local news, cable, and entertainment shows allowed the candidate to "touch a whole group of voters in a way they have never been touched before," explained one campaign press secretary.[72] Clinton repeatedly emphasized that "real" voters got to ask him questions that mattered to them—a blatant critique of traditional political journalism that then justified his strategy to ignore the Washington press corps.

Such arguments tapped into the very narrative cable advocates had used over the previous two decades: that cable could improve civic dialogue and solve the problems that network broadcast news—with its limited channel capacities and high expense—had created in American political life. The *Baltimore Sun* noted the changes on display with the Clinton campaign. "MTV and Arsenio Hall are part of a larger movement: the change from white-male hegemony to a multicultural America. The fragmenting of the TV audience into many different groups determined by age, sex, gender and other factors goes hand-in-hand with the fragmenting of the body politic."[73] The political media became more frivolous and divided, but it also became more diverse and accessible.

Perhaps most consequentially, it linked the democratic process more deeply to television profits, consumer demand, and narrowcasting. Dave Sirulnick was blunt about MTV's business strategy shaping its political coverage. "The rule of thumb is to anticipate what viewers will be interested in and to shun any news reporting that smacks of 'take your medicine,'" he explained, seeing this approach to news as a curating service for younger Americans to learn about the world while never turning the dial.[74] Another executive was even more direct. "The more full-service we are, the less our viewers ever have to leave our channel. We don't want our viewers going to ABC or NBC for the news."[75] Forming information silos was good for business, and Clinton's comeback campaign showed how it could be politically advantageous as well.

MTV's political coverage exposed the thin line between empowerment and indulgence as corporations sold access to political lifestyle media as a form of meaningful civic engagement. Critics called this out, lambasting "Choose or Lose" as celebrating the "egoistic, selfish materialism of American culture."[76] They highlighted how it encouraged a superficial understanding of politics, lamenting how such programming referenced the importance of individual rights without also discussing the civic responsibilities, particularly with voter education, that come with such rights.

Initially, it seemed that meeting voters on their preferred viewing channel might actually encourage civic engagement. Fueled by increased participation by younger Americans, voter turnout increased that year, jumping up almost five percentage points from 1988.[77] MTV used this data to laud its contribution to the political process, taking out advertisements that congratulated the seventeen million 18–29-year-olds who voted in the election. The cable network quickly moved to "cash in on its newfound respectability," as *Cablevision* put it, by hosting a new type of inaugural ball, the "Rock 'n' Roll Inaugural Ball." The high-profile event became the "hottest ticket in town," with Clinton showing up to credit the network for helping him win the presidency. "I think everyone knows MTV had a lot to do with the Clinton/Gore victory," he said on the stage.[78]

Clinton's celebration of MTV and the prominent role of cable networks at the inaugural festivities—Disney held events for children and HBO filmed an inaugural gala at the Lincoln Memorial—made industry observers hopeful that Gore's cable-bashing had given way to sympathy for the industry. "Now that cable has gotten the Clinton administration's attention," Craig Leddy wrote, "hopefully schmoozing will lead to more concrete discussions."[79]

As a follow-up to the "Choose or Lose" campaign, MTV News launched what it called "socially conscious programming" around topics like AIDS and racism in America. One special report hosted by Kurt Loder addressed the topic "Hate Rock" and racist ideas circulating in music across the globe.[80] Time and time again, such initiatives bolstered advertising sales, especially for businesses looking to appear socially responsible themselves.[81] It also kept viewers from turning the channel, providing the pretense that they could watch music videos and stay informed about the world around them.

Such programs continued to be profitable and politically advantageous, not just for Clinton but for his opponents.

———

Two months into the Clinton administration, George Stephanopoulos traveled from Washington to Long Island to attend an event at Hofstra University, where he had once studied. There, he accepted a bright blue Tiffany's box containing an engraved pewter bowl honoring his professional accomplishments. He was a rising star: after Hofstra, he became a Rhodes Scholar, then a presidential campaign adviser, and now director of communications in the Clinton White House.[82] During a twenty-minute speech that focused overwhelmingly on economic issues, Stephanopoulos also reminded the audience that Clinton was the first presidential candidate to appear on MTV. It showed that Clinton was "unafraid to go to the American people, to talk frankly, to go out and answer their questions and do what he can to make sure people stay involved." For the Clinton team, cable became a way to personalize politics by infusing new entertainment platforms with political messaging.[83]

Stephanopoulos pledged that the town hall cable style that helped Clinton win would be a defining feature of his presidency, and it was. While billed as a way to have open and transparent conversations, the administration had ulterior motives. Certainly, such a strategy continued to play to Clinton's strengths, as he thrived in settings where he could connect directly with people. Beyond that, his team could carefully select the audience and the topics based on their recent focus group and polling data (something the Clinton administration obsessed over).[84] Finally, it allowed the president to avoid conversations with professional journalists, whose investigations into the slew of Clinton scandals (which ranged from the operations of the White House Travel Office to real estate holdings) only intensified as the Clintons moved into 1600 Pennsylvania Avenue.

These lengthy talk-show-style events also helped him sell his policy agenda. When rolling out new healthcare legislation, for example, the administration held a media blitz that included purchasing large blocks of time on NBC, PBS, and NPR.[85] When President Clinton wanted to push the more controversial aspects of the bill, notably the question about abortion coverage, he then went on MTV to discuss the issue with audience members, who overwhelmingly supported such socially liberal policies.[86]

Again and again, Clinton turned to MTV to promote issues to younger Americans. Clinton pushed his national service initiative through a town hall with Tabitha Soren on MTV News called "Bill Clinton: Your Future, His Plan."[87] While press releases framed the interview as a conversation designed to "'get students' reaction to the plans President Clinton has set forth," it was actually a sales pitch designed to get youth buy-in for an initiative that depended on younger Americans pursuing public service in exchange for tuition support. To keep the audience's attention, Clinton mixed in a serious discussion of the initiative with stories about eating late-night pizza and a possible Beatles reunion at the White House.[88] When the rollout for the AmeriCorps program came at the end of the year, unsurprisingly it included advertising spots on MTV.[89]

Such an approach encouraged a more superficial discussion of policy that further blurred the line between public and private. For example, the following year, Clinton welcomed an audience of two hundred 16–20-year-olds to Washington to discuss the pending bipartisan crime bill that ultimately would dramatically expand mass incarceration through harsher sentences and billions of dollars to fund new prisons and the expansion of police forces.[90] Yet the most memorable part of the conversation came during a "rapid fire" round of questioning when Laetitia Thompson of Maryland asked what "the world's dying to know: Is it boxers or briefs?" As laughter filled the room, Clinton looked visibly shocked but still answered: "Usually briefs."[91]

This political environment also facilitated Clinton's undoing as private issues of marital infidelities soon became fodder for special counsel investigations and ultimately, impeachment.[92] It also revealed something distinctive about niche cable programs: the opportunity they afforded to test more controversial and outrageous ideas and statements, and simply see the response.[93] Shows like Bill

Maher's *Politically Incorrect*, which launched in 1993 on Comedy Central, became a way for right-wing figures like Ann Coulter and Laura Ingraham to experiment with selling fringe ideas and even profanity though a veneer of comedy.[94]

Even Newt Gingrich tried to follow in Clinton's footsteps, but he had less success. In 1993, he began hosting two shows on a new cable network, National Empowerment Television (NET), a conservative cable channel marketed as "C-SPAN with an attitude" and publicized as a challenge to the cynicism promoted by MTV.[95] Despite having wealthy conservative backers, the show struggled to overcome poor production quality and the persistent desire of hosts like Gingrich to advocate more than entertain. When NET folded, Gingrich decided to get on the MTV bandwagon. In the summer of 1995, he joined Tabitha Soren in what was promoted as a "rap" conversation called "Newt: Raw."[96] Having just become Speaker of the House following the midterm elections, Gingrich wanted to build popular support for the "Contract for America" agenda and sell copies of his new book *To Renew America*. While he had built his career through divisive attacks, as Speaker of the House, Gingrich's tune had changed. Now he wanted to govern and pass a program that he claimed 60 percent of Americans supported, per research allegedly conducted by Republican pollster Frank Luntz (in reality, Luntz only polled the slogans used, not the actual policies).[97]

The term "rap" was certainly a misrepresentation. Gingrich sat at a roundtable with six young adults as Soren moderated a conversation riddled with political conflict and disagreements over social issues.[98] While Clinton forged intimate connection with audience members, Gingrich cut people off and talked over those who disagreed with him. One young woman who grilled the Speaker on welfare policies left the conversation with a clear disdain for him and responded "hell no," when asked afterward if she would ever vote for him.[99] When a reporter asked him about what had now become the infamous "boxer or briefs" question, Gingrich scowled and shot back, "I think that's a very stupid question, and it's stupid for you to ask that question."[100]

Gingrich's style was better suited for conservative media, where he could confront enemies, refuse to compromise, and push ideological principles. His struggles and Clinton's effectiveness on MTV also exposed a broader difference between a Republican Party moving rightward toward ideological rigidity imposed by tapping into outrage and a Democratic Party attempting to broaden its political coalition through entertainment.

By the time Clinton launched his 1996 reelection bid, MTV had gotten what Soren would later acknowledge was "too much attention," ultimately influencing both campaign strategies and the election coverage in the mainstream media.[101] While it emulated C-SPAN's approach by following candidates around on a bus complete with a studio where all candidates eagerly appeared, other political media tried to copy MTV's informal style.[102] CNN hired three journalists in their twenties to "skew young" in political coverage (one was Kellyanne Fitzpatrick, later known by her married name Conway and the future campaign manager for Donald Trump's successful 2016 campaign).[103] Nickelodeon and Comedy Central also increased their political coverage. On *Kids Pick the President*, children called a toll-free number to vote for their favorite candidate, while *Indecision '96* expanded its earlier coverage by deploying comedians like Chris Rock to turn the campaign into "fodder" for comedy.[104]

NBC eagerly tapped into youth markets by merging cable with the internet world.[105] The network had a distinct advantage thanks to the 1992 cable legislation and its must-carry and retransmission consent rules. Here's how the rules played out in practice: Local broadcasters had two options. They could mandate carriage (must carry), something that unaffiliated local broadcasters desperate to expand their station's reach did (which meant that a small noncommercial or religious station could now secure valuable cable carriage). Or, affiliated broadcasters could demand payment for carriage (retransmission consent) for the network programming they disseminated, which of course cable operators wanted to carry because of consumer demand. In short, cable operators had to carry unpopular broadcast programs and pay for popular ones.[106] Rather than fork over the cash, cable companies negotiated an agreement with the national networks, offering them carriage of their own cable channels. Taking advantage of this, NBC first launched a channel called America's Talking on its new cable slot. In 1995 the network announced plans to restructure its cable programming through a partnership with Microsoft in an attempt to combine the excitement of the internet, the reach of cable television, and the credentials of the network news.[107]

MSNBC certainly capitalized on the fame of celebrity newscasters from the national broadcasting network, bringing in well-known names like Tom Brokaw, Katie Couric, and Bill Moyers to guest host segments. The main term used to sell MSNBC, however, was "interactive." On its corresponding website, viewers could access more information and share their questions and perspectives on the news as it unfolded. Internet made the engagement QUBE had promised almost two decades earlier now possible. Rather than the "rat-a-tat-tat of CNN," MSNBC would focus on providing depth around three to four stories a day, explained producers, with the companion website expanding coverage even more.[108] "We can tell you all about Steve Forbes' flat tax plan on the Nightly News and we can give you some analysis of that," a producer in charge of interactive programming explained. "But we can take it a step further on the Internet. We can give you a form, and you can fill in the blanks and print it out and find out how that tax plan will impact you personally."

The channel wanted to tap into the expansion of the internet and personal computer markets, which executives from NBC and Microsoft both understood as the "Gen X" world. Contributors wore Gap clothing on a set that looked like a Starbucks rather than a newsroom. The news became another commodity in Bill Gates's "metastasizing software empire," observed *Newsweek*.[109] The merger forced a conversation about what mattered most: customers or viewers; content or journalism. The two businesses had different cultures, acknowledged another MSNBC executive. "But, fundamentally, it's a media-news-information culture we're dealing with."[110]

The battle for viewers intensified as each of these nonstop news channels looked for ways to brand itself and its style of news. Cable insiders once again pointed to such programming diversity as a positive contribution to the democratic process—even as they mainly cared that this diversity padded their pocketbooks. *Cablevision's* Craig Leddy hammered this point home. "Voters are tired of being spoon-fed superficial broadcast TV reports focusing solely on the horse race," and cable interviews on MTV, CNN, and Comedy Central all provided "in-depth information and opportunities for voter interaction with candidates."[111] Candidates also had a plethora of outlets to connect to potential voters. It was a lucrative payday for cable companies too, something captured by the magazine's headline about the election: "Cable's Projected as Winner in '96: Forget the donkey and elephants—cable expects political ad sales results to be bullish."[112] Indeed, advertising spending on cable television tripled from four years earlier.[113]

And so, the 1996 election should have been a boon to democracy with the logic that diversity on the dial, expanded coverage, and personalized news could come together to inform voters and promote civic engagement. But the numbers told a different story. Fewer than 50 percent of voters went to the polls, even lower than the dip witnessed in 1988.[114]

What happened? Twenty years later, Tabitha Soren called out how the MTV promise of democratic engagement fundamentally conflicted with the business of cable television. "The pretense of a lot of political coverage today is that it aims to improve and edify our civic life," she wrote in an editorial for the *New York Times*. "The reality is that it's just whoring for our attention."[115] And she was right. Long-form cable programming had the potential to bring more depth to political coverage, and C-SPAN certainly did this for a very narrow sliver of the electorate. MTV's more popular political programming did something different. By pandering to what executives thought their audience wanted, it let market demand shape political coverage and rewarded those who could command attention on the camera. While Clinton had both policy and performative chops, this wouldn't always be the case, as Soren noted, while writing during the 2016 election.

Perhaps most dangerous was *the façade* that such political coverage did inform viewers who came for the fun show but left with a shallow understanding of the candidates and the political process.

———

On February 8, 1996, the two most powerful men in the country walked into a packed room at the Library of Congress with "Hail to the Chief" playing loudly as hundreds of audience members clapped thunderously. They stood in front of two computer screens bearing the presidential seal, and Al Gore took center stage.

Referencing how far the country had come since 1934 when Franklin Roosevelt signed the Communications Act into law with little fanfare, Gore promised that the Telecommunications Act of 1996, which Bill Clinton was about to sign, would unleash "an entirely new world, a world in which we use technology to put us more directly in contact with each other. A world in which our ability to create and receive information will be limited not by the bounds of our technology but only by the infinite boundaries of our imagination."[116] The vice president had dedicated tremendous time and energy to negotiations around the issue, and he celebrated the compromises between private industry and government as well as Republicans and Democrats. He pledged that the bill's "DNA" centered on delivering the "public interest values of democracy, education, and economic and social well-being for all of our citizens."

Gore then turned on the computer screen where comedian Lily Tomlin appeared in character as "Ernestine the Telephone Operator." In a performance she made famous almost thirty years earlier on *Rowan & Martin's Laugh-In*, Tomlin jested with the vice president, asking him if he was "surfing the net" for images of global warming. "You crazy guy! It's true what I've been telling my friends," she joked. "You're not stiff, you're just a techno-nerd." Decades earlier, Richard Nixon had used that show to forge a more intimate connec-

Vice President Al Gore looks on as President Clinton uses an electronic pen to sign the Telecommunications Act of 1996, Thursday, February 8, at the Library of Congress in Washington, D.C.
Photo Credit: AP Photo/Doug Mills.

tion with Gore and Clinton's generation. Now these two "Baby Boomers" used such entertainment as a campaign *and* governing strategy.

Bill Clinton scribbled his signature with one last symbolic statement: he signed with the very pen that President Eisenhower had used to usher into law the 1957 National Interstate and Defense Highways Act. The message was clear: this bill would unleash the infrastructure for the twenty-first century.

It did. But despite Gore's promise that a commitment to the public interest was built into the bill's DNA, consumer interest was the driving factor. In fact, he saw them as one and the same.[117] The 1934 Communications Act had allowed commercialism and advertising to underpin the broadcast economy, but it also mandated that the media monopolies it allowed to emerge had responsibilities to promote the public interest as well.[118] Certainly, this monopolistic system was flawed, as critics across the political spectrum had repeatedly pointed out. Public affairs programs offered a narrow, white, male, elitist, and exclusionary view of current events, while politicians like Lyndon Johnson manipulated the system for their individual economic and political benefit. By contrast, the 1996 act eliminated any public interest requirements, allowing private businesses to focus merely on providing consumer choice without any expectation or incentives to create tools or programs that informed citizens.

The bill lifted the shackles of cable legislation from four years earlier and allowed telecommunications industries (telephone, broadcasting, and cable) to compete with one another by offering integrated services. It was built on the premise that competition would keep rates down, something Gore had advocated during the 1989 cable hearings before he decided to shift gears to focus attention to regulating the "big bad monopoly" (the latter fit the populist message of the Clinton and Gore campaign).

It also introduced new rules on programming, even as it upheld the retransmission consent and must-carry provisions that cable programmers hated. Controversially, Title V, known as the Communications Decency Act, clamped down on "indecent" programming. Another clause introduced a ratings system provision, which would alert viewers on programming content. Finally, it also mandated television manufacturers to equip televisions with a "violence chip" (or V-chip) that would allow parents to block certain channels.[119] Clinton and Gore widely celebrated such programming regulations, and yet, the courts soon ruled them unconstitutional. Meanwhile, Section 230 of the Communications Decency Act, which excluded internet service providers and websites from being liable for the information shared or posted on them, would democratize internet content in ways that would propel social justice but also allow vulgar, radical, and violent ideas to percolate, and gain support, as well.[120]

For many in the cable industry, the bill's passage was anticlimactic, despite the hype that Gore and Clinton tried to inject into the signing ceremony. It was a legislative battle decades in the making, and the result of what Decker Anstrom—who had assumed the reins of the NCTA and led legislative discussions on the bill—called years of "bloody, disruptive, public whipping" by national politicians.[121]

Nothing illustrated this more starkly than Gore's reception at the National Cable Television Association's annual convention on May 4, 1996. Brian Roberts, the president of Comcast, introduced the vice president and celebrated the bill as an act of reconciliation. Rather than thinking of Gore as the "cable basher," Roberts encouraged his colleagues to see him as a visionary leader eager to "work together to move this legislation forward and not gripe by looking backwards."[122] Amid loud applause, the vice president strolled onto the stage, smiling widely as he shook Roberts' hand. Gore admitted to having "disagreements" with some in the industry, jesting that "some of you may have even seen me as Washington's answer to Darth Vader" (a joke that fell flat). He too proposed a new way forward: a "corporate citizenship" for the industry to build the information superhighway and fill it with content. "Cable has set the pace for much of what President Clinton and I have been trying to accomplish to make television more nourishing for children and more useful for our democracy."

Many seasoned cable veterans refused to let "bygones be bygones" and called out the hypocrisy of Gore's political posturing. Craig Leddy compared Gore to the character made famous by Jim Carrey's dark performance of an obsessive cable repairman in the recent movie *The Cable Guy*. "His politically slick performance," wrote Leddy in a scathing review of Gore's speech, "made it appear that Al Gore is the real Cable Guy, a slightly demonic, deal-wielding nudge that won't go away."[123] Gore's attempt to take credit for building the information highway that cable companies made possible infuriated many in the industry. "Thanks for nothing," Leddy concluded.

Gore's appearance at the NCTA reflected just how politically and economically powerful the cable industry had become by 1996. Sure, someone like John Malone could be a good villain on the campaign trail, but Gore and Clinton needed him and other cable executives to execute their media strategy *and* policy goals.

In the end, the Telecommunications Act certainly served the bottom line of corporations looking to pursue new markets and the self interest of elected officials hoping to use cable networks to promote their campaigns and policies. But such economic and political developments also depended on feeding a public appetite for entertainment and distraction and treating the news as a market commodity, not a civic necessity.[124] This was the cultural consequence of deregulation. Time and time again, the threat of congressional action or FCC rulemaking had pushed the industry to fulfill a social contract and provide programming that demonstrated its commitments to the public interest. The new media landscape took away this stick and enlarged the carrot: profits.

Such dramatic changes played out with little public attention or concern, perhaps unsurprising during a year in which the movie *Jerry Maguire* made the line "show me the money" a cultural phenomenon.[125] Media critics tried to sound the alarm with prescient warnings about corporate consolidation they feared was coming to media and technology industries. "Everyone sits around commenting on the coming of a new telecommunications age," argued Marvin Kitman, a columnist for *Newsday*. "It's not new. It's the same old plundering of public resources. Only we have funny-looking real estate now, real estate that can't be seen."[126]

Media critic Patricia Aufderheide agreed, calling attention to how a consumerist understanding of the public interest had triumphed, and the consequences.[127] She explained how the legislation hinged on the idea that mere access to more programming would advance the public interest without requiring providers to invest in education, training, or activities that would help communications technology actually do this. Nor did the legislation clarify how technology could or should address structural issues perpetuating inequality, like poverty, racism, and sexism.[128] Aufderheide anticipated that political ferment would follow because "the law had changed the terms of doing business, but it had not established any consistent zone of responsibilities for the social effects of the communications processes that these businesses put into motion."

It didn't take long for such predictions to come true. In the spring of 1997, John Malone joined CEOs from Comcast, Cox Communications, Time Warner Cable, and the head of the industry-funded CableLabs for a dinner party with Bill Gates that would transform the industry.[129] These cable executives hoped to convince the titan of the tech world to invest in cable infrastructure so that together, cable operators and Silicon Valley companies could deliver digital broadband services that offered high-speed internet and even more cable programming. The dinner set the stage for a groundbreaking summer announcement. Not only did Microsoft have a stake in cable programming with MSNBC, now it would forge a partnership with Comcast to own part of the hardware.

At the same time, cable companies started to swap operations so they could cluster their systems in regions across the country to better compete against telephone companies. In what TCI's Leo Hindery called the "most dramatic swapping in the history of any industry," cable executives sat in closed-door corporate rooms trading cities ("You take Philadelphia, I'll take San Antonio") to "enhance their regional concentration over time."[130] Soon after, mergers between telephone and cable companies began taking place, with TCI and AT&T striking a deal in 1998, setting the stage for even bigger telecommunications monopolies and ushering in what critics have called a "New Gilded Age."[131]

Such partnerships, along with CableLabs research, soon made digital service a reality. By the end of the century, 9.7 million subscribers had digital boxes and access to over one hundred channels, and both numbers continued to expand dramatically.[132] And yet, a central question remained: did such expanded consumer options on television advance democracy, as so many cable advocates had always promised it would?

Walter Cronkite had his doubts. In a widely celebrated 1998 event on the "State of Television News," the legendary network newscaster asked the titan of the cable industry, John Malone, whether market forces could deliver the "very heavy responsibility in our democracy of keeping the people informed adequately enough so that they can perform their role in democracy at the voting polls."[133] Cronkite lauded the growth of cable programming but also worried about the day that viewers could "punch up and get nothing but golf, for we will have a lot of really good golfers but they aren't going to know what the hell is going on in the rest of the world."

Malone scoffed. "The consumer is king," he argued. "The consumer will ultimately demand convenience, accuracy . . . and quality." He was right about the importance of consumption in twenty-first-century politics, but wrong about what consumers wanted.

Conclusion

DEMOCRACY IN CABLE AMERICA

Roger Ailes was furious. He had just watched the glitzy and highly touted unveiling of the new venture between NBC and Microsoft—MSNBC—and realized that it would not include him. In fact, it would replace America's Talking, the cable network he had helmed for NBC over the past few years. He exploded watching the press conference. "Fuck them," he told his assistant.[1] The man who prided himself on being a "counterpuncher" knew his tumultuous days at NBC were numbered. Within a month, he reached a separation agreement with the company that paid his $1 million salary and barred him from moving to CNN, Dow Jones, or Bloomberg.[2]

Ailes had no interest in those existing media outlets, however. By the end of January, the news came out. He would work with Rupert Murdoch to launch a cable news competitor to MSNBC and CNN. A decade earlier, Murdoch, an Australian media mogul, had the audacity to challenge the Big Three networks and establish an independent broadcast network, Fox Broadcasting Company. Murdoch later turned to cable television and happily used the retransmission consent rule to acquire carriage for his FX channel. And yet, he also craved the social and political prestige he felt came with entering television news. Like Ailes, Murdoch also wanted to counter the liberal bias he believed shaped the mainstream media. And so, the two men used their media expertise and conservative political outlooks to shape the formation of the Fox News Channel (FNC).

Ailes had been dreaming about a conservative news network for decades. Long before David Caldwell had introduced the idea of PRES to Reagan, Ailes had floated the idea of GOP TV to Richard Nixon after working as his media adviser during the 1968 campaign. With more people relying on television news and finding it more "believable than any other medium," Ailes saw an opportunity to create their own television program featuring "pro-Administration" news that would bypass the networks.[3]

Nixon's team passed on the idea, seeing its execution (including an airplane and truck delivery system) as too costly. Such a program would have also generated too much controversy. Even Richard Nixon understood the need to keep his efforts to manipulate his public image, divide Americans, and pursue revenge politics out of the public eye. Cable television changed the dynamics over the next two decades, though. Yes, it certainly provided the technology to disseminate such propaganda. But, more significantly, experiments on the cable dial—from the GOP's Operation Uplink to Gingrich's C-SPAN rants to Clinton's cozy relationship with MTV—made partisan television more commonplace.

Indeed, Ailes had helped to usher in these changes as he climbed the ranks of the GOP with his savvy suggestions on how to stage media appearances and sell political advertisements during the 1980s. And he knew exactly when and how to tap into the potential of cable television to exploit Americans' darker impulses, as his work with the Bush campaign in 1988 showed. From the beginning, Ailes was clear in his political approach to television: he wanted to exploit viewers' passivity. "People are lazy," he wrote early on in his career. "With television, you just sit—watch—listen. The thinking is done for you."[4] Now, Ailes wanted to use the veil of viewer empowerment (something clear in Fox News's other less famous tagline "We Report: You Decide") to do the thinking for viewers and make television news more engaging, addictive, and profitable.

The launch of Fox News also exposed something fundamental about the business of cable television and its commitment to civic initiatives following the passage of the 1996 Telecommunications Act. Just to get off the ground, Fox News needed carriage and the cable dial was extremely crowded. And then, none other than John Malone stepped in to help. At the end of June in 1996, TCI and Fox News announced that they had a deal in which the cable giant would carry Murdoch's channel in exchange for an undisclosed sum (rumored to be around $200 million) and an option to acquire a 20 percent stake in the business. The move opened access to around fifteen million homes.[5] To make space, Malone dropped the Lifetime channel, which angered many female viewers, who wrote letters, made phone calls, and even turned out for protests in Oregon and Texas.[6] The following year, the company also dropped C-SPAN on many systems. As Frank Rich, a *New York Times* columnist, observed, "Conglomerates, not competition, now drive TV: prices are higher, choice is less, and 'better quality' means more Murdoch and less C-Span. Public service or even public relations may stand little chance against the imperatives of the bottom line."[7] Luckily for the public affairs network, it had vocal and loyal viewers who launched a "Citizens for C-SPAN" letter-writing and phone campaign to raise enough ruckus for TCI's new president, Leo Hindrey, to step in and promise carriage and financial support for C-SPAN.[8] Nevertheless, the incident exposed how, when push came to shove, corporate earnings mattered more than any professed commitments to public service.

Fox News would soon show that to be the case on a much bigger scale as it created an opportunity for an even more combative and explosive political style—which had proved popular, profitable, and politically effective in talk radio—to enter the world of cable television. This was by design. Ailes was close with Rush Limbaugh and had even produced a television show for the radio star. Limbaugh then urged his listeners to demand that cable operators carry the channel by saying it would provide television news "for the independent thinker."[9] He also assured listeners that "Fox News is fair news," in direct contrast to the liberal media, against whom he ranted each day.

The scandal-ridden Clinton administration helped Fox find its footing as a news outlet that appealed to conservatives. Initially, Ailes carefully walked the line between news and propaganda, as he had watched exploits like National Empowerment Television fail because they were too ideologically driven. Like conservative media activists had for decades, he stressed the importance of balance.[10] Accuracy and facts mattered significantly less than a liberal-versus-conservative debate on issues, especially during opinion programming, which openly embraced an infotainment model.[11] Commentators like Fox News host Sean Hannity would perhaps discuss real news issues, like the Iraq war, but they also fabricated ones, like the 2004 Swift Boat controversy, in which Hannity "leaked" a forthcoming ad about Democratic presidential nominee John Kerry that featured Vietnam veterans attacking his wartime record. As the segment turned the latter topic into a campaign issue, Ailes relished how his cable news channel was "beginning to change the agenda of what is news."[12]

By the 2004 election, Fox News had emerged as a breeding ground for aspiring Republican politicians, and a lucrative career path for those who lost elections but caused a scene in the process. More importantly, the network affected what its viewers thought—to the benefit of Republicans. That year, Fox News viewers and Limbaugh listeners were more likely to endorse Republican campaign messages and reject Democratic ones than were nonviewers and nonlisteners, a trend that would only intensify.[13] Meanwhile, Fox News commentators and talk radio hosts listened to one another's shows on the radio, watched them on television, and read the same articles in the *Wall Street Journal* (which Murdoch bought in 2007); they consumed one another's perspectives and ran in the same social circles, which soon included stumping for Republican candidates.

FNC made clear the extent to which cable news had fundamentally changed how millions of Americans engaged in politics. It didn't seek to inform citizens. It wanted to sell and intensify a carefully curated political identity.[14] This was good for the television business as Republicans trusted Fox News more than any other outlet.[15] But, since Americans simultaneously reported that they found cable news a helpful source of information to understanding politics, this powerful echo chamber has been bad for democracy as it has opened new avenues for misinformation to circulate.[16] Over the next decade, especially after the election of the first African American president and the rise of the first woman Speaker of the House, Fox News saw the business potential of tapping into white identity politics by fueling racism, sexism, and eventually, with the political rise of Donald Trump, illiberalism.[17]

For decades, the cable industry looked for ways to ingratiate itself into the political process, but not even Bill Daniels—a staunch Republican—could have predicted the depths of entanglement that emerged with Fox News and the White House during Donald Trump's administration. Under the 45th president, Fox News commentators assumed a role that far surpassed how network executives or Hollywood entertainers had previously advised presidents.[18] While the actor Robert Montgomery had once helped Dwight Eisenhower navigate television appearances, and William Paley had caved to pressures from Lyndon Johnson about news programming on the Vietnam War, the relationship between Trump and Fox News was fundamentally different. Fox stars—notably Sean Hannity, Tucker Carlson, and Laura Ingraham—operated as a shadow cabinet for Trump, shaping not just his media choices but advising him on policy. The cable news network became a pipeline for White House staffers as well, with former Fox co-president Bill Shine even assuming the role of communications director and deputy chief of staff.[19]

As a result, a Fox-Trump echo chamber emerged in which the president tweeted in response to Fox programming and Fox stars referenced Trump's tweets, even at times speaking directly to him on their shows.[20] With such a relationship, the line between news and White House propaganda didn't just fade. It disappeared and the Trump drama—lies over COVID-19, racist rants about African countries and immigration policy, and efforts to overturn the 2020 election—emboldened his supporters and enraged his critics.[21]

It was the ultimate manifestation of political narrowcasting: a cable channel and a president each catering directly to one another.[22] It boosted the business of television, even as the rise of social media and the emergence of streaming services have simultaneously upended the cable industry itself as millions of Americans have cut the cord. Nevertheless, the demand for personalized programming has intensified, and the values that cable television brought to media and politics—disruption, branding, targeting, and fracturing—have now overwhelmed both worlds.

Donald Trump's presidency has made clear the consequences. Certainly his celebrity and his use of new media, notably Twitter, helped him circumvent the political and media establishments just as figures like John F. Kennedy and Richard Nixon did before him. Unlike his predecessors, however, he emerged as a public figure during a time in which politicians and the public alike believed that profits and ratings could boost democracy. He also blended the range of experiments on the cable dial—partisan propaganda, outrage, and entertainment—to go beyond merely trying to control the media narrative. Like cable channels, he wanted to promote his brand and craft a personal loyalty to him that seemingly knew no bounds. And indeed, even a violent insurrection could not sever it for millions of Americans.

The lesson is that political and media values don't just coincide— they cocreate one another, and cable television changed both. The broadcasting and Hollywood studio eras were a time when news and entertainment producers looked to appeal to the broadest audience possible. Performance and stagecraft mattered, of course, but so too did an ability to connect to a wide range of people. The shift to niche and narrowcasting programming on the cable dial created a media world that prioritized cult followings and fealty to individual brands.[23] Reality television flourished on the cable dial because it was cheap and it brought shock and awe to audiences craving both authenticity and the drama that people like Newt Gingrich also delivered on a daily basis. In a world in which political media programs are "whoring for our attention," as Tabitha Soren noted, the line between fact and fiction disappeared and the notion of "alternative facts" emerged.[24]

This was the future that the famed media critic Neil Postman feared in 1985 when he penned a powerful critique of how the expansion of television allowed show business to infuse all aspects of civic life by co-opting "serious modes of discourse—news, politics, science, education, commerce, religion—and turn[ing] them into entertainment packages."[25] He contended that shows like *60 Minutes* and local *Eyewitness News* programs threatened civic health because they created the expectation that political information and political leadership should also entertain. Just as dangerously, viewers also left with the *illusion* that they were informed on public affairs.

Postman wrote *Amusing Ourselves to Death* just as cable television was entering the lucrative urban markets across the country. Cable advocates had long promised that they would advance democracy by expanding access to information. Some people truly believed this and worked toward this goal. However, such a promise was always linked to growing the business of television. And instead of a richer democracy—one with better educated Americans who debate issues and hear from politicians in depth—cable has delivered a divided, polarized, angry America, where people doom scroll on their favorite social media platform (another segmented market-place) controlled by various private businesses and their agendas.

NOTES

Introduction

1. C-SPAN Video, "Cable Television Political Workshop," March 1, 1984, https://www.c-span.org/video/?124204-1/cable-television-political-workshop.

2. 1st Cable Television Political Workshop Agenda, March 1, 1984. Folder 6, Box 67, Robert and Elizabeth Dole Archive and Special Collections, Robert J. Dole Institute of Politics, The University of Kansas (hereafter Robert Dole Papers).

3. Thomas Frank, *The Conquest of Cool: Business Culture, Counterculture and the Rise of Hip Consumerism*, University of Chicago Press, 1997, 19–20. Here, Frank also discusses these findings as insights from the extensive work of prominent cultural historians Warren Susman, William Leach, and T. J. Jackson Lears.

4. Frank, *The Conquest of Cool*. For more recent work, see Lizabeth Cohen, *A Consumers' Republic: The Politics of Mass Consumption in Postwar America*, Random House, 2003.

5. 1st Cable Television Political Workshop Agenda, March 1, 1984. Folder 6, Box 67, Robert Dole Papers.

6. Susan J. Douglas, *Listening In: Radio and the American Imagination*, University of Minnesota Press, 2004.

7. Charles L. Ponce de Leon, *That's the Way It Is: A History of Television News in America*, University of Chicago Press, 2016; Christopher B. Daly, *Covering America: A Narrative History of a Nation's Journalism*, University of Massachusetts Press, 2012, 287–321.

8. See, for example, Susan J. Douglas, *Where the Girls Are: Growing Up Female with the Mass Media*, Crown, 1995; Michele Hilmes, *Radio Voices: American Broadcasting, 1922–1952*, University of Minnesota Press, 1997; James L. Baughman, *Television's Guardians: The FCC and the Politics of Programming, 1958–1967*, University of Tennessee Press, 1985; James L. Baughman, *Same Time, Same Station: Creating American Television, 1948–1961*, The Johns Hopkins University Press, 2007; Aniko Bodroghkozy, *Equal Time: Television and the Civil Rights Movement*, University of Illinois Press, 2012.

9. Lizabeth Cohen makes this important observation about the application of market segmentation to politics as dividing people along race, class, gender, and economic lines in *Consumers' Republic*. See especially 404–406.

10. "Political Cablecasting," NCTA Cablecasting Guidebook, 1973, Barco Library, The Cable Center, Denver, Colorado (hereafter Barco Library, The Cable Center).

11. Daniel T. Rodgers, *Age of Fracture*, Harvard University Press, 2012, 75–76.

12. Paul Starr, *The Creation of the Media: Political Origins of Modern Communications*, Basic Books, 2005.

13. Sedition Act, 1798, https://www.archives.gov/milestone-documents/alien-and-sedition-acts. See also Katlyn Marie Carter, "What the 1798 Sedition Act Got Right—and What It Means Today," *Washington Post*, January 14, 2021, https://www.washingtonpost.com/outlook/2021/01/14/what-1798-sedition-act-got-right-what-it-means-today/.

14. Katlyn Marie Carter, "Houses of Glass: Secrecy, Transparency, and the Birth of Representative Democracy," book manuscript under contract with Yale University Press. On public opinion and the founding generation, see Lindsay M. Chervinsky, *The Cabinet: George Washington and the Creation of an American Institution*, Harvard University Press, 2020. On concerns over misinformation in the early republic, see Jordan E. Taylor, *Misinformation Nation: Foreign News and the Politics of Truth in Revolutionary America*, The Johns Hopkins University Press, 2022.

15. David Greenberg, *Republic of Spin: An Inside History of the American Presidency*, W. W. Norton, 2016; Lizabeth Cohen, *Making a New Deal: Industrial Workers in Chicago, 1919–1939*, Cambridge University Press, 1990; Kathryn Cramer Brownell, *Showbiz Politics: Hollywood in American Political Life*, University of North Carolina Press, 2014, 12–41.

16. C-SPAN Video, "Cable Television Political Workshop."

17. Judith Miller, "But Can You Dance to It? MTV Turns to News," *New York Times*, October 11, 1992, A-31.

18. Lily Geismer, *Left Behind: The Democrats' Failed Attempt to Solve Inequality*, Public Affairs, 2022; Gary Gerstle, *The Rise and Fall of the Neoliberal Order: America and the World in the Free Market Era*, Oxford University Press, 2022; Rodgers, *Age of Fracture*, 75–76.

19. Markus Prior, *Post-Broadcast Democracy: How Media Choice Increases Inequality in Political Involvement and Polarizes Elections*, Cambridge University Press, 2007.

20. James Poniewozik, *Audience of One: Donald Trump, Television, and the Fracturing of America*, Liveright, 2019.

21. Chad Raphael, "The Political Economic Origins of Reali-TV," *Reality TV: Remaking Television Culture*, ed. Susan Murray and Laurie Ouellette, NYU Press, 2008, 123–140.

22. The importance of seeing media culture as central to democracy and a deeper consideration of this fundamental paradox can be found in Zac Gershberg and Sean Illing, *The Paradox of Democracy: Free Speech, Open Media, and Perilous Persuasion*, University of Chicago Press, 2022.

23. Journalists have chronicled the business history and political impact of the cable industry, with recent books focusing on Ted Turner and the launch of CNN, the role of Roger Ailes and Fox News, and, more recently, the network's

connection to Donald Trump. See the extensive works by Ken Auletta, including *Three Blind Mice: How the TV Networks Lost Their War*, Vintage, 2010; *Media Man: Ted Turner's Improbable Empire*, W. W. Norton, 2005; and *Backstory: Inside the Business of the News*, Penguin, 2004. See also Lisa Napoli, *Up All Night: Ted Turner, CNN, and the Birth of 24-Hour News*, Harry N. Abrams, 2021; Gabriel Sherman, *The Loudest Voice in the Room: How the Brilliant, Bombastic Roger Ailes Built Fox News*, Random House, 2014; and Brian Stelter, *Hoax: Donald Trump, Fox News and the Dangerous Distortion of the Truth*, Atria/One Signal, 2020. Communications scholars and political scientists have examined the programming contributions of the cable dial and the emergence of conservative, and more recently, liberal political echo chambers. This literature is extensive, but some key works include Megan Mullen, *Television in the Multichannel Age: A Brief History of Cable Television*, Blackwell, 2008; Patrick Parsons, *Blue Skies: A History of Cable Television*, Temple University Press, 2008; Kathleen Hall Jamieson and Joseph N. Cappella, *Echo Chamber: Rush Limbaugh and the Conservative Media Establishment*, Oxford University Press, 2010; and Stefano DellaVigna and Ethan Kaplan, "The Fox News Effect: Media Bias and Voting," *Quarterly Journal of Economics* 122, 2007, 1187–1234. More recent works include John McMurria, *Republic on the Wire: Cable Television, Pluralism, and the Politics of New Technology, 1948–1984*, Rutgers University Press, 2017; Jill Edy and Patrick Meirick, *A Nation Fragmented: The Public Agenda in the Information Age*, Temple University Press, 2019; and Dannagal Goldthwaite Young, *Irony and Outrage: The Polarized Landscape of Rage, Fear, and Laughter in the United States*, Oxford University Press, 2020.

24. Ezra Klein, "I Didn't Want It to Be True, but the Medium Really Is the Message," *New York Times*, August 7, 2022, https://www.nytimes.com/2022/08 /07/opinion/media-message-twitter-instagram.html; John M. Culkin, "A School-man's Guide to Marshall McLuhan," *Saturday Review,* March 18, 1967, reprinted in *Reading and Interpretation of Critical Issues in Modern American Life*, ed. Robert J. Wechman, Associated Educational Services Corporation, 1968, 5A.

25. Historians have shown how television is a political institution shaped by cultural values and political agendas, which in turn influence changing media institutions and their operations. See the extensive work of Heather Hendershot, including *What's Fair on the Air? Cold War Right-Wing Broadcasting and the Public Interest*, University of Chicago Press, 2011; *Open to Debate: How William F. Buckley Put Liberal America on the Firing Line*, Broadside Books, 2016; and most recently, *When the News Broke: Chicago 1968 and the Polarizing of America*, University of Chicago Press, 2023. See also the extensive work of Richard R. John, including *Network Nation: Inventing American Telecommunications*, Harvard University Press, 2015; Paul Starr, *The Creation of the Media*; Nicole Hemmer, *Messengers on the Right: Conservative Media and the Transformation of American Politics*, University of Pennsylvania Press, 2016; Allison Perlman, *Public Interests: Media Advocacy and Struggles over U.S. Television*, Rutgers University Press, 2016; Brian Rosenwald, *Talk Radio's America: How an Industry Took Over a Political Party That Took Over the United States*, Harvard University Press, 2019; Matthew Pressman, *On Press: The Liberal Values that Shaped the News*, Harvard University Press, 2018; Oscar Winberg,

"Archie Bunker for President: Television Entertainment and the Transformation of American Politics in the 1970s," PhD diss., Åbo Akademi University, Finland, 2021; and Sage Goodwin, "Making the News: The Development of Network Television News and the Struggle for Black Freedom in the 1950s and 1960s," PhD diss., University of Oxford, 2022.

26. On the need to rethink the role of ideological divides as shaping recent American political history, see Brent Cebul, Lily Geismer, and Mason B. Williams, eds., *Shaped by the State: Toward a New Political History of the Twentieth Century*, University of Chicago Press, 2019.

27. Edward Murrow address before the RTNDA Convention, October 15, 1958, https://www.rtdna.org/content/edward_r_murrow_s_1958_wires_lights _in_a_box_speech.

Act I

1. Patrick Parsons, *Blue Skies: A History of Cable Television*, Temple University Press, 2008, 1–3.

2. Newton Minow Oral History, 1999, Hauser Collection, Barco Library, The Cable Center.

3. See for example: Ralph Lee Smith, "Deadlier than a Western: The Battle over Cable TV," *New York Times*, May 26, 1968. Folder, The Battle over Cable TV, Box Series 89, Frederick Ford Collection, Barco Library, The Cable Center.

4. Stephen Singular, *Relentless: Bill Daniels and the Triumph of Cable TV*, James Charlton, 2003.

5. Bill Daniels Oral History, 1986, Penn State Collection, Barco Library, The Cable Center.

6. On how other industries organized and lobbied for change, see, for example, Katherine Rye Jewell, *Dollars for Dixie: Business and the Transformation of Conservatism in the Twentieth Century*, Cambridge University Press, 2017; and Jennifer Delton, *The Industrialists: How the National Association of Manufacturers Shaped American Capitalism*, Princeton University Press, 2020.

7. Parsons, *Blue Skies*, 102–107.

8. Megan Mullen, *Television in the Multichannel Age: A Brief History of Cable Television*, Blackwell, 2010.

9. Bill Daniels Oral History, 1990, Barco Library, The Cable Center.

Chapter 1

1. "Report Minow, Adlai's Partner, Will Head the FCC," *Chicago Daily Tribune*, January 9, 1961, 3.

2. Newton Minow Oral History, 1999, Hauser Collection, Barco Library, The Cable Center.

3. Kathryn Cramer Brownell, *Showbiz Politics: Hollywood in American Political Life*, University of North Carolina Press, 2014, 85–91.

4. J. Leonard Reinsch Oral History, March 13, 1967, Harry S. Truman Presidential Library, https://www.trumanlibrary.gov/library/oral-histories/reinsch.

5. In Minow's oral history, he notes how CBS had the largest cable system in North America with its investment in a Vancouver station. See, for example, "CBS Buys Chunk of Vancouver CATV," *Broadcasting*, October 19, 1964, 10. Between 1960 and 1965, broadcasters eagerly eyed the cable industry. Because of FCC concerns about concentration of ownerships in areas with both cable and broadcast systems, most broadcasters bought CATV operations outside their broadcasting markets. By 1969, broadcasters owned 32.3 percent of CATV systems. Patrick Parsons, *Blue Skies: A History of Cable Television*, Temple University Press, 2008, 184–186. The following year the FCC would initiate changes in ownership requirements and ban local cross-ownership of broadcasting stations and cable systems, forcing many large broadcasting companies to divest of cable holdings. This ruling also prohibited networks from owning cable stations, forcing CBS to sell off its holdings in what then became Viacom. See Benjamin M. Compaine, *Who Owns the Media?: Concentration of Ownership in the Mass Communications Industry*, Knowledge Industry Publications, 1982, 385–389.

6. James L. Baughman, *Television's Guardians: The FCC and the Politics of Programming, 1958–1967*, University of Tennessee Press, 1985, 152–165.

7. Newton Minow, "Television and the Public Interest," speech delivered to the National Association of Broadcasters, May 9, 1961, Washington, D.C., https://www.americanrhetoric.com/speeches/newtonminow.htm.

8. Newton Minow Oral History.

9. Minow, "Television and the Public Interest."

10. Michael Curtin, *Redeeming the Wasteland: Television Documentary and Cold War Politics*, Rutgers University Press, 1996, 7; James L. Baughman, *The Republic of Mass Culture: Journalism, Filmmaking, and Broadcasting in America Since 1941*, The Johns Hopkins University Press, 2006, 96.

11. Curtin, *Redeeming the Wasteland*.

12. Michele Hilmes, "NBC and the Network Idea: Defining the 'American System,' in *NBC: America's Network*, University of California Press, 2007, ed. Michele Hilmes, 7–24; Paul Starr, *The Creation of the Media: Political Origins of Modern Communications*, Basic Books, 2005, 327–384; Jennifer Holt, "A History of Broadcast Regulations: Principles and Perspectives," in *A Companion to the History of American Broadcasting*, ed. Aniko Bodroghkozy, Wiley, 2018, 171–192.

13. On the scholarly debates over scarcity, see Holt, "A History of Broadcast Regulations," 173–174. See also Starr, *Creation of the Media*, 329–330.

14. Allison Perlman, *Public Interests: Media Advocacy and Struggles over U.S. Television*, Rutgers University Press, 2016, 4–5.

15. Starr, *Creation of the Media*, 220–222; Richard R. John, *Network Nation: Inventing American Telecommunications*, Harvard University Press, 2015.

16. Starr, *Creation of the Media*, 328.

17. Specifics of the Radio Act of 1927 can be found in Starr, *Creation of the Media*, 343.

18. Mark Lloyd, *Prologue to a Farce: Communication and Democracy in America*, University of Illinois Press, 2006, 111–113. On the broadcast reform movement of the early 1930s, see Robert W. McChesney, *Telecommunications, Mass Media, and Democracy: The Battle for Control of U.S. Broadcasting 1928–1935*, Oxford University Press, 1995, 177–187. On the privileging of national interests over local ones, see Perlman, *Public Interests*, 15–16; Lizabeth Cohen, *Making a New Deal: Industrial Workers in Chicago, 1919–1939*, Cambridge University Press, 1990, 323–333.

19. All of these examples, plus a larger discussion of the criticism that emerged of radio in the 1940s, can be found in Victor Pickard, *America's Battle for Media Democracy: The Triumph of Corporate Libertarianism and the Future of Media Reform*, Cambridge University Press, 2015, 9–37.

20. Starr, *Creation of the Media*, 380–382.

21. Baughman, *Television's Guardians*, 10.

22. Alan Brinkley, *Voices of Protest: Huey Long, Father Coughlin & The Great Depression*, Vintage Books, 1983.

23. Quoted in Heather Hendershot, *What's Fair on the Air? Cold War Right-Wing Broadcasting and the Public Interest,* University of Chicago Press, 2011, 16. For a broader discussion of the concerns about editorializing and the origins of the Fairness Doctrine, see 16–20. See also Pickard, *America's Battle for Media Democracy*, 98–123.

24. In *America's Battle for Media Democracy*, Pickard writes that the doctrine continues to be invoked by progressives as the "highwater mark for enlightened media policy," 98. In the postwar period, frustrations with this policy motivated conservatives to organize politically, as Nicole Hemmer shows in *Messengers of the Right: Conservative Media and the Transformation of American Politics*, University of Pennsylvania Press, 2016; and as Hendershot shows in *What's Fair on the Air?*

25. Pickard, *America's Battle for Media Democracy*, 5.

26. Baughman, *Television's Guardians*, 11.

27. Hendershot makes this key point that "'regulation' should be understood for what it was—a euphemism for 'censorship,'" *What's Fair on the Air?*, 20.

28. Parsons, *Blue Skies*, 8–36.

29. Baughman, *Republic of Mass Culture*, 41.

30. Les Brown, *Televi$ion: The Business behind the Box*, Harcourt Brace Jovanovich, 1971, 16.

31. Discussed in Oral History Panel, "Development of Cable in Pennsylvania," conversation with George Gardner, Bob Tudek, Bob Tarlton, Irene Gans, Joe Gans, Len Ecker, Stratford Smith, and Jim Duratz, Hauser Collection, Barco Library, The Cable Center. See also John McMurria, *Republic on the Wire: Cable Television, Pluralism, and the Politics of New Technologies, 1948–1984*, Rutgers University Press, 2017, 34–61. See also Newton Minow Oral History.

32. Baughman, *Television's Guardians*, 36–39.

33. For an overview of cable's origins, see Parsons, *Blue Skies*, 54–71.

34. Parson's experiences in starting his cable system are detailed in his oral history: Leroy "Ed" Parsons Oral History, June 19, 1986, Barco Library, The Cable Center.

35. Leroy "Ed" Parsons Oral History.

36. Leroy "Ed" Parsons Oral History.

37. "Development of Cable in Pennsylvania Oral History Panel."

38. Parsons, *Blue Skies*, 61. The Cable Center recognizes men like Bob Tarlton in Pennsylvania and Jimmy Davison in Arkansas along with Parsons as "founders of CATV." Their successes also came by learning from other engineers and entrepreneurs, men like Milton J. Shapp, the founder of Jerrold Electronics, which became a key supplier of amplifiers for cable operators, and the team of Martin Malarkey and Archer Taylor, who would create the industry's first CATV engineering consulting firm, Malarkey & Associates. For an overview of this official history as told by The Cable Center, see Larry Satkowiak, *The Cable Industry: A Short History through Three Generations*, The Cable Center, 2015, 5–8.

39. Parsons, *Blue Skies*; Baughman, *Television's Guardians*. On businesses constructing a civic role for themselves in the postwar period, see Elizabeth A. Fones-Wolf, *Selling Free Enterprise: The Business Assault on Labor and Liberalism, 1945–1960*, University of Illinois Press, 1994.

40. Baughman, *Television's Guardians*, 13.

41. Baughman, 14.

42. Vance Kepley Jr., "The Weaver Years at NBC," *Wide Angle* 12, no. 2, April 1990, 55; Michael Socolow, "'We Should Make Money on Our News': The Problem of Profitability in Network Broadcast Journalism History," *Journalism* 11, no. 6, 2010, 675–691.

43. On the personal motivations behind developing newsrooms to chronicle public affairs and bring "a vicarious sense of gravitas to all those involved," see Christopher B. Daly, *Covering America: A Narrative History of a Nation's Journalism*, University of Massachusetts Press, 2012, 292–293.

44. Sig Mickelson, "Television and the Voter," Address to Round Table Luncheon of the Radio and Television Executives Society, New York, NY, October 28, 1959. Folder, TV Arrangements, Media Plan Summary, Box 395, Television and Radio Division, Democratic National Committee, John F. Kennedy Presidential Library, Boston, MA (hereafter JFKPL).

45. Mickelson, "Television and the Voter."

46. Ralph Freeman, "Postwar Economic Trends in the United States," in John Patrick Diggins, *The Proud Decades: America in War and Peace, 1941–1960*, W. W. Norton, 1989, 186.

47. Mickelson, "Television and the Voter."

48. On the profitability of television news, see Socolow, "'We Should Make Money on Our News.'" On the efforts by those excluded to build alternative media institutions, see Devorah Heitner, *Black Power TV*, Duke University Press, 2013; Hemmer, *Messengers of the Right*.

49. Newton N. Minow, John Bartlow Martin, and Lee M. Mitchell, *Presidential Television*, Basic Books, 1973, 74.

50. C-SPAN: "Eisenhower Cabinet Meeting," https://www.c-span.org/video/?15025-1/eisenhower-cabinet-meeting. On the impact of these television events in shaping news, see Stephen J. Whitfield, *The Culture of the Cold War*, 2nd ed., The Johns Hopkins University Press, 1996, 156–157.

51. Joe S. Foote, *Television Access and Political Power: The Networks, the Presidency, and the Loyal Opposition*, Praeger, 1990.

52. Brownell, *Showbiz Politics*, 158–187.

53. Minow, Martin, and Mitchell, *Presidential Television*, 51.

54. Newton N. Minow and Craig L. LaMay, *Inside the Presidential Debates: Their Improbable Past and Promising Future*, University of Chicago Press, 2008, 29.

55. Theodore H. White, *The Making of the President 1960*, Harper Perennial Reissue Edition, 2009, 280–281.

56. James L. Baughman, *Same Time, Same Station: Creating American Television, 1948–1961*, The Johns Hopkins University Press, 2007, 296–298.

57. Quoted in Minow and LaMay, *Inside the Presidential Debates*, 35.

58. Minow and LaMay, *Inside the Presidential Debates*, 35–39.

59. Don Hewitt's Oral History, in *Hollywood and Politics: A Sourcebook*, ed. Donald Critchlow and Emilie Raymond, Routledge, 2009.

60. Michael Schudson, *The Power of News*, Harvard University Press, 1996; David Greenberg, "Torchlight Parades for the Television Age: The Presidential Debates as Political Ritual," *Daedalus* 138, no. 3, 2009, 6–19.

61. Brownell, *Showbiz Politics*.

62. Minow, Martin, and Mitchell, *Presidential Television*, 39.

63. Minow, Martin, and Mitchell, *Presidential Television*, 41; David Greenberg, *Republic of Spin: An Inside History of the American Presidency*, W. W. Norton, 2016, 340–354.

64. Baughman, *Republic of Mass Culture*, 96.

65. Donald G. Tacheron and Morris K. Udall, *The Job of the Congressman: An Introduction to Service in the U.S. House of Representatives*, The Bobbs-Merrill Company, 1966, 100.

66. Michael Schudson, "Congress and the News Media," in *The American Congress: The Building of Democracy*, ed. Julian E. Zelizer, Houghton Mifflin Harcourt, 2004, 650–651.

67. Francis E. Rourke, "Congressional Use of Publicity," in *Congress and the News Media*, ed. Robert O. Blanchard, Hastings House Publishers, 1974, 128.

68. For a detailed overview of the history of televised congressional hearings, see Ronald Garay, *Congressional Television: A Legislative History*, Praeger, 1984.

69. Douglass Cater, "The Congressional Hearing as Publicity Vehicle," in *Congress and the News Media*, 346–351.

70. Garay, *Congressional Television*, 46–50.

71. Ben Bagdikian, "Congress and the Media, Partners in Propaganda," in *Congress and the News Media*, 388–398.

72. Bagdikian, "Congress and the Media"; and Mark J. Green, James M. Fallows, and David R. Zwick, ". . . And, Frankly, Getting Reelected," in *Congress and the News Media*, 384–387.

73. Garay, *Congressional Television*, 8–9.

74. Mark J. Green, Bruce Rosenthal, and Lynn Darling, "Who Runs Congress?," in *Congress and the News Media*, 275–282.

75. Delmer Dunn, "Symbiosis: Congress and the Press," in *Congress and the News Media,* 282.

76. Green, Fallows, and Zwick, ". . . And, Frankly, Getting Reelected."

77. Tim Anderson and Arthur Magida, "Alvin E. O'Konski: Republican Representative from Wisconsin," Ralph Nader Congress Project, *Citizens Look at Congress,* Grossman Publishers, 1972.

78. Anderson and Magida, "Alvin E. O'Konski."

79. "Lyndon Johnson, Broadcaster Once Removed," *Broadcasting,* January 29, 1973, 24.

80. Robert Caro, *The Years of Lyndon Johnson: Means of Ascent,* Knopf, 1990, 80–118.

81. Mark I. Gelfand, "Lyndon B. Johnson," in *Presidential Misconduct: From George Washington to Today,* ed. James M. Banner Jr., The New Press, 2019, 366–368.

82. Robert Dallek, *Lyndon B. Johnson: Portrait of a President,* Oxford University Press, 2005, 75.

83. Dallek, 75.

84. Dallek, 77.

85. "Lyndon Johnson, Broadcaster."

86. Dallek, *Lyndon B. Johnson,* 75.

87. Dallek, 76.

88. John Campbell Oral History, April 20, 2002, Hauser Project, Barco Library, The Cable Center.

89. Louis Kohlmeier, "Johnson and the FCC," *Wall Street Journal,* March 24, 1964, 14.

90. Kohlmeier, 14.

91. Kohlmeier, 14.

92. "Lyndon Johnson, Broadcaster," 24.

93. See Vice-President's Daily Diary entry, 11/28/1962, Pre-Presidential Daily Diary Collection; Vice-President's Daily Diary entry, 12/14/1962, Pre-Presidential Daily Diary Collection; Vice-President's Daily Diary entry, 12/18/1962, Pre-Presidential Daily Diary Collection; Vice-President's Daily Diary entry, 1/29/1963, Pre-Presidential Daily Diary Collection; Vice-President's Daily Diary entry, 2/4/1963, Pre-Presidential Daily Diary Collection. Lyndon B. Johnson Presidential Library (hereafter LBJPL), https://www.discoverlbj.org/item/vpdd -19630204.

94. Carol McMurtry, "Cable TV Contract Signed with City Despite Protests," *The Austin Statesman,* January 29, 1963, 13. See also Kohlmeier, "Johnson and the FCC," 14. This debate is also discussed in John Campbell's oral history as well as a version of that oral history published in *How CATV Came to Texas,* Createspace Independent Pub, 2005, 90–91, Barco Library, The Cable Center.

95. Parsons, *Blue Skies,* 184–186.

96. "Dispute Keys on 21 Points," *The Austin Statesman,* January 30, 1963, 27; McMurtry, "Cable TV Contract Signed," 13.

97. "Development of Cable Television in Texas," oral history roundtable featuring John Campbell, Ben Hooks, Jake Landrum, Bill Arnold, Ken Gunter, Herb Jackson, and Ben Conroy, Hauser Collection, Barco Library, The Cable Center; Kohlmeier, "Johnson and the FCC," 14.

98. "Johnsons' Television Station in Austin May Get Competition," *New York Times*, November 10, 1963, 65.

99. Campbell, *How CATV Came to Texas*, 97.

100. This timeline is discussed in Campbell, *How CATV Came to Texas*, 98–103. It also appears in Kohlmeier, "Johnson and the FCC," 14.

101. "Johnsons' Television Station," 65.

102. Nan Robertson, "F.C.C. Upholds Mrs. Johnson on Her TV Station," *New York Times*, December 14, 1963, 55.

103. For an overview of this operation and the connection between the broadcasting and cable business, see Robertson, "F.C.C. Upholds Mrs. Johnson on Her TV Station," 55.

104. "Lawyer for TV Cable Alleges Capital Cable and Johnson Family Station Misled FCC," *Wall Street Journal*, April 29, 1964, 2.

105. Kohlmeier, "Johnson and the FCC," 14.

106. Campbell, *How CATV Came to Texas*, 105.

107. Kohlmeier, "Johnson and the FCC," 14.

108. Kohlmeier, 1.

109. Kohlmeier, 1.

110. Oral history transcript, J. Waddy Bullion, interview 1 (I), 5/28/1969, by David G. McComb, LBJ Library Oral Histories, LBJPL, https://www.discoverlbj.org/item/oh-bullionj-19690528-1-09-45.

111. "Capital Cable Refuses to Give FCC Details of an Agreement," *The Austin Statesman*, April 8, 1964, A40.

112. Gelfand, "Lyndon B. Johnson," 366–369.

113. "Kohlmeier of *Wall Street Journal* Awarded Pulitzer Prize for Johnson Wealth Series," *Wall Street Journal*, May 4, 1965, 2.

114. Keith Wheeler and William Lambert, "How L.B.J.'s Family Amassed Its Fortune," *Life*, August 21, 1964, 63.

Chapter 2

1. Martin Mayer, "Big Play for Pay TV's $1.50 Splendors," *Saturday Evening Post*, May 2, 1964, 71.

2. Speech outline for "The Gilded Curtain," n.d. (mid-1950s), Folder 10, Box 126, National Association of Broadcasters Records, Wisconsin Center for Film & Theater Research, University of Wisconsin–Madison (hereafter WCFTR).

3. Lizabeth Cohen, *Making a New Deal: Industrial Workers in Chicago, 1919–1939*, Cambridge University Press, 1990, 302.

4. Speech outline for "The Gilded Curtain."

5. Stan Searle, "STV: An Uphill Battle," *TV & Communications*, October 1964, 9.

6. John McMurria, "A Taste of Class: Pay-TV and the Commodification of Television in Postwar America," in *Cable Visions: Television Beyond Broadcasting*, ed. Sarah Banet-Weiser, Cynthia Chris, and Anthony Freitas, New York University Press, 2007, 44–65.

7. Gary R. Edgerton, *The Columbia History of American Television*, Columbia University Press, 2009, 158–167.

8. Vance Kepley Jr., "The Weaver Years at NBC," *Wide Angle* 12, no. 2, 1990, 57.

9. Pat Weaver, *The Best Seat in the House: The Golden Years of Radio and Television*, Knopf, 1993, 247.

10. Weaver, *The Best Seat in the House*, 260; "In Pat Weaver's Own Wide World," *Life*, July 18, 1955, 108–114; "NBC's Sylvester (Pat) Weaver," *Newsweek*, July 18, 1955, 49–52.

11. James L. Baughman, *Same Time, Same Station: Creating American Television, 1948–1961*, The Johns Hopkins University Press, 2007, 110–111.

12. Baughman, 110–112.

13. Kepley Jr., "The Weaver Years at NBC," 53–55.

14. Baughman, *Same Time, Same Station*, 112–114.

15. Patrick Parsons, *Blue Skies: A History of Cable Television*, Temple University Press, 2008, 110–112; Memorandum from J. Roger Wollenberg to Sylvester L. Weaver, November 13, 1957. Folder 11, Box, 11, Sylvester "Pat" Weaver Papers, WCFTR.

16. Michele Hilmes, *Hollywood and Broadcasting: From Radio to Cable*, University of Illinois Press, 1999, 127–128.

17. Parsons, *Blue Skies*, 112.

18. Parsons, 110.

19. Memorandum from Henry J. Kaiser to Sylvester Weaver and Edgar F. Kaiser, November 7, 1957. Folder 11, Box, 11, Pat Weaver Papers, WCFTR.

20. Memorandum from J. Roger Wollenberg to Sylvester L. Weaver, November 13, 1957. Folder 11, Box, 11, Pat Weaver Papers, WCFTR.

21. Memorandum from Fred Wile to Pat Weaver, February 6, 1958. Folder 11, Box, 11, Pat Weaver Papers, WCFTR.

22. "2 Network Heads Oppose Toll Video," *New York Times*, January 23, 1958, 54.

23. "Network Presidents State Views Against Pay TV," statements of Robert W. Sarnoff, Leonard Goldenson, and Frank Stanton before the House Committee on Interstate & Foreign Commerce, January 21–22, 1958. Reprinted in a special supplement of *Television Digest with Electronics Reports*, January 25, 1958. Folder 11, Box, 11, Pat Weaver Papers, WCFTR.

24. "2 Network Heads Oppose Toll Video," 54.

25. Hilmes, *Hollywood and Broadcasting*, 130–134.

26. "Network Presidents State Views against Pay TV."

27. McMurria, "A Taste of Class," 47–48.

28. Parsons, *Blue Skies*, 186–189.

29. Hilmes, *Hollywood and Broadcasting*, 116–139.

30. Charles Wigutow, "The Not So Quiet Growth of Cable Television," *TV & Communications*, May 1964, 18.

31. Milton Shapp unpublished autobiography, n.d., Barco Library, The Cable Center.

32. Milton Shapp, "Two Necks—Same Noose," *Broadcasting*, June 28, 1965, 32–34.

33. Parsons, *Blue Skies*, 185.

34. Hilmes, *Hollywood and Broadcasting*, 128.

35. David Gunzerath, "'Darn That Pay TV!' STV's Challenge to American Television's Dominant Economic Model," *Journal of Broadcasting & Electronic Media* 44, no. 4, 2000, 661; David H. Ostroff, "A History of STV, Inc. and the 1964 California Vote against Pay Television," *Journal of Broadcasting* 27, no. 4, 1983, 377.

36. Gunzerath, "'Darn That Pay TV!,'" 660.

37. McMurria, "A Taste of Class," 53–58.

38. Gunzerath, "'Darn That Pay TV!,'" 661.

39. Gunzerath, 662.

40. On the budget, see Gunzerath, 665. Examples of all of these materials can be found in: Folder, "Campaign for Free TV" Committee for Free TV, Committee against Proposition 15, Office of the Secretary of State, Sacramento, California.

41. Herbert E. Alexander, *Financing the 1964 Election*, Citizens' Research Foundation, 1966, 46. Because of a lack of Democratic financial reporting, these are just estimates.

42. "'Darn That Pay TV!'" flyer. Folder, Prop. 15—Promotional Materials. Dockweiler Family Papers, CSLA-12. Department of Archives and Special Collections, William H. Hannon Library, Loyola Marymount University (hereafter Dockweiler Family Papers).

43. "Voters to Decide STV's Future," *Broadcasting*, November 2, 1964, 52–54.

44. "Say a Lot, Learn Little," *Broadcasting*, January 20, 1964, 61. Transcripts of the panel conversation can be found in: "Condensed Remarks," at the Hollywood chapter of the National Academy of Television Arts and Sciences, January 14, 1964. Folder, Prop. 15—Promotional Materials. Dockweiler Family Papers.

45. McMurria, "A Taste of Class," 53–58.

46. "NAB Joins STV Foes; Pat Weaver Fights Back," *TV & Communications*, April 1964, 28.

47. "Say a Lot, Learn Little," 61.

48. Transcripts of the panel conversation can be found in: "Condensed Remarks," at the Hollywood chapter of the National Academy of Television Arts and Sciences, January 14, 1964. Folder, Prop. 15- Promotional Materials. Dockweiler Family Papers.

49. "Condensed Remarks."

50. McMurria, "A Taste of Class," 49–50.

51. "20 Minute Talk on Free TV," Folder, Prop. 15—Promotional Materials. Dockweiler Family Papers.

52. For a longer history of the debates surrounding the term "free enterprise" and how conservatives used it to build a movement to dismantle the New Deal

state, see Lawrence B. Glickman, *Free Enterprise: An American History*, Yale University Press, 2019.

53. McMurria, "A Taste of Class," 544–565.

54. "STV Baseball Finds Favor on West Coast," *Broadcasting*, August 24, 1964, 68. On the 40,000 hook-up orders, see Searle, "STV: An Uphill Battle."

55. Subscriber's Choice, September 9–22, 1964, Volume 1, Number 3, Folder 1, Box 18, Pat Weaver Papers, WCFTR.

56. "STV Signs 30,000 Subscribers," *TV & Communications*, September 1964, 10.

57. "A Rumble over Pay in California," *Broadcasting*, March 23, 1964, 55.

58. Kathryn Cramer Brownell, *Showbiz Politics: Hollywood in American Political Life*, University of North Carolina Press, 2014.

59. Gunzerath, "'Darn That Pay TV!,'" 663.

60. Ostroff, "A History of STV," 377.

61. Searle, "STV: An Uphill Battle," 9.

62. "Network Conspiracy Charged," *TV & Communications*, October 1964, 14.

63. "A Fight against Pay TV," *Broadcasting*, February 3, 1964, 37.

64. "A Fight against Pay TV," 37.

65. "What to Do with Community Television?," *Broadcasting*, March 24, 1964, 60.

66. "Broadcasters Disagree on Regulation of CATV and Pay-TV," *TV & Communications*, June 1964, 7.

67. Searle, "STV: An Uphill Battle," 4.

68. NAB Views on CATV and Pay Television: Remarks by William Carlisle, NAB vice president, before the Southeast Radio-TV Seminar, *TV & Communications*, August 1964, 16–17.

69. "The Economic Impact of CATV," *Broadcasting*, October 26, 1964, 74–75.

70. Searle, "STV: An Uphill Battle," 4.

71. "20 Minute Talk on Free TV."

72. "STV's Backers Plan 'Phonathon,'" *Broadcasting*, October 26, 1964, 87.

73. For these numbers see Gunzerath, "'Darn That Pay TV!,'" 665–667.

74. "20 Minute Talk on Free TV." See also flyer, "Vote Yes on the Television Initiative, Keep TV Free in the Home" by the Citizens Committee for Free TV. Folder, Prop. 15—Promotional Materials. Dockweiler Family Papers.

75. Emilie Raymond, "'No on 14': Hollywood Celebrities, the Civil Rights Movement, and the California Open Housing Debate," in *Media Nation: The Political History of News in Modern America*, ed. Bruce J. Schulman and Julian E. Zelizer, University of Pennsylvania Press, 2017, 114–125.

76. S. L. Weaver, D. E. O'Neill, and T. F. Greenhow v. Frank M. Jordan, Sac. 7682. Folder, Free TV Act 1964, Box Series 89, Frederick Ford Collection, Barco Library, The Cable Center.

77. Raymond, "'No on 14,'" 124.

78. David C. Smith, "California's Overloaded Ballot Stirs Calls for Reform of State's Initiative Process," *Wall Street Journal*, November 2, 1964, 4.

79. "Will Vote Halt Pay TV's Growth?," *Broadcasting*, November 9, 1964, 21.

80. "Will Vote Halt Pay TV's Growth?," 22.

81. Ostroff, "A History of STV," 381–383.

82. S. L. Weaver, D. E. O'Neill, and T. F. Greenhow v. Frank M. Jordan, Sac. 7682.

83. Weaver, *The Best Seat in the House*, 274.

84. Gunzerath, "'Darn That Pay TV!,'" 670.

85. Bruce Merrill, Editorial, *TV & Communications*, July 1964, 24.

Chapter 3

1. Article on J. Leonard Reinsch by Norman Shavin, reprinted from *Atlanta Magazine*, August 1965. Vertical File: J. Leonard Reinsch, Barco Library, The Cable Center. See also Richard Rutter, "Personalities: Formidable Radio-TV Team," *New York Times*, August 23, 1964, F3.

2. Kathryn Cramer Brownell, *Showbiz Politics: Hollywood in American Political Life*, University of North Carolina Press, 2014, 151–157.

3. J. Leonard Reinsch Oral History, March 13, 1967, Harry S. Truman Presidential Library, https://www.trumanlibrary.gov/library/oral-histories/reinsch.

4. J. Leonard Reinsch Oral History.

5. J. Leonard Reinsch, "Broadcasting the Political Conventions," *Journal of Broadcasting & Electronic Media* 12, no. 3, June 1968, 219–223.

6. Rutter, "Personalities: Formidable Radio-TV Team."

7. Article on J. Leonard Reinsch by Norman Shavin.

8. Article on J. Leonard Reinsch by Norman Shavin.

9. Proceedings of the 13th Annual Convention of the National Community Television Association, June 14–19, 1964, A-21, Barco Library, The Cable Center.

10. Proceedings of the 13th Annual Convention.

11. Proceedings of the 13th Annual Convention.

12. Frederick W. Ford Oral History, Federal Communications Commission Project, 1980. Columbia Center for Oral History, New York. On the broader faith during the New Deal era on the importance of "expert commissioners to shape business practices in accordance to the public interest," see Thomas K. McGraw, *Prophets of Regulation: Charles Francis Adams, Louis D. Brandeis, James M. Landis, Alfred E. Kahn*, Harvard University Press, 1986, 152.

13. James L. Baughman, *Television's Guardians: The FCC and the Politics of Programming, 1958–1967*, University of Tennessee Press, 1985, 45–53.

14. "Cable TV Trade Group Finally Confirms Ford Is Its New President," *Wall Street Journal*, January 25, 1965, 24.

15. Patrick Parsons, *Blue Skies: A History of Cable Television*, Temple University Press, 2008, 214.

16. Letter from Milton Shapp, May 27, 1965, Box Series 89, Frederick Ford Collection, Barco Library, The Cable Center.

17. Brent Cebul and Mason B. Williams, "'Really and Truly a Partnership': The New Deal's Associational State and the Making of Postwar American Politics," in *Shaped by the State: Toward a New Political History of the Twentieth Century*, ed. Brent Cebul, Lily Geismer, and Mason B. Williams, University of Chicago Press, 2019, 96–122.

18. Milton Friedman, *Capitalism and Freedom*, 40th Anniversary Edition, University of Chicago Press, 2002 (originally published in 1962), 8.

19. Cebul and Williams, "'Really and Truly a Partnership.'"

20. National Community Television Association Membership Bulletin, Vol. 8, No. 5, February 18, 1966, Barco Library, The Cable Center.

21. Ford's response is found in National Community Television Association Membership Bulletin, Vol. 8, No. 5, February 18, 1966, Barco Library, The Cable Center. Quote from Jerrold's president is found in Parsons, *Blue Skies*, 218.

22. Parsons, *Blue Skies*, 218–219.

23. Proceedings of the 15th Annual Convention of the National Community Television Association, June 26–29, 1966, A-10, Barco Library, The Cable Center.

24. Proceedings of the 15th Annual Convention of the National Community Television Association, June 26–29, 1966, A-11, Barco Library, The Cable Center.

25. National Community Television Association Membership Bulletin.

26. "National Public Relations Program for Community Antenna Television," June 1966, CATV Public Relations, Box Series 89, Frederick Ford Collection, Barco Library, The Cable Center.

27. "National Public Relations Program."

28. "National Public Relations Program."

29. Memorandum from Richards Associates to Public Relations Committee, September 23, 1966. Folder, CATV Public Relations, 1966–1969, Box Series 89, Frederick Ford Collection, Barco Library, The Cable Center.

30. "National Cable TV Week," *TV Communications*, January 1967, 8.

31. "The Wonderful World of Cable TV." Folder, The Wonderful World of Cable TV, Box Series 89, Frederick Ford Collection, Barco Library, The Cable Center.

32. See examples of this in Folder, Congressman Campaign—"Tune into the Wonderful World of Cable," Box Series 89, Frederick Ford Collection, Barco Library, The Cable Center.

33. Letter from Robert Everett to Frederick Ford, January 19, 1967. Folder, Congressman Campaign—"Tune into the Wonderful World of Cable," Box Series 89, Frederick Ford Collection, Barco Library.

34. Parsons, *Blue Skies*, 217–219.

35. Proceedings of the 15th Annual Convention of the National Community Television Association, June 26–29, 1966, D-47–D-49, Barco Library, The Cable Center.

36. Proceedings of the 15th Annual Convention of the National Community Television Association, June 26–29, 1966, D-51, Barco Library, The Cable Center.

37. Parsons, *Blue Skies*, 233.

38. The October 1967 edition of *TV & Communications* has a range of articles dealing with these cablecasting alternatives; see 37–59. See also Parsons, *Blue Skies*, 98.

39. "National Survey Indicates Major Move into Cablecasting," *TV & Communications*, October 1967, 37–41.

40. Letter from William Adler to Fred Ford, August 26, 1966. Folder, Community Service Committee, Box Series 89, Frederick Ford Collection, Barco Library, The Cable Center.

41. William Adler Oral History, November 22, 2001, Hauser Collection, Barco Library, The Cable Center.

42. Letter from William Adler to Fred Ford.

43. Ira Kamen, "The Promotional Value of a Community Channel," *TV Communications*, May 1967, 58.

44. Baughman, *Television's Guardians*, 150–152.

45. Nicholas Johnson, *How to Talk Back to Your Television Set*, Little Brown and Company, 1970, 21.

46. Johnson, 58.

47. "Commissioner Johnson: The Future of Cable Television as a Regulated Industry," *TV Communications*, November 1967, 56–66. Johnson also discusses "CATV: Promise and Peril" in *How to Talk Back*, 152–168, an essay that also appeared in the *Saturday Review* in 1967.

48. National Community Television Association Membership Bulletin, Vol. 8, No. 5, February 18, 1966, Barco Library, The Cable Center.

49. Sol Schildhause Oral History, 1991, Penn State Collection, Barco Library, The Cable Center.

50. Stanley Searle, "Subject to Reason," *TV & Communications*, February 1967, 8.

51. "National Public Relations Program for Community Antenna Television," June 1966, CATV Public Relations, Box Series 89, Frederick Ford Collection, Barco Library, The Cable Center.

52. Ralph Lee Smith, *The Wired Nation: Cable TV: The Electronic Communications Highway*, Harper Colophon Books, 1972. The ideas originally appeared in an article in *The Nation* on May 18, 1970, and then formed the basis of a longer book.

53. Thomas Streeter, "Blue Skies and Strange Bedfellows: The Discourse of Cable Television," in *The Revolution Wasn't Televised: Sixties Television and Social Conflict*, ed. Lynn Spigel and Michael Curtin, Routledge, 1997, 221–242.

54. Tim Wu, *The Master Switch: The Rise and Fall of Information Empires*, Vintage, 2011, 5–6; Richard R. John, *Network Nation: Inventing American Telecommunications*, Harvard University Press, 2015; Paul Starr, *The Creation of the Media: Political Origins of Modern Communications*, Basic Books, 2005; Susan J. Douglas, *Listening In: Radio and the American Imagination*, University of Minnesota Press, 2004.

55. Streeter, "Blues Skies and Strange Bedfellows."

56. Aniko Bodroghkozy, *Equal Time: Television and the Civil Rights Movement*, University of Illinois Press, 2013, 2.

57. Bodroghkozy, 41.

58. Bodroghkozy, 150.

59. Sage Goodwin, "Making the News: The Development of Network Television News and the Struggle for Black Freedom in the 1950s and 1960s," PhD diss., University of Oxford, 2022; Milan Meeske, "Black Ownership of Broadcast Stations: An FCC Licensing Problem," *Journal of Broadcasting* 20, no. 2, spring 1976, 261–271.

60. Goodwin, "Making the News"; Allison Perlman, *Public Interests: Media Advocacy and Struggles over U.S. Television*, Rutgers University Press, 2016, 64.

61. Devorah Heitner, *Black Power TV*, Duke University Press, 2013, 9.

62. Yuya Kiuchi, *Struggles for Equal Voice: The History of African American Media Democracy*, State University of New York Press, 2013, 71–72.

63. Kiuchi, 78.

64. Perlman, *Public Interests*, 49–51.

65. Quoted in Aniko Bodroghkozy, *Equal Time*, 61.

66. David Greenberg, "The Idea of 'The Liberal Media Bias,' and Its Roots in the Civil Rights Movement," *The Sixties* 1, no. 2, 2008, 167–186; Heather Hendershot, *What's Fair on the Air? Cold War Right-Wing Broadcasting the Public Interest*, University of Chicago Press, 2011; Gabriel Sherman, *The Loudest Voice in the Room: How the Brilliant, Bombastic Roger Ailes Built Fox News*, Random House, 2015; Nicole Hemmer, *Messengers of the Right: Conservative Media and the Transformation of American Politics*, University of Pennsylvania Press, 2016.

67. Heather Hendershot, *When the News Broke: Chicago 1968 and the Polarizing of America*, University of Chicago Press, 2023.

68. Goodwin, "Making the News."

69. Baughman, *Television's Guardians*, 157.

70. Baughman, 159.

71. Allison Perlman, "The Politics of/within Educational Television in the 1960s," Exhibit for the American Archive of Public Broadcasting, https://americanarchive.org/exhibits/conservatism/politics-net; see also Perlman, *Public Interests*, 13–45.

72. Allison Perlman, "On the Right: NET and Modern Conservatism," Exhibit for the American Archive of Public Broadcasting, https://americanarchive.org/exhibits/conservatism.

73. Debate: Baldwin vs. Buckley, June 14, 1965, https://americanarchive.org/catalog/cpb-aacip_151-sn00z71m54; Nicholas Buccola, *The Fire Is upon Us: James Baldwin, William F. Buckley Jr., and the Debate over Race in America*, Princeton University Press, 2019.

74. Baughman, *Television's Guardians*, 153–158.

75. Perlman, *Public Interests*, 45.

76. Josh Shepperd, "Public Broadcasting," in *A Companion to the History of American Broadcasting*, ed. Aniko Bodroghkozy, Wiley-Blackwell, 2018, 220.

77. Laurie Ouellette, *Viewers Like You? How Public TV Failed the People*, Columbia University Press, 2002, 57–58.

78. Perlman, *Public Interests*.

79. Ouellette, *Viewers Like You*, 6. The larger battle that Richard Nixon waged against public television can be found in David M. Stone, *Nixon and the Politics of Public Television*, Garland Publishing, 1985.

80. Patrick Parsons calls June 1968 "one of the industry's most tumultuous months" and provides an overview of these court decisions and their consequences, *Blue Skies*, 246–252.

81. Parsons, 256–257.

82. Henry Geller, "The Mandatory Origination Requirement for Cable Systems," August 1974, Barco Library, The Cable Center.

83. Laura R. Linder, *Public Access Television: America's Electronic Soapbox*, Praeger Publishers, 1999, 7.

84. Lyle O. Keys, "A Basic Video Primer for CATV Technicians," *TV Communications*, February 1972, 80. See also Parsons, *Blue Skies*, 256–257.

85. "Access Issue: No Longer a Problem," *TV Communications*, March 1972, 34.

86. NCTA Local Origination Directory. Folder, Local Origination Directory, Box Series 89, Frederick Ford Papers, Barco Library, The Cable Center.

87. As Thomas Streeter shows in "Blue Skies and Strange Bedfellows," these studies, however, frequently reinforced one another, creating a "common consensus" among this coalition. This rhetoric inspired huge investments into the cable industry and influenced the FCC 1972 Second Order Decision to lift regulations on the cable industry that had formerly restricted it from the top one hundred markets.

88. Heitner, *Black Power TV*, 9.

89. Fred Turner, *From Counterculture to Cyberculture: Stewart Brand, the Whole Earth Network, and the Rise of Digital Utopianism*, University of Chicago Press, 2006.

90. Tom Wolfe, *The New Journalism*, Harper & Row Publishers, 1973; Bruce J. Schulman, *The Seventies: The Great Shift in American Culture, Society, and Politics*, Free Press, 2001, 144–158; Bradford D. Martin, *The Theater Is in the Street: Politics and Public Performance in 1960s America*, University of Massachusetts Press, 2004; Deirdre Boyle, *Subject to Change: Guerrilla Television Revisited*, Oxford University Press, 1997.

91. Martin, *The Theater Is in the Street*.

92. Michael Shamberg, *Guerrilla Television*, Henry Holt & Company, 1971; Boyle, *Subject to Change*, 36.

93. Hemmer, *Messengers of the Right*; Boyle, *Subject to Change*, 32.

94. Boyle, *Subject to Change*, 96–98.

95. "The Mayor's Advisory Task Force on CATV and Telecommunications: A Report on Cable Television and Cable Telecommunications in New York City," September 14, 1968, 2, Barco Library, The Cable Center.

96. Details about the franchise terms and history are outlined in "Major's Advisory Task Force on CATV," 14.

97. Parsons, *Blue Skies*, 311.

98. Parsons, 312.

99. "Mayor's Advisory Task Force on CATV," 6–10.

100. Vincent J. Cannato, *The Ungovernable City: John Lindsay and His Struggle to Save New York*, Basic Books, 2001, 114.

101. "Mayor's Advisory Task Force on CATV," 62–63.

102. "Mayor's Advisory Task Force on CATV," 47.

103. Stanley Penn, "Scandals and Allegations Intensify the Bid to Divest Towns of Authority over CATVs," *Wall Street Journal*, April 20, 1971, 38.

104. Monroe E. Price, "Requiem for the Wired Nation: Cable Rulemaking at the FCC," *Virginia Law Review* 61, no. 3, April 1974, 541–577.

Chapter 4

1. Gladwin Hill, "Nixon Denounces the Press as Biased," *New York Times*, November 8, 1962, 1.

2. Remarks of Clay Whitehead, director of Office of Telecommunications Policy at the Sigma Delta Chi Luncheon, Indianapolis, Indiana, December 18, 1972. Folder, Speech—Indiana Broadcasters Association, December 18, 1972, Box 42, Clay T. Whitehead Papers, Library of Congress, Washington, D.C. (hereafter CTWP).

3. "The Whitehead Years," *Cablevision*, March 28, 1977, 52–56.

4. For more about policy shifts in the 1970s and the ways in which they reshaped boundaries for what seemed politically possible and reasonable, see Elizabeth Popp Berman, *Thinking Like an Economist: How Efficiency Replaced Equality in U.S. Public Policy*, Princeton University Press, 2022, 4.

5. Bruce J. Schulman, *The Seventies: The Great Shift in American Culture, Society, and Politics*, Free Press, 2001, 23–52.

6. Richard M. Nixon, *Six Crises*, Doubleday, 1962, 344.

7. Michael Schudson, *The Power of News*, Harvard University Press, 1996, 116–117; Kathryn Cramer Brownell, "The Making of the Celebrity Presidency," in *Recapturing the Oval Office: New Historical Approaches to the American Presidency*, ed. Brian Balogh and Bruce J. Schulman, Cornell University Press, 2015, 164.

8. Kathryn Cramer Brownell, *Showbiz Politics: Hollywood in American Political Life*, University of North Carolina Press, 2014, 200–207.

9. Memo from Bill Gavin to Len Garment, Re: Nixon notes. N.d. [1968]. Folder, Bill Gavin, 2 of 3, Box 69, Name File Box 3 of 29, 1968 Campaign File, Len Garment, White House Central Name File, Richard M. Nixon Library (hereafter RMNL). See also a discussion of media strategies in Joe McGinniss, *The Selling of the President, 1968*, Trident Press, 1969.

10. "Politics Provides Programs for Service-Minded Systems," *TV & Communications*, August 1968, 26.

11. "Republicans Set up First National CATV-Use Program," *TV & Communications*, November 1968, 32–34.

12. Memorandum from B. Jay Baraff to Jay Parker, September 10, 1968. Folder, Use of CATV in Nixon Campaign, Box Series 89, Frederick Ford Collection, Barco Library, The Cable Center.

13. "Republicans Set up First National CATV-Use Program."

14. Memorandum from B. Jay Baraff to Jay Parker, September 10, 1968.

15. Letter from Bill Daniels to Maurice Stans, June 6, 1969. Folder, Association Correspondence, Box 8, Sol Schildhause Collection, Barco Library, The Cable Center.

16. Robert A. Searle, "Perspective on the News," *TV & Communications*, December 1968, 10.

17. William Safire, *Before the Fall: An Inside View of the Pre-Watergate White House*, Belmont Tower Books, 1975, 343.

18. Memorandum from Nixon to Haldeman, January 6, 1970, quoted in Chester Pach, "'Our Worst Enemy Seems to Be the Press': TV News, the Nixon Administration, and U.S. Troop Withdrawal from Vietnam, 1969–1973," *Diplomatic History*, June 2010, 556.

19. John Anthony Maltese, *Spin Control: The White House Office of Communications and the Management of Presidential News*, 2nd ed., University of North Carolina Press, 1994, 28.

20. Maltese, *Spin Control*, 34.

21. Jeb Stuart Magruder, *An American Life: One Man's Road to Watergate*, Atheneum, 1974, 64–66.

22. For an overview of the dirty tricks, see Michael Koncewicz, *They Said No to Nixon: Republicans Who Stood Up to the President's Abuses of Power*, University of California Press, 2018, 31–71.

23. Wafa Unus argues that Klein played a prominent role in shaping Nixon's media strategy in *A Newsman in the Nixon White House: Herbert Klein and the Enduring Conflict between Journalistic Truth and Presidential Image*, Lexington Books, 2018. However, as other scholars, notably Mark Feldstein and David Greenberg, have shown, Klein never gained the level of influence that Haldeman and Colson had in Nixon's inner circle. Mark Feldstein, *Poisoning the Press: Richard Nixon, Jack Anderson, and the Rise of Washington's Scandal Culture*, Farrar, Straus, and Giroux, 2010; David Greenberg, *Nixon's Shadow: The History of An Image*, W. W. Norton, 2003.

24. William E. Porter, *Assault on the Media: The Nixon Years*, University of Michigan Press, 1976, 95.

25. Magruder, *An American Life*, 72–77.

26. Harry S. Ashmore, *Fear in the Air: Broadcasting and the First Amendment: The Anatomy of a Constitutional Crisis*, W. W. Norton, 1973.

27. Quoted in Ashmore, *Fear in the Air*, 12.

28. Spiro Agnew, "Television News Coverage," November 13, 1969, https://www.americanrhetoric.com/speeches/spiroagnewtvnewscoverage.htm.

29. Nicole Hemmer, *Messengers of the Right: Conservative Media and the Transformation of American Politics*, University of Pennsylvania Press, 2016; Heather Hendershot, *What's Fair on the Air? Cold War Right-Wing Broadcasting and the Public Interest*, University of Chicago Press, 2011.

30. Hemmer, *Messengers of the Right*, 221.

31. Porter, *Assault on the Media*, 270–273.

32. Koncewicz, *They Said No to Nixon*. See also Paul Matzko, *The Radio Right: How a Band of Broadcasters Took on the Federal Government and Built the Modern Conservative Movement*, Oxford University Press, 2020, 213–217. As Matzko notes, scholars debate over how involved Nixon was directly in ordering these rule changes, but as Koncewicz also contends, such actions reflect the culture of corruption and win by any means necessary atmosphere that pervaded the Nixon administration.

33. Benjamin M. Compain, *Who Owns the Media? Concentration of Ownership in the Mass Communications Industry*, 2nd ed., Knowledge Industry Publications, 1982, 388.

34. For an overview of these policies and the battle over them, see Michele Hilmes, *Hollywood and Broadcasting: From Radio to Cable*, University of Illinois Press, 1999, 186–190. For how these fit into Nixon's war on network television, see Porter, *Assault on the Media*, 154–159.

35. Oscar Winberg, "Archie Bunker for President: Television Entertainment and the Transformation of American Politics in the 1970s," PhD diss., Åbo Akademi University, Finland, 2021, 34–35.

36. Porter, *Assault on the Media*, 154.

37. Walter Pincus and George Larder Jr., "Nixon Hoped Antitrust Threat Would Sway Network Coverage," part of "The Nixon Tapes" series from *Washington Post*, December 1, 1992, A1, https://www.washingtonpost.com/wp-srv/national/longterm/nixon/120197tapes.htm.

38. Quoted in Ashmore, *Fear in the Air*, 13.

39. Talking points re: meeting with Whitehead and Colson, February 3, 1973. Folder 2, Box 47, CTWP.

40. On the culture of corruption purposefully created by Nixon, see Koncewicz, *They Said No to Nixon*.

41. Details of Whitehead's biography can be found in the biography section of Clay Whitehead Papers, http://claytwhitehead.com/biography/. On Nixon's attitudes about MIT, see Koncewicz, *They Said No to Nixon*, 73.

42. "Whitehead Years," 54.

43. Taped conversation with Clay Whitehead, Brian Lamb, Henry Goldberg, and Jason (no last name but identified as a research assistant), 2008. Folder, Susan Burgess Materials and Interviews, Box 60, CTWP.

44. Lyndon B. Johnson, Special Message to the Congress on Communications Policy, online by Gerhard Peters and John T. Woolley, The American Presidency Project, https://www.presidency.ucsb.edu/node/237955.

45. Francis Rourke and Roger Brown, "Presidents, Professionals, and Telecommunications Policy Making in the White House," *Presidential Studies Quarterly* 26, 1996, 544.

46. Rourke and Brown, "Presidents, Professionals," 544. On the controversy the report provoked among task force members, see Memorandum from Charles Zwick to Under Secretary Rostow, December 4, 1968. Folder 11, Box 12, CTWP.

47. Letter from Leonard Goldenson to Clay Whitehead, September 16, 1969. Folder 8, Telecommunications Industry Replies to Letters, Box 16, CTWP.

48. Taped Conversation with Tom Whitehead, Brian Lamb, and Henry Goldberg, n.d. (2003). Folder, Interviews, Box 60, CTWP.

49. Parsons, *Blue Skies*, 328–333.

50. "A Hot New Breath down FCC's Neck," *Broadcasting*, September 28, 1970, 23–24.

51. Alfred P. Sloan Foundation Press Release, June 10, 1970. Folder, Commission on Cable Communications, 1970, Box 26, CTWP.

52. "On the Cable: The Television of Abundance," Report of the Sloan Commission on Cable Communications, 1971, 152; author interview with Monroe Price, May 28, 2020.

53. "On the Cable," 116–117.

54. Herbert E. Alexander, *Financing the 1968 Election*, Heath Lexington Books, 1971, 95.

55. Robert E. Mutch, *Buying the Vote: A History of Campaign Finance Reform*, Oxford University Press, 2014, 132–133.

56. "On the Cable," 120–121.

57. "On the Cable," 167–170.

58. Neil Postman, *Amusing Ourselves to Death: Public Discourse in the Age of Show Business*, Penguin Books Anniversary Edition, 2005 (originally published in 1985).

59. The initial discussion of the cabinet committee can be found in Letter to Robert Finch from Clay Whitehead, June 7, 1971. Folder, Cable Trends, Box 2, WHCF, FG 6–14, RNPL.

60. Sol Schildhause and Jerold L. Jacobs, "Federal Regulations for Cable Television Systems," May 1972. Folder 4, Box 1, Sol Schildhause Collection, Barco Library, The Cable Center.

61. Parsons, *Blue Skies*, 266; Letter from Clay Whitehead to John Pastore, November 15, 1971. Folder, Organization of the OTP Office (2 of 2), Box 33, CTWP.

62. Bruce Owen, "Project BUN—Background Paper," December 5, 1972. Folder, Project BUN, Box 36, CTWP.

63. For more details on the discussion of starting the White House's own news network, see Gabriel Sherman, *The Loudest Voice in the Room: How the Brilliant, Bombastic Roger Ailes Built Fox News*, Random House, 2014, 60–78.

64. Taped Conversation with Tom Whitehead, Brian Lamb, and Henry Goldberg.

65. WH TEL, December 27, 1972, 035-17. Transcription and source shared generously by Oscar Winberg.

66. Material on the OTP and Project B.U.N. is drawn from Kathryn Cramer Brownell, "'Ideological Plugola,' 'Elitist Gossip,' and the Need for Cable Television," in *Media Nation: The Political History of News in Modern America*, ed. Bruce J. Schulman and Julian E. Zelizer, University of Pennsylvania Press, 2017, 160–175.

67. Memorandum re: Broadcasting Policy and Network Power, addendum to Owen's "Project BUN."

68. Memorandum from Clay Whitehead to John Ehrlichman, December 6, 1972. Folder, CTW OTP Senate Confirmation and Miscellaneous Materials, Box 27, CTWP.

69. The planning of the speech and different versions of it as well as reactions, interview requests, and news clippings in response to this speech are found in: Folder, Speech—Indiana Broadcasters Association, December 18, 1972, Box 42, CTWP.

70. James Kilpatrick, "Whitehead off Base in Attack on TV Industry," *The Evening Star and Daily News*, December 26, 1972. Folder, Speech—Indiana Broadcasters Association, December 18, 1972, Box 42, CTWP.

71. Transcript, *Firing Line* (taped February 1, 1973, and aired February 16) with guest Clay Whitehead. Southern Educational Communications Association, Hoover Institution Library and Archives, Stanford University, Stanford, California.

72. Memorandum from Clay Whitehead to John Ehrlichman, December 6, 1972.

73. Memorandum re: Meeting the President, February 5, 1973. Folder, Congressional Testimony and Meeting with Nixon, Box 47, CTWP.

74. Berman, *Thinking Like an Economist*, 4.

75. Taped Conversation with Tom Whitehead, Brian Lamb, and Henry Goldberg.

76. "Cable: Report to the President by the Cabinet Committee on Cable Communications," 1974. Folder, Report to the President, the Cabinet Committee on Cable Communication, Box 36, CTWP.

77. Bruce M. Owen, *Economics and Freedom of Expression: Media Structure and the First Amendment*, Ballinger, 1975.

78. Editorial, January 19, 1974. Folder, Cable Television and Regulation 2, Box 21, Frederick Lynn May Collection, Gerald Ford Presidential Library (hereafter GFPL).

79. Douglass Cater, "Anatomy of a Government Document: The Cabinet Committee Report on Cable Communications," February 13, 1974. Folder, Congress /1/6/74–9/2/74, Box 5, Sol Schildhouse Collection, Barco Library, The Cable Center.

80. Excerpts from Dialogue, Aspen Institute Program on Communications and Society, "Conference on Cabinet Committee Report on Cable Communications," 4. Folder, Congress /1/6/74–9/2/74. Box 5, Sol Schildhouse Collection, Barco Library, The Cable Center.

81. "Conference on Cabinet Committee Report on Cable Communications," 9.

82. "Whitehead Years," 52–56.

83. All these attacks on the media are outlined in Porter, *Assault on the Media*.

84. Winberg, "Archie Bunker for President"; Brownell, *Showbiz Politics*.

Act II

1. Brian Lamb Oral History, The Archive of American Television, https://interviews.televisionacademy.com/interviews/brian-lamb?clip=71388#interview-clips.

2. Charles C. Joyce Jr., "Ad Hoc Review Group for Organization for Telecommunications within the Executive Branch," February 9, 1976. Folder, Federal Regulatory Reform-Office of Telecommunications Policy Study, Box 20, Edward C. Schmults Papers, Gerald R. Ford Presidential Library (hereafter GRFPL).

3. Brian Lamb, "Washington Wire," *CATV*, September 1, 1975, 4.

4. "The Whitehead Years," *Cablevision*, March 28, 1977, 52–56. Folder, Communications Reform-OTP, Box 36, Domestic Policy Staff, Simon Lazarus's 1976 Campaign Transition Files, Jimmy Carter Presidential Library (hereafter JCPL).

5. "Cable: Still Something Drab Sounding to Influential Newspapermen," *CATV*, December 1, 1975, 14.

6. Lamb, "Washington Wire," 4.

7. Deirdre Boyle, *Subject to Change: Guerrilla Television Revisited*, Oxford University Press, 1997; Laura R. Linder, *Public Access Television: America's Electronic Soapbox*, Praeger, 1999.

8. Brian Lamb Oral History.

Chapter 5

1. AP Archive, "Nixon Impeachment Hearings, May 9, 1974," accessed October 11, 2022, https://www.youtube.com/watch?v=VKrLM5cqM6Q.

2. For a discussion of Watergate coverage and footage, see "'Gavel to Gavel': Watergate and Public Television," American Archive of Public Broadcasting, Library of Congress, https://americanarchive.org/exhibits/watergate/the -watergate-coverage.

3. Mike Mansfield, "Impeachment on TV: In the Public Interest," *New York Times*, May 26, 1974, 173.

4. R. W. Apple Jr., "TV and Impeachment: Hearings Found to Give House an Image of an Institution Worthy of Respect," *New York Times*, August 2, 1974, 13.

5. House Report 94-539, "Congress and Mass Communications." Serial Set, Volume 13101-1, October 7, 1975. Washington: U.S. G.P.O.

6. Michael Schudson, *The Rise of the Right to Know: Politics and the Culture of Transparency, 1945–1975*, Harvard University Press, 2018.

7. Communications Subcommittee, Senate Commerce Committee, "Equal Time for Congress: Congressional Hearings 1970," in *Congress and the News Media*, ed. Robert O. Blanchard, Hastings House Publishers, 1974, 116. Portions of this chapter appear in Kathryn Cramer Brownell, "Watergate, the Bipartisan Struggle for Media Access, and the Growth of Cable Television," *Modern American History* 3, no. 2–3, 2020, 175–198, doi:10.1017/mah.2020.18.

8. The Senate hearings and an overview of them by Senate historian Donald Ritchie can be found in the C-SPAN, "American History TV," January 29, 2016, https://www.c-span.org/video/?404591-1/donald-ritchie-1966-vietnam-hearings -general-maxwell-taylor. For more details on Senator Fulbright and his connection with the networks, see William Small, "Congress, Television and War Protests," in *Congress and the News Media*, 352–356. See also Ralph Engelman, *Friendlyvision: Fred Friendly and the Rise and Fall of Television Journalism*, Columbia University Press, 2009, 198–233.

9. Engelman, *Friendlyvision*, 211–213.

10. Letter from Thom Keith to Bill Daniels, January 31, 1969. Folder, Daniels and Associates, Box Series 89, Frederick Ford Collection, Barco Library, The Cable Center. These documents support the story outlined in the authorized biography of Daniels from his estate: Stephen Singular, *Relentless: Bill Daniels and the Triumph of Cable TV*, Bill Daniels Estate, 2003, 118–120.

11. Singular, *Relentless*, 120.

12. Singular, 119.

13. Letter from Bill Daniels to Key Members of the National Cable Television Association. Folder, Daniels and Associates, Box Series 89, Frederick Ford Collection, Barco Library, The Cable Center.

14. Memo from Bill Daniels to the Cable Industry, August 19, 1969. Folder, Use of CATV in Nixon Campaign, Box Series 89, Frederick Ford Collection, Barco Library, The Cable Center.

15. Memorandum from Chuck Walsh to Pennsylvania CATV Operators with Cablecasting Facilities, November 19, 1969. Folder, Memo from NCTA on Political Cablecasting, Box Series 89, Frederick Ford Collection, Barco Library, The Cable Center.

16. Herbert S. Dordick and Jack Lyle, "Access by Local Political Candidates to Cable Television: A Report of an Experiment," RAND Corporation, Santa Monica, California, 1971, 16, Barco Library, The Cable Center.

17. Dordick and Lyle, "Access by Local Political Candidates," 19–20.

18. Jaime Sánchez Jr., "Revisiting McGovern-Fraser: Party Nationalization and the Rhetoric of Reform," *Journal of Policy History* 32, no. 1, Cambridge University Press, 2020, 1–24.

19. Oscar Winberg, "Archie Bunker for President: Television Entertainment and the Transformation of American Politics in the 1970s," PhD diss., Åbo Akademi University, Finland, 2021.

20. Sánchez, "Revisiting McGovern-Fraser," 14.

21. Letter to R. H. Nolte, Institute of Current World Affairs, from Eden Lispon, September 22, 1972. Folder, Sparklies, Theodore H. White Papers, John F. Kennedy Presidential Library.

22. Paid Advertisement, "National Cable TV Week Feb. 13–19," *The New Mexican*, February 13, 1972, D4.

23. "Campaigning on Cable Television" pamphlet. Folder, Campaigning on Television, Box 2, George Barco Collection, Barco Library, The Cable Center.

24. Letter from Charles Walsh to Dick Williams, January 24, 1972. Folder, CATV, 1972, Box 176, George McGovern Papers, Princeton University Special Collections Library.

25. Warren Weaver Jr., "Cable TV Getting Political Test in New Hampshire," *New York Times*, February 29, 1972.

26. Overview of TVTV. Folder, TVTV, Maureen Orth Private Papers.

27. Deirdre Boyle, *Subject to Change: Guerrilla Television Revisited*, Oxford University Press, 1997, 37.

28. Overview of TVTV.

29. Elizabeth Cobbs Hoffman, *All You Need Is Love: The Peace Corps and the Spirit of the 1960s*, Harvard University Press, 1998.

30. Max Frankel, "Majority Is 1,618," *New York Times*, July 11, 1972, 1.

31. Boyle, *Subject to Change*, 56.

32. "Political Cablecasting," NCTA Cablecasting Guidebook, 1973, Barco Library, The Cable Center.

33. "TV: A 'Scrapbook' of the Democratic Convention: One Hour Documentary on Cable Tonight," *New York Times*, August 17, 1972, 71.

34. Discussion of the public response to the documentary airing on broadcast stations can be found in: Boyle, *Subject to Change*, 62–63.

35. Boyle, 63.

36. "Political Cablecasting."

37. "Political Cablecasting."

38. Warren Weaver Jr., "Cable Television Offers Boon for Financially Pressed Candidates," *New York Times*, November 5, 1972, news clipping included in "Campaigning on Cable Television" pamphlet. Folder, Campaigning on Television, Box 2, George Barco Collection, Barco Library, The Cable Center.

39. "Cable and the Congressman," *TV & Communications*, November 1974, 38.

40. Rob Stengel, "CATV Gears up for Political Cablecasting in Campaign '76." Folder, Advertising Brochures, Campaigning on Cable Television, President Ford Committee Records, GRFPL.

41. Tim Shuey, "Political Cablecasting: A State Network," *Over the Cable*, National Cable Television Association, 1974, 7–9, Barco Library, The Cable Center.

42. Tim Shuey comments on the panel, "Successful Cablecasting Programs," *Over the Cable*, National Cable Television Association, 1974, 12, Barco Library, The Cable Center.

43. Advertisement, *Salina Journal*, April 30, 1974, 15.

44. On loosening PEG requirements, see Patrick R. Parsons, *Blue Skies: A History of Cable Television*, Temple University Press, 2008, 357–358. On the legal challenges to public access that hurt guerrilla TV productions, see Boyle, *Subject to Change*, 183–196.

45. "Campaigning on Cable Television."

46. Brownell, "Watergate, the Bipartisan Struggle."

47. Bob Woodward and Carl Bernstein, "Nixon and His Aides Believe Hearing Is a Witch-Hunt," *Washington Post*, July 21, 1973, in *Congress and the News Media*, 486–487.

48. Spiro Agnew, "TV's Incandescent and Damaging Presence in the Hearing Room," speech before the National Association of Attorneys General, St. Louis, Missouri, June 11, 1973, in *Congress and the News Media*, 472–479.

49. Mike Mansfield, "Impeachment on TV: In the Public Interest," *New York Times*, May 26, 1974, 173.

50. These viewer letters are discussed in James MacGregor, "Blessing in Disguise: Watergate Is a Boon to Public Television," *Wall Street Journal*, June 15, 1973, 1. David M. Stone also discusses the public response in Stone, *Nixon and the Politics of Public Television*, Garland Publishing, 1985, 291–295.

51. Kathryn Cramer Brownell, "'Ideological Plugola,' 'Elitist Gossip,' and the Need for Cable Television," in *Media Nation: The Political History of News in Modern America*, ed. Bruce J. Schulman and Julian E. Zelizer, University of Pennsylvania Press, 2017.

52. Stanley M. Besen and Bridger M. Mitchell, "Watergate and Television: An Economic Analysis," *Communication Research* 3, no. 3, July 1976, 243–260.

53. Memorandum from Paul MacAvoy to the Domestic Council Review Group on Regulatory Reform, December 23, 1975. Folder, Cable Television, Box 88, Paul W. MacAvoy Files, GRFPL.

54. "Gerald R. Ford's Remarks Upon Taking the Oath of Office as President," August 9, 1974, https://www.fordlibrarymuseum.gov/library/speeches/740001.asp.

55. Paul Sabin, *Public Citizens: The Attack on Big Government and the Remaking of American Liberalism*, W. W. Norton, 2021; Jason Stahl, *Right Moves: The Conservative Think Tank in American Political Culture Since 1945*, University of North Carolina Press, 2016.

56. Many of these policy ideas come out of collaborations with the American Enterprise Institute, see Stahl, *Right Moves*, 82–85.

57. Paul W. MacAvoy, ed., *Deregulation of Cable Television: Ford Administrative Papers on Regulatory Reform*, American Enterprise Institute for Public Policy Research, 1977, 96.

58. MacAvoy, 96.

59. Letter from Ralph Baruch to Lynn May, October 10, 1975. Folder, Cable TV and Regulation-4, Box 21, Frederick Lynn May Collection, GRFPL.

60. Letter from Edward M. Allen to F. Lynn May, October 28, 1975. Folder, Cable TV and Regulation-4, Box 21, Frederick Lynn May Collection, GRFPL.

61. Memorandum from Jonathan C. Rose to F. Lynn May, March 29, 1976. Folder, Cable Television and Regulation-9, Box 22, Frederick Lynn May Collection, GRFPL.

62. Biographical information on F. Lynn May, GRFPL, https://www.fordlibrarymuseum.gov/library/guides/findingaid/maylfiles.asp.

63. F. Lynn May, "Speech to the Western Cable Television Show and Convention," November 14, 1976; Memorandum from Jonathan C. Rose to F. Lynn May, March 29, 1976. Folder, Cable Television and Regulation-9, Box 22, Frederick Lynn May Collection, GRFPL.

64. See, for example, an exchange of letters from August 30, 1974, to October 17, 1974, in Folder, Cable Television and Regulation-1, Box 20, Frederick Lynn May Collection, GRFPL.

65. Richard E. Cohen, "Regulatory Report/Broadcast, Cable Industries Face Off on Cable Reform Plan," February 7, 1976, *National Journal*. News clipping, Folder, Cable Television and Regulation-7, Box 21, Frederick Lynn May Collection, GRFPL.

66. Cohen, "Regulatory Report/Broadcast."

67. Brian Lamb, "Taylor's Waves Turn the Tide," *Cablevision*, November 3, 1975.

68. "Who's Ahead in Making Case on De-Regulation of Cable?," *Broadcasting*, October 27, 1975, 32–34.

69. Letter from William Carlisle to Dave Crockett, September 29, 1975. Folder, Cable Television Regulatory Reform-Background Material on Cable Issue, Box 19, Edward C. Schmults Papers, GRFPL. See also "Who's Ahead in Making Case," 32–34.

70. Memorandum from Robert W. Ross re: Broadcast Industry Profits for 1974, October 30, 1975; Memorandum from Jonathan C. Rose to Calvin J. Collier re: Proposed Cable Television Legislation, October 28, 1975. Folder, Cable Television Regulatory Reform-Background Material on Cable Issue, Box 19, Edward C. Schmults Papers, GRFPL.

71. Memorandum from John Eger to F. Lynn May and Paul MacAvoy, October 23, 1975. Folder, Cable TV and Regulation, 4, Box 21, Frederick Lynn May Collection, GRFPL.

72. Memorandum on Deregulation of Cable Television, December 4, 1975. Folder, Cable TV and Regulation-6, Box 21, Frederick Lynn May Collection, GRFPL.

73. Letter from F. Lynn May to Mr. Schroeder, November 18, 1975; Letter from F. Lynn May to Richard Dudley, November 19, 1975, both in: Folder, Cable TV and Regulation-5, Box 21, Frederick Lynn May Collection, GRFPL.

74. "Who's Ahead in Making Case," 32–34.

75. Letter from David C. Adams to Paul MacAvoy, December 22, 1975. Folder, Cable TV and Regulation-6, Box 21, Frederick Lynn May Collection, GRFPL.

76. "White House Seems Willing to Kill Half of All Stations to Unleash Cable," *Broadcasting*, December 15, 1975. News clipping, Folder, Cable TV and Regulation-6, Box 21, Frederick Lynn May Collection, GRFPL.

77. Memorandum from Paul MacAvoy to the Domestic Council Review Group on Regulatory Reform, December 23, 1975. Folder, Cable Television, Box 88, Paul W. MacAvoy Files, GRFPL.

78. Allison Perlman, *Public Interests: Media Advocacy and Struggles over U.S. Television*, Rutgers University Press, 2016, 92–97.

79. Elizabeth Popp Berman, *Thinking Like an Economist: How Efficiency Replaced Equality in U.S. Public Policy*, Princeton University Press, 2022.

80. Report: "The Domestic Council Review Group's Examination of Cable Television De-Regulation," March 25, 1976. Folder, Cable Television and Regulation-9, Box 22, Frederick Lynn May Collection, GRFPL.

81. Cover, *CATV*, April 26, 1976.

82. Brian Lamb, "White House Excuses—A Lot of Baloney," *Cablevision*, April 19, 1976. Folder, Cable Television and Regulation-9, Box 22, Frederick Lynn May Collection, GRFPL. In this same folder, there is also a clipping from Brian Lamb's media report that corroborates this story.

83. Irwin B. Arieff, "The Inside Story: Why Ford Backed Down on Cable," advance copy of the story to appear in July 1976 publication of *Videography*. News clipping, Folder, Cable TV and Regulation- 9, Box 22, Frederick Lynn May Collection, GRFPL.

84. Kathryn Cramer Brownell, "Gerald Ford, *Saturday Night Live*, and the Development of the Entertainer-in-Chief," *Presidential Studies Quarterly* 46, no. 4, December 2016, 925–942.

85. Memorandum from F. Lynn May for Jim Cannon, November 15, 1976. Folder, Cable Television and Regulation-9, Box 22, Frederick Lynn May Collection, GRFPL.

86. John A. Lawrence, *The Class of '74: Congress after Watergate and the Roots of Partisanship*, The Johns Hopkins University Press, 2018; Sam Rosenfeld, *The Polarizers: Postwar Architects of Our Partisan Era*, University of Chicago Press, 2018; Julian E. Zelizer, *On Capitol Hill: The Struggle to Reform Congress and Its Consequences, 1948–2000*, Cambridge University Press, 2006.

87. Lily Geismer, *Left Behind: The Democrats' Failed Attempt to Solve Inequality*, Public Affairs, 2022.

88. Oral History with Timothy E. Wirth, 2006. Carnegie Library for Local History, Boulder, Colorado.

89. 1964 President's Commission on White House Fellowships, text reprinted, https://www.whitehouse.gov/get-involved/fellows/.

90. Oral History with Timothy E. Wirth, 2006.

91. Timothy Wirth Oral History, 2000, Hauser Collection, Barco Library, The Cable Center.

92. Rachel Guberman, "The Real Silent Majority: Denver and the Realignment of American Politics after the Sixties," PhD diss., University of Pennsylvania, 2015, Proquest Dissertation Publishing, AAI3722661. On Daniels and the building of Daniels and Associates in Denver, see Singular, *Relentless*.

93. Amos Hostetter Oral History, 1999, Hauser Collection, Barco Library, The Cable Center.

94. Parsons, *Blue Skies*, 328.

95. Parsons, 289.

96. Timothy Wirth Oral History, 2000.

97. Thomas Wheeler Oral History, 2000, Hauser Collection, Barco Library, The Cable Center.

98. Thomas Wheeler Oral History, 2000.

99. Susan Crawford, *Captive Audience: The Telecom Industry and Monopoly Power in the New Gilded Age,* Yale University Press, 2013, 40.

100. Parsons, *Blue Skies*, 349–352.

101. Parsons, 350.

102. Quoted in Parsons, 352.

103. Berman, *Thinking Like an Economist*, 198–200.

104. Memorandum from Jerry Colbert to Thomas P. O'Neill Jr., February 17, 1976. Folder 5-TV Coverage of the House, Box 53, Thomas "Tip" O'Neill Congressional Papers, Archives and Manuscript Department, John J. Burns Library, Boston College (hereafter Tip O'Neill Papers).

105. Letter from Thomas O'Neill to House Colleagues, March 15, 1977. Folder 11, Box 351, Tip O'Neill Papers.

106. "TV Coverage of House Chamber Appears to Have a Real Future," *Staff: A Congressional Staff Journal as a Process for Communication*, 95th Congress, Issue 2, Folder 11, Box 351, Tip O'Neill Papers.

107. J. Brooks Flippen, *Speaker Jim Wright: Power, Scandal, and the Birth of Modern Politics*, University of Texas Press, 2018.

108. Mary Russell, "House Votes Own Control of Chamber TV Cameras," *Washington Post*, June 15, 1978.

109. Supplement to the Legislative Report for the Week of October 24, 1977. Folder 11, Box 351, Tip O'Neill Papers.

110. *Congressional Record*, October 27, 1977. P. 35426.

111. Stephen Frantzich and John Sullivan, *The C-SPAN Revolution*, University of Oklahoma Press, 1996, 34.

112. *Congressional Record*, October 27, 1977. P. 35433.

113. Frantzich and Sullivan, *The C-SPAN Revolution*, 34–35.

114. *Congressional Record*, October 27, 1977, P. 35433.

115. Frantzich and Sullivan, *The C-SPAN Revolution*, 35.

116. Brian Lamb, "Television in the House: A Quick Way to Introduce Congress to Cable," *Cablevision*, November 7, 1977, 16.

117. Oral History with Brian Lamb, Archive of American Television, https://interviews.televisionacademy.com/interviews/brian-lamb?clip=71394#interview-clips.

118. Michael O'Daniel, "Cable Has a Secret," *Emmy*, November/December 1984. Folder 24-Various News Clippings 1984, Box 1, C-SPAN Archives.

119. Letter from C-SPAN to Tip O'Neill, March 5, 1982. Folder 1, C-SPAN 1982, Box 34-15, Subseries 18-Miscellaneous Files, Tip O'Neill Papers.

Chapter 6

1. Patrick R. Parsons, *Blue Skies: A History of Cable Television*, Temple University Press, 2008, 276–277.

2. United States v. Irving B. Kahn and Teleprompter Corporation, 472 F.2d 272 (2d Cir. 1973), Court of Appeals for the Second Circuit, 472 F.2d 272 Docket Number: https://www.courtlistener.com/opinion/307845/united-states-v-irving-b-kahn-and-teleprompter-corporation/.

3. Clarence Peterson, "Suspicions Peril Future of Cable TV," *Chicago Tribune*, Feb. 4, 1971, B21.

4. "Blue Sky through a Green Filter," remarks by Irving B. Kahn at the Texas Cable TV Association Annual Convention, February 27, 1975, Irving Kahn Papers Collection, Barco Library, The Cable Center. See also Parsons, *Blue Skies,* 341–342.

5. Parsons, 326.

6. Larry Kramer, "Welcome to the World of Cable Television," *Washington Post*, April 9, 1978. Folder, Cable Television in 1979: An Industry Profile-1, Box L-9, Gerald R. Ford Post-Presidential Office Files, GRFPL.

7. Thomas Whiteside, "Cable Television," *New Yorker*, May 20, 1985, 64.

8. "History of Cable TV Subscribers and Revenues," Estimates of Paul Kagan Associates, 1982, *The Cable TV Financial Databook*, 1983, Barco Library, The Cable Center.

9. "The Happiness of Pursuit," Irving B. Kahn Address, September 20, 1979, FF75, Irving Kahn Papers, Barco Library, The Cable Center.

10. Memorandum from Les Read to Peter Frame, March 11, 1985. Folder, HBO History-First Satellite Launch, Vero Beach, FL, Leslie Read Papers, Barco Library, The Cable Center.

11. This phrase was used in HBO advertising for *TVC*, October 1975. The issue focused extensively on pay cable operations.

12. This story is discussed in great depth in Whiteside, "Cable Television," 60–69. See also Parsons, *Blue Skies*.

13. Parsons, 335.

14. Parsons, 330–338.

15. Financial numbers are from Parsons, 337–338.

16. Leslie Read Oral History, 1990, Penn State Collection, Barco Library, The Cable Center.

17. Parsons, *Blue Skies*, 339.

18. Lizabeth Cohen, *A Consumers' Republic: The Politics of Mass Consumption in Postwar America*, Random House, 2003, 296–297.

19. Joseph Turow, *Breaking up America: Advertisers and the New Media World*, University of Chicago Press, 1997, 25–26.

20. Turow, *Breaking up America*, 13.

21. Andrew N. Case, "'The Solid Gold Mailbox': Direct Mail and the Changing Nature of Buying and Selling in Postwar United States," *History of Retailing and Consumption* 1, 2015, 28–46.

22. "Selling HBO Door to Door." Folder, HBO Sales Literature, Leslie Read Collection, Barco Library, The Cable Center.

23. John Billock Oral History, 2001, Hauser Collection, Barco Library, The Cable Center.

24. Pay Television Statistics. Folder, Cable Television in 1979: An Industry Profile-1, Box L-9, Gerald R. Ford Post-Presidential Office Files, GRFPL.

25. Parsons, *Blue Skies*, 355–356.

26. Whiteside, "Cable Television," 64.

27. Bill Mesce Jr., *Inside the Rise of HBO: A Personal History of the Company that Transformed Television*, McFarland & Company, 2015, 2.

28. Parsons, *Blue Skies*, 339.

29. "Black Ownership . . . Black Subscribers . . . Black Gold in Columbus," *Cablevision*, October 9, 1978, 36.

30. Don Anderson discusses the HBO and Time Inc. mentality about investing in Black programming to tap into urban markets extensively in his oral history. Barco Library, The Cable Center. Another Black executive, Gayle Greer, shared similar stories about working as a Black woman at Time Inc. in her oral history. Gayle Greer Oral History, 1999, Hauser Collection, Barco Library, The Cable Center. On the broader history of how Black capitalists shaped advertising and commercial industries, see Brenna Wynn Breer, *Represented: The Black Image-makers Who Reimagined African American Citizenship*, University of Pennsylvania Press, 2019.

31. Turow, *Breaking up America*, 34.

32. Jeremy Galbreath, "Interactive Television: The State of the Industry," *Educational Technology* 36, no. 2, 1996, 24–35.

33. Marilynn Preston, "QUBE Is TV's Biggest News, but Will It Really Fly?," *Chicago Tribune*, December 27, 1977, A10.

34. Les Brown, "TV Lets Homes Boo, Buy, Vote," *New York Times*, April 13, 1978, C22.

35. Iver Peterson, "Carter Speech Scores in a Midwest TV Poll," *New York Times,* July 16, 1979, A11.

36. Photograph of QUBE Demonstration of Columbus Alive Program in 1978, Searle Photograph Collection, Barco Library, The Cable Center.

37. Preston, "QUBE Is TV's Biggest News."

38. Eric Pace, "Advertising: Growth in Direct Marketing," *New York Times*, September 9, 1981, D20. See also Case, "'The Solid Gold Mailbox,'" 42.

39. Mark Lloyd, *Prologue to a Farce: Communication and Democracy in America*, University of Illinois Press, 2006, 183–185; Parsons, *Blue Skies*, 410.

40. C-SPAN, "First Cable Television Political Workshop," March 1, 1984, https://www.c-span.org/video/?124204-1/cable-television-political-workshop; 1984 Cable TV Fact Book. Folder 6, Box 67, Robert Dole Papers.

41. These numbers were pulled from the 1978 TV Factbook and included in the list of 1978 cable television developments. Folder, Cable Television in 1979: An Industry Profile-1, Box L-9, Gerald R. Ford Post-Presidential Office Files, GRFPL.

42. Robert Schmidt, "Television in the 1980s," *Washington Post*, June 18, 1978. Folder, Cable Television in 1979: An Industry Profile-1, Box L-9, Gerald R. Ford Post-Presidential Office Files, GRFPL. A range of other news clippings in Folder 2 highlight the educational component of cable television.

43. Virginia Degner, "Seniors Boast 'First-in-the-Nation' TV Show," *Reporter* (Castro Valley, CA), February 23, 1978. News clipping, Folder, Cable Television in 1979: An Industry Profile-2, Box L-9, Gerald R. Ford Post-Presidential Office Files, GRFPL.

44. Fred Dawson, "The Franchise Story," *Cablevision*, May 19, 1980, 87.

45. Quoted in Stephen Frantzich and John Sullivan, *The C-SPAN Revolution*, University of Oklahoma Press, 1996, 36.

46. "C-SPAN's Historic Undertaking," *Cablevision*, February 12, 1979, 37.

47. Arthur Hill, "C-SPAN—A Return to Participatory Democracy," *TVC*, March 1, 1979. News clipping, Folder, C-SPAN Launch Kit, Box 229, C-SPAN Archives, Special Collections Research Center, Fenwick Library, George Mason University (hereafter C-SPAN Archives).

48. Letter to Brian Lamb from Thomas G. Gherardi, December 7, 1978. Folder 26, C-SPAN Launch Kit, Box 229, C-SPAN Archives.

49. Press release draft. Folder, C-SPAN Launch Kit, Box 229, C-SPAN Archives.

50. Hill, "C-SPAN—A Return to Participatory Democracy."

51. Memorandum, C-SPAN, March 27, 1979. Folder, C-SPAN Launch Kit, Box 220, C-SPAN Archives.

52. Pete Tittle, "Hey, You Wanna Be a Television Star?," *News*, Beloit, Wisconsin, n.d. Folder, Cable Television in 1979: An Industry Profile-2, Box L-9, Gerald R. Ford Post-Presidential Office Files, GRFPL.

53. "C-SPAN's Historic Undertaking," *Cablevision*, February 12, 1979, 39.

54. "Congressional Video," *Washington Star*, August 10, 1979; and "Live from Capitol Hill," *Washington Post*, September 6, 1979. Folder 1, News Clippings 1979–1982, Box 1, C-SPAN Archives.

55. Mimi Noel, "Hamming It Up: House TV Show Is Usually off the Air," *Roll Call*, September 20, 1979. Folder 1, News Clippings 1979–1982, Box 1, C-SPAN Archives.

56. Joanne Ostrow, "From House to Home," *Videography*. Folder 1, News Clippings 1979–1982, Box 1, C-SPAN Archives.

57. "House TV Show a Hit, Speaker Wants It Cut," *Associated Press*, reprinted in *Washington Star*, August 4, 1979. Folder 1, News Clippings 1979–1982, Box 1, C-SPAN Archives.

58. "Congressional Video"; "Live from Capitol Hill."

59. "Live from Capitol Hill."

60. Steven V. Roberts, "House G.O.P. Freshmen Are Speaking Up on Party Issues," *New York Times*, October 29, 1979, A16.

61. Joanne Ostrow, "From House to Home."

62. On CNN's impact on journalism, see Christopher B. Daly, *Covering America: A Narrative History of a Nation's Journalism*, University of Massachusetts Press, 2012, 403–411. See also Lisa Napoli, *Up All Night: Ted Turner, CNN, and the Birth of 24-Hour News*, Harry N. Abrams, 2021.

63. Daly, *Covering America*, 407. See also Ted Turner Oral History, 2001, Hauser Collection, Barco Library, The Cable Center.

64. Barbara Ruger, "CNN: Cable's Most Heralded Event," *Cablevision*, June 16, 1980, 14.

65. "CNN Prepares for June Debut," *Cablevision*, May 19, 1980, 196.

66. Charles L. Ponce de Leon, *That's the Way It Is: A History of Television News in America*, University of Chicago Press, 2016, 172. On the centrality of right-to-work laws in attracting businesses to Georgia and other Sunbelt cities, see Elizabeth Tandy Shermer, "Sunbelt Boosterism," in *Sunbelt Rising: Industrial Recruitment, Economic Development and Growth Politics in the Developing Sunbelt*, ed. Michelle Nickerson and Darren Dochuck, University of Pennsylvania Press, 2011, 34–32.

67. "CNN Premiere," June 1, 1980, accessed August 12, 2021, https://www.youtube.com/watch?v=oguIxHS5u3A.

68. Napoli, *Up all Night*, 202.

69. "Cable News Network Debuts June 1," *Firing Line*, June 1980. Folder, *Firing Line* for NCTA Members, 1980, Box 90, NCTA Collection, Barco Library, The Cable Center.

70. "Cable News Network Debuts June 1."

71. "NCTA Provides Input During Republican Party Platform Committee Hearing," June 1980. Folder, *Firing Line* for NCTA Members, 1980, Box 90, NCTA Collection, Barco Library, The Cable Center.

72. Fred Dawson, "NCTA Convention Wrap-Up," *Cablevision*, June 16, 1980, 34–35.

73. "History of Cable TV Subscribers & Revenues," in *The Kagan Cable TV Financial Databook*, ed. Sharon Armbrust and Alice Schneider, Paul Kagan Associates, 1987. Provided by Barco Library, The Cable Center.

74. Network TV: Evening News Overall Viewership Since 1980, Pew Research Center, July 9, 2015, https://www.pewresearch.org/journalism/chart/network-tv-evening-news-overall-viewership-since-1980/.

75. Tony Schwartz, "The TV News, Starring Ted Turner," *New York Times*, May 25, 1980, 1.

76. See, for example, advertisements for CNN, *Cablevision*, August 25, 1980; as well as "CNN Schedules Cable Ad Seminar," *Cablevision*, October 27, 1980, 26.

77. "WTBS, CNN Strive for Market Research," *Cablevision*, August 25, 1980, 33.

78. "The Happiness of Pursuit," an address by Irving B. Kahn. Folder 75, Irving Kahn Papers, Barco Library, The Cable Center.

79. "Pursuit of Advertising Intensifies Beyond Expectation," *Cablevision*, August 18, 1980, 26.

80. Turow, *Breaking up America*, 37–39.

81. Norma Pecora, "Nickelodeon Grows Up: The Economic Evolution of a Network," in *Nickelodeon Nation: The History, Politics, and Economics of America's Only TV Channel for Kids,* ed. Heather Hendershot, NYU Press, 2004, 16.

82. "Cable Television's Expanding Diversity," Folder, Cable Television in 1979: An Industry Profile-1, Box L-9, Gerald R. Ford Post-Presidential Office Files, GRFPL.

83. Nickelodeon advertisement, *Cablevision*, November 17, 1980.

84. For more specific details on the history and legacy of ESPN, see Travis Vogan, *ESPN: The Making of a Sports Media Empire*, University of Illinois Press, 2015.

85. Vogan, *ESPN*, 11–20.

86. "Survey of Attitudes Toward Cable Television," 1979, Peter D. Hart Research Associates. Folder: HBO History, Articles, and Timelines, Leslie Read Collection, Barco Library, The Cable Center.

Chapter 7

1. "Tom Wheeler's 'Regimen with a Difference,'" *TV & Communications*, July 15, 1979, 32–38.

2. "Visions '79: NCTA Gambles on Las Vegas," *TV & Communications*, May 1979, 46–47. For a discussion of the NCTA convention hosting a record number of policymakers, see Newsletter from NCTA on Visions '79, May 2, 1979. Folder, NCTA Las Vegas, 5/20/79, Box 18, Records of the Assistant to the President for Communication, Jimmy Carter Presidential Library (hereafter JCPL).

3. NCTA program, "Visions 1979." Folder, Cable Television in 1979: An Industry Profile-1, Box L-9, Gerald R. Ford Post-Presidential Office Files, GRFPL.

4. "Las Vegas, Nevada—Host to NCTA's Biggest Bash Yet," *TV & Communications*, June 1, 1979, 11; Paul FitzPatrick, "28th Annual NCTA Convention," *Cablevision*, 86.

5. Michael A. Davis, "The Post-Presidential Years of Gerald R. Ford," in *Companion Guide to Gerald Ford and Jimmy Carter*, ed. Scott Kaufman, John Wiley & Sons, 2016, 513–631.

6. Excerpts of his speech appear on Paul FitzPatrick, "28th Annual NCTA Convention," *Cablevision*, June 18, 1979, 86.

7. "The President Honors Cable TV, and Cable Meets the Challenge," *TV & Communications*, July 1, 1979, 41.

8. C-SPAN, Cable Television Issues, May 23, 1979, https://www.c-span.org/video/?124052-1/cable-television-issues.

9. Issue introduction, *Cablevision*, June 4, 1979, 4.

10. FitzPatrick, "28th Annual NCTA Convention," 86.

11. Thomas Dowden Oral History, 1990, Penn State Collection, Barco Library, The Cable Center.

12. Thomas Dowden Oral History.

13. Letter from Tom Dowden to Douglas Dittrick, August 9, 1976. Folder, Cable Communication, Box 423, 1976 Presidential Campaign, Pre-Presidential Papers, JCPL.

14. Letter from Thomas Dowden to cable operators, August 16, 1976. Folder, Cable Communication, Box 423, 1976 Presidential Campaign, Pre-Presidential Papers, JCPL; Letter from Tom Dowden to Douglas Dittrick, August 9, 1976, JCPL.

15. Letter to cable operators, n.d. Folder, Cable Communication, Box 423, 1976 Presidential Campaign, Pre-Presidential Papers, JCPL.

16. Amber Roessner, *Jimmy Carter and the Birth of the Marathon Media Campaign*, LSU Press, 2020.

17. Letter from Thomas Dowden to Gerald Rafshoon, September 6, 1978. Folder, Correspondence July 1978–May 1980, Thomas Dowden Collection, Barco Library, The Cable Center.

18. Letter from Thomas Dowden to Gerald Rafshoon, September 6, 1978.

19. "The President Honors Cable TV, and Cable Meets the Challenge," *TV & Communications*, July 1, 1979, 41.

20. Roessner, *Jimmy Carter.*

21. Brian Lamb, "Government and the Media," *The Media Report* 3, no. 10, July 16, 1976. Folder, OTP, Box 4, Barry Jagoda Papers, JCPL.

22. Memorandum from Alan Fein to Rick Neustadt re: Carter remarks on Cable TV. Folder, Cable 2 of 2; Box 7, Domestic Policy Staff Richard Neustadt File, JCPL.

23. Lamb, "Government and the Media."

24. Tim Wu, *The Master Switch: The Rise and Fall of Information Empires*, Vintage, 2011, 191–193.

25. Richard G. Gould, Draft Policy Statement: Competition in Communications, September 16, 1976. Folder, Communications Industry, Box 4, 1976 Presidential Campaign, Pre-Presidential Papers, JCPL.

26. Memorandum from Alan Fein to Rick Neustadt.

27. Barry Jagoda, *Journeys with Jimmy Carter and other Adventures in Media*, Koehler Books, 2020, 111.

28. "Carter's Plans for OTP," *Television Digest*, January 3, 1977. News clipping, Folder, OTP, Box 4, Barry Jagoda Papers, JCPL.

29. Memorandum for the President from Stu Eizenstat and Rick Neustadt, February 7, 1977. Folder, OTP, Box 4, Barry Jagoda Papers, JCPL.

30. Communications Issues Brief. Folder, Television, Box 127, 1976 Presidential Campaign, Pre-Presidential Papers, JCPL.

31. Brian Lamb, "Inside the Media," *The Media Report* 3, no. 18, November 1976.

32. Memorandum from Lynn May re: OTP Study, February 12, 1976. Folder, Federal Regulatory Reform-Office of Telecommunications Policy Study, Box 20, Edward C. Schmults Papers, GRFPL.

33. Letter from Bill Monroe to Barry Jagoda, June 29, 1977, found in both Folder, OTP, Box 4, Barry Jagoda Papers, JCPL; and Jagoda, *Journeys with Jimmy Carter*, 26.

34. See, for example, Memorandum from Stu Eizenstat to Rick Neustadt re: OTP Reorganization. Folder, Communications Reform-OTP, Box 36, Domestic Policy Staff, Simon Lazarus's 1976 Campaign Transition Files, JCPL.

35. "The Whitehead Years," *Cablevision*, March 28, 1977. Folder, Communications Reform-OTP, Box 36, Domestic Policy Staff, Simon Lazarus's 1976 Campaign Transition Files, JCPL.

36. Frances E. Rourke and Roger E. Brown, "Presidents, Professionals, and Telecommunications Policy Making in the White House," *Presidential Studies Quarterly* 25, no. 2, spring 1996, 539–549.

37. Rourke and Brown, 539–549.

38. Rourke and Brown, 539–549.

39. On the bipartisan embrace of deregulation during the 1970s, see Rachel Louise Moran, "Fears of a Nanny State: Centering Gender and Family in the Political History of Regulation," in *Shaped by the State*, ed. Brent Cebul, Lily Geismer, and Mason B. Williams, University of Chicago Press, 2019, 317–343; Daniel T. Rodgers, *Age of Fracture*, Harvard University Press, 2012, 41–63.

40. Reed W. Smith, "Charles Ferris: Jimmy Carter's FCC Innovator," *Journal of Radio & Audio Media* 21, no. 1, 2014, 149–162. On Jimmy Carter's effort to reorganize the executive branch and cut down the bureaucracy, see Ronald P. Seyb, "Reform as Affirmation: Jimmy Carter's Executive Branch Reorganization Effort," *Presidential Studies Quarterly* 31, no. 1, 2001, 104–120.

41. Charles D. Ferris: Staff Director, Senate Democratic Policy Committee (1963–1977), Oral History Interviews, April 5, 2004, to September 23, 2009, Senate Historical Office, Washington, D.C.

42. "Profile on Charles D. Ferris." Folder, Telecommunications Cable Television, 3/77–8/77, Box 86, Domestic Policy Staff, Steven Simmons File, JCPL.

43. Donald A. Ritchie, "The Media Will Be Key to Overcoming a Senate Filibuster on Voting Rights," *Washington Post*, April 12, 2021, https://www.washingtonpost

.com/outlook/2021/04/12/media-will-be-key-overcoming-senate-filibuster
-voting-rights/.

44. "Charles D. Ferris: Staff Director."

45. Smith, "Charles Ferris," 150.

46. Oral History with Charles Ferris, June 29, 2010, conducted by Reed Smith
and shared generously with the author by Reed Smith.

47. Thomas K. McGraw, *Prophets of Regulation: Louis D. Brandeis; James M.
Landis; Alfred E. Khan*, Harvard University Press, 1986.

48. Elizabeth Popp Berman, *Thinking Like an Economist: How Efficiency
Replaced Equality in U.S. Public Policy*, Princeton University Press, 2022; Rodgers, *Age of Fracture*.

49. Smith, "Charles Ferris," 153. See also Oral History with Charles Ferris.

50. Patrick Parsons, *Blue Skies: A History of Cable Television*, Temple University
Press, 2008, 363.

51. Parsons, 365.

52. Oral History with Charles Ferris.

53. Memo on FCC Rules in the Cable Broadcasting Area, June 21, 1977. Folder,
Cable TV 4/1977–5/1978, Box 8, Domestic Policy Staff, Richard Neustadt Files, JCPL.

54. *Cablevision*, October 9, 1978.

55. See, for example, Minutes of Broadcasting Task Force Meeting of May 23,
1977. Folder, Broadcasting Reform Task Force, Box 7, Domestic Policy Staff, Richard Neustadt Files, JCPL.

56. Memo from Rick Neustadt to Stu Eizenstat and Louis Martin, August 10,
1979, Folder- BE3-4, Executive 1.20.77-8.31-80, Box BE-6, Subject File Business-Economics, White House Central Subject File, JCPL. On the efforts by the NAACP
to draw attention to the dearth of minority media ownership in broadcasting during the 1970s, see Perlman, *Public Interests,* 96–99.

57. Letter from William Johnson to Robert Sachs, which was then forwarded
to Rick Neustadt, December 6, 1977. Folder, Cable TV-7/19/77–5/8/78, Box 8,
Domestic Policy Staff, Richard Neustadt Files, JCPL.

58. See, for example, Minutes of Broadcasting Task Force Meeting of May 23,
1977.

59. "Black-Owned TV Station Is on Air," *Circleville Herald*, September 26,
1978, 5.

60. "First Minority Cable TV Merits Columbus Support," *Call and Post*, January 14, 1978, 2B.

61. Letter from Martha Mitchell to Rene Anselmo, January 31, 1978. Folder,
BE3–4, Executive 1.20.77–8.31.80, Box BE-6, Subject File Business-Economics,
White House Central Subject File, JCPL.

62. Lily Geismer, *Left Behind: The Democrats' Failed Attempt to Solve Inequality*,
Public Affairs, 2022, 331.

63. For the history of cable television prior to 1974, see *Cable in Columbus:
What's Happening/What Can Happen*, Report by the Design Center for Community
Communications, 1974, Barco Library, The Cable Center.

64. On how this played out in Detroit and Boston, see Yuya Kiuchi, *Struggles for Equal Voice: The History of African American Media Democracy*, State University of New York Press, 2013.

65. On this activism in Columbus, see "First Minority Cable TV."

66. "First Minority Cable TV."

67. "Black Ownership . . . Black Subscribers . . . Black Gold in Columbus," *Cablevision*, October 9, 1978, 35.

68. On the system of "predatory inclusion" and the ways in which the banking industry undermined Black economic opportunities, see Keeanga-Yamahtta Taylor, *Race for Profit: How Banks and the Real Estate Industry Undermined Black Home Ownership*, University of North Carolina Press, 2019.

69. "Black Ownership," 35.

70. Memorandum Drew Days to Julia Dobbs, October 2, 1980. Folder, BE 3–4 General 1.20.77–1.20.81, White House Central Subject File-Businesses-Economics-BE 7, JCPL. See also Allison Perlman, *Public Interests: Media Advocacy and Struggles over U.S. Television*, Rutgers University Press, 2016, 94–122; Devorah Heitner, *Black Power TV*, Duke University Press, 2013; Billy R. Glasco Jr., "Louis E. Martin: The Godfather of Black Politics," (accessed November 18, 2020), https://www.blackpast .org/african-american-history/martin-louis-e-1912-1997/; https://rediscovering -black-history.blogs.archives.gov/2020/11/18/louis-e-martin/.

71. Victoria Gits, "Conglomerates Take Cable's Bait," *Cablevision*, December 15, 1980, 129.

72. Gilbert Price, "Sale of KBLE to Help Other Johnson Efforts," *Call and Post*, September 5, 1985, 2A.

73. A Cablevision Staff Report, "Cable: The New Force in Election Politics," *Cablevision*, June 30, 1980, 38.

74. Letter from Thomas Dowden to Gerald Rafshoon, July 17, 1978. Folder, Correspondence July 1978–May 1980, Thomas Dowden Collection, Barco Library, The Cable Center.

75. Memorandum from Steve Selig, March 24, 1980. Folder, Turner, R.E. White House Central Name File, JCPL.

76. Roessner, *Jimmy Carter and the Birth of the Marathon Media Campaign*, 201–203. Michael Socolow, "The Media Must Make It Easier to Track President Trump's Covid-19 Failures," *Washington Post*, April 20, 2020, https://www .washingtonpost.com/outlook/2020/04/20/media-must-make-it-easier-track -president-trumps-covid-19-failures/.

77. Memorandum from Ray Jenkins to the President, May 30, 1980. Folder, Interview Cable News Network, Box 63, Subject File Jody Powell, JCPL.

78. Video, WHCA-C: Cable News Network with President Carter, White House Communication Agency Video Collection, JCPL.

79. Transcript, CNN Interview with President Jimmy Carter, May 31, 1980. Folder, Interview Cable News Network, Box 63, Subject File Jody Powell, JCPL.

80. Barbara Ruger, "CNN: Cable's Most Heralded Event," *Cablevision*, June 16, 1980, 14.

81. "Cable: The New Force," 38.

Chapter 8

1. C-SPAN Video. "Rep. Al Gore (D-TN) Gives first House Floor Speech Televised on C-SPAN," March 19, 1979, https://www.c-span.org/video/?c4600904/rep-al-gore-house-floor-speech-televised-span.

2. Albert Gore Jr., "The Impact of Television on the Conduct of the Presidency, 1947–1969," Undergraduate Honors Thesis, Harvard College, March 1969.

3. Gore Jr., "The Impact of Television," 65.

4. For a look at the Gay Cable Network, see Lauren Herold, "Cable Comes Out: LGBTQ Community Television on New York Public Access Stations," PhD diss., Northwestern University, 2021. On the growth of Spanish International Network, see America Rodriguez, *Making Latino News: Race, Language, Class*, SAGE, 1999. On evangelical cable stations, see Darren Dochuck, *From Bible Belt to Sunbelt: Plain-Folk Religion, Grassroots Politics, and the Rise of Evangelical Conservatism*, W. W. Norton, 2012, 343; and Patrick R. Parsons, *Blue Skies: A History of Cable Television*, Temple University Press, 2008, 385. On Black Entertainment Television, see Berett E. Smith-Shomade, *Pimpin' Ain't Easy: Selling Black Entertainment Television*, Routledge, 2007.

5. Joseph Turow, *Breaking Up America: Advertisers and the New Media World*, University of Chicago Press, 1997.

6. Michael J. Socolow, "We Should Make Money on Our News: The Problem of Profitability in Network Broadcast Journalism History," *Journalism* 11, no. 6, 2010, SAGE, 675–691.

7. Tony Schwartz, "The TV News, Starring Ted Turner," *New York Times*, May 25, 1980, 1.

8. Sharon Geltner, "Television Verité," *Washington Journalism Review*, September 1984. Article Reprinted in "Special Coverage on C-SPAN," *Cablevision*, September 20, 1982, 30–34.

9. Victoria Gits, "A Day on the Road with C-SPAN's Brian Lamb," *Cablevision*, September 20, 1982; Michael O'Daniel, "Cable Has a Secret," *Emmy*, November/December 1983, 49. Folder 24, Box 1, C-SPAN Archives.

10. Sally Bedel Smith, "Personalities at CNN Increase Ratings," *Chicago Tribune*, December 25, 1984, D14; Geltner, "Television Verité."

11. Geltner, "Television Verité." On the decline of objectivity, see Nicole Hemmer, *Messengers of the Right: Conservative Media and the Transformation of American Politics*, University of Pennsylvania Press, 2016; Matthew Pressman, *On Press: The Liberal Values That Shaped the News*, Harvard University Press, 2018.

12. Quoted in Lisa Napoli, *Up All Night: Ted Turner, CNN, and the Birth of 24-Hour News*, Harry N. Abrams, 2021, 199.

13. "Cable: The New Force in Election Politics," *Cablevision*, June 30, 1980, 38.

14. Kagan Benchmark Cable Subscriber Stats, 1980–2015, Barco Library, The Cable Center.

15. "Cable: The New Force," 39.

16. "C-SPAN: Carving out a New Programming Niche," *Broadcasting*, n.d. [September 1980]. News Clippings 1979–1982, Box 1, C-SPAN Archives.

17. Boris Weintraub, "TV in Congress—Measuring the Impact," *Washington Star*, March 19, 1980. News Clippings 1979–1982, Box 1, C-SPAN Archives.

18. Lee Margulies, "Cable Keeps a Promise," *Los Angeles Times*, March 13, 1981. News Clippings 1979–1982, Box 1, C-SPAN Archives.

19. John Carmody, *The TV Column*, April 18, 1980. News Clippings 1979–1982, Box 1, C-SPAN Archives.

20. Charles L., Ponce de Leon, *That's the Way It Is: A History of Television News in America*, University of Chicago Press, 2016, 170–171.

21. Simon Applebaum, "CNN Fame Grows in Press Circles," *Cablevision*, February 2, 1981, 16.

22. Budgets are referenced in Napoli, *Up all Night*, 201.

23. Sally Bedell Smith, "CNN Raising Its Identity Quotient," *New York Times*, December 19, 1984, C26.

24. Ernest Leiser, "The Little Network That Could," *New York Times*, March 20, 1988, 30–38.

25. Ponce de Leon, *That's the Way It Is*, 175. On political cable commentary shows allowing the expansion of fringe ideas, see Nicole Hemmer, *Partisans: The Conservative Revolutionaries Who Remade American Politics in the 1990s*, Basic Books, 2022.

26. Ponce de Leon, *That's the Way It Is*, 178.

27. Heather Hendershot, *Open to Debate: How William F. Buckley Put Liberal America on the Firing Line*, Broadside Books, 2016; Ponce de Leon, *That's the Way It Is*, 188.

28. Hemmer, *Partisans*, 72–74.

29. Simon Applebaum, "CNN Fame Grows in Press Circles," *Cablevision*, February 2, 1981, 16.

30. Craig T. Allen, *News Is People: The Rise of Local TV News and the Fall of News from New York*, Wiley-Blackwell, 2001.

31. Bruce J. Schulman, *The Seventies: The Great Shift in American Culture, Society, and Politics*, The Free Press, 2001, 51; Ron Powers, *The Newscasters: The News Business as Show Business*, St. Martin's Press, 1977.

32. Ponce de Leon, *That's the Way It Is*, 176–177.

33. Parsons, *Blue Skies*, 504.

34. Ponce de Leon, *That's the Way It Is*, 181.

35. "Barbara Walters Debuts on ABC News," October 4, 1976, https://abcnews.go.com/US/video/barbara-walters-debuts-abc-news-1976-69034551.

36. Ponce de Leon, *That's the Way It Is*, 141–143.

37. C-SPAN Video, "Congressional Hearing on Early Election Projections," February 27, 1984, https://www.c-span.org/video/?124198-1/early-election-projections.

38. Susan Spillman, "Cable News: Westinghouse and ABC Make it a Race," *Cablevision*, August 24, 1981, 100–108.

39. Spillman, "Cable News," 100–108.

40. David Stoller, "Turner Throws down the Gauntlet," *Cablevision*, July 5, 1982, 15; Spillman, "Cable News: Westinghouse and ABC," 100–108.

41. Simon Applebaum, "Ready for the Fight," *Cablevision*, October 5, 1981, 22.

42. Patrick Gushman, "Function Follows Form," *Cablevision*, January 4, 1982, 13–17.

43. Ponce de Leon, *That's the Way It Is*, 185.

44. Video appears before Turner's Oral History event at the Cable Center.

45. "Light at the End of the Tunnel," *Cablevision*, January 4, 1982, 16.

46. Details on the marketing plan, subscriber incentives appear in "Marketing News," *Cablevision*, July 5, 1982, 24.

47. Jean Bergantini Grillo, "SNC Goes Live," *Cablevision*, July 5, 1982, 17.

48. "Comp Wars," *Cablevision*, January 17, 1983, 61.

49. Travis Vogan, *ESPN: The Making of a Sports Media Empire*, University of Illinois Press, 2015, 175.

50. "Turner the Victor in Cable News Battle," *Broadcasting*, October 17, 1983, 27.

51. Ponce de Leon, *That's the Way It Is*, 186.

52. "The End of the Cable News War," *Cablevision*, October 24, 1983, 18.

53. CBS floated a plan in 1982, and NBC tried to develop one in 1985. See Ernest Leiser, "The Little Network That Could," *New York Times*, March 20, 1988, 30–38.

54. "Turner Faces Operator Ire," *Cablevision*, December 26, 1983, 22.

55. "C-SPAN Approves 24 Hour Program Day," *Cablevision*, January 19, 1981, 12–14.

56. Gary Rothbart, "C-SPAN Troubles," *Cablevision*, April 19, 1982, 23.

57. "Top Fan Believes in C-SPAN," *Cablevision*, September 20, 1982, 60.

58. David Freed, "Cable Blackout Leaves a Hunger," *Rocky Mountain News*, April 13, 1982. Folder 8, Box 1, C-SPAN Archives.

59. "Cable Keeps a Promise," *Cablevision*, September 20, 1982, 48.

60. "Special Report: Public Affairs Network Goes 24 Hours," *Cablevision*, September 20, 1982, 52.

61. Craig Leddy, "First C-SPAN Invitational," *Cablevision*, March 28, 1983, 18.

62. Sharon Geltner, "Television Verité," *Washington Journalism Review*, September 1984.

63. C-SPAN, "First C-SPAN Call-In," October 7, 1980, https://www.c-span.org/video/?187989-1/span-call.

64. "Special Report: Public Affairs," 55.

65. Michael O'Daniel, "Cable Has a Secret," *Emmy*, November/December 1983, 50. Box 1, Folder 24, C-SPAN Archives.

66. Brian Rosenwald, *Talk Radio's America: How an Industry Took Over a Political Party That Took Over the United States*, Harvard University Press, 2019.

67. T. R. Reid, "Congress: Best Little Soap Opera on Cable," April 29, 1984, *Washington Post*. Box 2, Folder 2, C-SPAN Archives.

68. Announcement and Official Rules for C-SPAN's Fifth Anniversary Competition, March 19, 1984. Folder 4, Box 91, C-SPAN Archives.

69. "I Watch C-SPAN Because . . ." Contest Results. Folder 4, Box 91, C-SPAN Archives. All of the following quotes with names are from the publicized top ten runner-up essays. Names are only provided for the letters that were published in

contest results. Names on other letters cited that were not published are retracted due to archive privacy policy.

70. Letter from Pleasant Hill, California, April 23, 1984. Folder 4, Box 91, C-SPAN Archives.

71. Michael Robinson and Maura Clancey, "The C-SPAN Audience After Five Years." Folder 10, Box 194, C-SPAN Archives.

72. Matthew Baum and Samuel Kernell, "Has Cable Ended the Gold Age of Presidential Television?" *The American Political Science Review* 93, no. 1, March 1999, 99–114.

73. This quote is from Michael Robinson and Maura Clancey, "The C-SPAN Audience After Five Years." On budget cuts and hollowing of community centers, see Bruce J. Schulman, "The Privatization of Everyday Life," in *Living in the Eighties*, ed. Gil Troy and Vincent J. Cannato, Oxford University Press, 2009, 167–180; Robert D. Putnam, *Bowling Alone: The Collapse and Revisal of American Community*, Simon & Schuster, 2000.

74. Herold, "Cable Comes Out."

75. Herold, 229–233.

76. Herold, 250–252.

77. Herold, 260–262.

78. Author interview with Maureen Orth, August 8, 2022.

79. Press release, "Newsweek Video Sells News Programs to Hearst/ABC Video Services," March 9, 1982, Maureen Orth Personal Papers; Ilene Smith, "'Is There Life After Lunch?' Daytime Backers Say Yes," *TVC*, February 15, 1982, 86–87.

80. Parsons, *Blue Skies*, 458.

81. Smith, "'Is There Life After Lunch?',", 86.

82. Smith, 86.

83. Maureen Orth Personal Papers.

84. Parsons, *Blue Skies*, 444. See also Jill Marks, "1981: The Year in Programming," *TVC*, January 15, 1982, 46–53.

85. Marks, "1981: The Year in Programming," 46–53.

86. Parsons, *Blue Skies*, 385.

87. Louise Manon Bourgault, "An Ethnographic Study of the 'Praise the Lord Club,'" PhD diss., Ohio State University, 1980. On ways that evangelicals used entertainment to reach new audiences, see Dochuck, *From Bible Belt to Sun Belt*, 340–345.

88. Trinity Broadcasting Network, launched by Paul and Jan Crouch on May 1, 1977, was actually the first evangelical station to use satellite. See Dochuck, *From Bible Belt to Sunbelt*, 343.

89. Brian Lamb, "Satellite Technology for Christ . . . 'You're Kidding,'" *Cablevision*, January 30, 1978, 41.

90. David Price, "Divining for Dollars," *Cablevision*, February 22, 1982, 21.

91. Lamb, "Satellite Technology for Christ."

92. Monroe Price, "The Cable Connection: A New Pulpit for Politicians," *Wall Street Journal*, May 24, 1984, 30.

93. Kagan Benchmark Cable Subscriber Stats.

94. Amber Roessner, *Jimmy Carter and the Birth of the Marathon Media Campaign*, LSU Press, 2020.

95. Eric Mink, "C-SPAN: Unique Coverage," *St. Louis Post Dispatch*, February 22, 1984. Box 1, Folder 24, C-SPAN Archives.

96. Susan Cobb, "Cable Nets off to a Fast State with Coverage of Iowa Caucus," *Multichannel News*, February 27, 1984. Box 1, Folder 24, C-SPAN Archives.

97. Editorial, "Showing It as It Really Is," *Des Moines Register*, March 1, 1984. Box 1, Folder 24, C-SPAN Archives.

98. Brooke Gladstone, "Monitoring the Political Pulse," *Cablevision*, January 16, 1984, 20–24.

99. C-SPAN, "New Hampshire Primary," February 24, 1984, https://www.c -span.org/video/?123812-1/hampshire-primary.

100. "Chief Calls C-SPAN 'Video Verite,'" *Milwaukee Sentinel*, March 1, 1984. Box 1, Folder 24, C-SPAN Archives.

101. Christopher B. Daly, *Covering America: A Narrative History of a Nation's Journalism*, University of Massachusetts Press, 2018, 401–403.

102. Gladstone, "Monitoring the Political Pulse," 20–24.

103. Kathryn Cramer Brownell, "Going Beyond the Headlines: The C-SPAN Archives, Grassroots '84, and New Directions in American Political History," in *The C-SPAN Archives: An Interdisciplinary Resource for Discovery, Learning, and Engagement*, ed. Robert X. Browning, Purdue University Press, 2014, 45–58.

104. News Coverage, *Cablevision*, November 15, 1982, 13.

105. Gladstone, "Monitoring the Political Pulse," 20–24.

106. Steve Knoll, "Gearing Up for Election Year," *New York Times*, January 29, 1984. Box 1, Folder 24, C-SPAN Archives.

107. Heather Hendershot, *When the News Broke: Chicago 1968 and the Polarizing of America*, University of Chicago Press, 2022.

108. Steve Knoll, "Gearing Up for Election Year."

109. Perlman, *Public Interests*, 124.

110. Jill MacNelce, "GOP vs. Networks at Dallas," *USA Today*, n.d. [1984]. Folder 3, Box 5, C-SPAN Archives.

111. Gladstone, "Monitoring the Political Pulse," 20–24.

112. "CNN, C-SPAN Rival (Surpass?) Big Three at Dems' Convention," *Cablevision*, August 20, 1984, 28–32.

113. "CNN, C-SPAN Rival (Surpass?)," 28–32.

114. "CNN, C-SPAN Rival (Surpass?)," 28–32.

115. Gore Jr., "The Impact of Television," 70–71.

Act III

1. Letter from David Caldwell to Michael McManus, May 9, 1984. FG 128-4085000-409999, Box 60, White House Office of Records Management (WHORM)-Subject File, Ronald Reagan Presidential Library (hereafter RRPL).

2. Proposal by Communications by Design, September 22, 1983. FG 128-4085000-409999, Box 60, WHORM, RRPL.

3. Letter from David Caldwell to David Gergen, October 24, 1983. FG 128-4085000-409999, Box 60, WHORM, RRPL.

4. Letter from David Caldwell to Michael McManus, May 9, 1984.

5. David Greenberg, *Republic of Spin: An Inside History of the American Presidency*, W. W. Norton, 2017, 408–415.

6. Memorandum from Larry Speakes to Jim Brady re: Communications Plan for the President's Economic Speech, February 5, 1981. Folder, Communications Strategy 1 of 8, Box 1, Larry Speakes Files, RRPL.

7. Letter from David Caldwell to Michael McManus, May 1, 1984. FG 128-4085000-409999, Box 60, WHORM-Subject File, RRPL.

8. Kathleen Hall Jamieson, *Packaging the Presidency: A History and Criticism of Presidential Campaign Advertising*, 3rd ed., Oxford University Press, 1996, 448–449.

9. "Ronald Reagan and David Brinkley," ABC News, December 22, 1988, https://tvnews.vanderbilt.edu/broadcasts/657338; Lou Cannon, *President Reagan: The Role of a Lifetime*, Public Affairs, 2000, 32.

10. Kathryn Cramer Brownell, *Showbiz Politics: Hollywood in American Political Life,* University of North Carolina Press, 2014, 195–198. Thomas W. Evans, *The Education of Ronald Reagan: The General Electric Years and the Untold Story of His Conversion to Conservatism*, Columbia University Press, 2006.

11. Nicole Hemmer, *Partisans: The Conservative Revolutionaries Who Remade American Politics in the 1990s*, Basic Books, 2022, 34–41.

12. Special Report: Local Origination Efforts, "Government in Action: A Local View," *Cablevision*, September 20, 1982, 92.

13. Howard Fields, "Showboating Congressmen Use C-SPAN and Help It," *Cable Age*, August 6, 1984. Folder 5, Box 5, C-SPAN Archives; T. R. Reid, "Congress: Best Little Soap Opera on Cable," *Washington Post*, April 29, 1984. Folder 2, Box 2, C-SPAN Archives.

14. See for example, his address to the NCTA convention in 1983, C-SPAN, May 5, 1982, "Cable Television Greeting," https://www.c-span.org/video/?88302-1/cable-television-greeting.

15. Bruce J. Schulman, "The Privatization of Everyday Life," in *Living in the Eighties*, ed. Gil Troy and Vincent J. Cannato, Oxford University Press, 2009, 167–180.

Chapter 9

1. C-SPAN, "First Cable Television Political Workshop," March 1, 1984, https://www.c-span.org/video/?124204-1/cable-television-political-workshop.

2. Newt Gingrich, "Campaign Speech to College Republicans in Atlanta," June 24, 1978, reprinted in Meg Jacobs and Julian E. Zelizer, *Conservatives in Power: The Reagan Years, 1981–1989*, Bedford/St. Martin's, 2010, 83–85.

3. Zachary C. Smith, diss., "From the Well of the House: Remaking the House Republican Party, 1978–1994," Boston University, Proquest Dissertations Publishing, 2011.

4. Strategy Notes, Folder, Task Force Stuff, Box 147, Newt Gingrich Papers, State University of West Georgia and generously shared with the author by Brent Cebul.

Written sometime between 1979 and 1982. See also Nicole Hemmer and Brent Cebul, "They Were Made for Each Other," *New Republic*, July 11, 2016, https://newrepublic .com/article/134983/newt-gingrich-laid-groundwork-donald-trump-rise.

5. Franklin J. Havlicek, ed., *Election Communications and the Campaign of 1992*, Chicago American Bar Association, 1984, 53.

6. Smith, "From the Well of the House."

7. Printed in Walter Scott Personality Parade, September 14, 1980. Republished, for example, in the *Sioux City Journal*, September 14, 1980, 86.

8. C-SPAN, "First Cable Television Political Workshop."

9. John M. Florescu, "Cable TV: Meet the Politician's New Helper on the Campaign Trail," *Boston Globe*, January 3, 1982, 8.

10. Richard Armstrong, *The Next Hurrah: The Communications Revolution in American Politics*, Beech Tree Books, 1988, 170.

11. Florescu and Barney discuss all the specifics of the cable strategy at length during the C-SPAN, "First Cable Television Political Workshop."

12. Letter from Thomas W. McGee to Democratic colleagues, October 21, 1982. Folder 3, Box 21, Gary Hart Papers, Norlin Library, University of Colorado, Boulder (hereafter Gary Hart Papers).

13. Jeffrey B. Abramson, F. Christopher Arterton, and Gary R. Orren, *The Electronic Commonwealth: The Impact of New Media Technologies in Democratic Politics*, Basic Books, 1988, 100–101.

14. James M. Perry, "Politicians Are Turning to Cable as Alternative to Costly Networks," *Wall Street Journal*, June 3, 1982, 27.

15. Perry, "Politicians Are Turning to Cable," 27.

16. UPI Wire Story, March 1984. Folder 17, Box 1, C-SPAN Archives.

17. Gerald Seib, "Central America Issue Heats Up as President Follows His Instincts," *Wall Street Journal*, April 27, 1983, 1.

18. Samuel Kernell, *Going Public: New Strategies of Presidential Leadership*, CQ Press, 2006; Michael Schudson, *The Power of News*, Harvard University Press, 1996, 130–141.

19. "Transcript of Democrats' Response to Reagan Speech on Central America," *New York Times*, April 28, 1983, A13.

20. C-SPAN, House Session, April 28, 1983, https://www.c-span.org/video/ ?170642–1/house-session.

21. Discussion of William Alexander as "blazing the trail" for using Special Orders to compete with Reagan can be found in T. R. Reid, "Congress," C-SPAN Archives.

22. Joe S. Foote, *Television Access and Political Power: The Networks, the Presidency, and the "Loyal Opposition,"* Praeger, 1990, 34. As Foote notes, the "opposition" to presidential addresses frequently invoked the Fairness Doctrine to assert a different perspective on issues during nonelection years and used an equal time request during election years. "Opposition requests fell into the vacuum between the 'equal time' rule and the mainstream of the fairness doctrine," and networks intentionally wanted to keep the "rules of access vague and ambiguous" to afford them more leeway over making decisions on these requests.

23. Foote, *Television Access and Political Power*, 113. On politicians tapping into the media bias for drama, see Amber Roessner, *Jimmy Carter and the Marathon Media Campaign*, LSU Press, 2020.

24. "The TV Advantage of the Presidency," *Broadcasting*, October 8, 1984. News clipping, Folder, Network Fairness Doctrine, 1984–1985, Box 235, Legislative Files, Tip O'Neill Papers.

25. "TV Advantage of the Presidency."

26. Reid, "Congress."

27. C-SPAN, "First Cable Television Political Workshop."

28. Letter from Bill Alexander to Democratic Colleagues, May 8, 1984. *Congressional Record*, May 10, 1984, 11895.

29. C-SPAN House Session, May 16, 1984, https://www.c-span.org/video/?171086-1/house-session.

30. Reid, "Congress."

31. Dian Granat, "Televised Partisan Skirmishes Erupt in House," *Congressional Quarterly*, February 11, 1984. Folder 35, Box 2, C-SPAN Archives. For how C-SPAN fit into the broader goals of conservative members of Congress trying to revamp the Republican Party, see Smith, "From the Well of the House."

32. Granat, "Televised Partisan Skirmishes."

33. Reid, "Congress."

34. Memo from Dave Obey to House Members, August 2, 1983. Folder, Network Fairness, Box 235, Tip O'Neill Papers.

35. Strategy Notes, Folder, Task Force Stuff. See also Hemmer and Cebul, "They Were Made for Each Other."

36. Letter to "Fellow Republicans" from Newt Gingrich, March 18, 1982. Folder, Newt Gingrich, Kirk O'Donnell Files, Staff Files, Tip O'Neill Papers.

37. Letter to "Fellow Republicans."

38. Smith, "From the Well of the House."

39. T. R. Reid, "House Democrats Set to Huddle, Call TV Signals," *Washington Post*, May 9, 1984. Reprinted in the *Congressional Record*, May 19, 1984, 11896.

40. Letter from Tim Wirth to Tip O'Neill, May 9, 1984. Folder, Network Fairness, Box 235, Tip O'Neill Papers.

41. C-SPAN, House Session, May 10, 1984, https://www.c-span.org/video/?124921-1/house-session.

42. See, for examples and quotations, in T. R. Reid, "'Minority Objector' Consciously Flays Foes with House Rules," *Washington Post*, March 21, 1984; "Televised Partisan Skirmishes."

43. Smith, "From the Well of the House," 109.

44. House Session, May 10, 1984.

45. Granat, "Televised Partisan Skirmishes." See also Zack C. Smith, "House Republicans' Leadership Fight Signals a New Direction," *Washington Post*, May 12, 2021, https://www.washingtonpost.com/outlook/2021/05/12/house-republicans-leadership-fight-signals-new-direction/.

46. Letter from Robert Michel to Tip O'Neill, May 11, 1984. Folder, Network Fairness, Box 235, Tip O'Neill Papers.

47. Transcript, "Speaker's Press Conference," May 14, 1985. Folder, Network Fairness, Box 235, Tip O'Neill Papers.

48. O'Neill acknowledges he should have told Michel in the *Congressional Record*, May 14, 1984, 3790. The other framing of the remarks comes from his press conference on May 14.

49. Letter from Robert Michel to Tip O'Neill, May 11, 1984.

50. C-SPAN, "House Session," May 15, 1984, https://www.c-span.org/video/?171083-1/house-session.

51. Smith, "From the Well of the House," 116–117.

52. Smith, 118.

53. Tom Shales, "As the Hill Turns: C-SPAN's Riveting Mini-Series: Tips' Tiff and a House Divided," *Washington Post*, May 17, 1984. Folder 2, Cam Scam, 1984, Box 2, C-SPAN Archives.

54. Shales.

55. Shales.

56. Editorial, "Wide-Angle Wares," *Cedar Rapids Gazette*, May 1984; editorial, "Watching House on TV? Look Out!," *Youngstown Indicator*, May 16, 1984; editorial, "Not-Ready-for-Prime-Time Congressmen," *Chattanooga Daily Times*, May 17, 1984. Folder 16, Cam Scam Editorials, Box 1, C-SPAN Archives. Over eighty editorials from local newspapers across the country are included in Folder 16, Cam Scam Editorials, Box 1, C-SPAN Archives.

57. Kathryn Cramer Brownell, "Watergate, the Bipartisan Struggle for Media Access, and the Growth of Cable Television," *Modern American History* 3, nos. 2–3, November 2020, 175–198; editorial, "Party Leaders Must End Disrupting Feud," *Olympian*, May 1984; editorial, "House Dispute Is Plain Silly," *Eagle*, May 18, 1984. Folder 16, Cam Scam Editorials, Box 1, C-SPAN Archives.

58. Editorial, "The People Watch Big Brother," *Camera*, May 21, 1984. Folder 16, Cam Scam Editorials, Box 1, C-SPAN Archives.

59. Editorial, *Dallas Morning News*, May 20, 1984. Folder 16, Cam Scam Editorials, Box 1, C-SPAN Archives.

60. David Crook, "House TV: Is the Show out of Control?" *Los Angeles Times*, reprinted in *C-SPAN Update*, June 4, 1984.

61. Quotes from senators regarding the question of television in the Senate. Folder 5, Box 61, C-SPAN Archives.

62. Resolutions Introduced in 99th Congress Concerning Senate TV. Folder 5, Box 61, C-SPAN Archives.

63. Quotes from senators regarding the question of television in the Senate.

64. Letter from James A. McClure to Republican Senate colleagues, September 14, 1981. Folder 15345, Box 588, James A. McClure Papers, University of Idaho Special Collections (hereafter James A. McClure Papers). See also J. Robert Vastine, Staff Director, Senate Republican Conference 1985–1991, Oral History Interviews, August 27 to October 25, 1993, Senate Historical Office, Washington D.C.

65. On the popularity of the radio actuality programs, see Communications Survey response, Folder 15348, Box 588, James A. McClure Papers.

66. Campaign News Operations, 1982, National Republican Senatorial Committee. Folder 19185, Box 679, James A. McClure Papers.

67. "Radio Actualities in Campaign News Operations," 1982, National Republican Senatorial Committee. Folder 19185, Box 679, James A. McClure Papers.

68. Warren Weaver Jr., "Video Game for Senate Republicans," *New York Times*, February 22, 1982, A14.

69. Perry, "Politicians Are Turning to Cable," 27.

70. "Reactions to Program Sought," *Cablevision*, February 8, 1982. News clipping, Folder 18262, Box 659, James A. McClure Papers.

71. Perry, "Politicians Are Turning to Cable"; David Shribman, "Senate GOP Plays Cable TV Circuit," *New York Times*, June 23, 1983, B8.

72. Clews referenced May 23, but Senate records show it was May 24, 1844, https://www.senate.gov/about/historic-buildings-spaces/capitol/first-telegraph-messages.htm.

73. Letter from Carter Clews to Broadcasters, May 24, 1982. Folder 18262, Box 659, James A. McClure Papers.

74. Letter from Carter Clews to Broadcasters, June 1, 1982. Folder 18262, Box 659, James A. McClure Papers.

75. Letter from Carter Clews to Broadcasters, October 4, 1982. Folder 18262, Box 659, James A. McClure Papers.

76. Shribman, "Senate GOP Plays Cable TV Circuit."

77. See advertisements for *Conference Roundtable* in Folder 18262, Box 659, James A. McClure Papers, University of Idaho Special Collections. For the McClure quote, see Shribman, "Senate GOP Plays Cable TV Circuit."

78. Advertisement for *Conference Roundtable Presents: Tuition Tax Credits*. Folder 18262, Box 659, James A. McClure Papers.

79. Shribman, "Senate GOP Plays Cable TV Circuit."

80. Letter from Carter Clews to Broadcasters, June 1, 1982.

81. Letter from Carter Clews to Broadcasters, June 28, 1982. Folder 18262, Box 659, James A. McClure Papers.

82. Letter from Carter Clews to Broadcasters, May 24, 1982.

83. Armstrong, *Next Hurrah*, 202.

84. "Special Report: Cable Keeps a Promise," *Cablevision*, September 20, 1982, 47–100.

85. Linda Stein, "The Honorable Want their D.C. TV," *Cablevision*, October 10, 1988, 62–64.

86. On the Democratic embrace of "big tent" coalition politics, see Matt Grossman and David A. Hopkins, *Asymmetrical Politics: Ideological Republicans and Group Interest Democrats*, Oxford University Press, 2016, 1–4. On the divides in the Democratic Party in the 1980s, see Lily Geismer, *Left Behind: The Democrats' Failed Attempt to Solve Inequality*, Public Affairs, 2022, 34–43.

87. "Confidential Senator Hart Cable Plan." Folder 19, Box 65, Gary Hart Papers.

88. Armstrong, *Next Hurrah*, 188–189.

89. Armstrong, *Next Hurrah*, 44–45. See also forthcoming work by L. Benjamin Rolsky, a portion published in "Conservatives Pioneered Direct Mail to

Stoke Discontent. It Worked," *Washington Post*, August 4, 2022, https://www.washingtonpost.com/made-by-history/2022/08/04/conservatives-pioneered-direct-mail-stoke-discontent-it-has-worked/.

90. Quoted from Rolsky, "Conservatives Pioneered Direct Mail."

91. Armstrong, *Next Hurrah*, 188–189.

Chapter 10

1. Lily Geismer, *Left Behind: The Democrats' Failed Attempt to Solve Inequality*, Public Affairs, 2022, 17–19.

2. Geismer, 26–34.

3. On relationships between New Democrats and the tech industry, see Margaret O'Mara, *The Code: Silicon Valley and the Remaking of America*, Penguin Press, 2019.

4. Gary Gerstle, *The Rise and Fall of the Neoliberal Order: America and the World in the Free Market Era*, Oxford University Press, 2022, 125–126. In fact, along with shepherding the Cable Act alongside Goldwater and liberal Republican Bob Packwood, Tim Wirth also emerged as a key voice in pushing for the breakup of AT&T's federally regulated monopoly, something that the Department of Justice finally made happen with an antitrust ruling in 1982.

5. See, for example, Jennifer Holt, *Empires of Entertainment: Media Industries and the Politics of Deregulation, 1980–1996*, Rutgers University Press, 2011; Richard W. McChesney, *Communication Revolution: Critical Junctures and the Future of Media*, The New Press, 2008.

6. On the juxtaposition of Minow and Fowler, see Holt, *Empires of Entertainment*, 54–58.

7. Mark S. Fowler and Daniel L. Brenner, "A Marketplace Approach to Broadcast Regulation," *Texas Law Review* 60, no. 2, 1982, 210.

8. Holt, *Empires of Entertainment*, 18, 56. See also John McMurria, "Regulation and the Law," in *Media Industries: History, Theory and Method*, ed. Jennifer Holt and Alisa Perren, Wiley-Blackwell, 2009. McMurria observes: "Federal regulation considered TV cables private wires not scarce public information conduits, viewers were paying individual consumers not collective publics, and cable operators were private companies with strict First Amendment protections, not public trustees with universal mandates," 176.

9. There is a rich literature that explores the debate over regulation, privatization, and the embrace of free market incentives. Some notable works include: Kim Phillips-Fein, *Invisible Hands: The Businessmen's Crusade against the New Deal*, W. W. Norton, 2009; Benjamin C. Waterhouse, *Lobbying America: The Politics of Business from Nixon to NAFTA*, Princeton University Press, 2013; Elizabeth Tandy Shermer, *Sunbelt Capitalism: Phoenix and the Transformation of American Politics*, University of Pennsylvania Press, 2013; and Katherine Rye Jewell, *Dollars for Dixie: Business and the Transformation of Conservatism in the Twentieth Century*, Cambridge University Press, 2017. For an overview of this historiography around businesses' involvement in shaping public policy and public life as well as insight

into scholars working on this issue, see *What's Good for Business: Business in American Politics Since World War II*, ed. Kim Phillips-Fein and Julian E. Zelizer, Oxford University Press, 2012.

10. Kimberly Phillips-Fein, "The History of Neoliberalism," in *Shaped by the State: Toward a New Political History of the Twentieth Century*, ed. Brent Cebul, Lily Geismer, and Mason B. Williams, University of Chicago Press, 2018, 347–362.

11. Bruce J. Schulman, "The Privatization of Everyday Life: Public Policy, Public Services and Public Space in Reagan's America," in *Living in the Eighties*, ed. Gil Troy and Vincent J. Cannato, Oxford University Press, 2009. 167–180.

12. Patrick Gushman, "Cable Texas Style," *Cablevision*, February 22, 1982, 4–10.

13. Details from the franchising process are from Affiliated Capital Corp. V. Houston, United States Court of Appeals for the Fifth Circuit, March 17, 1983. No. 81-2335. On Houston's multicultural growth during the 1970s, see John D. Márquez, *Black-Brown Solidarity: Racial Politics in the New Gulf South*, University of Texas Press, 2014.

14. "Houston Grants Solo Cable TV Franchise," *Del Rio News Herald*, May 2, 1973, 5.

15. Gayle Greer (The HistoryMakers A2013.038), interviewed by Larry Crowe, February 2, 2013, The HistoryMakers Digital Archive, session 1, tape 1, story 2, Gayle Greer describes her career.

16. "Houston Groups Challenge Awarding of Franchise," *Brownwood Bulletin*, June 12, 1973, 2.

17. Gayle Greer (The HistoryMakers A2013.038), interviewed by Larry Crowe, February 2, 2013, The HistoryMakers Digital Archive, session 1, tape 4, story 6, Gayle Greer talks about the power of organizing and impact of community.

18. Gushman, "Cable Texas Style," 4–10.

19. Affiliated Capital Corp. V. Houston.

20. Gushman, "Cable Texas Style."

21. Affiliated Capital Corp. V. Houston.

22. Gushman, "Cable Texas Style." See also Patrick Parsons, *Blue Skies: A History of Cable Television*, Temple University Press, 2008, 408.

23. Gushman, "Cable Texas Style."

24. Márquez, *Black-Brown Solidarity*, 116. On the history of racial discrimination in Houston, see also Tyina L. Steptoe, *Houston Bound: Culture and Color in a Jim Crow City*, University of California Press, 2015.

25. Affiliated Capital Corp. V. Houston.

26. "Cable Controversy Moves to Court," *Longview News-Journal*, January 14, 1981, 2.

27. Michael Botein and Ben Park, "What to Do When Cable Comes to Town: A Handbook for Local Officials," Communications Media Center, New York Law School, Barco Library, 1980, 3.

28. Hugh Panero and Fred Dawson, "Are They Doing the Job? The Cable Consultant," *Cablevision*, December 8, 1980, 27.

29. Fred Dawson, "The Franchise Story," *Cablevision*, May 19, 1980, 146.

30. Robin Cruise, "Franchising Wars Resurface," *Cablevision*, October 9, 1978, 26.

31. Dawson, "Franchise Story," 168.

32. Parsons, *Blue Skies*, 408–409.

33. Cruise, "Franchising Wars Resurface," 32.

34. Hugh Panero, "The Winning Combinations: What It Took to Win in Eight Big Cities," *Cablevision*, June 1, 1981, 328.

35. Dawson, "Franchise Story," 107.

36. Panero, "Winning Combinations," 328.

37. Dawson, "Franchise Story," 107.

38. Panero, "Winning Combinations," 332.

39. Parsons, *Blue Skies*, 412–413.

40. Dawson, "Franchise Story," 135.

41. "Wire Wars," *Cablevision*, December 15, 1980, 72; Jonathan Levy, *Ages of American Capitalism: A History of the United States*, Random House, 2021, 614.

42. Victoria Gits, "Conglomerates Take Cable's Bait," *Cablevision*, December 15, 1980, 129. On the romanticization of "mom 'n' pop" days, see Megan Mullen, "The Moms 'n' Pops of CATV," in *Cable Visions: Television Beyond Broadcasting*, ed. Sarah Banet-Weiser, Cynthia Chris, and Anthony Freitas, NYU Press, 2007, 24–43.

43. Fred Dawson, "Case of the Erupting Pie . . . ," *Cablevision*, May 7, 1984, 14.

44. Cable Telecommunications Act of 1982, https://www.congress.gov/bill /97th-congress/senate-bill/2172/all-info?r=42&s=1.

45. Parsons, *Blue Skies*, 476.

46. Gits, "Conglomerates Take Cable's Bait."

47. Craig Leddy, "Voice of the Cities," *Cablevision*, October 4, 1982, 86.

48. Craig Leddy, "New Look at Legislation," *Cablevision*, July 19, 1982, 16.

49. Craig Leddy, "Lobbying War," *Cablevision*, August 16, 1982, 59.

50. Dawson, "The Franchise Story," 146.

51. Summary of Action, Cable Communications Policy Act (S.66), Folder 14, Box 391, Robert W. "Bob" Packwood Papers, Willamette University Archives and Special Collections (hereafter Bob Packwood Papers).

52. Summary of Action, Cable Communications Policy Act (S.66), Folder 14, Box 391, Bob Packwood Papers.

53. "Cablevision Interviews Bob Packwood," *Cablevision*, August 1, 1983, 36–40. See also Craig R. Smith, "The Campaign to Repeal the Fairness Doctrine," *Rhetoric and Public Affairs* 2, no. 3, Fall 1999, 481–505.

54. "Cablevision Interviews Bob Packwood," 36–40.

55. "Congress Looks at Cable Franchising," *Firing Line*, NCTA Newsletter, September 1981. Folder, Firing Line for NCTA Members, Box 90, NCTA Collection, Barco Library, The Cable Center.

56. "Nader Attacks Cable Bill," *Cablevision*, September 26, 1983, 21.

57. Gerstle, *The Rise and Fall of the Neoliberal Order*, 159; Paul Sabin, *Public Citizens: The Attack on Big Government and the Remaking of American Liberalism*, W. W. Norton, 2021.

58. Press release, October 6, 1983. Folder 2, Cable TV, Box 983, Timothy Wirth Papers, University of Colorado Boulder Special Collections (hereafter Tim Wirth Papers).

59. Letter from Senator Packwood to Hernan Padilla, September 6, 1984. See also form letters to mayors included in the file. Folder 14, Box 391, Bob Packwood Papers.

60. Letter from Barry Goldwater to Mark Fowler, August 10, 1984. Folder 14, Box 391, Bob Packwood Papers.

61. Hale Montgomery, "It's a Mystery," *Cable Television Business*, December 1, 1984.

62. Senator Packwood Floor Speech, October 11, 1984. Folder 14, Box 391, Bob Packwood Papers.

63. Press Release, "Cable Deregulation Approved by Senate," October 11, 1984. Folder 14, Box 391, Bob Packwood Papers.

64. Press Release, "Cable Television Legislation Becomes Law," October 30, 1984. Folder 2, Cable TV, Box 983, Tim Wirth Papers.

65. "Congress Limits Local Control of Cable TV," *New York Times*, October 12, 1984, A15.

66. "Atlantic Cable Show Toasts S.66," *Cablevision*, November 12, 1984, 11.

67. "Cable Bill Impact: Financier Says Money Will Flow Like Wine," *Cablevision*, December 3, 1984.

68. Memorandum from James Mooney to NCTA Board and Members, December 24, 1986. Folder, NCTA President's Report, Box B, NCTA Files, Barco Library, The Cable Center.

69. Parsons, *Blue Skies*, 544.

70. Jeannine Aversa, "Cable Led '88 Price Hikes: Labor Dept.," *Multichannel News*, January 30, 1989, 1.

71. Chuck Moozakis, "Rate Hikes at a Glance," *Cable Television Business*, October 1987, 9.

72. Parsons, *Blue Skies*, 545.

73. Parsons, 545.

74. "Plotting Cable's Future," *Cable Television Business*, June 1, 1989, 29.

75. Parsons, *Blue Skies*, 554–555.

76. Michael Schrage, "Cable Gets to Pick and Choose," *Washington Post*, September 10, 1985, D1.

77. Parsons, *Blue Skies*, 563–565.

78. O'Mara, *The Code*, 193, 290–292.

79. O'Mara, 292.

80. John Malone Oral History, 2001, Hauser Collection, Barco Library, The Cable Center.

81. Mark Robichaux, *Cable Cowboy: John Malone and the Rise of the Modern Cable Business*, John Wiley & Sons, 2002, 1–3.

82. Robichaux, 75.

83. Parsons, *Blue Skies*, 443.

84. *1984 Cable TV Fact Book*, Folder 6, Box 67, Robert Dole Papers.

85. Robichaux, *Cable Cowboy*, 104.

86. Robichaux, 105.

87. Robert Johnson Oral History, 2003, Hauser Project, Barco Library, The Cable Center.

88. Richard Tedesco, "The Flowering of Basic Cable Underlines Power of Niche Strategy," *Cablevision*, November 6, 1989, 22.

89. C-SPAN, Cable Telecommunications Act, Day 1, Part 1, November 16, 1989, https://www.c-span.org/video/?9959-1/cable-telecommunications-act-day-1-part-1.

90. L. J. Davis, "Television's Real-Life Cable Baron," *New York Times*, December 2, 1990, 38.

91. C-SPAN, Cable Telecommunications Act, Day 1, Part 1.

92. C-SPAN, Cable Telecommunications Act, Day 1, Part 2, https://www.c-span.org/video/?11059-1/cable-telecommunications-act-day-1-part-2.

93. C-SPAN, Cable Telecommunications Act, Day 1, Part 1.

94. C-SPAN, Cable Telecommunications Act, Day 1, Part 2.

95. Parsons, *Blue Skies*, 412.

96. Geismer, *Left Behind*, 8–9, 50.

97. On this view of the 1990s, see "Congress Breaks with Cable Business Unfinished," *Multichannel News*, November 27, 1989. On the Hobson's Choice, see "Expect the Worst from The Hill," *Multichannel News*, November 20, 1989, 36.

Chapter 11

1. Quoted in Lily Geismer, *Left Behind: The Democrats' Failed Attempt to Solve Inequality*, Public Affairs, 2022, 21.

2. John A. Lawrence, *The Class of '74: Congress after Watergate and the Roots of Partisanship*, Johns Hopkins University Press, 2018.

3. C-SPAN, Wirth Retirement Announcement, April 8, 1992, https://www.c-span.org/video/?25458-1/wirth-retirement-announcement.

4. Christopher B. Daly, *Covering America: A Narrative History of a Nation's Journalism*, University of Massachusetts Press, 2012, 400–402.

5. Matt Bai, *All the Truth Is Out: The Week Politics Went Tabloid*, Vintage, 2015.

6. Reginald Stuart, "Fairness Doctrine Assailed by F.C.C.," *New York Times*, August 8, 1985, 1.

7. Julian E. Zelizer, "How Washington Helped Create the Contemporary Media: Ending the Fairness Doctrine in 1987," in *Media Nation: The Political History of News in Modern America*, ed. Bruce J. Schulman and Julian E. Zelizer, University of Pennsylvania Press, 2017, 185.

8. Nicole Hemmer, *Partisans: The Conservative Revolutionaries Who Remade American Politics in the 1990s*, Basic Books, 2022, 130; Zelizer, "How Washington Helped Create the Contemporary Media," 185–187.

9. Brian Rosenwald, *Talk Radio's America: How an Industry Took Over a Political Party That Took Over the United States*, Harvard University Press, 2019, 16.

10. On the roots of televised attack advertisements, see Robert Mann, *Daisy Petals and Mushroom Clouds: LBJ, Barry Goldwater, and the Ad That Changed American Politics*, LSU Press, 2011.

11. Kathleen Hall Jamieson, *Dirty Politics: Deception, Distraction, and Democracy*, Oxford University Press, 1992, 16–17.

12. Richard L. Berke, "50.16% Voter Turnout Was Lowest Since 1924," *New York Times*, December 18, 1988, 36.

13. Darrell M. West, *Checkbook Democracy: How Money Corrupts Political Campaigns*, Northeastern University Press, 2000, 16–17; Hemmer, *Partisans*, 43–44.

14. C-SPAN, "General Election Strategy," November 4, 1991, https://www.c-span.org/video/?22519-1/general-election-strategy-marketing-research.

15. West, *Checkbook Democracy*, 19–25.

16. Marc C. Johnson, *Tuesday Night Massacre: Four Senate Elections and the Radicalization of the Republican Party*, University of Oklahoma Press, 2021.

17. Rosenwald, *Talk Radio's America*.

18. C-SPAN, "General Election Strategy."

19. Jamieson, *Dirty Politics*, 37.

20. Joseph Crespino, "Ronald Reagan's South: The Tangled Roots of Modern Southern Conservatism," in *Living in the Eighties*, ed. Gil Troy and Vincent J. Cannato, Oxford University Press, 2009, 37–50. See also Joseph Crespino, *Strom Thurmond's America*, Hill and Wang, 2012.

21. Kathleen Hall Jamieson and Paul Waldman, "The Press as Storyteller," in *The Press Effect: Politicians, Journalists and the Stories That Shape the Political World*, Oxford University Press, 2003, 1–23.

22. Lisa Stein, "The Willie Horton Ad, a Cable Exclusive," *Cablevision*, December 5, 1988, 132.

23. C-SPAN, "General Election Strategy."

24. C-SPAN, "General Election Strategy."

25. Jamieson, *Dirty Politics*, 15–42.

26. C-SPAN, "General Election Strategy."

27. Stein, "Willie Horton Ad," 132.

28. Kathleen Hall Jamieson, *Packaging the Presidency: A History and Criticism of Presidential Campaign Advertising*, 3rd ed., Oxford University Press, 1996, 474.

29. C-SPAN, "General Election Strategy."

30. Stein, "Willie Horton Ad."

31. Advertisement: "Counterpunch." Folder 17, Box 1, Michael S. Dukakis Presidential Campaign Records, Northeastern University Archives and Special Collections (hereafter Dukakis Campaign Records).

32. Stein, "Willie Horton Ad."

33. Jamieson, *Dirty Politics*, 136–142.

34. Lily Geismer, *Don't Blame Us: Suburban Liberals and the Transformation of the Democratic Party*, Princeton University Press, 2015, 251–279.

35. Invoice, January 27, 1988. Folder 10, Box 1, Dukakis Campaign Records.

36. Notes re: February 7 event. Folder 10, Box 1, Dukakis Campaign Records.

37. February 6, 1988, *St. Paul Pioneer Press Dispatch*. News clipping, Folder 6, Box 1, Dukakis Campaign Records.

38. Memo from J. B. Lyon to Leslie Dach, January 26, 1988. Folder 6, Box 1, Dukakis Campaign Records.

39. Letter from Gregory Harney to Michael Dukakis, February 25, 1988. Folder 10, Box 1, Dukakis Campaign Records.

40. See correspondence re: Headquarters' Satellite Situation. Folder 16, Box 1, Dukakis Campaign Records.

41. "Cable Advertising Notes." Folder 5, Box 1, Dukakis Campaign Records.

42. "Cable Advertising Notes."

43. Press Release, October 18, 1988. Folder 148, Box 3, Dukakis Campaign Records.

44. Memo from Barbara Epstein and J. B. Lyon to State directors, October 16, 1988. Folder 148, Box 3, Dukakis Campaign Records.

45. Talking points. Folder 148, Box 3, Dukakis Campaign Records.

46. Memo from Barbara Epstein and J. B. Lyon to State directors, October 16, 1988. Folder 148, Box 3, Dukakis Campaign Records.

47. "Twenty Questions for AG/Rural Cable Show." Folder 148, Box 3, Dukakis Campaign Records.

48. "Area Folks Get Answers from Dukakis," *Lansing State Journal*, October 28, 1988. Press Clipping, Folder 150, Box 3, Dukakis Campaign Records.

49. Memo from Marilyn Yager and Barbra Epstein, October 30, 1988. Folder 150, Box 3, Dukakis Papers.

50. Press Release, October 24, 1988. Folder 150, Box 3, Dukakis Campaign Records.

51. Election Eve Town Meeting Proposal. Folder 150, Box 3, Dukakis Campaign Records.

52. Press Release, October 25, 1988. Folder 150, Box 3, Dukakis Campaign Records.

53. On the broader debate over new technology and democracy happening at the time, see, for example, F. Christopher Arterton, *Teledemocracy: Can Technology Protect Democracy?*, SAGE, 1987, 165.

54. Amber Roessner, *Jimmy Carter and the Birth of the Marathon Media Campaign*, LSU Press, 2020.

55. David R. Runkel, ed., *Campaign for President: The Managers Look at '88*, Auburn House Publishing Company, 1989, 136.

56. Andrew Rosenthal, "Campaign Tactics Provoke New Changes," *New York Times*, October 31, 1988, B6.

57. Mike Royko, "Down, Dirty a Clear Winner for Voters," *Chicago Tribune*, November 8, 1988, 3.

58. Richard Armstrong, *The Next Hurrah: The Communications Revolution in American Politics*, Beech Tree Books, 1988, 179.

59. Armstrong, 188–189.

60. Matt Grossman and David A. Hopkins, *Asymmetrical Politics: Ideological Republicans and Group Interest Democrats*, Oxford University Press, 2016, 14–16.

61. See forthcoming research by L. Benjamin Rolsky, a portion of it published in "Conservatives Pioneered Direct Mail to Stoke Discontent. It Worked," *Washington Post*, August 4, 2022, https://www.washingtonpost.com/made-by-history/2022/08/04/conservatives-pioneered-direct-mail-stoke-discontent-it-has-worked/.

62. C-SPAN, "General Election Strategy."

63. C-SPAN, "Why We Lost and How We Can Win," March 5, 1994, https://www.c-span.org/video/?55069-1/lost-win.

64. Joseph Turow, *Breaking Up America: Advertisers and the New Media World*, University of Chicago Press, 1998,, 125–127.

65. Stein, "Willie Horton Ad."

66. Berke, "50.16% Voter Turnout," 36.

67. "Statement of Senator Tim Wirth on S. 1880," September 28, 1990. Folder 19, Box 665, Tim Wirth Papers.

68. Mike Mills, "Cable TV Re-Regulation Bill May Be off Fall Lineup," *Congressional Quarterly*, September 29, 1990. Folder, 10, Box 367, Tim Wirth Papers.

69. Adriel Bettilheim, "Wirth Compromise Bill Backed by Cable Firms," *Denver Post*, October 2, 1990. Folder 10, Box 367, Tim Wirth Papers.

70. Paul Farhi, "Bill to Re-Regulate Cable Industry Dies," *Washington Post*, September 29, 1990. Folder 10, Box 367, Tim Wirth Papers.

71. Joan Lowy and John Brinkley, "Cable Industry Has Contributed $80,000 to Wirth's Campaign," *Washington Times*, October 4, 1990. Folder 9, Box 367, Tim Wirth Papers.

72. Letter from Tim Wirth to Jay Ambrose, October 3, 1990. Folder 10, Box 367, Tim Wirth Papers.

73. Letter from Tim Wirth to Jay Ambrose, October 3, 1990.

74. Political Cartoon, October 4, 1990, *Rocky Mountain News*. Folder 9, Box 367, Tim Wirth Papers.

75. Michael Schudson, *The Power of News*, Harvard University Press, 1996, 142–165; Matthew Pressman, *On Press: The Liberal Values That Shaped the News*, Harvard University Press, 2018, 219–231.

76. Lizabeth Cohen, *A Consumers' Republic: The Politics of Mass Consumption in Postwar America*, Random House, 2003, 396–397.

77. Thomas Frank, *One Market under God: Extreme Capitalism, Market Populism, and the End of Economic Democracy*, Random House, 2001, 2–3.

78. A legislative compromise that Wirth and Gore crafted to move forward on cable legislation that fall was ultimately derailed when President George H. W. Bush's threat to veto the bill promised to turn a legitimate policy debate into a partisan football, which neither side wanted. Senate Minority Leader Robert Dole agreed to work with the White House to delay a vote. Price Colman, "Cable Reregulation Still Kicking," October 12, 1990. Folder 19, Box 665, Tim Wirth Papers.

79. Colman, "Cable Reregulation Still Kicking"; Casey Anderson and Kelly Richmond, "Wirth Viewed as Capitol Hill Hatchet Man for Cable," *The Chieftain*, December 22, 1991. Folder 9, Box 367, Tim Wirth Papers.

80. Elizabeth Heilman Brooke, "A Media Ready Mayor's Mansion," *New York Times*, March 26, 1998, F13.

81. George Baldwin's "By George" column, *Albuquerque Tribune*, July 25, 1988, 12.

82. Heilman Brooke, "A Media Ready Mayor's Mansion."

83. Memorandum, December 4, 1990: Daniels Dinner. Folder 8, Box 666, Tim Wirth Papers.

84. "Talking Points on Message to Daniels Group." Folder 8, Box 666, Tim Wirth Papers; Kagan Benchmark Cable Subscriber Stats, 1980–2015, Barco Library, The Cable Center.

85. "Talking Points: Advice for 1991." Folder 19, Box 665, Tim Wirth Papers.

86. Gwen Ifill, "Gore Won't Run for President in 1992," *New York Times*, August 22, 1991, A20.

87. C-SPAN, Senate Session, January 27, 1992, https://www.c-span.org/video/?23978-1/senate-session.

88. C-SPAN, Senate Session, January 27, 1992.

89. Geismer, *Left Behind*.

90. Memorandum re: Reply to Cable Inquiries. Folder 10, Box 367, Tim Wirth Papers.

91. C-SPAN, Statement Regarding S. 12, January 31, 1991. Folder 34, Box 70, C-SPAN Archives.

92. Chris Nolan, "Wirth-less Cable," *Cablevision*, May 4, 1992, 12.

93. C-SPAN, Wirth Retirement Announcement, April 8, 1992, https://www.c-span.org/video/?25458-1/wirth-retirement-announcement.

94. Timothy Wirth Oral History, 2000, Hauser Collection, Barco Library, The Cable Center.

95. Chris Nolan, "Giving Until It Hurts," *Cablevision*, October 19, 1992, 30.

96. Chris Nolan, "Capitol Cookbook," *Cablevision*, October 19, 1992, 48.

Chapter 12

1. Rob Tannenbaum and Craig Marks, *I Want My MTV: The Uncensored Story of the Music Video Revolution*, Penguin, 2011, 498–504. On the MTV demographics, see Judith Miller, "But Can You Dance to It? MTV Turns to News," *New York Times*, October 11, 1992, SM30.

2. Tannenbaum and Marks, *I Want My MTV*, 55–58.

3. Miller, "But Can You Dance to It?"

4. Miller.

5. Elizabeth Kolbert, "Tabitha Soren: From MTV to NBC," *New York Times*, March 14, 1993, 1, 9.

6. See Tannenbaum and Marks, *I Want My MTV*, 500–501; Kolbert, "Tabitha Soren."

7. Tannenbaum and Marks, *I Want My MTV*, 247.

8. Kolbert, "Tabitha Soren."

9. C-SPAN, "Music Television Convention Coverage," August 16, 1992, https://www.c-span.org/video/?31202-1/music-television-convention-coverage.

10. Karen DeWitt, "MTV Puts the Campaign on Fast Forward," *New York Times*, February 8, 1992, 8.

11. C-SPAN, "Music Television Convention Coverage."

12. Tannenbaum and Marks, *I Want My MTV*, 501.

13. DeWitt, "MTV."

14. C-SPAN, "Music Television Convention Coverage."

15. "Grassroots Politicking: MTV Style," *Cablevision*, November 30, 1992, 63–66.

16. Lily Geismer, *Left Behind: The Democrats' Failed Attempt to Solve Inequality*, Public Affairs, 2022, 145.

17. Craig Leddy, "Damage Control," *Cablevision*, October 19, 1992, 4.

18. Kagan Benchmark Cable Subscriber Stats, 1980–2015, Barco Library, The Cable Center.

19. Richard Katz, "Money for Nothing?" *Cablevision*, December 14, 1992, 24.

20. Charles Ponce de Leon, *That's the Way It Is: A History of Television News in America*, University of Chicago Press, 2016, 190.

21. Ponce de Leon, 191–192.

22. Ponce de Leon, 197.

23. Ponce de Leon, 197–199.

24. Letter to the Editor by Lloyd Trufelman, *Cablevision*, August 10, 1992, 56.

25. Cable Television Public Affairs Association Pamphlet, 1986, Cable Television Public Affairs Association Files, Barco Library, The Cable Center; Cable Television Public Affairs Association Pamphlet, 1990, Cable Television Public Affairs Association Files, Barco Library, The Cable Center.

26. Newsletter, Cable Television Public Affairs Association, January 1991, Cable Television Public Affairs Association Files, Barco Library, The Cable Center.

27. Memorandum from Nancy Larkin to CTPAA Board Members, May 23, 1991. Folder, CTPAA 1991, Cable Television Public Affairs Association Files, Barco Library, The Cable Center; "The Local Angle," *Cablevision*, June 29, 1992, 44.

28. "Lifetime's Favorite Year," *Cablevision*, February 8, 1993, 32.

29. "Grassroots Politicking."

30. About Rock the Vote, accessed June 22, 2022, https://www.rockthevote.org/about-rock-the-vote/.

31. "Grassroots Politicking."

32. *Larry King Live*, CNN, February 20, 1992, https://advance.lexis.com/api/document?collection=news&id=urn:contentItem:3TD9-8N10-0066-J287-00000-00&context=1516831.

33. Margaret O'Mara, *Pivotal Tuesdays: Four Elections That Shaped the Twentieth Century*, University of Pennsylvania Press, 2015, 180–181.

34. On the "Celebrity CEO," see Gil Troy, *Morning in America: How Ronald Reagan Invented the 1980s*, Princeton University Press, 2005, 131–134.

35. Nicole Hemmer, *Partisans: The Conservative Revolutionaries Who Remade American Politics in the 1990s*, Basic Books, 2022, 88–89.

36. Hemmer, *Partisans*, 88–89; O'Mara, *Pivotal Tuesdays*, 178.

37. See a discussion of this media strategy with Frank Greer's Oral History, 2005, Miller Center for Public Affairs, University of Virginia, https://millercenter.org/the-presidency/presidential-oral-histories/frank-greer-oral-history.

38. William H. Chafe, *Bill and Hillary: The Politics of the Personal*, Duke University Press, 2014, 142.

39. *The War Room*, directed by Chris Hegedus and D.A. Pennebaker, 1993, Criterion Collection, DVD, 2012; Chafe, *Bill and Hillary*, 142.

40. Steve Daley, "Clinton Campaign Going after a TV Blitz," *Chicago Tribune*, June 10, 1992, N5.

41. C-SPAN, "Clinton Campaign Media Consultant," June 12, 1992, https://www.c-span.org/video/?26582-1/clinton-campaign-media-consultant.

42. Daley, "Clinton Campaign Going after a TV Blitz"; C-SPAN, "Clinton Teleconference with Talk Show Hosts," June 19, 1992, https://www.c-span.org/video/?26677-1/clinton-teleconference-talk-show-hosts; Brian Rosenwald, *Talk Radio's America: How an Industry Took Over a Political Party That Took Over the United States*, Harvard University Press, 2019, 42.

43. Rick Pu Brow, "Campaign Trailblazes New Age TV," *Los Angeles Times*, April 4, 1992, SDF1.

44. Miller, "But Can You Dance to It?"

45. Christine Hagstrom, "Choose or Lose: New MTV Message Hits Youth Vote," *Los Angeles Times*, June 21, 1992.

46. "Talk-Radio Meets Rock-TV," *The Economist*, September 5, 1992.

47. "MTV Crowd Questions Gore about Labels," *Associated Press*, October 22, 1992, 4A.

48. C-SPAN, "Music Television Convention Coverage."

49. C-SPAN, "The New Media in the 1992 Campaign," October 2, 1992, https://www.c-span.org/video/?32993-1/media-1992-campaign.

50. C-SPAN, "The New Media in the 1992 Campaign."

51. Steve Johnson, "Convention's Oddest of Couples: MTV and GOP," *Chicago Tribune*, August 18, 1992, NW1.

52. Johnson, "Convention's Oddest of Couples"; Miller, "But Can You Dance to It?"

53. Rosenwald, *Talk Radio's America*, 43–44.

54. Rosenwald, 44–45.

55. Rosenwald.

56. Edmund L. Andrews, "Bush Rejects Bill That Would Limit Rates on Cable TV," *New York Times*, October 4, 1992, 2.

57. Letter from George Bush to Robert Dole, September 17, 1992. Folder 5, Box 666, Tim Wirth Papers; Roll-Call of 74–25 Vote in the Senate, *New York Times*, September 23, 1992, D2.

58. George E. Curry, "Gore Blasts Cable TV Veto Threat," *Chicago Tribune*, September 29, 1992, N5.

59. Curry, "Gore Blasts Cable TV."

60. Letter from George Bush to Robert Dole, September 17, 1992.

61. Patrick R. Parsons, *Blue Skies: A History of Cable Television*, Temple University Press, 2008, 577.

62. Andrews, "Bush Rejects Bill," 30.

63. Breakfast invitation list. Folder 39, Box 404, Bob Dole Papers.

64. Letter to Senator Dole re: Cable Bill. Folder 38, Box 40, Bob Dole Papers.

65. Elaine S. Povich, "Bush Beaten on Cable Bill; 1st Veto Loss," *Chicago Tribune*, October 6, 1992, N1.

66. Povich, "Bush Beaten on Cable Bill."

67. Transcript, *Larry King Live*, Cable News Network, October 5, 1992.

68. Parsons, *Blue Skies*, 578–580.

69. Brian Lamb, "An Accidental Victim," *The Washington Monthly*, March 27, 1997, 21.

70. Howard Kurtz, "Campaign '92: In Final Blitz, a Blur of Polls, Pontification and Sound-Bite Slogans," *Washington Post*, November 2, 1992, A17.

71. Tannenbaum and Marks, *I Want My MTV*, 501; Hagstrom, "Choose or Lose."

72. C-SPAN, "The New Media in the 1992 Campaign."

73. David Zurawik, "MTV Shoulders Its Way into the Political Arena. Clinton Reaches Youthful Audience," *Baltimore Sun*, June 17, 1992, https://www.baltimoresun.com/news/bs-xpm-1992-06-17-1992169161-story.html.

74. Miller, "But Can You Dance to It?"

75. Zurawik, "MTV Shoulders Its Way."

76. Miller, "But Can You Dance to It?"

77. Voter Turnout in Presidential Elections, The American Presidency Project, University of California-Santa Barbara, https://www.presidency.ucsb.edu/statistics/data/voter-turnout-in-presidential-elections.

78. Quotation appears in "They Said It," President Bill Clinton at MTV's inaugural ball, January 20, 1993, *Cablevision*, February 3, 1993, 9.

79. Craig Leddy, "Schmooze or Lose," *Cablevision*, February 8, 1993, 4.

80. Deborah Russell, "MTV Experiments to Hold Viewers," *Billboard*, July 3, 1992, 1.

81. Russell, "MTV Experiments."

82. C-SPAN, "Clinton Administration," March 22, 1993, https://www.c-span.org/video/?39656-1/clinton-administration.

83. Markus Prior, *Post-Broadcast Democracy: How Media Choice Increases Inequality in Political Involvement and Polarizes Elections*, Cambridge University Press, 2007.

84. David Greenberg, *Republic of Spin: An Inside History of the American Presidency*, W. W. Norton, 2016, 416–426.

85. Bo Blew, "Private Foundations and the Health Security Task Force: Using C-SPAN to Understand Perceptions of Expertise," in *Democracy and the Media:*

The Year in C-SPAN Archive Research, ed. Robert Browning, Purdue University Press, 2021.

86. CBS News Transcripts, "Inclusion of Health-Care Coverage for Abortion in Government Plan Raising Protests," May 22, 1993.

87. "President Clinton Returns to MTV to Gain Support for Youth Program: MTV News Interview with the President Highlights Plans for National Youth Service," *Business Wire*, February 26, 1993.

88. "Clinton Sales Pitch Woos MTV Audiences," *Hamilton Spectator*, March 2, 1993.

89. Mary Jordan, "Youth Service Corps Officials Prepare for Recruiting Blitz," *Washington Post*, December 2, 1993.

90. Heather Ann Thompson, *Blood in the Water: The Attica Prison Uprising of 1971 and Its Legacy*, Pantheon Books, 2016, 563–565.

91. Peter Johnson and Alan Bash, "Carlin, Still Wryly Cursed with Blue Sense of Humor," *USA Today*, April 21, 1994.

92. Kathryn Cramer Brownell, "William J. Clinton," in *Presidential Misconduct: From George Washington to Today*, ed. James M. Banner Jr., The New Press, 2019, 431.

93. Russell, "MTV Experiments."

94. Hemmer, *Partisans*, 196–201.

95. "Conservative Starting Up TV Channel," *St. Louis Post-Dispatch*, November 28, 1993, 11A.

96. Walt Belcher, "Newt Follows Clinton's Path in MTV Visit," *Tampa Tribune*, July 6, 1995.

97. Hemmer, *Partisans*, 126.

98. Mark de la Vina, "Gingrich Visit Boosts Soren's Image," *Philadelphia Daily News*, 37.

99. Bryan Sierra, "Gingrich Goes 'Raw' for MTV," *United Press International*, July 13, 1995.

100. "Boxers or Briefs? Stupid Question, Gingrich Says," *Associated Press*, July 13, 1995.

101. Tabitha Soren, "Hillary Clinton and the Ghosts of MTV," *New York Times*, August 18, 2016.

102. Jim Forkan, "MTV Takes the Bus," *Cablevision*, March 25, 1996, 20–21.

103. Edward Lewine, "Young Hands Take America's Political Pulse," *New York Times*, June 23, 1996, H36.

104. Jim Cooper, "Eyes on the Prize," *Cablevision*, March 25, 1996, 25.

105. Tom Hopkins, "Television: NBC, Microsoft Launch Cable News Network," *Dayton Daily News*, July 16, 1996, 5C.

106. Parsons, *Blue Skies*, 598–600.

107. Hopkins, "Television: NBC, Microsoft"; John Lippman and Mark Robichaux, "Resistance Surfaces to NBC's Proposal for All News Channel with Microsoft," *Wall Street Journal*, June 3, 1996, B4.

108. Hopkins, "Television: NBC, Microsoft."

109. Rick Martin, "Rebooting the News," *Newsweek*, July 29, 1996, 77.

110. Lawrie Mifflin, "Journalist as Broker in Mixed Marriage Next Week of Microsoft and NBC News," *New York Times*, July 8, 1996, D8.

111. Craig Leddy, "Vote Now," *Cablevision*, March 25, 1996, 4.

112. Jim Forkan, "Cable's Projected as Winner in '96: Forget the Donkey and Elephants—Cable Expects Political Ad Sales Results to Be Bullish," *Cablevision*, March 25, 1996, 26.

113. Michael Katz, "Cable Looking to Triple Campaign Ad Take," *Broadcasting & Cable*, August 26, 1996, 51.

114. Voter Turnout in Presidential Elections.

115. Soren, "Hillary Clinton."

116. C-SPAN, "Telecommunications Bill Signing," February 8, 1996, https://www.c-span.org/video/?69814-1/telecommunications-bill-signing.

117. Patricia Aufderheide, *Communications Policy and the Public Interests*, Guilford Press, 1999, 5–36.

118. Aufderheide, *Communications Policy*, 13; Victor Pickard, *America's Battle for Media Democracy: The Triumph of Corporate Libertarianism and the Future of Media Reform*, Cambridge University Press, 2014, 208.

119. Parsons, *Blue Skies*, 634–635.

120. Jeff Kosseff, *The Twenty-Six Words That Created the Internet*, Cornell University Press, 2019, 3–5.

121. Decker Anstrom Oral History, 2000, Hauser Collection, Barco Library, The Cable Center.

122. C-SPAN, "The Future of Cable Television," April 29, 1996, https://www.c-span.org/video/?71503-1/future-cable-television.

123. Craig Leddy, "Thanks for Nothing," *Cablevision*, May 27, 1996, 6.

124. Ezra Klein, "I Didn't Want It to Be True, but the Medium Really Is the Message," *New York Times*, August 7, 2022, https://www.nytimes.com/2022/08/07/opinion/media-message-twitter-instagram.html.

125. Thomas Frank, *One Market under God: Extreme Capitalism, Market Populism, and the End of Economic Democracy*, Random House, 2001, 2.

126. Quoted in Gary Gerstle, *The Rise and Fall of the Neoliberal Order: America and the World in the Free Market Era*, Oxford University Press, 2022, 168–169.

127. Aufderheide, *Communications Policy*, 2.

128. Aufderheide, 103.

129. Parsons, *Blue Skies*, 636–637.

130. Leo Hindery Oral History, 2001, Hauser Collection, Barco Library, The Cable Center.

131. Susan Crawford, *Captive Audience: The Telecom Industry and Monopoly Power in the New Gilded Age*, Yale University Press, 2013, 76.

132. Parsons, *Blue Skies*, 658.

133. C-SPAN, "The State of Television News," September 15, 1998, https://www.c-span.org/video/?111881-1/state-television-news.

Conclusion

1. Gabriel Sherman, *The Loudest Voice in the Room: How the Brilliant, Bombastic Roger Ailes Built Fox News*, Random House, 2014, 168.

2. On being a counterpuncher, see Brian Stelter, *Hoax: Donald Trump, Fox New, and the Dangerous Distortion of Truth*, Atria/One Signal, 2020, 28. On the terms of the payout and Ailes's exit from NBC and his partnership with Murdoch, see Sherman, *Loudest Voice in the Room*, 168–174.

3. Sherman, *Loudest Voice in the Room*, 72–74.

4. Sherman, 72–74.

5. Bill Carter, "TCI Reaches Deal with Fox to Carry All-News Channel," *New York Times*, June 25, 1996, D6; see also Sherman, *Loudest Voice in the Room*, 185–186.

6. Sherman, *Loudest Voice in the Room*, 205.

7. Frank Rich, "Lamb to the Slaughter," *New York Times*, February 5, 1997, A23.

8. Patricia Aufderheide, "C-SPAN's Fight for Respect," *Columbia Journalism Review*, July/August 1997, 14.

9. Brian Rosenwald, *Talk Radio's America: How an Industry Took Over a Political Party That Took Over the United States*, Harvard University Press, 2019, 102.

10. Nicole Hemmer, *Messengers of the Right: Conservative Media and the Transformation of American Politics*, University of Pennsylvania Press, 2016.

11. Rosenwald, *Talk Radio's America*, 103.

12. Sherman, *Loudest Voice in the Room*, 285–287.

13. Kathleen Hall Jamieson and Joseph N. Cappella, *Echo Chamber: Rush Limbaugh and the Conservative Media Establishment*, Oxford University Press, 2010, xiv.

14. Zac Gershberg and Sean Illing, *The Paradox of Democracy: Free Speech, Open Media, and Perilous Persuasion*, University of Chicago Press, 2022, 187.

15. John Gramlich, "5 Facts about Fox News," Pew Research, April 8, 2020, https://www.pewresearch.org/fact-tank/2020/04/08/five-facts-about-fox-news/.

16. Jennifer Hoewe, Kathryn Cramer Brownell, and Eric C. Wiemer, "The Role and Impact of Fox News," *The Forum* 18, no. 3, 2020, 367–388.

17. Stelter, *Hoax*.

18. Kathryn Cramer Brownell, *Showbiz Politics: Hollywood in American Political Life*, University of North Carolina Press, 2014.

19. Jane Mayer, "The Making of the Fox News White House," *The New Yorker*, March 4, 2019, https://www.newyorker.com/magazine/2019/03/11/the-making-of-the-fox-news-white-house.

20. Stelter, *Hoax*.

21. Nicole Hemmer, "Why the Trump-Fox News Relationship Really Is Unprecedented," *CNN Opinion*, March 5, 2019, https://edition.cnn.com/2019/03/04/opinions/trump-fox-news-new-yorker-jane-mayer-hemmer/index.html.

22. James Poniewozik, *Audience of One: Donald Trump, Television, and the Fracturing of America*, Liveright, 2019.

23. See also Ezra Klein, "I Didn't Want It to Be True, but the Medium Really Is the Message," *New York Times*, August 7, 2022, https://www.nytimes.com/2022/08/07/opinion/media-message-twitter-instagram.html.

24. Tabitha Soren, "Hillary Clinton and the Ghosts of MTV," *New York Times*, August 18, 2016.

25. Neil Postman, *Amusing Ourselves to Death*, Penguin Books Anniversary Edition, 2005 (originally published in 1985), 44.

INDEX

Italic pages refer to figures or tables

A NOTE ON THE TYPE

This book has been composed in Adobe Text and Gotham. Adobe Text, designed by Robert Slimbach for Adobe, bridges the gap between fifteenth- and sixteenth-century calligraphic and eighteenth-century Modern styles. Gotham, inspired by New York street signs, was designed by Tobias Frere-Jones for Hoefler & Co.